European Business Environment

European Business Environment

Doing Business in the EU

Edited by Frans J.L. Somers

Sonja A. van Hall

Cor van Leeuwen

Egin E. Lengton

René W.H. van der Linden

First edition

Noordhoff Uitgevers Groningen/Houten

Cover design: G2K Designers Groningen/Amsterdam
Cover illustration: iStockphoto

If you have any comments or queries about this or any other publication, please contact: Noordhoff Uitgevers bv, Afdeling Hoger Onderwijs, Antwoord-nummer 13, 9700 VB Groningen, e-mail: info@noordhoff.nl

0 1 2 3 4 5 / 14 13 12 11 10

ISBN 978-90-01-76891-1
NUR 781

European integration is taught at many universities both inside and outside Europe. Most of the textbooks for these courses are written from an economic or political perspective and put a strong emphasis on common economic policies. This book focuses on the business perspective – specifically, on the effects of European integration on the European business environment and its implications for individual enterprises' international strategies. The European Union's aim of creating a borderless single (or internal) market with one common currency for all participating countries will of course have far-reaching consequences for enterprises doing business in the EU.

The single market

This book therefore puts the spotlight on the *single market*, as the central element of integration from a business point of view, and examines in detail how this market is functioning, especially for businesses. A separate chapter is devoted to each of the 'four freedoms' of the single market: *the free movement of goods, services, capital and people*. To introduce the four key chapters, the economic theory, historical development and judicial basis of integration in Europe are first discussed, with each of these topics being related explicitly to the business environment.

The book is amply illustrated with business case studies and examples. Every chapter starts with an opening case study, which is used to highlight the main issues dealt with in the chapter. Most of the cases are drawn from real life, and they relate to a wide range of countries and industries. Further case studies and short business examples are also introduced in the course of the chapter. The aim of this approach is to give the student a clear idea of the significance of European integration for business and an understanding of how the theory underlying this policy works out in practice for individual businesses. Each chapter ends with brief conclusions and some questions.

An integrative approach

The business environment has many dimensions, and accordingly this book takes an integrative approach. The single market is analysed from the economic, political, legal and marketing points of view, corresponding to the various disciplines of the contributing authors. The final text is, however, the outcome of close collaboration and discussion among the authors and editor, ensuring balanced coverage of the subject.

Relevant courses

This is an essential textbook for students on undergraduate and postgraduate degree programmes in European and international business. In addition, it offers valuable supplementary reading for all courses in European integration, European studies, the economics of the EU and other courses of which business forms an important aspect. The book is also relevant to courses at universities outside the EU, because it explicitly deals with opportunities for non-European companies operating within the EU.

Acknowledgements
First and foremost, I wish to thank all the contributors for their input. Their wide range of expertise has made this comprehensive book possible. They have put an enormous amount of work into writing and revision in order to achieve a consistent approach and satisfy their own high quality standards. Working in a multidisciplinary team is a challenging task, requiring patience, open-mindedness and determination, and the contributors have shown all of these in bringing the project to a successful conclusion.

Special thanks go to Otto Venema, our publisher at Noordhoff Uitgevers in the Netherlands. Otto initiated this project and has remained fully committed, supportive and inspiring throughout the writing process. Without his close involvement, this book could not have been published. I am also extremely grateful to Marijke Quarré, our editor at Noordhoff Uitgevers, who has given invaluable technical support during the production of the book.

Finally, I wish to thank my students at Leiden University and Hanze University Groningen, both in the Netherlands, and the students I have taught at universities abroad, who have inspired me over the years to publish on this fascinating and dynamic subject.

Frans Somers
Glimmen, July 2009

Frans J. L. Somers (volume editor; economics, marketing and law; chapters 1 and 9) studied quantitative economics and law at the University of Groningen and now works as an independent consultant advising universities and businesses, mainly with respect to their international marketing strategies. He has taught European economics and business at the University of Leiden and at Hanze University in the Netherlands and at universities in Prague, Budapest and Moscow. He is the author, co-author or editor of several textbooks, including *European Union Economies, a comparative study* (Addison Wesley Longman; editor).

Sonja A. van Hall (law; chapter 4 and legal sections of chapters 5 and 6) studied law at the Radboud University of Nijmegen and is now a lecturer in international law at the Hogeschool van Arnhem en Nijmegen (HAN University of Applied Sciences). In addition to her university post, Sonja van Hall is the (co-)author of several publications on legal aspects of international trade. In 2008 she wrote the textbook *Contracten in de internationale handel* (Contracts in international trade) for Noordhoff publishers. Sonja van Hall also acts as a legal adviser to businesses participating in international trade and international logistics and offers training courses to such businesses.

Cor van Leeuwen (marketing; manufacturing, export and marketing sections of chapters 5 and 6) studied biophysics at the University of Leiden and is currently senior lecturer at Rotterdam University (a university of applied sciences). He is a member of the curriculum, accreditation and quality control committees. For approximately 25 years he held various commercial and general management positions in the business-to-business and service sectors. In 2003 he changed career to become a university lecturer. His principal areas of interest are the internationalization of SMEs, marketing in life sciences and sustainability.

Egin E. Lengton (law; chapters 3 and 8) studied Dutch law at Maastricht University and business information science at the University of Twente. He is on the staff of the Arnhem Business School, where he teaches international and European law, and works concurrently as an independent legal adviser.

René W. H. van der Linden (economics; chapters 2 and 7) studied economics at the University of Amsterdam and is currently lecturer in economics and banking & finance at the InHolland University of Applied Sciences in Amsterdam/Diemen. He was previously with the Erasmus University Rotterdam and the Amsterdam Academy for Banking and Finance, a collaborative venture between InHolland and the Free University. As a member of the European Association of University Teachers in Banking and Finance ('Wolpertinger') he has published several papers on the Chinese economy and banking system.

Contents

This book analyses and discusses the European business environment and its impact on doing business in Europe. This environment is developing rapidly, and European political and economic integration is one of the main drivers for change. Because integration has many aspects, this book takes a multidisciplinary approach, analysing the European business environment from the macroeconomic, political, legal and marketing perspectives.

Two parts
The book is divided into two parts. To introduce the subject, the background to the European integration process is first discussed, from the theoretical, historical and organizational points of view, in part 1, 'The European integration process'.

The core of the book is the analysis of the functioning of the single – or internal or common – market and its impact on business. The 'four freedoms' of this market, being the free movement of goods, services, capital and people, are studied in detail in part 2, 'The single market and international business strategy'. What does the single market mean and how does it work in practice? Have the barriers to trade really been removed and can people move freely? Do we have fully integrated financial markets? And what is the significance of the single market for companies inside and outside the EU? What kind of strategies can be developed in order to benefit from economic integration in Europe?

Part 1
Part 1 starts with a general discussion of the subject. The main themes of the book are explored and linked to each other in chapter 1. In chapter 2 the rationale and principal concepts of the theory of integration are examined. What are the main advantages and disadvantages of economic and monetary integration? What stages of integration can be distinguished? How does economic integration relate to political decision making? What are the effects of integration on business strategy and performance?

In chapter 3 the actual development of economic integration in Europe is reviewed and put in its historical perspective. This development is compared and contrasted with the theory set out in chapter 2, especially the theoretical stages of economic integration, and linked to a number of milestones (the successive European treaties).

Chapter 4 deals with the organization and legal structure of the EU. The difference between the legislative, executive and judicial branches of power is explained. The legislative branch is the source of European law, which is contained in the treaties and in regulations and directives. Executive power is delegated to the Commission, which is responsible for the proper execution of EU law. Judicial power, finally, is held by the European Court of Justice, which ensures that EU law is observed and uniformly applied.

Part 2
In part 2 the single market is analysed in detail. A chapter is devoted to each of the four freedoms, analysing their functioning and significance for international business strategy. The *free movement of goods* is covered in chapter 5, which explains precisely what this means in legal terms. How does it relate to public law and to private law, such as international sales contracts? What are the exceptions? What can be done in the event of infringements of the free movement of goods by Member States? The second part of chapter 5 deals with manufacturing industry in Europe, including its import and export activities, and with the theoretical and practical aspects of the marketing of goods in the EU.

Chapter 6 focuses on the *free movement of services* in the EU. The structure of the chapter is similar to that of chapter 5. First, the nature and the legal basis of the free movement of services (including the exceptions) are explained. A discussion of European protection of the free movement of services follows. Section 6.3 explores the significance of service industries in the EU and their international dimension. The limited nature of international trade in services (apart from traditional sectors as tourism) is discussed, and the success and failure factors, including barriers to cross-border activities in this field, are examined. The chapter ends with a section on the marketing of services in the EU.

The *free movement of capital* refers to the free circulation of money and capital in the EU. This requires the full integration of banking and capital markets and a common currency. Chapter 7 analyses the EU's efforts to reach this goal, which is still far from achieved. The chapter examines in detail the present state of affairs, the effects of financial integration on the European economy and economic policy, and its impact on business. Special attention is given to the introduction of the euro, its impact on the economies of the euro-zone countries and its effects on the European business environment.

Chapter 8 discusses the *free movement of people*, which refers to the right of EU citizens not only to travel freely and live anywhere within the EU, but also to find and take up jobs and to provide services everywhere in the Union. This subject is examined in section 8.1. The free movement of people also includes the right of individuals and companies to establish businesses everywhere in the EU. This topic – and its influence on European company law – is discussed in section 8.2. The chapter ends with a discussion of cross-border labour and social security issues.

Finally, in chapter 9, the challenges of progressive EU integration for businesses operating in the EU are explored. The European business environment is nowadays very diverse, even more so since the accession of the new Member States in Central and Eastern Europe, with their emerging economies. Section 9.1 presents some of the opportunities arising from this situation, illustrating them with graphics and case studies. Section 9.2 reviews the rationale for selecting a target country for international operations within the EU and demonstrates that every Member State has (in principle) its own advantages and disadvantages, depending on a business's strategic aims.

Study guide and teaching approach

All the chapters in this book have a uniform structure. Every chapter opens with a case study, which is used throughout the chapter to illustrate the theory under discussion. The theoretical presentation of macroeconomic, legal and business aspects of the European business environment is also amply supported by graphics and tables.

After each specific facet of this environment has been explained, its impact on business and its relevance for business strategy are analysed. This analysis is illustrated by a number of additional business case studies and examples.

Every chapter ends with a short summary ('conclusions') and some questions. A list of abbreviations, a glossary and a Web guide are provided at the end of the book.

Website

This book is supported by a website: www.europeanbusinessenvironment.noordhoff.nl. The website makes available additional information, including recent articles, additional case studies and questions, and answers to the questions in the book. For lecturers, a secure, password-protected site offers supplementary teaching materials.

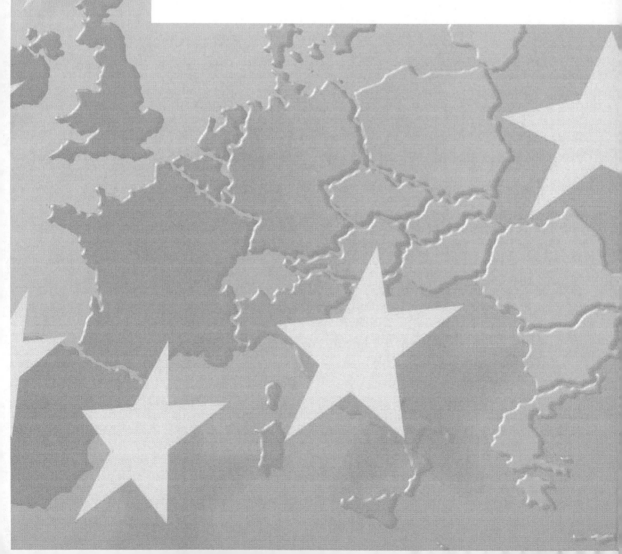

The European integration proces

1

The changing European business environment

1

'Selling to another country requires a strategy based on sound research.'

Interview with Frans Alting, Team leader for international trade, North Netherlands Chamber of Commerce

The North Netherlands Chamber of Commerce has a number of tasks. One of them is to support and advise companies planning to start or expand international operations. Originally, the focus was almost exclusively on supporting companies in the region with export activities related to goods. Recently attention has shifted to include other forms of international trade (services and imports). Frans Alting co-ordinates a team of five consultants in this field.

How important are exports these days for companies in the Netherlands, in particular for Small and Medium-sized Enterprises (SMEs)?
The percentage of SMEs involved in this form of international trade is relatively low: about 15% (excluding retail). But there are large variations around this average. For manufacturing industry it is about 40% and for wholesale about 25%. Service companies, on the other hand, are hardly involved in exports at all: only 2% of them.
The Dutch government aims at a percentage for all SMEs of 15% in the near future. This may not be easy to realize, because services are the most rapidly growing industries. That is why the Dutch Trade Board is very committed to promoting the export of services in particular. It is also a natural trend that the continuous growth and development of the service sector will lead to a further internationalization of services as well. Take for instance the IT business. IT companies were originally strongly focused on supporting local companies with the development and implementation of their computer systems. Today, software products are more and more sold internationally; in many cases these products require additional services in the field of implementation, including adaptation and tailoring to the needs of overseas customers.

Can selling to other countries in the EU still be considered as 'exporting'? Or is this just entering another market?
From a customs point of view, only selling goods to non-EU countries is considered as exporting. The euro has made international operations easier and less risky. Nevertheless, from a company's perspective, selling to other EU countries is still definitely exporting. Foreign markets – including foreign EU markets – are very different from the home market. Indeed, other cultures, languages, consumer preferences and distribution channels play a very important role in this. Normally, foreign companies lack sufficient knowledge of this new business environment. But on top of that there are still a lot of barriers related to differences in rules and regulations. In theory, these legal barriers should no longer exist according to the principles of the single market in Europe. The single market entails, among other things, mutual recognition of each other's standards and product norms, and European Standards have been defined for a number of products (CE marking).

In reality, there are many exceptions to the mutual recognition principle, however. And where an agreement has already been accepted for a specific group of products, countries are in many cases still allowed long transition periods before the arrangement comes into effect. A typical example could be the office chairs we are sitting on at the moment. Almost certainly this office furniture would not satisfy German ergonomic standards and hence cannot be sold in that country.

European Standards are only applicable to a limited number of products. Harmonization and standardization of product norms will not be easily achieved, even in Europe. Every country is inclined to use this kind of barrier to protect its own industry. Breaking them down involves tough negotiations. The single market is – despite the '1992 project' which was supposed to achieve it – far from completed. It is an ongoing process. The obstacles in the field of services are far higher still.

A company wanting to install a special sealed floor in a petrol station in Belgium will almost certainly be confronted with all kinds of special rules and regulations, concerning for instance the environment and the employment of staff; rules which may be quite different from the Dutch ones.

Another example: a Dutch business which would like to sell dustbins to the Municipality of Hamburg. The order will be placed as a result of a public tender. The tender will probably have to be made in German and the product must satisfy specific German standards, unknown to the Dutch supplier. If it comes to a contract, it should be specified whether the agreement comes under Dutch or German law. The German client may have a strong preference for German law and even prefer the product to be supplied via a German subsidiary of the Dutch business.

Selling to a customer in another country – even within Europe – means that you have to enter a completely different market, previously unknown to your company. That requires a strategy based on sound research. For SMEs in particular, developing and implementing such a strategy is a long-term investment, costing time and substantial amounts of money. In many cases, large companies already have a marketing department dealing with this kind of research and strategy, meaning that less additional investment is needed and (part of) the knowledge is already available within the company.

What are the main markets for companies starting to export?
Most of the companies going abroad for the first time just go to the neighbouring countries. For the Netherlands, Germany is the most important export market (around twenty-five per cent), followed by Belgium (around fifteen per cent). If they are successful, they might turn to more distant countries.

What are the most important reasons for companies to go abroad?
The most important reason is that companies want to grow. If the Dutch market is saturated, the obvious alternative would be exporting. Businesses considering exporting should have distinctive capabilities, meaning that they should have either a cost advantage or a superior product. In other

words, they should have a competitive advantage which could also be leveraged to foreign markets. A good network, special products or superior logistics (e.g. in the case of import–export businesses) could contribute to such a competitive advantage.

Sometimes there is a clear link with trade. Suppose a company started by importing cheap Chinese products for the Dutch market. If you manage to find other markets in Europe for these products as well (transit trade), you might realize economies of scale. That means that you can negotiate lower purchasing prices, offer a wider range of models and demand exclusivity from your supplier. An example of this is the trade in artificial (plastic) Christmas trees made in China.

For manufacturing industry, scale is a crucial factor. Most producers cannot survive on small volumes, among other reasons because they must cover the costs of their investment in machinery and research & development.

A declining market can also be a good reason for exporting. If the business is going very well, there is no need for foreign adventures; on the other hand, if it is going very badly, there are normally no resources for going abroad. However, in an economic downturn such as we are facing today, businesses' first reaction is to cut costs. The second might be to look for new markets abroad, in order to restore their previous sales level. For that reason, an economic recession could be an incentive for further internationalization.

How do companies start exporting?
In many cases by coincidence. An employee of the company meets someone at a business meeting or other event. It could also be a matter of strategy: most companies are not particularly interested in the mass production of standard products. Generally, they can make more money by making specialist products for a niche market. But a niche market could be very small in the Netherlands. That is why it makes sense to try to find similar markets abroad. In that way you can have both a differentiation strategy and a large market as well. This can be considered a logical and natural development.

Some companies must even internationalize right from the start, particularly if they make very specialized products. Typical examples are companies in advanced sectors, such as hi-tech, biochemistry or medical devices. The Dutch market is simply too small for them. In many cases these are start-ups linked to universities or other knowledge centres.

Can you tell something about the experiences of companies starting to internationalize? What are the pitfalls and what are the success factors?
Failures are mostly related to bad preparation. Some companies just apply a kind of trial-and-error approach. They happen to meet a business contact: an agent, importer or company active in the same business. They do not really check it out and do not start with solid market research or a study of the different options. In the end, it turns out that they committed themselves to the wrong partner. The choice of the wrong distribution channel can also play a role. A key factor for success is the opposite approach: sound research

and good preparation before you make any move. Good entrepreneurship is generally required.

International trade is mostly associated with exporting. What about importing? How important is importing for companies, in particular for SMEs?
Importing is of crucial importance in the Netherlands. In many cases, exporting and importing are linked. This is related to the Dutch trading spirit. Dutch companies import goods in order to resell them abroad (transit trade). This business only makes sense, however, if the Dutch company manages to give the products some added value, whether in terms of logistics, upgrading, marketing concept, packaging or other innovations.

The Netherlands is a trading nation. About sixty-five per cent of our national product is related to international trade. But we are only able to increase our exports if imports are growing too. That is another reason why the Chamber of Commerce has chosen a different approach for its consulting role: the former *export advisers* have become advisers on *international trade*.

Do companies in general look for support when starting international operations?
Many do, although some companies still just go it alone. For smaller companies particularly, this is not really a wise thing to do. Better would be to get some support from experienced organizations which have an overseas network. This can be obtained from (semi-)governmental organizations, such as the chambers of commerce, the Dutch Agency for International Business and Co-operation (EVD), investment and development agencies (such as NOM, the Investment and Development Agency for the Northern Netherlands) and organizations dealing with innovation (such as Syntens) or from private consultancy companies.

The North Netherlands Chamber of Commerce co-operates closely with the other (semi-)governmental organizations mentioned above, because many of their activities are linked. For instance, exporting is also a kind of innovation. On the other hand, if you are making innovative products, you have to go abroad anyway, because the market in the Netherlands is too small for your niche product. And, last but not least, if you are active abroad you may be confronted with new competitors, new ideas and other challenges. This could be an extra incentive to innovate further, in order to stay ahead of the competition. So in fact it is a kind of virtuous circle, where innovation leads to exporting and exporting to innovation.

That is also the main reason why the Chamber of Commerce has chosen an integral and comprehensive approach to its consultancy practice, and also to its organization and co-operation with external partners. You can no longer isolate international trade from a company's other core activities these days.

In this chapter the background to European integration, the main issues and their relationship to the European business environment are explained and analysed. These issues are explored in more detail in the following chapters.

Section 1.1 focuses on the single market, which is considered to be the central element of European economic integration. Its main principles and its significance for business are explained. In section 1.2 the rationale for economic integration in Europe is discussed, including the assumed benefits and costs, from both economic and business points of view. Section 1.3 examines the background to European co-operation, including the political and economic aspects.

1.1 The single market

The European Union (EU) is of growing importance for the daily life of ordinary European citizens. Today, more than half of new rules and regulations come from 'Brussels'. European citizens are free to travel and settle in other EU countries and to find jobs there. About forty per cent of all products sold in the EU are obliged to satisfy EU norms concerning, for instance, safety, health and the environment. Consumers are also protected in many other ways, e.g. in the field of product liability and adequate product information. The majority of EU citizens – more than 300 million – use the same currency: the euro. The EU is also concerned with environmental protection, equal treatment of men and women, working conditions and social welfare.

European integration is shaping a new business environment as well. Particularly since the latest enlargement rounds, which led to the accession of a number of emerging economies in the eastern part of Europe, a vast number of new business opportunities have arisen. The present-day EU offers great potential for the development of new markets, the expansion of sales or imports, the relocation of production facilities, outsourcing, the recruitment of foreign employees and external financing. As the interview with Frans Alting of the North Netherlands Chamber of Commerce shows, dealing with other countries – even within the European Union – is far more complex than just doing business on the domestic market. It requires a sound strategy.

On top of this, ongoing integration can become a threat to businesses, especially if their markets become internationalized and they do not adjust to the changing circumstances. Competition in home markets can become fiercer due to the appearance of foreign enterprises and the falling production costs of internationalizing domestic competitors. These competitors may, for instance, have access to cheaper inputs from elsewhere in the EU or they may have relocated part of their production to low-cost environments abroad. In short, it will be difficult for most companies to simply ignore ongoing European integration.

The central element in European integration from a business point of view is the single market, with its *'four freedoms'*: the free movement of (1) goods, (2) services, (3) capital and (4) people.

Free movement of goods means that goods can (in theory) be freely exported from one European country to another, without being hindered by all kinds of obstacles. The most obvious barriers to trade are tariffs, quotas and border controls. These barriers have been completely abolished within the EU. Many other hurdles had to be removed as well; for instance, countries might have different product norms. The EU tried to solve this problem by setting common EU standards (known as *Conformité Européenne*, or CE marking) for an increasing number of products. The leading principle, however, is that Member States must (in principle) accept each other's standards for the remaining products. Taxes can also be a hindrance: large differences in sales taxes can give businesses in some countries a competitive advantage. This is why Value Added Tax (VAT) has been more or less harmonized: all countries have set a minimum rate of 15%. Many other obstacles have also been addressed , but a number still remain. See, for instance, the examples of petrol stations and dustbins in the interview with Frans Alting in the opening case study. Some of these barriers – such as administrative measures – can have a hidden character. Countries are inclined to protect their own industries, even if this is not official policy.

Free movement of services implies that restrictions on the provision of services in Member States by companies or individuals resident in the EU are prohibited. Polish construction companies should be able to offer their services in France, German doctors in the United Kingdom, and Finnish companies should be able to offer their training, maintenance and consultancy services in the Netherlands (see case study 9.1, Wärtsilä). In many cases, the free movement of services and the free movement of people (freedom to settle) are related. There are nonetheless quite a number of exceptions to the general rule. Not all services qualify for the free movement principle. Examples are transport and financial services, which are subject to specific regulations and policies. There are also numerous other barriers related to the free movement of services, such as the qualifications of the service providers and other standards, consumer protection, and general concepts such as public interest. Many barriers still remain in this field.

Free movement of capital refers to the free circulation of money and capital across borders, the right to establish financial service companies and to supply cross-border services throughout the Member States, and the existence of common supervisory regulations. Banks and other financial institutions should be able to set up branches or take over competitors in all Member States, and EU citizens and businesses should be able to open bank accounts, transfer money, borrow and invest everywhere in the EU. The aim is to create an open, integrated, competitive and efficient European market for financial services. But the single market for capital is far from complete yet. On the one hand, all restrictions on the free circulation of capital and money have been abolished. In addition, exchange-rate risks no longer exist within the euro zone. EU citizens and businesses are indeed entitled to make financial transactions everywhere in the Union. But on the other hand the financial service industry is still highly fragmented, owing to the complex supervision and regulation of the financial system, which in many cases remains the responsibility of national supervisory bodies. Member States are very much inclined to favour their domestic financial service industry, thereby interfering with an open market and fair competition.

Free movement of people, finally, includes the right of every EU citizen to move and reside freely within the territory of the Member States. Indeed, citizens can travel throughout Europe (almost) without any restrictions, as long as they do not stay longer than three months in any one country. Most countries have completely abolished their border controls for persons (within the framework of the Schengen Agreement).

For longer periods of residence, all kind of conditions and restrictions apply. Most important is the condition that foreigners (and their family members) should be able to support themselves economically. This can be achieved by being (self-)employed or having other financial resources and being properly insured. Workers are allowed to move freely and to stay and work in a Member State under the same conditions as local workers. EU citizens and businesses are also free to establish businesses in other Member States (in principle) without obstacles of any kind. The Finnish company Wärtsilä (see case study 1.1) for instance, is free to set up training facilities in the Netherlands and to employ both Dutch and other EU citizens there. Nevertheless, all movement and residence rights can be denied on grounds of public policy, public security and public health, and there are also temporary limitations for citizens of some new Member States. Other restrictions may also apply.

Case study 1.1 **Wärtsilä expands services offering in the Netherlands**

Wärtsilä is expanding its service capacity in the Netherlands with new, larger premises and a modern training centre. On April 9th Wärtsilä opened a new Wärtsilä Land & Sea Academy training centre at Waalwijk in the Netherlands. With this large-scale training establishment, Wärtsilä is able to offer its customers, its own employees and educational institutions a broad package of technical training programmes. In addition, Wärtsilä opened new and larger service premises in IJmuiden in March.

International training centre in Waalwijk
The Wärtsilä Land & Sea Academy at Waalwijk covers an area of 2,000 square metres and contains nine classrooms, four conference rooms and a large workshop. The new centre is one of 10 Wärtsilä training centres worldwide. 'In 2009, we expect to welcome some 800 to 1,000 students to Waalwijk. We are very pleased to have the Wärtsilä Land & Sea Academy here, where we can provide, among other things, training programmes in propulsion, automation and engine products,' says Job van der Burgt, Vice President Services, Wärtsilä in the Netherlands. The Wärtsilä Land & Sea facility offers product-specific training programmes in the area of diesel engines and propulsion.

New facilities in IJmuiden
Last week, Wärtsilä opened its new modern service premises in IJmuiden, also in the Netherlands, which cover an area of 3,000 square metres. The new premises include office space, an in-house classroom and an impressive workshop. The larger workshop enables the company to deliver a broad range of services. The workshop has state-of-the-art machines and portable tools to carry out repairs and maintenance work. The IJmuiden service location-delivers spare parts, service support and technical expertise primarily to vessels working in dredging, fishing and inland shipping applications. The location makes Wärtsilä well placed to

serve its customers in the Netherlands and to provide a rapid response to the demand for services. Because of its favourable location, IJmuiden is a well-established base of operations for shipping leaving Amsterdam for the North Sea, and for vessels returning to port.

Wärtsilä in brief

Wärtsilä enhances the business of its customers by providing them with complete lifecycle power solutions. Wärtsilä focuses on the marine and energy markets with products and solutions as well as services. Through innovative products and services, Wärtsilä sets out to be the most valued business partner of all its customers. This is achieved by the dedication of close to 19,000 professionals manning 160 locations in 70 countries around the world. Wärtsilä is listed on the NASDAQ OMX in Helsinki, Finland.

Wärtsilä (Yantai)

Source: Wärtsilä press release, 9th April 2009

1.2 Aims of European integration

Why is the EU aiming at economic integration and a single market in the first place? From an economic point of view, a single market should in theory contribute to a number of positive effects. Most of these effects are interrelated and a number of them are supposed to mutually reinforce each other. They can be divided into effects on the micro or industry level and effects on a macro level:

Micro and industry level:
1 More competition
2 Improved efficiency
3 Increased specialization

4 Economies of scale and scope
5 Increased productivity

Macro level:
6 Additional intra-EU trade
7 More international investment
8 Better allocation of factors of production (labour and capital)
9 Lower inflation
10 Increased competitiveness
11 Higher economic growth
12 More jobs and less unemployment.

More competition could be considered to be at the core of these assumed positive effects, because it triggers a number of other developments. Opening up markets to foreign competitors means that competition will increase. Domestic suppliers will be forced to increase efficiency or come up with product innovations. This will generally lead to downward pressure on prices, reducing *inflation* (no. 9). Companies might also decide to *specialize* (3) in products or services for which they might have more distinctive capabilities. These capabilities might be influenced by the country in which they are established; for example, the availability of cheap labour or specific know-how, training facilities or a network of related industries.

Free access to a larger market might also result in sales volumes increasing. Production can take place on a larger scale or over a larger product range (scope). Overall, this will lead to lower average costs, because overheads such as research & development (R&D) and administration can be spread across a larger number of products (*economies of scale*, 4) or across a wider product range (*economies of scope*, 4). Greater efficiency, specialization and economies of scale and scope could in turn lead to *increased productivity* (5).

On the macro level, opening markets will normally result in *more trade* within the economic bloc (6: trade creation). There may also be negative effects, however, because of the replacement of cheaper suppliers outside the bloc by more expensive ones inside the bloc – depending on the external tariffs of the trading bloc (trade diversion: see section 2.3). Generally, an open market implies that the barriers to foreign investment have also been removed and that foreign investors are treated in the same way as domestic investors. This will in principle lead to *more (foreign) direct investment* (FDI, 7) in sales offices, production units, etc. Some of these investments take place within the framework of consolidation of production: since the barriers to trade have been removed, it is no longer necessary to have a different production facility in every single country. Is it better to concentrate the production in one or a few locations which have specific cost advantages, and to serve the markets in the trading bloc from there. Generally, concentration may also offer more opportunities to realize economies of scale and scope. Other investments may be triggered by the need for product innovation in order to stay ahead of the competition.

Better allocation of factors of production (8) is a result of specialization and relocation: capital and labour will be employed in places where they give their highest return. For instance, (relatively) labour-intensive production units (e.g. assembly lines for car manufacture) should be established where labour is abundant and cheap (the eastern part of the EU) and R&D facilities in places where scientific knowledge is widely available (major cities in Western Europe).

More efficiency, increased specialization, economies of scale and scope, increased productivity and lower inflation will in turn increase the international *competitiveness* (10) of the businesses in the integrated trading bloc. Businesses will be better equipped to compete on world markets and to export to countries outside the bloc. All these factors together should – on the macro level – result in higher economic growth and more jobs.

Although the single market is thought to have many positive effects, it can have a number of disadvantages as well. The most important is that opening up markets can lead to all kinds of (macroeconomic) *imbalances*. Taking away barriers means that domestic producers can no longer be protected. More competition can lead to the bankruptcy of individual enterprises and even the disappearance of whole sectors of industry. If this is not compensated by new economic activities, it could result in the stagnation of countries or regions and also to high levels of unemployment. These regional disparities can become persistent. The single market is not just an opportunity; for individual companies and citizens it is a threat as well. They can never just sit back and watch. A good business today might be at risk tomorrow if the management does not anticipate changes in the European business environment. The whole idea of the single market is largely based on a *free market philosophy*, with limited opportunities for national governments to intervene and protect domestic industries and employment. In a way, a free market is a kind of jungle: only the strongest will survive.

Opening up markets and stimulating cross-border trade is also facilitated by the use of a single currency. That is one of the main reasons why the euro was introduced in 1999 (for bank transfers; euro notes and coins became legal tender in 2002), within the framework of (European) Economic and Monetary Union (EMU). At the time of writing, the euro has been adopted as the sole legal tender in 16 EU countries: Austria, Belgium, Cyprus, Finland, France, Germany, Greece, Ireland, Italy, Luxembourg, Malta, the Netherlands, Portugal, Slovakia, Slovenia and Spain. Eight other countries will follow as soon as they have fulfilled a number of strict entry criteria.

The main advantages of the euro for the realization of the internal market are that it will lead to:
1 Elimination of transaction costs
2 Elimination of currency risks
3 Greater price and market transparency
4 Lower borrowing costs due to more efficient financial markets
5 Lower administration costs.

Elimination of transaction costs (no. 1) and *lower administration costs* (5) will reduce the cost of international trade. *Elimination of currency risks* (2) will reduce the risk of cross-border operations. Lower cost and risk can be expected to stimulate international trade.

Greater price and market transparency (3) will intensify competition. As discussed above, more competition is assumed to have positive effects on efficiency, innovation, specialization, productivity and inflation, and (indirectly) on economic growth and employment. Finally, *lowering borrowing costs* (4) is supposed to reduce production costs and stimulate demand.

Altogether, EMU is assumed to contribute to a more competitive environment in the internal market. Different currencies and exchange rates can be considered a form of hindrance to international trade – even more so if governments and/or central banks (monetary authorities) manipulate exchange rates in order to stay competitive, as has frequently been done in the past by such countries as Italy and Spain (so-called 'competitive devaluations'). A single market cannot be complete without removing this barrier to trade.

From a macroeconomic point of view, a single currency may have disadvantages as well (see section 2.3). Countries are no longer able to set their own monetary policies, and there are no longer any exchange rates, which can have a dampening effect on economic shocks (see sections 2.3 and 7.6).

1.3 The background to European integration

European integration did not begin purely for economic reasons. Political factors may have played an even more important role, not only at the start of the process, but also along the way. The European integration movement has it roots in the aftermath of the Second World War. It was most important to prevent new wars in Europe and also to avoid isolation and poverty in European countries, particularly Germany. Economic and political co-operation could make a strong contribution to a more stable, safer, democratic and prosperous Europe. This is why European integration more or less began with the placing of the French and German coal and steel industry, vital for warfare, under a common High Authority, by means of the Treaty of Paris of 1952. Political and in particular economic co-operation was extended in 1958 with the establishment of the European Economic Community (EEC) by the original six participating countries – France, Germany, Italy, the Netherlands, Belgium and Luxembourg – under the Treaty of Rome. Integration in Europe has since not only deepened, but also widened: the number of Member States has increased from the original six in 1958 to 27 today.

Most enlargement rounds had not only economic but also clear political motives. This was perhaps less true of the first (the entry of the UK, Ireland and Denmark in 1973), but Greece (1981) and Spain and Portugal (1986) were strongly welcomed after they had overthrown their dictatorships. EU membership was supposed to guarantee that these countries would not return to undemocratic systems. Much the same applies to the enlargement rounds of 1995, 2004 and 2007. The 1995 round took place soon after the end of the Cold War in the early 1990s, which opened the way to membership for the former neutral countries Sweden, Finland and Austria. The last rounds to date took place in 2004 and 2007, when many former socialist countries in Central and Eastern Europe (plus Cyprus and Malta) joined the Union. The EU was prepared to accept these countries for reasons of security and stability, even if a number of them were not quite ready at the time (e.g. Bulgaria and Romania). The discussions about the present candidates, Croatia and Turkey, are also significantly influenced by political factors, such as their degree of democracy, human rights, religion and the cultural identity of Europe.

Some developments in the EU, on the other hand, were largely driven by economic factors. Most important were the completion of the single market and the establishment of EMU. Taking the single market first, it was felt during the severe economic recession of the early 1980s that the problems in Europe were intensified by the fragmented European home market, which was still characterized by many internal barriers to trade. Businesses in Europe were losing ground to their main competitors in the USA and Japan. The intended common market, as envisaged by the Treaty of Rome in 1958, had not really materialized. That is why the process of removing obstacles to the four freedoms was speeded up by the adoption of the Single European Act (SEA) of 1985, which was intended to pave the way for the completion of the Single European Market (SEM) in 1992. The main aim of the SEM was to encourage a more competitive and dynamic economic environment. Achievement of this goal involved the establishment of EMU as well, requiring far-reaching co-ordination of monetary and economic policies among the Member States. By means of the Treaty on European Union (TEU), adopted in 1992 and ratified in 1993, it was decided to establish EMU no later than 1999. This was realized according to plan, involving the setting up of a European Central Bank (ECB), a common monetary policy and a common currency (the euro).

Have all the goals of the single market project now been reached? Definitely not. There still remain a large number of obstacles; some are quite obvious and others more or less hidden. They range from non-implementation of Community legislation by Member States and delayed or non-acceptance of each other's standards to administrative, linguistic and cultural barriers of all kinds. Realization of the single market will – in the words of Frans Alting of the Chamber of Commerce – be 'an ongoing process' and probably never fully completed. But is clear that the barriers have been significantly reduced, leading to a huge increase in intra-Community trade.

Conclusions

European integration has been driven by political and economic motives. Economic and political co-operation should contribute to a more stable, safer, democratic and prosperous Europe. From a business point of view, the central element in economic integration is the single market, with its four freedoms. The single market is supposed to stimulate trade and international competition and to have positive effects on business efficiency, economic growth and employment. European EMU, with its single currency, is considered to support the functioning of the single market.

The single market, for all its advantages; could also lead to severe imbalances. Countries and businesses may not be able to cope with the increased international competition, leading to regional industrial decline and unemployment. On top of that, EMU, with its single currency and centralized monetary policy, will lead to a loss of sovereignty, loss of independent monetary policy and fewer opportunities for national governments to adjust to economic problems stemming from abroad.

For business, too, there will be many new opportunities but also threats in the increasingly competitive European business environment. In that sense, 'Europe' is a must: the vast majority of companies cannot sit and wait for foreign competitors to come and take over their markets, deriving their competitive advantage from optimal product locations elsewhere. A more proactive strategy is generally highly advisable. Such a strategy should be based on sound research and thorough knowledge of the changing European business environment.

Questions

1.1   In practice it turned out to be more difficult to realize free movement of services than free movement of goods. What could be the reasons for this?

1.2   Discuss which of the four freedoms of movement might have been relevant for Wärtsilä when it set up the operations in the Netherlands mentioned in case study 1.1.

1.3   Explain why getting involved in international business operations will probably increase the competitiveness of a business in the home market too.

1.4   Explain why multiple currencies can be considered as a barrier to trade and an instrument for protection of the domestic economy.

The theory of integration

A technical barrier to trade: when is a liqueur not a liqueur?

One very common type of frictional barrier concerns health and safety regulations that have the side effect of hindering trade. Perhaps the most notorious of these was a German regulation forbidding the importation of certain low-alcohol spirits, including the sweet French liqueur cassis, used in making the popular white-wine drink kir. This regulation was challenged before the European Court of Justice (ECJ) as a barrier to trade. When challenged on this regulation, the West German government argued that the prohibition was necessary to protect public health (since weak spirits more easily promote alcohol tolerance) and to protect consumers (since consumers might buy weak spirits thinking that they were strong). The West German company Rewe-Zentral AG wanted to import cassis, but found that under West German law it could not do so. The problem was that cassis did not contain enough alcohol to be classed as a liqueur but also fell outside any other category of alcoholic drink permitted by West German law. Rewe started legal proceedings in Europe to challenge the German law. The basis of Rewe's case was that this law discriminated against non-German companies.

In 1979, the court ruled that the measure prohibiting the importation of certain low-alcohol spirits was not necessary, since the widespread availability of low-alcohol drinks (e.g. beer) in Germany made the prohibition ineffective in furthering public health. It also found that putting the alcohol content on the label was sufficient to protect consumers, so the import ban was not necessary for consumer protection. The court ruling resulted in this frictional barrier being removed. More importantly, it established the basic principle known as 'mutual recognition', whereby goods that are lawfully sold in one Member State of the European Union (EU) shall be presumed to be safe for sale in all EU countries. Exceptions to this principle require explicit justification.

The European Union consists of 27 countries and is one of the world's most highly integrated trading blocs or preferential trading arrangements. Although the EU clearly encourages trade between its Member States, many countries outside the EU complain that it benefits its members at the expense of the rest of the world. Chapter 2 describes the theory of integration, with its costs and benefits. Section 2.1 details the static and dynamic effects of European economic integration. Section 2.2 explains the main features of the various stages in the process of European integration, from a free trade area to total economic integration, describes its opponents and proponents and explains its impact on individuals and businesses. Section 2.3 describes the 'three-pillar concept' of EU organizational structure, in which the Treaty of Maastricht (1992) drew a clear line between supranational (or federal) and intergovernmental policy areas. The road to European Economic and Monetary Union (EMU), its advantages and disadvantages, and the preconditions for forming an optimum currency area are addressed in section 2.4. Section 2.5 looks at the EU from a global perspective and compares it with other trading blocs, such as the North American Free Trade Agreement (NAFTA). EU trade disputes and the role of the World Trade Organization (WTO) are also covered. Finally, section 2.6 discusses the europeanization of business in terms of internationalization, rationalization, harmonization, standardization and consolidation; this will be addressed more in detail in later chapters.

2.1 The concept of economic integration: static and dynamic effects

Economic integration refers to the elimination of economic frontiers between two or more economies. Independent nation states thus form a *preferential trading system*, also called a *trading bloc*, and commit themselves to systematically removing and eradicating the barriers that are distorting their mutual trade flows. Moreover, the member countries of a given group may contemplate higher and more complex levels of integration by attempting to harmonize their economic and/or political policies. The terms 'regional economic integration' or 'economic regionalism' can be employed to distinguish this specific course of action from the worldwide integration of national economies, accompanied by general market convergence and driven by *globalization*. Economic regionalism intrinsically divides the world economy into *preferred trading partners* and those that are discriminated against. This in effect fragments the global marketplace and establishes a set of competing protectionist trading blocs whose integration varies in its depth, breadth and expansion. These trading blocs, based on regional groupings of countries (i.e. a European region centred on the European Union, an Asian region on Japan and a North American region on the USA, etc.), are examples of *preferential trading arrangements*. Such arrangements involve restrictions on trade with the rest of the world and the lowering or removal of restrictions between the members.

The underlying motive for countries to join these regional groupings or preferential trading arrangements is that the larger market offers opportunities to achieve greater efficiency, reap the benefits of *economies of scale and scope* and stimulate economic growth. *Economies of scale* occur when increasing the scale of production leads to a lower cost per unit of output. *Economies of scope* occur when increasing the range of products produced by a business reduces the cost of each one (by making efficient use of complementarities; for instance, a bank combines its financial services with securities and insurance in an efficient way). The opposite situation is called *diseconomies of scale and scope* respectively. Economies of scope are not the same as the growth strategy of diversification, which is intended to spread risk. Scope economies are related to the lower costs associated with selling complementary products, while diversification benefits are presumed to arise from totally different products. As an industry sector grows in size, this can lead to *external* economies of scale and/or scope for enterprises belonging to that sector, as opposed to *internal* economies of scale and/or scope, which are related only to the size of the enterprise itself. In a situation of external economies of scale and/or scope, an enterprise, whatever its own individual size, benefits from the large size of the whole sector's infrastructure. From this point onwards, the phenomenon *economies of scale and scope* will generally be mentioned in one breath, since in most cases businesses are aiming to achieve both at the same time. If this is not the case, the two terms will be used separately.

The gains arising from regional economic integration can be classified as either *static efficiency* or *dynamic efficiency*. Static or allocative efficiency denotes the optimal allocation of scarce resources to obtain the best possible combination of outputs (in terms of income, value added or employment) from the existing inputs or factors of production (in terms of the labour force, capital and raw materials). Furthermore, static efficiency gains stem from the improvement and fine-tuning of operations while the technology and factors of production remain fixed. Therefore, in the theory of static efficiency, it is assumed that the competitive environment does not change in the short term. Static or direct effects of a preferential trading arrangement are *trade creation* and *trade diversion*, which are explained in more detail in section 2.2. Although the European integration process is quite often assessed on the basis of short-term static effects, the real benefits of the integration process will be felt more in the long term. Member States such as Spain, Portugal and Ireland in particular have greatly benefited from these dynamic effects over a longer period of time.

The concept of dynamic efficiency is closely linked to innovation when a longer time span is taken into consideration. Gains from dynamic efficiency arise when regional economic integration induces changes in the quantity and quality of factors of production, technological progress and changes in the competitive environment. The rationale here is that, when the market grows and competition between enterprises intensifies as a result of the elimination of trade barriers, the formerly protected enterprises need to become more efficient and look for entirely new ways of doing business. Thus, the heightened pressures of competition act as an incentive for enterprises to innovate.

In many cases, economic integration is justified on the grounds of static efficiencies; however, the gains stemming from dynamic efficiencies in fact make an even greater contribution to a member country's prosperity and economic performance. Whereas static efficiency refers to the short term and reaches its limit relatively quickly, dynamic gains are recurrent and benefit the economy over the longer term. The longer-term or dynamic economic effects of a preferential trading system are stressed above all by the proponents or supporters of the European integration process, also known as *'Europhiles'*. They often see monetary union as a vital element in their vision of a united Europe and focus on the increased market size, which may enable an enterprise in a member country to exploit *internal economies of scale and scope* in both production and marketing operations. This gives it greater market share or power and increased efficiency in these activities. For instance, whereas a German enterprise may be only moderately efficient when producing 10,000 units of a product strictly for the German market, it greatly increases its efficiency by producing 50,000 units for the much larger EU market.

The phenomena *internationalization* and *globalization* are often mentioned in one breath, although their meaning is different. Internationalization is a process whereby a business enters a foreign market, while globalization refers to a worldwide integration of national economic systems. Internationalization within the trading bloc helps to teach businesses how to compete more effectively outside the bloc as well. These businesses enjoy additional benefits through increased access to factors of production that now flow freely across national borders within the bloc. Other examples of these long-term economic effects are further *external economies of scale* through improvements in the infrastructure (better roads, railways, financial services, etc.); increased competition between member states, which may stimulate efficiency, attract foreign direct investments (FDIs) and reduce the power of monopolies; the fact that a more intensified integration process may encourage a more rapid spread of technology; elimination of the costs of currency conversion and exchange-rate uncertainty between members; and lower inflation and interest rates. Foreign enterprises prefer to invest in countries that are part of an economic bloc, because factories that they build outside the bloc receive preferential treatment for exports to other member countries. For example, many non-EU businesses, including General Mills, Samsung and Tata, have invested heavily in the EU in order to take advantage of Europe's economic integration. By setting up operations in a single EU country, these companies gain free access to the entire EU market.

Opponents or critics of the European integration process, also known as 'Eurosceptics', however, see a monetary union as a surrender of sovereignty and a threat to nationhood. They stress the longer-term economic disadvantages of a preferential trading arrangement. According to these critics, despite the gains, the European integration process goes hand in hand with underestimated problems of inequality of wealth and income distribution and more concentrated economic power. For instance, bloc trading may encourage *oligopolistic collusion* (collusion between the few very large suppliers in a market) and mergers and takeovers. This has the effect of keeping prices to the consumer high and can result in the creation of very large companies (such as Airbus), which may become excessively bureaucratic and inefficient. Another argument against further moves towards European integration is that, as a result of the single currency and monetary policy, the Member States will lack their own independent monetary and exchange-rate policy and will have fewer tools at their disposal. This could become a serious problem if economies such as Spain and Portugal have relatively high inflation rates caused by cost-push pressures. *Cost-push inflation* is associated with continuing rises in the costs of production (independently of demand), such as an increase in oil excise duty, wage rises or energy price increases. This would make it more difficult for these countries to keep their goods competitive with the rest of the preferential trading system. With separate currencies, these countries could allow their currencies to depreciate, which is not possible within the euro area. Finally, the aim of a common market is to encourage more *factor mobility* – the free flow of factors of production, such as labour, capital and land. *Factor immobility* occurs when factors of production respond slowly to changes in demand and supply. Labour, for example, may be highly immobile both occupationally and geographically, due to regulation of the labour market and the powerful role of the trade unions. Despite the gains of increased market opportunities, opponents or critics of the single market project argue that, in a Europe of oligopolies, unequal ownership of resources, rapidly changing technologies and factor immobility, the removal of internal barriers to trade has merely exaggerated the problems of inequality of wealth and economic power. Basically, the Eurosceptics argue that the current EU is not an optimum currency area (see section 2.4).

It is very difficult to evaluate the arguments and counter-arguments of the proponents and opponents of the European integration process. Many of these arguments are open to question. To decide whether membership has been beneficial to a country requires a prediction of what things would have been like if it had not joined. Many of the advantages and disadvantages are very long term and depend on future attitudes, institutions, policies and global events. In addition, some of the costs and benefits of deeper European integration are distinctly political, such as 'greater political power' or 'loss of sovereignty'.

The 'Cassis de Dijon' case (the opening case study for chapter 2) created an opportunity to implement the concept of *mutual recognition* and pushed forward further harmonization of European common policies. Mutual recognition means that, if one member country determines that a product is fit for sale, all other EU members are also obliged to do so under the provisions of the Treaty of Rome. Because France had determined Cassis de Dijon to be a legitimate liqueur, West Germany was obliged to allow its sale as well. This EU principle of mutual recognition states that one country's rules and regulations must apply throughout the EU and that, if they conflict with those of another country, individuals and companies should be able to choose which to obey – usually the ones which are least constraining. The Cassis de Dijon case has had a big impact on European business (see also section 5.3 and case study 5.5 from a legal perspective). It has meant that that national governments can no longer devise special rules and regulations that exclude competitors from EU countries. A possible disadvantage of mutual recognition is the danger that national governments could end up competing against each other to provide the lightest set of regulations, in order to attract enterprises to invest in their country. This could be to the detriment of consumers and workers. Thus some common sets of rules and regulations are still required. The introduction of *qualified majority voting* in place of *unanimous approval* on issues of rules and regulations (which does not apply to the harmonization of taxes) is an important feature of the Single European Act (SEA) of 1987 and has helped to achieve agreement on regulations. Under the unanimous approval system, the dissent of a single Member State meant that no agreement was reached; this is not the case with qualified majority voting, in which each Member State has a specified number of votes. In addition, the SEA aimed at removing tariff barriers (TBs) and non-tariff barriers (NTBs), such as subsidies and quotas.

2.2 Stages in the European integration process

Regional economic integration can take many forms, ranging from bilateral agreements to the creation of a single federal state. At this point, it is important to highlight a distinction between *negative integration* and *positive integration* (without imposing any value judgement) as two typologies of European integration (see table 2.1). Negative integration follows the rationale of the common market and has a deregulatory or 'market-making' nature. It refers to deregulation and the removal of discrimination in national economic rules and policies under joint surveillance. By intervening against national barriers to the free movement of goods, services, capital and persons (the so-called 'four freedoms'), negative integration greatly reduces the range of national policy choices and represents a fundamental loss of political control over a market economy. This loss of national regulatory power is crucial in avoiding market-distorting state interventions, such as financial support for an unprofitable national industry or discriminatory measures against foreign capital and labour. Negative integration is generally quite effective in achieving liberalization in such fields as competition policy, by removing TBs and NTBs, often in tandem with supranational agencies such as the European Commission and the European Court of Justice (ECJ). A weaker, non-binding example of negative European integration is the EU's railways policy. However, there is currently new interest in the railway sector, with the expansion of high-speed rail services linking Europe's major cities and the development of the rail equivalent of the Trans-European Network (TEN) of motorways.

Positive integration, on the other hand, comes into the picture further on in the integration process. It involves standardizing and harmonizing certain national policies among the Member States, as well as setting up at least some supranational institutions (see chapter 3 for a description from a legal perspective). The unwanted side effects of liberalization processes, in particular as a result of the 'four freedoms', require a certain level of re-regulation at the European level. Positive integration is hence 'market-shaping' because it aims to intervene in the economy and involves greater institutional adaptation at the domestic level to a specific European model. The domestic implementation of positive European policies requires a much more co-ordinated effort, depending on the extent to which there is a 'match' or 'mismatch' between European and national policies. The single monetary policy conducted by the European Central Bank (ECB) is an example of the EU taking further binding steps to deepen European integration. Obviously, the Member States' national governments and/or national central banks are faced with diminishing constitutional sovereignty over this particular common policy of the EU. An example of a weaker form of positive integration is the Bologna Treaty (1999). The main aim of the Bologna Treaty is to create a common European higher education area with comparable and compatible systems of academic degrees and quality assurance standards within Europe.

Table 2.1 **Typology of European integration**

	Negative (Deregulatory)	**Positive** (Regulatory)
Strong (binding)	e.g. competition policy	e.g. monetary policy (ECB)
Weak (non-binding)	e.g. railways policy	e.g. higher education policy (Bologna Treaty)

The Hungarian economist Béla Balassa (1928–1991) developed a basic model to aid understanding of the process of economic integration and give an idea of the key implications of each stage on policy making. Additionally, his model enables us to categorize different regional blocs according to how far the countries making up the group have progressed in reducing trade barriers and the extent to which they have implemented common policies. The five evolutionary stages of regional preferential trading arrangements identified by Balassa are shown in table 2.2.

Table 2.2 **Béla Balassa's stages of regional preferential trading arrangements**

Stage of economic integration	Definition	Some features
Free trade area or *association* (FTA), e.g. European and North American FTAs (EFTA and NAFTA), ASEAN and CER	Tariffs and quotas on imports from area members abolished; FTA members retain national tariffs (and quotas) against non-member countries	No positive integration; Differing external tariffs could cause *deflection of trade*
Customs union (CU), e.g. Mercosur (Latin America)	Suppression of discrimination against CU members in product markets; Equalization of tariffs (and no common quotas) in trade with non-members	No positive integration; CU = FTA plus common external tariffs (CETs); CETs could cause *trade creation* and *trade diversion*
Common market (CM), e.g. EU-27, European Economic Area (EEA): EU-27 plus 3 EFTA states	A CU which abolishes restrictions on movement of factors of production	No positive integration; Free flow of goods, services, capital and persons (the 'four freedoms')
Economic union (EcU): remains an ideal; yet to be achieved	A CM with 'some degree of harmonization of national economic policies in order to remove discrimination due to disparities in these policies'	Positive integration introduced
Total economic union (TEcU) or *Political union*	'Unification of monetary, fiscal, social and countercyclical policies'; 'Establishment of a supranational authority whose decisions are binding on the Member States'	Supranational regulatory body (e.g. ECB)

The stages of regional preferential trading arrangements are presented in a slightly different way from Béla Balassa's in table 2.3. This table identifies five possible levels of regional integration as a continuum, with economic interconnectedness progressing from a low level of integration (the FTA) through higher levels to the most advanced form of integration, political union or total economic union (TEcU). Political union represents the ultimate degree of integration between countries, which has not yet been achieved. These levels of the economic integration process have been classified according to several steps which will deepen economic integration: elimination of TBs and NTBs, such as quotas; CETs; the 'four freedoms'; harmonization of economic policies (e.g. tax, social security and pensions); and unification of policies and political institutions (e.g. the common monetary policy of the euro zone countries conducted by the ECB).

Table 2.3 **Stages of the economic integration process classified by several criteria**

Levels (columns) and Stages (rows) of integration	No tariffs or quotas (no TBs or NTBs)	CETs	'Four freedoms'	Harmonization of economic policies	Unification of policies and political institutions
FTA	Yes	No	No	No	No
CU	Yes	Yes	No	No	No
CM	Yes	Yes	Yes	No	No
EcU	Yes	Yes	Yes	Yes	No
TEcU	Yes	Yes	Yes	Yes	Yes

As can be seen in figure 2.1, the European economic integration process has created several, sometimes overlapping, preferential trading agreements at different stages or levels of economic integration. The following agreements and Member States apply in 2009:
- European Free Trade Association (EFTA): Iceland, Liechtenstein, Norway and Switzerland
- European Union (EU-27): Austria, Belgium, Bulgaria, Cyprus, Czech Republic, Denmark, Estonia, Finland, France, Germany, Greece, Hungary, Ireland, Italy, Latvia, Lithuania, Luxembourg, Malta, Netherlands, Poland, Portugal, Romania, Spain, Sweden, Slovenia, Slovakia, United Kingdom (UK)
- European Economic Area (EEA) = EU-27 plus Iceland, Liechtenstein and Norway
- Euro zone or EMU members = Austria, Belgium, Cyprus, Finland, France, Germany, Greece, Ireland, Italy, Luxembourg, Malta, Netherlands, Portugal, Slovakia, Slovenia, Spain
- Schengen Area: EU excluding Bulgaria, Cyprus, Ireland, Romania and UK, plus Iceland, Norway and Switzerland.

Figure 2.1 The relationship between various supranational European organizations

Source: http://en.wikipedia.org/wiki/File:Supranational_European_Bodies.png

The Schengen Area is a group of twenty-five European countries (see figure 2.2) which have abolished all internal border controls. It originated in an agreement signed in the Luxembourg town of Schengen in 1985, which has since been absorbed into the EU. All EU members except Ireland, UK, Bulgaria, Cyprus and Romania, have done so. Three non-Member States, Iceland, Norway and Switzerland, have also implemented the Schengen rules. Implementing the Schengen rules involves eliminating border controls with other Schengen members while simultaneously strengthening border controls with non-Member States. The rules include provisions for common policy on temporary entry of persons (including the Schengen visa), harmonization of external border controls, and cross-border police and judicial co-operation (see 8.1.3 for more details). A typical Schengen border crossing has no border control post and only a standard EU state sign welcoming the visitor.

Figure 2.2 **The Schengen Area**

2.2.1   Free trade area (FTA)

A *free trade area* is an intergovernmental arrangement whereby all tariff barriers and quotas (i.e. quantitative restrictions) impeding trade between the participating member states are removed. However, where imports from non-members are concerned, each member country retains the right to set its external tariff levels independently, irrespective of the policies applied by the other members. Members of FTAs are often vulnerable to the problem of *deflection of trade*, in which non-members reroute (or deflect) their exports to the member country with the lowest external trade barrier (see section 2.5.5). This means that provisions have to be made to prevent external imports entering the FTA via the country with the lowest external tariff. The European Free Trade Association (EFTA), the North American Free Trade Agreement (NAFTA), the Association of South-East Asian Nations (ASEAN) and the Australia and New Zealand Closer Economic Relations trade agreement (CER) are examples of free trade areas.

The members of EFTA are Iceland, Liechtenstein, Norway and Switzerland. Within EFTA, Iceland, for example, may use high tariffs or quotas to discourage imports of a given product from non-members, while Norway may impose few restrictions on imports of the same product from non-members. Taking advantage of the latter's low barriers, non-members may deflect their exports destined for Iceland by first shipping the goods to Norway and then re-exporting them from Norway to Iceland. This type of deflection of trade is more significant in trade with the NAFTA member countries, Canada, the USA and Mexico. To prevent trade deflection from undermining their members' trade policies towards non-members, most FTAs specify *rules of origin*, which detail the conditions under which a product is classified as a member product or a non-member product.

2.2.2 Customs union

A *customs union* (CU) combines the elimination of internal trade barriers between its members with the adoption of common external trade policies towards non-members. Because of the uniform treatment of products from non-member countries, a CU avoids the trade deflection problem. An enterprise from a non-member country pays the same tariff on exports to any member of the CU. A CU is basically an FTA combined with the adoption of common external tariffs (CETs) and quotas, which are imposed by all members on non-member countries. In other words, as well as committing to tariff-free circulation of goods and services within their collective borders, the member countries also agree to establish an unified set of tariff and non-tariff barriers with respect to imports originating from third-party countries.

Typically, a CU involves some degree of political integration, since its members implement a common external trade policy and consequently the participating countries are obliged to give up a degree of national political autonomy. Determining the most appropriate CET is challenging, because member countries must agree on the tariff level. In addition, governments must agree on how to distribute proceeds from the tariff among member countries.

Historically, the most important CU was the 'Zollverein' created in 1834 by several independent principalities in what is now Germany. The eventual unification of Germany in 1871 was hastened by this CU, which tightened the economic bonds among the German principalities and facilitated their political union. A more recent example of a CU is the Mercosur Accord, an economic bloc that has been promoting trade between Argentina, Brazil, Paraguay, Uruguay and Venezuela since 2006.

The difference between an FTA and a CU is, in brief, that the first is politically straightforward but an administrative headache, while the second is just the opposite. Once a CU is established, tariff administration is relatively easy: goods must pay tariffs when they cross the border of the union, but from then on can be shipped freely between countries. A cargo that is unloaded at Marseilles or Rotterdam must pay duties there, but will not face any additional charges if it then goes on by road to Munich. To make this simple system work, the countries must agree on tariff rates: the duty must be the same whether the cargo is unloaded at Marseilles, Rotterdam or Hamburg, because otherwise the importer would choose the point of entry that minimized their payments. So a CU requires that its member states agree to charge the same tariffs. This is not easily done: countries are, in effect, ceding part of their sovereignty to a supranational entity. In Europe, this has been possible for a variety of reasons, including the belief that economic unity would help cement the postwar political alliance between European democracies. Clearly, these conditions are lacking elsewhere, which partly explains why economic integration in Europe has developed through more stages than in the other trading blocs.

2.2.3 Common market

A *common market* (CM) is the third step along the path to total economic integration. Like a CU, a CM, also known as a *single* or *internal market*, establishes a common trade policy towards non-members plus free mobility of the factors of production within the designated group of member countries. A CM goes a step further by eliminating barriers that restrict the movement of labour, capital and technology among its members. Workers may move away from their home country and practise their profession or trade in any of the other member countries. Enterprises may locate production facilities, invest in other businesses and utilize their technologies anywhere within the CM. Productivity within the CM is expected to rise because the factors of production are free to locate where the returns to them are the highest. The Single European Market (SEM) which followed the SEA established the 'four freedoms', thereby creating a common market, in 1992. A worker from an EU country has the right to work in other EU countries, and EU enterprises can freely transfer funds among their subsidiaries within the trading bloc. Common markets are hard to create because they require substantial co-operation from the member countries on socio-economic policies. Moreover, because labour and capital can flow freely inside the bloc, benefits to individual members vary, because skilled labour may move to countries where wages are higher and investment capital may flow to countries where returns are greater. For example, Germany has seen a sharp inflow of workers from Poland and the Czech Republic, because workers from the latter countries can earn substantially higher wages in Germany than they can at home.

A full common market also requires a common system of taxation and common laws and regulations governing production (e.g. product specifications), employment, dismissal of labour, mergers and take-overs, and monopolies and restrictive practices. A common market requires the same rules of play in order to guarantee fair competition on a 'level playing field'. The liberalization of seaports within the EU is an example of a common EU policy designed to achieve a level playing field. This implies creating similar conditions for competition in the areas of dockside buildings, allocation of land, co-financing by (local) government, regulations, imposition of customs duties, etc.

A perfect common market will involve the total absence of border controls between member states, the freedom of workers to work in any member country and the freedom of enterprises to expand into any member state. Another important feature of a full common market is the absence of special treatment by member governments of their own domestic industries. Government procurement policies can function as an indirect form of NTB, especially in countries with a relatively large public sector (such as the Scandinavian countries and the Netherlands). Governments are big purchasers of goods and services, and support domestic industries by adopting procurement policies that restrict purchases to domestic suppliers. For example, several governments require that air travel purchased with government funds be with domestic carriers. In a perfect common market, the government should buy from whichever companies within the market offer the most competitive deal and not favour domestic suppliers. In the past, governments have frequently been found to award contracts to domestic enterprises. However, with the emergence of the SEM and a European common procurement policy this is diminishing. The result of this common procurement policy will be greater efficiency, lower costs and an economically stronger common market. On the other hand, when this strategy is implemented, many enterprises are likely to find themselves losing business to competitors in other EU countries who can provide higher quality and better service at lower cost.

An example of a CM is the European Economic Area (EEA), which was established on 1st January 1994 between the EU and Iceland, Liechtenstein and Norway (three of the four EFTA members). Since 1st May 2004 the EEA has united the 27 EU Member States and the three EFTA member countries into an internal market which promotes the free movement of goods, services, labour and capital among its members in an open and competitive environment. The purpose of the EEA is in essence to allow its members to participate in the EU's internal market without becoming EU members. The aim of the EEA is to promote a continuous and balanced strengthening of trade and economic relations between the member countries, with a view to creating a homogenous EEA. In order to ensure equal conditions for businesses across the whole internal market, the EEA agreement includes rules on competition and state aid. It also includes horizontal provisions relevant to the four freedoms, as well as co-operation outside the four freedoms in so-called 'flanking areas' such as social policy, consumer protection and environment policy. Norway negotiated a number of critical exceptions to the internal market in the fields of common trade policy, agriculture and fisheries, and free movement of workers. The EEA agreement allows for EEA–EFTA participation in EU programmes and agencies, albeit with no right to vote. The EEA–EFTA member countries also make financial contributions towards the reduction of economic and social disparities in the EEA. The agreement covers most important aspects of the EU's relations with the EEA–EFTA member states.

The EEA agreement contains common rules for public procurement in countries within the EEA, covering public-sector purchases of goods, services and construction projects. Norway, like the EU countries, has also acceded to the common procurement policy. Legislation governing public procurement in Norway consists of rules covering the purchase of goods and services, regulations on construction project contracts and special rules applying to government supply sectors.

2.2.4 Economic union with common EU policies

An *economic union* represents full integration of the economies of two or more countries and can be described as a CM combined with some degree of harmonization of national fiscal, social and monetary policies with a view to avoiding the discrimination that may result from discrepancies in these policies (positive integration). Harmonization entails common rules and consistent policies, which inevitably lead to greater uniformity across the members of the economic union (including the principle of mutual recognition).

Harmonization of common EU policies is intended to fine-tune legislation in the various EU Member States in order to encourage the development of the 'four freedoms'. The most important common EU policy is the Common Agricultural Policy (CAP), adopted and implemented by the EU in order to support sufficient food supply, a fair standard of living for farmers, adequate growth in agricultural productivity, and stable and reasonable prices for consumers. Other important common policies of the EU are fisheries, competition, transport and cohesion (or regional policies), including a cohesion fund as a means of providing economic development aid to Member States whose per capita gross domestic product (GDP) is less than 90% of the EU average. The initial recipients of development aid included Spain, Portugal, Greece and Ireland, although Ireland's access to this aid terminated in 2004 because its booming economy elevated Ireland's per capita income above the average for the EU. The aim of the cohesion fund is to support the infrastructure projects and to enhance measures that help to protect and improve the quality of the environment, such as improving the quality of water supply and the treatment of waste. The new members of the EU-27 also qualify for aid from the cohesion fund. Other common EU policies focus on harmonization of taxation (see section 2.2.8), in particular Value Added Tax (VAT), and on social policy, covering such areas as decent levels of income for both the employed and the unemployed, freedom of movement of labour between Member States, freedom to belong to a trade union and equal treatment of men and women in the labour market.

The harmonization of social policies has long been the subject of intense debate. The Treaty of Rome was very ambitious in the area of economic integration, but not in the harmonization of social policies, which has always had a low priority. With respect to this 'omitted' aspect of European integration there are two schools of thought, namely the 'harmonize-before-liberalizing school' versus 'the no-need-to-harmonize school'. According to the first approach, international differences in wages and social conditions give an 'unfair' advantage to countries with more market-oriented social policies. If countries initially have very different social policies, lowering trade barriers will give those countries with low social standards an advantage, assuming that exchange rates and wages do not adjust, for example due to intervention by the authorities.

The 'no-need-to harmonize' school of thought, whose ideas prevailed in the Treaty of Rome, argues that wages and social policies are reflections of differences in productivity and social preferences, which will be adjusted by transparent and flexible labour markets. According to this point of view, enterprises will hire workers up to the point where the total cost of employing workers equals the value they create for the business. As far as the enterprise is concerned, it is not important whether the cost of a worker stems from social policy or from wages paid directly to the worker. Different countries have different productivity levels and this is why wages can differ. If one country has more expensive social policies, the workers in that country will end up taking home as wages a smaller share of the value they create for the enterprise. The reason is that the enterprise pays the costs of the social policy out of the value that the workers themselves create for the business. Of course, this way of reasoning requires an understanding of how (labour) markets work, so it is less easily grasped, which explains why this aspect of European integration has been given a lower priority or has been omitted from the programme.

The difference between a common market and an economic union is rather unclear and difficult to pinpoint, taking into consideration the impact of a common social policy on the EU integration process. The scope of a common market is sometimes extended to include a fixed exchange rate between the member countries' currencies, which might involve a single currency for the whole market (e.g. the euro). A common market can also include common macroeconomic policies, and hence the abolition of separate fiscal and/or monetary intervention by individual member states. On the road to a single monetary union, 16 of the 27 EU members have adopted the euro, a single European Central Bank (ECB) with a unified monetary policy and a common exchange rate with non-members. Since January 1999 these countries have joined the European Economic and Monetary Union (EMU), forming the euro zone. The official abbreviation EMU is somewhat misleading, since it is indeed a European monetary union, but not a true economic union in the sense that the Member States have the same fiscal policies. Each EMU member has its own fiscal policy, which should be fine-tuned with the common monetary policy. An example of a measure in which the fiscal policies of EU members need to be in line with common policy is the EU Stability and Growth Pact (SGP), which aims to guarantee the hardness of the euro.

2.2.5 The EU Stability and Growth Pact

If a particular government persistently runs a budget deficit, the national debt will rise. If it rises faster than GDP, it will account for a growing proportion of GDP. 'Servicing' this debt, i.e. paying the interest on it, is then likely to become an increasing problem. If the government succeeds in borrowing more and more, the national debt will rise faster and so it will have to pay higher interest rates in order to attract finance; hence, investment by the private sector could be crowded out. Since the market of the euro zone will gradually become a level playing field for all EMU members, a rise in interest rates in one Member State might easily create a burden for investors, including the governments of the other Member States. By signing the Treaty of Maastricht in 1992, the EU countries agreed that, to be eligible to join EMU, they must have sustainable deficits and debts. The aim of the SGP is not only to create a level playing field in the financial markets of the EU, but also to curb inflation, since government debts can lead to inflationary effects as a result of more expansionary expenditure. This explains why the SGP includes some of the *convergence criteria* of the Treaty of Maastricht (see section 2.4).

For years, criticism of the SGP turned on whether it was flexible enough. In the Treaty of Amsterdam (1997), the EU countries agreed that governments adopting the euro should seek to balance their budgets, averaged over the course of the business cycle, and that deficits should not exceed 3% of GDP in any one year. A country's deficit is only allowed to exceed 3% if its GDP has declined by at least 2%. Otherwise, countries with deficits exceeding 3% are required to make deposits of money with the ECB. These deposits then become fines if the excessive budget deficit is not eliminated within two years.

There are two main reasons for targeting a zero budget deficit over the business cycle. The first is to allow automatic stabilizers to work without 'bumping into' the 3% deficit ceiling in years when economies are slowing. The second is to achieve a reduction in government debts as a proportion of GDP (assuming that GDP grows on average at around 2–3% per year). The big question is whether the SGP is sufficiently flexible. From 2002 onwards, both Germany and France breached the 3% ceiling. This was partly the result of slow growth and rising unemployment, and hence falling tax revenue and rising benefit payments. Not surprisingly, both countries were reluctant to cut government expenditure to bring the deficit in line, for fear of dampening an already sluggish economy. Despite various promises by the two countries to rein in expenditure, they continued to have deficits in excess of 3%.

Eventually, in March 2005 a deal was reached between European finance ministers. It allowed Germany to exclude reunification costs and France to exclude military and aid costs from the calculation of government expenditure. This compromise brought the deficits of the two countries below the 3% ceiling and allowed them to avoid adopting a tighter fiscal policy.

Since the financial crisis of 2007–09, many EU countries (including France, Spain, Ireland, Greece, Latvia and Malta) have received warnings over their rising budget deficits and debts, but it is obvious that the European Commission is unwilling to impose fines during this extraordinary economic recession, since strict application of the rules might be counterproductive. Basically, the EU considers the SGP as a tool for combating recession which should be used flexibly and not as a straitjacket.

In November 2008 the Commission announced a €200 billion fiscal stimulus plan, mainly in the form of increased expenditure. €170 of the money would come from member governments and €30 from the EU. The money would be used for a range of projects, such as vocational training, help for small businesses, developing green energy technologies and energy efficiency. These measures would push most EMU countries' budget deficits well above the 3% ceiling, but since the recession in EU countries was predicted to deepen in 2009, with real GDP forecast to decline by more than 2% in the euro zone as a whole and by 5.4% in Germany and 3% in France (see table 9.1), this was not seen to breach the SGP.

2.2.6 Total economic integration (political union)

The final stage of economic integration is characterized by full supranational decision making. Member states and national economies effectively merge into one another, forming one unitary state. A supranational political authority is established, which replaces national sovereignty and decides all matters pertaining to economic policy. Decisions made by this overarching political authority are binding on all member states (see section 2.3).

The five Balassa categories are often interpreted as five sequential stages, tracing a path that gradually leads towards deeper forms of integration. However, this is not to say that the order should be rigidly followed. From the very beginning, the EU was based on the idea of a customs union with the objective of becoming a common market, and therefore effectively 'jumped over' the FTA stage. At present, the EU can be categorized as a single, internal or common market and the euro zone as a monetary union (EMU) within the EU-27. (Béla Balassa did not distinguish between economic and monetary union.)

2.2.7 Static and dynamic effects of economic integration

Regional economic integration reduces or eliminates tariff and non-tariff barriers to trade for member countries. It produces both *static effects* and *dynamic effects*. Static effects are the shifting of resources from inefficient to efficient businesses as trade barriers fall. Dynamic effects are the overall growth in the market and the impact on a business of expanding production and of the business's ability to achieve greater economies of scale and scope.

It is important to note that, contrary to the naive neoliberalist view that perceives free trade to be an unequivocally good thing and consequently considers any move towards freer trade desirable, the static or short-term effects of regional integration can in fact be either welfare-enhancing or, in some instances, welfare-reducing. The welfare-enhancing effects derive from *trade creation*, while the welfare-reducing effects result from *trade diversion*. If the latter were to occur, regional integration would not be in the best interest of all member countries. This theoretical framework analysing the ambiguity of the welfare effects was first introduced by Jacob Viner (1892–1970), and as a result the concept became known in 1950 as Viner's Ambiguity.

2.2.7.1 Trade creation and its strategic implications

Trade creation is a situation where, upon joining a regional trade bloc, a given country's trade shifts from a higher-cost domestic producer to a lower-cost producer in another country within the trading bloc. In this scenario, regional integration leads to a change in trading patterns that enables countries to concentrate on producing goods for which they have a natural comparative advantage. As the term implies, trade creation refers to trade that would not have materialized without the existence of the preferential trading system.

The strategic implication of trade creation is that companies which might not have been able to export to another country, even though they might be more efficient than producers in that country, are now able to export when barriers come down. Thus there will be more demand for their products. It is also possible for investment to shift to countries that are more efficient or that have a comparative advantage in one or more of the factors of production.

2.2.7.2 Trade diversion

Trade diversion, on the other hand, occurs when, following the establishment of a trading bloc, the importing country decides to acquire products from a higher-cost trading bloc partner, instead of from the lower-cost producer outside the trading bloc from which it had been importing them, even though the non-member producers might be more efficient in the absence of trade barriers. Hence, trade is being diverted away from a more efficient supplier in a non-member country towards a less efficient supplier in one of the member countries, due to the differential treatment of extra-bloc and intra-bloc imports. Had the tariffs been eliminated against all countries, instead of just the subset that comprises the free trade area, the same imports could have been obtained at less cost. The economic welfare of the importing country is therefore being reduced as a result.

Suppose that, before the formation of NAFTA, Canada and the USA were each self-sufficient in the production of wine. Suppose further that neither country imported wine from the other because of a 100% tariff. Now suppose that, on the formation of NAFTA and the elimination of the tariff, Canada began importing wine from the USA. This is an example of trade creation. Prior to NAFTA, Canada had imported all its wine from France because Canada's tariff on wine imports from France was only 50%, making French wine cheaper than US wine. But NAFTA's launch eliminated the US tariff and made US wine cheaper than French wine. Canada may therefore discontinue its wine imports from France in favour of imports from the USA. This is an example of trade diversion.

When Mexico joined NAFTA, in 1994, it gained a competitive edge over producers in non-NAFTA countries, which were still subject to US tariffs. Consequently, Mexico's exports to the USA increased substantially. However, this came at the expense of some other developing countries' exports. An example of trade diversion in the EU is the trade in olive oil, tomatoes and textile products between the EU and Morocco and Tunisia before and after Spain and Portugal entered the EU in 1986. Since Spain and Portugal became members of the EU most of these products have been imported from these new members, whereas before their entry to the EU they were produced more efficiently at lower cost in Morocco and Tunisia. These countries were then forced to look for other export destinations, such as the USA and the Middle East.

As these examples show, the formation of a preferential trade agreement will typically bring about both effects, trade creation and trade diversion, simultaneously and the net effect on economic welfare will be determined by the relative magnitude of each. Clearly, then, it is uncertain whether a given country is going to be worse off or better off. When trade diversion takes place there may still be a net gain, but there may instead be a net loss, depending on various circumstances and determining factors. Two important factors that will determine whether trade creation or trade diversion will occur when a country joins a customs union are the size of the customs union's external tariff and the cost differences between goods produced within and outside the union. A customs union is more likely to lead to trade diversion rather than trade creation:

- when the union's external tariff is very high. Under these circumstances, the abolition of the tariff within the union is likely to lead to a large reduction in the price of goods imported from other members of the union.
- when there is a relatively small cost difference between goods produced within and outside the union. Here, the abolition of even relatively low tariffs within the union will lead to internally produced goods becoming cheaper than externally produced goods.

2.2.7.3 Dynamic effects of integration

Dynamic effects of integration occur when trade barriers come down and the size of the market increases (see table 2.4). Because of the large size of the market, businesses can increase their production, which will result in a lower cost per unit. In order to survive in a larger market, businesses must produce more cheaply and become more efficient. This could result either in more trade between member countries or in an increase in foreign direct investment (FDI) as the market grows and it becomes feasible for companies to invest in the larger market. Another important effect of regional economic integration is the increase in efficiency due to increased competition. Many multinational enterprises (MNEs) in Europe have attempted to grow through mergers and acquisitions (M&As) in order to achieve the necessary size to compete in the larger market.

Table 2.4 **Static and dynamic effects of a preferential trade agreement**

	Trade impact	Investment impact
Trade barriers reduce for member countries (static effect)	Trade creation	Investment shift from less efficient to more efficient businesses
+		
Trade barriers remain higher for non-member countries (static effect)	Trade diversion	FDI from businesses outside the free trade agreement increases to avoid barriers
↓		
Market size increases (dynamic effect)	Trade creation	Member-country businesses increase FDI to achieve economies of scale

2.2.7.4 The domino effect of regionalism: changing EU trading patterns

Although there is, in general, considerable ambiguity as to the net impact of a trading bloc on the participating countries, the effect on third-party countries, the outsiders, is clearly damaging. The formation of a trading bloc could result in what are known as *'beggar-my-neighbour'* effects, which increase the welfare of a country or a group of countries (e.g. the EU) at the expense of other countries (e.g. the USA) as the differential tariff treatment improves the relative competitiveness of intra-bloc imports at the expense of imports from outside the trading bloc. This is by and large the case, even without excessive protectionist measures being taken by the member countries. Clearly, this effect partly explains how the EU's trading patterns have changed over time. However, there is no real empirical evidence of 'beggar-my-neighbour' policies and the European Commission claims to have encouraged further liberalization of world trade by making efforts in this direction through a larger trading bloc.

The resulting trade diversion, which reduces non-member exporters' profits, generates politico-economic pressure on the outsider countries, either to join an existing trading bloc or alternatively to form a new, competing one. These pressures grow every time a new member joins a trading bloc, as the bloc's increasing size and scope place the outsider countries at a disadvantage in an ever greater number of markets. The larger the trading bloc, the more vulnerable the countries outside it become in terms of trade flows. Therefore, each successive enlargement or each event that deepens the integration of existing bloc members increases the pressure on non-participants to jump on board and join the bloc, leading to new membership applications. This partly explains the acceleration of EU enlargement in 2004, when ten new Member States joined, and again in 2007 with the accession of Bulgaria and Romania. Economic regionalism may trigger a series of membership applications from countries that were formerly quite happy to stay out. This is called the *'domino effect'* of regionalism: one act of integration triggers another. In Europe, the dynamics of the domino effect have been witnessed in the progressive enlargement of the EU. Policymakers worry that the EU, NAFTA and other trading blocs could turn into economic fortresses, resulting in a decline in trade between blocs (*inter-trade*) that exceeds the gains from trade within the blocs (*intra-trade*). This point is often stressed by opponents of further European integration.

2.2.8 The impact of the European common market on individuals and businesses

From the viewpoint of an individual enterprise, regional integration is a two-edged sword. Lowering TBs and NTBs within the trading bloc opens the markets of all member countries to every enterprise in a member country. Businesses can reduce their average production, marketing, distribution and research & development (R&D) costs by capturing economies of scale and scope as they expand their customer base within the trading bloc. Although businesses in EU member countries have gained improved access to a larger market, they also face increased competition in their home markets from businesses in other member countries, which threatens less efficient businesses.

A regional trading bloc such as the EU may also attract FDI from non-member countries, as businesses outside the bloc seek the benefits of insider status by establishing manufacturing facilities within the EU. Most non-European multinationals, including General Mills, Toyota and Samsung, have invested heavily in the EU to take advantage of Europe's increased economic integration. These investments bolster the productivity of European workers and increase the choices available to European consumers, but they threaten established European business-es such as Unilever, Renault and Siemens. Since the publication in 1985 of the White Paper on Completing the Internal Market, intended to accelerate progress on ending all trade barriers and restrictions on the free movement of goods, services, capital and labour among members, many US and Japanese companies have set up operations in the EU.

The common or single market means a lot for both individuals and businesses. Before 1993, if you were travelling in Europe, you had a 'duty-free allowance'. This meant that you could only take goods up to the value of €600 across borders within the EU without having to pay duties in the country into which you were importing them. Now you can take as many goods as you like from one EU country to another, provided they are for your own consumption. However, to prevent fraud, Member States may ask for evidence that the goods have been purchased for the traveller's own consumption if the quantity exceeds a specified limit.

Before 1993, all goods traded in the EU were subject to VAT at every internal border. This involved some 60 million customs clearance documents annually, at a cost of some €70 per consignment. All of this has now disappeared: goods can pass from one Member State to another without any border controls. In fact, the concepts of 'importing' and 'exporting' within the EU no longer officially exist. All goods sent from one EU country to another are charged VAT only in the country of destination. They are exempt from VAT in the country where they are produced.

One of the most important requirements for fair competition in the single market is the convergence of tax rates. Although rates of income tax, corporate tax and excise duties still differ between Member States, there has been some narrowing in the range of VAT rates: there is now a lower limit of 15% on the standard rate of VAT. What is more, the Member States have agreed to abolish higher rates of VAT on luxury goods and to have no more than two lower rates of at least 5% on 'socially necessary' goods, such as food and water supply.

How to do business with the EU: implications for corporate strategy
Especially for non-EU MNEs, doing business in the EU can influence corporate strategy in three ways:
1. Determine where to produce products. One strategy is to produce products in a central location in the EU, to minimize transportation costs and the time it takes to move products from one country to another. However, the highest costs are in Central Europe. For instance, manufacturing wages in the German car industry exceed €30 per hour, compared with much lower wages in Eastern European EU countries. This is why Toyota opted to set up operations in lower-wage countries such as the Czech Republic and Poland.
2. Determine whether to grow through new investments, through expanding existing investments or through joint ventures and mergers. US companies are buying EU companies and vice versa to gain a market presence and to get rid of competition. For instance, in order to take advantage of the European car manufacturers' supplier network, Toyota has entered into a joint venture with PSA Peugeot–Citroën to build a new factory in the Czech Republic. In general, the European car market is more fragmented than the North American market, while the Japanese market is the most consolidated. The five largest European brands, Renault, Volkswagen, Peugeot, Fiat and Citroën, together account for only 44% of the European market.
3. Balance 'common denominators' with national differences. Besides national differences which are mainly due to language and history, there are also widely differing growth rates in the EU. Many smaller countries, such as Belgium and Ireland, have experienced unprecedented growth because their EU membership has increased their attractiveness for FDI, helped them to develop global perspectives and sheltered them from economic risks. In terms of products, Toyota is busy designing a European car, but for which Europe? Tastes and

preferences vary greatly between northern and southern EU countries. Toyota, however, is attempting to use its production location and design to facilitate a pan-European strategy.

2.3 Two schools of European integration: federalism versus intergovernmentalism

Ever since the Second World War, the European integration process has always hesitated between two opinions or two approaches. These two schools of European integration can be summarized as a tendency in favour of more federalism and a tendency in favour of more intergovernmentalism. Basically, the two sides are debating whether the European integration process should go into the direction of further economic integration combined with political integration (federalism) or further economic integration without political integration (intergovernmentalism). In the European Union, the Council of Ministers is an example of a purely intergovernmental body while the Commission, the European Parliament and the European Court of Justice represent the supranational mode of decision making.

The federalist school of thought, strongest in Germany, stresses that in order to prevent another business cycle of recovery combined with national rivalry, which might lead to a third world war, nation states should be embedded in a federalist structure. This means that European policies should be conducted by supranational organizations embodying some of the powers that had traditionally been exercised exclusively by nation states (such as the ECB, which currently conducts the monetary policy of the euro zone).

The school of intergovernmentalism, led largely by British thinkers, continues to view nation states as the most effective and most stable form of government. On this view, European integration should take the form of closer (economic) co-operation conducted strictly on an intergovernmental basis, i.e. all power should remain in the hands of national officials and any co-operation must be agreed unanimously by all participants. The main differences between federalism (or supranationalism) on the one hand and intergovernmentalism on the other hand are the following:
- Federalists assume that economic integration creates pressure for integration in other sectors (one of which is the political sector) and they therefore argue that politics follows economics. The intergovernmental approach presents the idea of economics and politics being independent of one another and therefore concludes that economic integration does not necessary lead to political integration.
- Federalists argue that supranational organizations should be the key actors in common European policies, while intergovernmentalists consider that nation states and their governments should fulfill this role.
- Federalists view the EU as a quasi-state in which Member State governments still hold the power and must share it with other actors, while intergovernmentalists see decision-making power especially as belonging to Member States.

- Federalists strongly support majority voting, arguing that where decisions must be made by several governments acting unanimously it could take years to reach some decisions (if at all), while intergovernmentalists favour decision making by unanimity.
- Federalism opposes the claim that only national governments can possess the necessary democratic legitimacy to exercise sovereignty. Supporters of federalism or supranationalism do not fear loss of sovereignty (autonomy); in fact, they support the idea that states should voluntarily give up some of their sovereignty and hand it over to collective institutions, in return for the many gains, prosperity and collective strength that such integration provides. Supporters of intergovernmentalism argue that EU integration should only involve the pooling of sovereignty, which strengthens the nation state, not the giving up of any part of it.

The various stages in the European integration process, explained in section 2.2, have involved taking steps in the different directions of federalism and intergovernmentalism in different areas of the integration process. This has resulted in differing approaches to common EU policy, such as in the common agricultural policy and the common foreign affairs policy. An important economic advantage of the EU's implementation of federalism is that it accommodates regional preferences and diversity through the *subsidiarity principle*, which is enshrined in the Treaty of Maastricht (1992). Within the context of the EU integration process, the principle of subsidiarity means that decisions should be made as close to the people as possible, and that the EU should not take action unless doing so is more effective than taking action at national, regional or local level.

In the intergovernmental approach there is no sharing of sovereignty. Each Member State retains its own power over the decisions made about any application or agreement. The intergovernmental system is needed to keep national policies as closely co-ordinated as possible with the core decision-making process. A weakness of intergovernmental systems is the lack of effective powers of enforcement to ensure that every nation state obeys the common rules agreed by the Council of Ministers. Disputes and settlements are handled by the European Court of Justice. The Treaty of Maastricht (1992) drew a clear line between supranational and intergovernmental policy areas by creating what is known as the *'three-pillar concept'* of EU organizational structure. The treaty, which came into force in November 1993, rests on the following three pillars, designed to further European economic and political integration (see figure 2.3):
- a new agreement to create a common foreign and security policy among members
- a new agreement to co-operate on police, judicial and public safety matters (home affairs)
- the old familiar European Community, with new provisions to create an economic and monetary union among member countries.

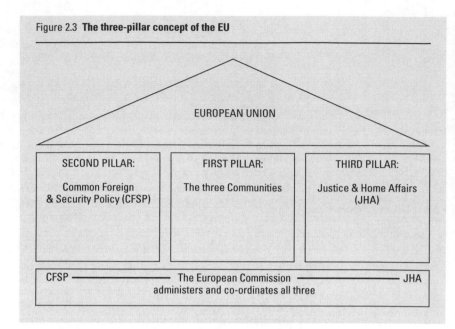

Figure 2.3 **The three-pillar concept of the EU**

EUROPEAN UNION

SECOND PILLAR:

Common Foreign
& Security Policy (CFSP)

FIRST PILLAR:

The three Communities

THIRD PILLAR:

Justice & Home Affairs
(JHA)

CFSP —————————— The European Commission —————————— JHA
administers and co-ordinates all three

In a nutshell, the policies of deeper integration up to and including the Treaty of Maastricht (the 'European Communities') are in the first pillar and continue to be subject to the supranationality of the Treaty of Rome. The intergovernmental policy areas are in the second and third pillars (common foreign and security policy in the second pillar and co-operation in the fields of justice and home affairs in the third). This 'three-pillar concept' is based on the 'Four Treaties' and the EU is the 'roof' covering the three pillars. The Four Treaties are the treaties establishing the European Coal and Steel Community (ECSC), the European Economic Community (EEC) and the European Atomic Energy Community (Euratom) and the Treaty on European Union or Treaty of Maastricht (TEU).

The European Commission, the day-to-day executive body of the EU, administers and co-ordinates all three pillars. Some find the following cynical phrase to be useful in remembering the numbering of the EU pillars: 'economics comes first, justice comes last and security is in the middle'. The three-pillar structure resolved the controversy over further integration through federalism or intergovernmentalism. This reduced the resistance of the UK and other supporters of intergovernmentalism to discussing closer integration in such areas as police co-operation and foreign policy co-operation. There is no possibility of the European Court of Justice or the European Commission using its authority to force deeper integration on reluctant members in pursuit of the duties assigned to them by the Treaty of Rome. It cannot be predicted which route the EU will follow or which system will be applied. However, if the plan to create a single constitution applying to all members of the EU is accepted and implemented, it will be a big step towards the federalist system. When an EU constitution is implemented, national laws will be overruled by European law, which means that nation states will lose sovereignty. The political debate over the 'three-pillar concept' in the context of a timeline of EU treaties and levels of European integration is explained in more detail in chapter 3 (see figure 3.1).

2.4 The road to EMU: preconditions for achieving an optimal currency area

It is important to understand why a large currency area such as the euro zone is desirable and what are the preconditions for achieving an optimum currency area (OCA). An OCA can be described as the conditions to be met in order to realize the maximum benefits from having a single currency (such as the euro) relative to the costs. The problem is that the bigger the OCA, the more likely it is that conditions in different parts of the area will diverge. Some parts of the OCA may have higher unemployment and require expansionary policies. Other parts may have low unemployment and suffer from inflationary pressures which may require tighter policies. It is important to understand the trade-off between costs and benefits as an OCA grows larger, in terms of a greater range of income differences on the one hand and a greater effectiveness of money in the real economy on the other hand. A larger OCA enhances the effectiveness of money, since money's impact on the real economy becomes greater in terms of its effect on inflation rates, income growth and expansion of employment. Setting out the path to EMU, the Treaty of Maastricht included plans to achieve monetary union in three stages. After attempts to co-ordinate monetary policy and encourage greater co-operation between EU central banks in stage 1, the Member States sought to meet five *convergence criteria* in stage 2:
- Inflation: should be no more than 1.5% above the average inflation rate of the three EU countries with the lowest inflation.
- Interest rates: the rate on long-term government bonds should be no more than 2% above the average of the three countries with the lowest inflation rates.
- Budget deficit: should be no more than 3% of GDP at market prices.
- National debt: should be no more than 60% of GDP at market prices.
- Exchange rates: the currency should have been within the normal Exchange Rate Mechanism (ERM) bands for at least two years with no realignments or excessive intervention.

The Council of Ministers had to decide which countries had met the convergence criteria and were thus eligible to progress to stage 3. At the beginning of stage 3, on 1 January 1999, the countries that met the five criteria would fix their currencies permanently to the euro and their national currencies would therefore effectively disappear. At the same time, a European System of Central Banks (ESCB) was created, consisting of the ECB and the national central banks (NCBs) of the EU Member States (the ECB plus the NCBs of the EMU members is called the 'Eurosystem'). The monetary policy of the ECB is independent of governments and EU political institutions. The euro zone started with 11 of the then 16 Member States in January 1999; only the UK, Denmark, Sweden and Greece (joining in 2001) did not join the euro zone. Currently, 16 of the 27 Member States have adopted the euro, including Cyprus, Greece, Malta, Slovakia and Slovenia (in 2009).

Although the EMU members unambiguously met the interest rate and inflation criteria, many Eurosceptics have their doubts as to whether they all genuinely met the other three criteria. First, many EMU members (such as Finland, Italy and Slovenia) had not been in the ERM for at least two years. Second, only four EU countries had national debts that did not exceed 60% (France, Finland, Luxembourg and the UK). However, the Treaty of Maastricht allowed countries to exceed this proportion as long as the debt was 'sufficiently diminishing and approaching the reference value at a satisfactory pace'. Critics argued that this phrase was interpreted too loosely. Third, some countries only managed to achieve a deficit of 3% or less by taking one-off measures, such as imposing a special tax in Italy and counting privatization receipts in Germany. The concern was that countries which only just met this criterion at time of entry would find it difficult to keep on track in times of recession or depression. This proved to be the case for France and Germany from 2002 to 2005: their budget deficits and debts rose substantially above the convergence criteria in order to reduce their high unemployment rates and push up their growth rates.

In June 1997 the EU countries agreed on the Stability and Growth Pact (SGP), according to which EMU governments should seek to balance their budgets (or even aim for a surplus) averaged over the course of the business cycle and budget deficits should not exceed 3% of GDP in any one year (see section 2.2.5). Countries with deficits exceeding this limit were required to make deposits of money with the ECB, which would become fines if the excessive budget deficit was not eliminated within two years. In 2005, Portugal, Germany and France had all exceeded this amount, but the Council of Ministers had not voted to fine those states. Subsequently, reforms were adopted to allow more flexibility and ensure that the deficit criteria took into account the economic conditions of the Member States, as well as additional factors. The main criticism of targeting a zero budget deficit over the business cycle has been that this would promote further *deflationary fiscal policies* which might be inappropriate at a time when there were fears of a world recession. Deflationary or tight fiscal policies involve a reduction in government expenditure (e.g. subsidies) and/or an increase in taxes or other income. This leads to lower demand over supply of goods and services, which will lower their prices (other things being equal).

2.4.1 Advantages and disadvantages of EMU: How desirable is the euro area?

EMU has several benefits and costs, which are usually stressed by its proponents and opponents respectively. Several of the major advantages are the elimination of the cost of currency conversion; increased competition and efficiency of production, leading to greater transparency in pricing and greater downward pressure on prices in high-cost businesses and countries; elimination of exchange-rate uncertainty between members, which reduces destabilizing speculation and encourages trade and investment between EMU countries; increased inward investment from the rest of the world (e.g. more FDIs); and lower levels and convergence of inflation and interest rates. The fact that the ECB is independent of short-term political manipulation designed to boost employment rates has resulted in a relatively low average inflation rate in the euro zone. This should help to convince financial markets that the euro will maintain its strength relative to other currencies. The result is lower long-term rates of interest, which will further encourage investment in the EMU countries. Although the ECB does not explicitly target the euro exchange rate, through its *monetary targeting* policy strategy (see section 7.5) the average inflation rate in the euro zone will be stabilized between 0% and 2% and this will indirectly affect the euro exchange rate. This explains why the current president of the ECB, Jacques Trichet, was worried about rising inflation rates in the euro zone due to cost-push factors such as rising energy (oil) and food prices in 2007, but was willing to lower the rates when average EMU inflation was falling due to the financial crisis and resulting economic slowdown of 2007–09.

As explained in section 2.1, many Eurosceptics consider EMU to be a surrendering of national political and economic sovereignty and not an optimum currency area at all. The lack of independent monetary and exchange-rate policies at the national level is considered as a serious shortcoming of EMU. When certain members are faced with greater inflationary cost-push pressures than others (due to strong trade unions, for example), they will find it more difficult to make their goods competitive with the rest of the world. This will lead to greater divergence in welfare between different EMU members and require more emphasis on regional policies. Europhiles, however, argue that it is better to tackle the problem of high inflation in 'depressed' regions of Europe through increased competition than merely to feed that inflation by keeping separate currencies and allowing repeated devaluations, with all the uncertainty that they bring. With free movement of labour and capital, resources are likely to be attracted to those countries or sectors with the highest added value or competitive cost advantage. For example, the movement of Polish workers to Germany and the Netherlands and of Romanian workers to Italy could help to narrow the gap between the richer and the poorer Member States. Critics of EMU counter this by arguing that labour is relatively immobile in Europe because of the cultural and language barriers. Thus an unemployed worker in Wales could not easily move to a job in Italy or Finland, so the EU is not an OCA.

A more serious issue raised by opponents of EMU is the *'one-size-fits-all'* problem, referring to the fact that the same interest rate must apply to all EMU countries. Since the aims of curbing inflation (and strengthening the currency) on the one hand and lowering unemployment rates on the other hand are quite often in conflict with each other, one country might require a higher interest rate, while another needed a lower interest rate in order to prevent a recession. A counter-argument on this issue is that the ECB, which is accountable for price stability within the euro zone, should be fully independent of the national governments, which are responsible for the employment rates in their member countries. The SGP should be used to prevent excessive differences arising between members' government spending financed on the capital market.

Besides the 'one-size-fits-all' problem, another difficulty arises for EMU members in adjusting to a shock when that shock affects members to different degrees. Such so-called *asymmetric shocks* are most likely to be associated with shifts in spending patterns due to changing tastes or technologies which affect only one country in a currency area. Different members of the currency area may experience different-sized shocks to their economies, whether from outside the currency area (e.g. a fall in the price of one of their major exports) or from inside (e.g. a prolonged strike). Another example of an asymmetric shock is a sudden change in the price of oil, which will affect the economy of an oil-exporting country such as the UK differently from oil-importing countries.

When an asymmetric shock affects the euro zone, formulating a policy response is difficult, because there is little scope for independent monetary or exchange-rate management. For instance, if southern EMU countries are experiencing high inflation and northern EMU countries are experiencing deflation, any ECB policy that aims to reduce the problem in one region is likely to make it worse in another region.

The OCA theory emphasizes the role of asymmetric shocks and proposes criteria by which to judge the costs and the desirability of sharing the same currency. The occurrence of asymmetric shocks in the euro zone is a concern but can be dealt with through fiscal and monetary policies.

Case study 2.1 What are the advantages and disadvantages of EMU?

What are the benefits and costs to a country of joining a monetary union such as the European EMU? With respect to the economic benefits and costs, the best way to examine this question is by means of a framework developed by Robert Mundell, an economist at Columbia University, who devised the concept of an 'Optimum Currency Area'

Benefits:
- Elimination of foreign exchange transaction (currency conversion) costs within the euro zone. Prior to the advent of the euro, enterprises conducting cross-border business within Europe were forced to pay fees to bankers, typically ranging from 0.4% to 2% of the transaction value, whenever they wished to convert French francs into Belgian francs, Dutch guilders into Austrian schillings and so on.
- Elimination of exchange-rate uncertainty relating to the country's currency against the euro, which should improve the quality of information on which consumers and enterprises base their decisions. Many enterprises bore exchange-rate risks in currency conversion transactions, although the foreign exchange market developed a variety of techniques to reduce or hedge these risks. The creation of the euro eliminated a lot of currency conversion and hedging costs.

- Greater price transparency when all goods are priced in euros, which may lead to increased competition within the single market.
- Participation in more integrated market-based European financial markets as a result of the elimination of currency risk. This has led to more efficient European financing of business activities.
- Joining a low-inflation area, provided the ECB keeps inflation in check, which contributes to the economic efficiency and credibility of the central bank.

Costs:
- The country can no longer conduct monetary policy on its own behalf.
- The country may have to substantially limit its use of expansionary fiscal policies under the SGP.
- The exchange rate is no longer available to cushion asymmetric shocks. For example, a decline in demand for the country's exports, which is specific to the country, would lead to an automatic depreciation of the currency if the exchange rate were floating. This would cushion the effect on the economy. On the other hand, if the country is part of an EMU, there is no longer a pound sterling, for example, to depreciate against other currencies, so the cushioning mechanism would be lost.

Whether the economic benefits exceed the costs depends on four factors:
1 the degree of trade integration with the other countries in the euro zone
2 the degree of labour mobility with the other countries in the euro zone
3 the number of 'asymmetric shocks' that hit the country
4 the flexibility of wages within the country.

The bottom line is that, based on the current state of knowledge, it is impossible to compute the economic benefits and costs of joining a monetary union with any degree of precision. From a strictly economic point of view, therefore, one cannot legitimately say whether or not the UK should adopt the euro.

This leaves open the question of whether the UK would reap any net political gain from adopting the euro. Some highly respected economists have made interesting remarks about the politics of EMU which might give an insight into the question 'Should the UK adopt the euro?':
1 'Politically, monetary unification has been seen as a practical and symbolic step toward the development of a capacity to formulate social and foreign policies at the European level.' (Eichengreen & Frieden)

2 'Political leaders in Europe see EMU as a way to further the political agenda of a federalist European political union, which will have a common foreign and military policy and a much more centralized determination of what are currently nationally determined economic and social policies.' (Feldstein)

3 'European economic integration has always been a politically motivated enterprise [...] If EMU succeeds on its economics, the political vision that gave birth to the project will be well served.' (Obstfeld)

4 'The euro is foremost a political project that is deeply entangled in European history.' (Chabot)

5 'If EMU succeeds, it will promote European political as well as economic integration, fostering peace and prosperity in a region that could some day include Eastern Europe. If EMU fails, however, its driving force, the goal of European political unification, will be set back.' (Krugman & Obstfeld)

6 'EMU should be understood as a bargain between Germany and France, where France wants monetary integration to recapture some control over the continent's monetary policy (which it gave up to Germany under EMS), while Germany wants political integration in order to acquire a foreign policy role in the context of an EU foreign policy.' (Eichengreen)

If you are a political conservative, you will probably side with Feldstein and view adopting the euro with alarm. Others might feel that the UK will be left behind politically and lose its voice in European affairs if it does not adopt the euro.

2.4.2 Preconditions for an optimum currency area

Several criteria for an OCA have been advanced. Three well-known classic economic criteria are the *labour mobility criterion* (proposed by Robert Mundell), the *openness criterion* (proposed by Ronald McKinnon) and the *production diversification criterion* (proposed by Peter Kenen).

Robert Mundell's *labour mobility criterion* looks at how to minimize the costs of sharing the same currency within a currency area in terms of reduced unemployment. The idea is that the costs of sharing the same currency would be eliminated if the factors of production, capital and labour were fully mobile across borders. If, for instance, country A is booming, while country B suffers from weak demand and unemployment, and if labour can move from B to A fairly easily, the regional imbalance can be corrected without the need for country B to adopt fiscal and/or monetary policies, and perhaps accept inflation, to stimulate demand. Since it is conventionally assumed that (financial) capital is mobile (in particular since the deregulation and liberalization of the capital markets during the 1980s), the real hurdle is lack of labour mobility, which is caused by several factors. First, not only do cultural and linguistic differences across borders restrain migration, but institutional barriers further discourage labour mobility (e.g. varying labour market regulations and traditions, differences in welfare systems between members and difficulties in reaching agreements between enterprises, trade unions and governments). Changes in legislation can facilitate cross-border labour mobility and increase the size of an OCA. Second, the goods produced in country A may differ from those produced in country B (e.g. the cheese produced in Italy is different from that in the Netherlands), so it may take some time to retrain workers. Third, labour needs equipment to be productive. Although financial capital can move freely and quickly (there are no longer any exchange controls in the EU), installed physical capital (means of production such as plants and equipment) is not mobile. It takes time to build plants and change the location of economic activities. The Mundell criterion thus focuses on labour's market willingness to move in response to asymmetric shocks. Labour mobility is not a panacea, but just one of the many factors that mitigate the costs of an asymmetric shock in the currency area.

Greater labour mobility within an OCA can also have adverse effects when it causes a region with low productivity to experience a rapid rise in wages because unemployment has made skilled workers leave. The movement of workers from eastern to western Germany since German reunification in 1990 is a case in point. The EU enlargement of 2004 is another example of an event which caused many Eastern European (especially Polish) workers to search for better job opportunities in Western Europe. Labour mobility is not always an appropriate solution to temporary fluctuations in the demand for labour, because the costs of moving are considerable and because it could threaten the 'catching up' process of economically weaker EMU Member States. Unlike the USA and Canada, the current EMU cannot be qualified as an OCA on the criterion of labour mobility owing to rigidities in the labour market and cultural and linguistic difficulties. Differences in unemployment levels are not fully reflected in differences in real wages (i.e. nominal wages adjusted for the cost of living). This means that asymmetric shocks, when they occur, are likely to be met by unemployment in countries facing a loss of competitiveness.

Ronald McKinnon's *openness criterion* emphasizes that, when a country's economy is small and very open to trade, it has little ability to change the prices of its goods on international markets. In that situation, giving up the exchange rate as a tool for adjusting its competitiveness does not entail a serious loss of policy independence. Relatively small and open economies, with a high degree of interdependence with other countries, can benefit the most from expanding demand in a neighbouring country and can relatively easily form an OCA. Examples in the EU are Belgium, Denmark, Ireland and the Netherlands, which have very high exposure to the outside world measured in terms of exports and imports as a percentage of GDP. These countries with a relatively high export versus import ratio are highly dependent upon trade and as such are very vulnerable when the business cycle of their trading partners deteriorates. Small fluctuations in the exchange rate will immediately affect their price levels. For example, a depreciation of the currency by a small, open economy is more rapidly dissipated by price increases (*import-price-push inflation*), since its relatively high import ratio must entail a larger direct upward effect of import prices on consumer prices, which could pass through into higher wage costs (*wage-push inflation*).

According to Peter Kenen's *production diversification criterion*, the countries most likely to be affected by severe shocks are those that have specialized in a narrow range of goods. A country whose economy is highly specialized and highly interdependent with other countries cannot achieve gains through exchange-rate adjustments at all. Suppose that France produces all the perfume in the EU and the UK all the whisky. In that case, a depreciation of the pound sterling cannot increase the production of the UK perfume industry, which does not exist, or of its whisky industry, which already has the entire EU market. In such an extreme case, a depreciation of the domestic currency can only increase prices and will have no real effect even in the short term. However, although there are some products whose production in the EU is country-specific, most products are produced in several Member States and exchange-rate changes do not necessarily increase the degree of diversification in an economy. A country in which one industry produces a substantial part of its GDP but has a small share of its foreign markets may advantageously use exchange-rate adjustments to cope with a shock affecting that industry. For example, if the steel industry were in a global recession, the country in which steel production was proportionally the largest might benefit most by the depreciation of its currency, which would increase its share of the world's consumption of steel. This would mitigate unemployment in the undiversified, steel-dependent country.

To sum up: the more integrated and industrially similar the member states become, the less useful exchange-rate flexibility between them is likely to be. Exchange-rate adjustments designed to increase production also become less useful when the concerning trading countries are more diversified. This explains why the Kenen criterion states that countries whose production and exports are widely diversified and of similar structure form an OCA in which exchange rate policy no longer exists.

In the UK, Eurosceptics see the passing of numerous new laws and regulations by centralized EU authorities as a direct threat to British self-governance. The UK is a sovereign state and the British electorate has little control over legislative measures by EU federal authorities in continental Europe. The UK has resisted joining EMU because such a move would reduce the power that it currently holds over its own currency, economy and monetary regime.

Since none of the criteria above is likely to be fully satisfied, no currency area is ever optimum. When separate countries contemplate the formation of a currency area, they need to realize that there will be times when disagreements arise which may follow national lines. When the common monetary policy gives rise to conflicts of national inter-est, the countries forming a currency area need to accept the costs in the name of their common destiny (the solidarity criterion). The costs of asymmetric shocks (and hence the costs of the euro zone) will be greater, the less the mobility of labour and capital, the less the flexibil-ity of prices and wages, and the fewer the alternative policies that are available (such as fiscal and regional policies).

The theory of an OCA provides a useful framework for thinking about the considerations that determine whether a group of countries will gain or lose by fixing their mutual exchange rates. The extent to which the euro zone becomes such an OCA will depend mainly on the accu-mulation of market-integrated policies that started in the 1960s with the customs union and the CAP and is now being taken further with the Treaty of Lisbon to promote growth and employment.

Although it is hard to determine quantitatively whether the euro zone is an OCA or not, as there are OCA criteria which may be only par-tially fulfilled, by combining the theory with information about the actual economic performance of the EMU countries it will become more obvious whether the euro zone qualifies as an OCA. One way of measuring this is to look at the extent of intra-European trade. At the time of the introduction of the euro, in 1999, most EU members exported between 10 and 20% of their production to other EU mem-bers. That percentage is far larger than the extent of EU–US trade but smaller than the amount of trade between regions of the USA.

Europhiles stress that multiple currencies made big price discrepancies possible, but that these should disappear under the single currency. In the case of some goods (such as consumer electronics) there has been considerable price convergence across EU countries since the euro's introduction. With other goods, including cars, similar items can still sell for widely differing prices in different European locations (owing partly to differences in excise duties and partly to the fact that the EU car industry is characterized as fairly domestically oriented).

The volume of intra-trade presents a more optimistic picture. While the extent of trade has fluctuated since the mid 1980s, the pronounced growth of trade after the creation of EMU suggests that the single cur-rency itself may have encouraged trade among EU countries, when then moved closer to forming an OCA. Although the creation of EMU has had a considerable effect on trade creation, it seems unlikely that the combination of the creation of a common market (in 1992) and the single currency (in 1999) has yet turned the EMU countries into an OCA. Based on the following factors, the current EMU still cannot be considered an OCA:
- Labour is relatively immobile. Although border controls no longer form the main barriers to labour mobility within the EU, differ-ences in language and culture discourage labour movements between EU countries. This partly explains why differences in regional unemployment rates in the USA are smaller and less per-

sistent than differences in national unemployment rates in the EU. Even within EU countries, labour mobility appears limited, partly because of government regulations.

- There are structural differences between Member States. The labour force of the northern EU countries is more academically skilled, while that of the southern countries is more vocationally skilled. EU products that make intensive use of vocationally skilled labour (such as shoes and leather products) are thus likely to come from Portugal, Spain, Greece or southern Italy. The proponents of the EMU project stress that, in time, the completion of the single European market will either remove these differences by redistributing capital and labour across Europe or increase them by encouraging regional specialization to exploit economies of scale and scope.
- The degree of interest-rate responsiveness to both the investment and the supply of money varies between Member States.
- Exports to countries outside the euro zone account for differing proportions of the members' GDP, and thus their economies are affected differently by any change in the euro's exchange rate against other countries.
- Wage rates are relatively inflexible and real wage costs do not always reflect differences in productivity growth.
- Under the SGP the scope of using *discretionary fiscal policies* is curtailed. Discretionary fiscal policies are deliberate changes in tax rates or the level of government expenditure in order to influence actual demand or GDP.

The first years of the euro were characterized by widely differing growth performance among EMU members. The ECB's monetary policy stance was probably not appropriate for all members. One result was divergences in inflation rates (in particular between countries such as the Netherlands, with relatively low inflation, and Ireland and Portugal, with relatively high inflation in the first years of EMU). However, rates have gradually converged in the second half of the current decade (see section 7.6).

Case study 2.2 UK convergence criteria for EMU membership: passing the five economic tests

The UK has a long history of ambivalence towards the concept of European unification. It did not join the EEC until 1973, having been vetoed by France a decade earlier. Shortly after finally joining, the UK held a referendum on the possibility of pulling out. In 1990 Britain entered the European Monetary System (EMS), fixing sterling to the Deutsche Mark (DM) at a rate that some observers thought overvalued the pound. Slow growth resulted, and two years later, in September 1992, the UK government abandoned the EMS with some relief and allowed sterling to float downward under pressure of a currency crisis.

For a long time there has been a national divide over entry into the euro zone and with it the adoption of the euro. This disagreement could not be better illustrated than by the former prime minister Tony Blair, a proponent of EMU membership, and his chancellor of the exchequer and eventual successor, Gordon Brown. The official position of the Labour government is that it is in favour of the UK joining 'when the time is right'. For the time to be right, *'five economic tests'* must be passed. These relate to:
- convergence between the UK and EMU;
- flexibility to cope with economic change;
- the effect on investment;
- the impact on the UK financial services industry;
- the impact on employment.

If all these five tests are met in a 'clear and unambiguous' way, the UK government will recommend joining and the decision will be taken by the electorate in a referendum. In 2003, after four years' experience of the euro zone, the UK Treasury carried out a detailed economic study of the five tests (see below).

1 Convergence: Are business cycles and economic structures compatible, so that we and others could live comfortably with euro interest rates on a permanent basis?

This is probably the key test. It essentially asks whether the business cycle in the UK is convergent with that (or those) of the euro zone countries. If the UK economy is in a rapid expansion phase, while the euro area is in recession, then the UK requires higher interest rates to dampen its excessive expansion, while the euro-zone countries require lower interest rates to boost aggregate demand. Clearly, with a single interest rate, there would be a problem if the UK's cycle were out of synch with the euro area.

Asssessment (2003): According to the government's assessment, there had been substantial (although not sufficient) movement towards convergence of the UK and euro-zone business cycles since 1997. Indeed, the UK economy showed more convergence here than did the economies of some individual euro-zone countries. Moreover, apart from not being in the ERM, the UK met the remaining original Maastricht criteria for euro membership.

One of the main remaining problems, however, is the lack of convergence in the housing markets, with most UK mortgage lending being at variable interest rates, while much of the lending for house purchase in the euro area is at fixed rates. This could make a common euro-zone interest rate inappropriate for the UK. This test was thus judged to have been failed.

2 Flexibility: If problems emerge, is there sufficient flexibility to deal with them?

The main issue here is that of asymmetric shocks. If the UK is affected differently by an economic shock (such as an oil price increase or a rise in US interest rates), is there sufficient economic flexibility to adjust to this? In other words, are prices sufficiently flexible; is there sufficient labour mobility; is the economy generally sufficiently adaptable to new economic circumstances? This is the same issue that faces regions within a country. If one part of a country (such as an industrial belt or a mining area) is affected differently from another (such as a region with a high number of service industries), is there

sufficient flexibility to deal with this and prevent a rise in regional unemployment and deprivation?

Assessment (2003): UK labour market flexibility had increased markedly in recent years, with a resulting fall in the equilibrium unemployment level. However, the assessment pointed to a lack of flexibility throughout much of the euro area, making it necessary for the UK to exercise even greater flexibility. For this reason, it was considered that UK flexibility was still inadequate. This test was also judged to have been failed.

3 Investment: Would joining EMU create better conditions for businesses making long-term decisions to invest in Britain?

The question here is whether adopting the euro would encourage both inward investment (e.g. from the USA and Japan as well as from the other euro-zone countries) and investment by UK businesses. Proponents of the EMU project argue that staying out has discouraged inward investment, as overseas businesses would prefer to invest in the huge euro area, where there is no risk of internal exchange-rate fluctuations. Opponents of the EMU project argue that what is important is the quality of the workforce and the transport, communications and financial infrastructure.

Assessment (2003): This argued strongly that euro membership would increase investment into the UK Over time, EMU was likely to boost cross-border investment flows and foreign direct investment (FDI) in the euro area. The assessment also maintained that 'There is a risk that the longer membership of the euro is delayed, the longer the potential gains in terms of increased inward investment are postponed.' Nevertheless, given a lack of overall convergence so far, it was judged that this test too had been failed. However, 'if sustainable and durable convergence is achieved, then we can be confident that the quantity and quality of investment would increase, ensuring that the investment test was met'.

4 Financial services: What impact would entry into EMU have on the competitive position of the UK's financial services industry, particularly the City's wholesale markets?

The issue here is what the likely impact of the pound's disappearance would be on the UK's large financial services industry. Would the bulk of the business move to Frankfurt, or would the City of London end up attracting more business by being within the euro area?

Assessment (2003): According to the assessment, this was the one test that was passed.

EMU entry should enhance the already strong competitive position of the UK's wholesale financial services sector by offering additional benefits. While the UK's retail financial services sector should remain competitive either inside or outside the euro area, entry would offer greater potential to compete and to capture the effects of greater EU integration arising from the single currency and other attempts to complete the single market, in particular the Financial Services Action Plan (FSAP) described in section 7.4. These benefits are withheld while the UK is not in EMU.

5 Growth, stability and employment: will joining EMU promote higher growth, stability and a lasting increase in jobs?

The issue here is whether, on balance, the UK's macroeconomic situation would be better if the country adopted the euro. Would the economy grow faster, be more stable and have higher long-term employment? This is probably the hardest test to assess, because it involves making a long-term judgement. the comparative performance of the UK and euro-zone countries since 1999 gives some indication, but it does not demonstrate conclusively whether the UK would have been better or worse off inside the euro area since 1999. What the future position would be is even more difficult to judge.

Assessment (2003): The test was failed, largely because of the lack of sustained and durable convergence, i.e. the failure of Test 1. Despite the progress made since 1997, the lack of sustainable and durable convergence meant that, for the UK, macroeconomic stability would be harder to maintain inside EMU than outside, were the UK to decide to join at that time. The assessment also criticized the rigid nature of the EU's monetary and fiscal policy framework. In particular, it criticized the ECB's objective of price stability and the 3% deficit limit under the SGP. The uncertainty created by the ECB's price stability objective and the potential constraints on the use of fiscal policy for stabilization under the current interpretation of the SGP increased the chances that output and employment would be less stable inside EMU. Nevertheless, the government argued that membership had the potential to bring significant gains in terms of growth, stability and employment, once Test 1 had been met.

On the surface, the government's stance on the euro is simple: if the five economic tests are passed, a referendum will be held, with the government recommending a 'Yes' vote. In practice, it is more complicated. There are two key reasons for this.

The first is that whether each test is passed is largely a question of judgement. The outcomes are not easily quantified and thus people can make judgements according to their own perspective. The opponents of entry to the euro zone take a much tougher approach to the tests than proponents will be inclined to do. The test of flexibility is a case in point. Europhiles argue that flexibility has increased substantially, making the UK economy well able to adjust to shocks. Eurosceptics argue that much greater flexibility is needed in eurozone countries if the UK is not to suffer. But just how is flexibility to be measured and what constitutes 'sufficient' flexibility? Then there is the final test: this involves looking well into the future, and forecasters frequently get that wrong, even in the short term!

The second reason why it is not simply a question of passing five tests and then holding a referendum is the political situation. As long as public opinion remains strongly against euro membership, the government is unlikely to risk holding a referendum, even if it believes its tests have been passed. Here the vagueness of the tests is clearly an advantage to the government: it can claim that the tests have not yet been met, but that the economy is moving in the right direction to meet them. It can keep this up for a long time! If public opinion eventually moves in favour of the euro, then it can claim that the tests have finally been met. As one might expect, Britain looks unlikely to hold a referendum on the euro any time soon.

2.5 Regional economic integration worldwide: a global perspective on the EU

Regional economic integration refers to the growing economic interdependence that results when two or more countries within a geographic region form an alliance aimed at reducing barriers to trade and investment. The free trade that results from economic integration helps countries to attain higher living standards by encouraging specialization, lower prices, greater choice, increased productivity and more efficient use of goods, services and factors of production. The total output of the integrated trading bloc becomes greater than that achievable by the individual member countries. It is estimated that about 40% of world trade today is under some form of trading bloc. The EU is the world's largest trading bloc, accounting for about 20% of global trade (2006), around 17% in goods and 26% in services (see figure 2.4). Since the EU claims free trade among its members to be its main objective, the EU is therefore keen to liberalize world trade for the benefit of rich and poor countries alike.

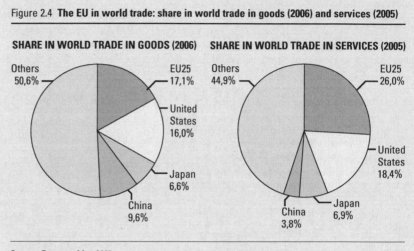

Figure 2.4 **The EU in world trade: share in world trade in goods (2006) and services (2005)**

SHARE IN WORLD TRADE IN GOODS (2006)

Others 50,6%
EU25 17,1%
United States 16,0%
Japan 6,6%
China 9,6%

SHARE IN WORLD TRADE IN SERVICES (2005)

Others 44,9%
EU25 26,0%
United States 18,4%
Japan 6,9%
China 3,8%

Source: Eurostat, May 2007

Trade boosts world growth to everybody's advantage. It brings consumers a wider range of products to choose from. Competition between imports and local products lowers prices and raises quality. Liberalized trade enables the most efficient EU enterprises to compete fairly with rivals in other countries. To help developing countries, the EU is ready to open its market to their exports even if they cannot reciprocate. The disappearance of trade barriers within the EU has made a significant contribution to its prosperity and has reinforced its commitment to global liberalization. As the EU countries removed tariffs on trade among themselves, they also unified their tariffs on goods imported from outside. This means that products pay the same tariff whether they enter the EU via the ports of Genoa or Hamburg. As a result, a car from Japan which pays import duty on arrival in Germany can be shipped to Belgium or Poland and sold there in the same way as a German car. No further duty is charged.

The EU, especially the economy of EMU countries, is relatively open in comparison to the USA and Japan. In 2006, the combined value of imports and exports of goods and services was equivalent to around 42% of GDP, compared with around 32% and 28% for Japan and the USA respectively. The euro zone also accounted for 18% of the value of world exports, compared with approximately 12% for the USA, 6% for Japan and 10% for the ten largest oil-exporting countries. Moreover, the trade openness of the euro area has increased noticeably since 1998, particularly as a result of rapidly growing trade with new EU members and China. Intra-EMU trade has increased sharply since 1998, and in 2007 trade among the EMU countries represented about 50% of total EMU trade.

The EU's three most important trading relationships, based on the value of trade flows, are those with China, Japan and the USA. Trade relations with China have changed dramatically over the last 20 years, going from a sizable trade surplus in the 1980s to a widening deficit with China in the 2000s. Overall, China is now the EU's second-largest trading partner (after the USA), and the EU became China's largest trading partner in 2004. The EU's trade deficit with China reflects, at least in part, the effect of trade barriers or market access obstacles in China. The EU's list of trade barriers encountered by its merchants in China includes barriers in the pharmaceutical, automotive, agriculture and fisheries, chemicals and electronics sectors. EU policy in this area aims at the liberalization of markets, as does the policy of the WTO. Key objectives include the removal of barriers to the import of specific goods (price controls, discriminatory registration requirements, arbitrary sanitary standards); the removal of obstacles to investment (geographical restrictions, joint venture requirements, discriminatory licensing procedures, outright closure of certain sectors to foreigners, restrictive foreign exchange regulations); and the improvement of the business environment (protection of intellectual property rights).

Both the absolute and the relative size of intra-EU trade has increased greatly at the expense of non-European countries in general, in terms of their exports to and imports from the EU. Trading between the existing EU-15 countries and the new, developing EU countries has risen a lot since the EU enlargement of 2004. The EU and the USA are the world's largest economies and each other's largest trading partner. Their combined GDP accounts for approximately 57% of world GDP and 40% of world trade. In addition, these two economies greatly influence world trade patterns, since either the EU or USA is the largest trading partner for most other economies. The fact that there are huge cross-Atlantic trade and FDI flows does not mean that there are no disputes, but they have affected only 2% of US–EU trade. Trade disputes have arisen over products as diverse as bananas, beef, steel and aeroplanes (see case study 2.3).

2.5.1 EU trade disputes and the role of the WTO

The WTO, established in 1995, provides a forum for negotiating agreements aimed at reducing obstacles to international trade and ensuring a 'level playing field' for all, thus contributing to economic growth and development. It also provides a legal and institutional framework for the implementation and monitoring of these agreements, as well as for settling trade disputes arising from their interpretation and application. The WTO currently has 153 members, 117 of which are developing countries or separate customs territories. The proponents of global liberalization of trade are disappointed by the proliferation of regional trade agreements or bloc trading. Since 1947, the General Agreement on Tariffs and Trade (GATT) and the WTO have achieved great success in fostering economic integration on a global scale. The WTO recognizes that regional integration can play an important role in liberalizing trade and fostering economic development. However, existing WTO rules have been less effective in dealing with groups of countries, and the WTO has failed to ensure compliance with WTO rules by all members of a trading bloc. Slow progress in liberalizing trade in goods and services, especially in agricultural products, has prompted many developing countries to seek alternatives to the multilateral trading system favoured by the WTO. Today, the WTO remains in negotiation with economic blocs, with the aims of exercising better control over their evolution and minimizing the risks associated with regional economic integration.

Some consider the current EU as a means for Europe to counterbalance the power and international influence of the USA. Forming an economic bloc also enables countries to obtain greater bargaining power in world affairs and thereby political power. In trade negotiations within the WTO, the EU enjoys greater influence than any individual member country. Broadly speaking, countries are more powerful when they cooperate than when they operate as individual entities.

Case study 2.3 **EU trade disputes and the role of the WTO**

Several rounds of negotiations have taken place over trade disputes between the EU and other WTO members, especially the USA. The following trade disputes between the EU and USA are all well known and have been much discussed.

Banana trade dispute
The EU–US banana war started in 1993, when the EU adopted a tariff and quota system that favoured banana producers in the African, Caribbean and Pacific group of states (ACP). Latin American producers (owned by US companies) were able to produce at lower cost, but the payment of tariffs made their bananas more expensive. The USA took the case to the WTO court and won. The EU did not comply, announcing that its move was part of a plan to support developing economies, and the USA imposed tariffs on the EU in response. The WTO judged in this case on 14th November 2008 that bananas imported from Ecuador should in fact be free of duty.

Hormone-treated beef
This trade dispute has been going on for 15 years. The EU refuses to import any animal products (live or processed) that have received growth hormones, due to concern over public health. The USA claiming that the EU has never proved that hormone-treated beef is actually unhealthy. The EU has been subjected to sanctions amounting to $117 million and the case remains unresolved. In a recent development, the departing Bush administration ratcheted up the pressure on its European counterparts, lodging a legal complaint against the EU at the WTO for blocking imports of American chicken. The litigation followed an earlier US decision to revise the list of European goods liable to trade sanctions as a result of this long-running case. The revision included a massive rise in import tariffs on Roquefort, the celebrated French cheese.

Genetically modified foods
A more recent trade dispute has arisen in the field of public health. The EU has banned all imports of seeds or foods containing genetically modified (GM) material (e.g. strains of maize and soya), claiming that this could contaminate the entire food supply once introduced. The USA argues that the public should have the freedom to choose, but the EU remains insistent on its principles. The USA has long complained that various EU hygiene rules keep its top five farm exports (beef, pork, poultry, soya and corn) out of European markets. A WTO hearing on 16th October 2008 produced no real conclusions and merely a suspension of obligations for the EU.

The European Airbus consortium

Supporters of *strategic trade theory* hold that comparative advantage need not be the result of luck or circumstance, but may in fact be created by government. By diverting resources into selected industries, usually hi-tech and high-skilled ones, a comparative advantage can be created through intervention. An example of such intervention was the European aircraft industry, and in particular the creation of the European Airbus consortium. This was established in the late 1960s, its four members being Aérospatiale (France), British Aerospace (now BAE Systems UK), CASA (Spain) and DASA (Germany). The setting up of this consortium was seen as essential to the future of the European aircraft industry, for three reasons:

to share high R&D costs, to generate economies of scale and scope, and to compete successfully with the market's major players in the USA, Boeing and McDonnell Douglas (which have since merged). By 2001 the consortium's market share was as high as 55%. Boeing has accused Airbus of breaking the WTO subsidy code and of being founded upon unfair trading practices and therefore not entitled to receive the level of government support it enjoys. The latest chapter in this case is the development of the new superjumbo (A3XX). The issue has yet to be heard by the WTO, and negotiations aimed at settling the Boeing–Airbus dispute have ended in disarray with each side still blaming the other.

2.5.2 A firm commitment

The EU has been a key player in international trade liberalization negotiations. The latest of these, the so-called Doha Development Round, began in 2001. The aim of the negotiations, held within the framework of the WTO, is to reduce tariffs and remove other barriers to world trade. Following earlier rounds, the EU's average tariff on industrial imports has now fallen to 4%, one of the lowest in the world. Progress in the Doha Round has been slow, however. Wide and persistent differences have opened up between the rich and poor countries on issues concerning access to each other's markets and the long-running question of agricultural subsidies. Negotiations have lurched from crisis to crisis. The EU has invested heavily in trying to make the Doha Round a success and the EU is also a firm believer in the WTO's rule-based system, which provides a degree of legal certainty and transparency in the conduct of international trade. The WTO sets up rules whereby its members can defend themselves against unfair practices such as 'dumping' (selling goods at below cost price) by means of which exporters compete against local rivals. It also provides a settlement procedure for disputes.

Trade rules are multilateral, but trade itself is bilateral, between buyers and sellers, exporters and importers. This is why the EU, in addition to the WTO's multilateral negotiations, has also developed a network of bilateral trade agreements with individual countries and regions across the world. The EU has partnership and co-operation agreements with its neighbours in the Mediterranean basin (the Euro-Mediterranean Partnership, Euromed, 2008), and with Russia, the other republics of the former Soviet Union, the ACP, the EEA, Mercosur, Mexico and South Africa.

The EU has established customs unions with Andorra, San Marino and Turkey. The customs union with Turkey (1995) covers trade in manufactured products between Turkey and the EU, and also entails alignment by Turkey with certain EU policies, such as technical regulation of products, competition and intellectual property rights. Trade between the EU and Turkey in agriculture and steel products is regulated by separate preferential agreements. The customs union has significantly increased the volume of trade between Turkey and EU Member States, and today more than half of Turkey's trade is with the EU.

The EU has specific trade agreements with its major trading partners among the developed countries, including the USA and Japan. Trade is handled through WTO mechanisms, although the EU has many agreements in individual sectors with both countries. The WTO framework also applies to trade between the EU and China, which joined the WTO in 2001.

2.5.3 Anti-dumping and countervailing duties: barriers to trade

Anti-dumping (AD) and countervailing duties (CVDs) are important examples of barriers to trade where WTO principles have a significant impact on EU practice. It is useful to examine why AD duties and CVDs are imposed. The WTO allows importing countries to protect their producers from unfair competition, such as dumping goods in an attempt to gain market share and drive out local competition. Importing countries are allowed to impose additional duties on products that have received export subsidies or are dumped. Before these duties are imposed, however, the country must show that its domestic industry has suffered material injury from dumped or subsidized imports. Although products at artificially low prices offer consumers in the importing countries a 'good buy', this type of competition is considered to be unfair to domestic producers, who object to dumping if the domestic market of the exporting country is closed to them. Domestic producers also object to subsidized imports, which can be offset by CVDs. These duties are intended to restrict international trade where imports subsidized by a foreign government have a negative impact on domestic competition.
The WTO has now developed a code on CVDs and AD duties that expedites the process of determining whether exports have been dumped or subsidized and whether the domestic industry has been injured. This subject is exceedingly complex. For example, if the EU waives VAT on exports by EU producers, it is debatable whether this is a subsidy or not. If Canada subsidizes production in a specific sector in one of its depressed regions for domestic reasons, are the exports of a subsidized enterprise

subject to CVDs? If the UK government subsidizes the domestic steel industry and incurs losses by selling at home and abroad at prices below full cost, are its exports subject to CVDs and AD duties? The problem is also complicated by the difficulty of determining what material injury is and how it should be measured.

2.5.4 Trading blocs worldwide

In order to benefit further from economies of scale and scope, countries on all continents have attempted to form trading blocs, mostly in the form of FTAs, such as CER and EFTA. EFTA (established in 1960) currently consists of Iceland, Liechtenstein, Norway and Switzerland; most of its former members eventually left EFTA to join the EU. EFTA members co-operate with the EU via bilateral free trade agreements and, since 1994, through the EEA arrangement, which allows for free movement of goods, services, labour and capital throughout the combined area of EFTA and the EU.

Examples in Latin America and the Caribbean include the Latin American Integration Association (LAIA), the Andean Community, the Central American Common Market and the Caribbean Community (CARICOM). CARICOM was set up in 1973 to lower trade barriers and establish a common external tariff (CET). A southern common market, Mercosur, was formed in 1991. This consists of Argentina, Brazil, Paraguay and Uruguay and accounts for some eighty per cent of South America's GDP. Mercosur aims eventually to become an economic union.

In 1993, six Asian nations (Brunei, Indonesia, Malaysia, the Philippines, Singapore and Thailand) agreed to work towards an Asian FTA. ASEAN now has ten members, including Cambodia, Laos, Myanmar and Vietnam, and is dedicated to increasing economic co-operation within the region. The ultimate plan is to establish a common market.

The most significant move towards establishing a more widespread regional economic organization in East Asia has been the creation of the Asia-Pacific Economic Co-operation forum (APEC). APEC links the economies of the Pacific rim, including Asian, Australian and North and South American countries. Unlike the EU and NAFTA, APEC is likely to remain solely an FTA and not to develop into a customs union, let alone a common market.

In Africa, the Economic Community of West African States (ECOWAS) has been attempting to create a common market between its 15 members, with the ultimate goal of introducing a common currency, the eco, in 2009.

2.5.5 Comparison between the EU and NAFTA

The EU is by far the most developed trading bloc, and two of the best-known examples of regional integration resulting from bloc trading are the EU and NAFTA. NAFTA came into being in 1994 and consists of Canada, Mexico and the USA. These three countries have agreed to abolish tariffs among themselves in the hope that increased trade and co-operation will follow. New NTBs will not be permitted either, but many existing ones can remain in force, thus preventing the development of true free trade between the members. Some industries, such as textiles, steel and agriculture, will continue to have major NTBs.

The NAFTA members hope that, with a market similar in size to the EU, they will be able to rival the EU's economic power in world trade. Other countries may join in the future, so NAFTA may eventually develop into a western hemisphere FTA. NAFTA is, however, at most only a free trade area and not a common market. This is because each member state of NAFTA has its own external tariff, while the EU has CETs with non-members. Unlike the EU, NAFTA does not have a single or internal market with free movement of goods, services, capital and labour, and NAFTA does not seek to harmonize laws and regulations, except in very specific areas such as environmental management and labour standards.

Under NAFTA, many US companies in industries covered by the agreement relocated their production to Mexico, the trading bloc member with the lowest wage rates. As a result, many enterprises in the US tomato-growing industry went out of business as the industry shifted south to Mexico. This example from the 1990s demonstrates very clearly how further steps towards regional integration could affect the business world and corporate strategy.

Mexico potentially has the most to gain from the agreement. With easier access to the US and Canadian markets, and with its increased attractiveness to foreign investors, especially US multinationals looking to reduce labour costs, the Mexican economy could reap huge benefits. Despite the largely positive effects of NAFTA, the Mexican economy nevertheless faces a number of real and potential threats from the agreement. For example, as trade barriers fall, Mexico's smaller and less efficient producers are being exposed to competition from their bigger and more efficient US and Canadian rivals.

One vital shortcoming of a free trade agreement such as NAFTA, when compared to customs unions or common markets such as the EU, is the existence of *deflection of trade* and the need for *rules of origin*. When countries enter into a free trade agreement, they remove all tariff barriers between the participating countries, thereby reducing the tariffs on intra-area imports to zero. Yet each member country retains its right to charge different tariffs on imports from extra-area countries. The tariff levels on imports originating from non-member countries can therefore vary substantially. This preferential tariff treatment may tempt third-party countries to take advantage of the divergence between the external tariffs and attempt to commit 'tariff cheats'. *Deflection of trade* occurs when imports from third-party countries enter the FTA via the member country with the lowest external tariffs. This country therefore serves as an entry point into the FTA and the goods are then exported duty-free to the actual destination country within the FTA. By this means the extra-FTA country effectively circumvents the high tariffs of the destination country.

Deflection of trade deprives countries with high external tariffs of the tariff revenue. As a result, FTA countries have to preserve intra-area customs posts in order to try to prevent deflection of trade. FTA countries also need to establish and implement *rules of origin* or *local content rules*, which provide the criteria for determining whether or not given imports are eligible to qualify for tariff-free border treatment. The CET set by customs unions effectively avoids deflection of trade and the country of origin problem, as all imports into the customs union are treated equally.

2.5.6 Trade and development

The EU's trade policy is closely linked to its development policy. The EU has granted duty-free or cut-rate access to its market for most imports from developing countries under its Generalized System of Preferences (GSP). It goes even further for the world's 49 poorest countries, all of whose exports (with the sole exception of arms) enter the EU duty free.

The EU has developed a new trade and development strategy with its 78 partners in the ACP which aims to integrate them into the world economy. It also has a trade agreement with South Africa that will lead to free trade, and it is negotiating a free trade deal with the six members of the Gulf Co-operation Council (GCC), Bahrain, Kuwait, Oman, Qatar, Saudi Arabia and the United Arab Emirates. The EU has agreements with Mexico and Chile and has been trying to negotiate a deal to liberalize trade with the Mercosur group.

2.6 The europeanization of business

Europeanization can be defined as the emergence and development at the European level of distinct structures of governance overlaying the domestic structures of Member States. Since the EU increasingly is making its presence known in the global business environment, this phenomenon is called the europeanization of business. The EU accounts for roughly 20% of world exports and imports and 30% of the world's FDI. It is the world's largest trading economy and the world's prime source of FDI outflows. A significant number of EU regulations have an impact in the USA, Japan, China and elsewhere because of the EU's size and importance as a trading partner. Today the EU has the necessary economic force to make many of the rules that influence world trade. For example, EU rules forced Microsoft to alter its contracts with software makers and even forced McDonald's to stop serving soft plastic toys with its Happy Meals. Most notably, in 2001 the European Commission voted to veto a proposed merger between two US companies, General Electric and Honeywell, which had been approved by the US Justice Department. The merger between General Electric and Honeywell, as it was proposed, would have severely reduced competition in the aerospace industry and resulted ultimately in higher prices for customers, particularly airlines. If the merger had taken place the new company would not have been able to operate in the EU.

In the case of Microsoft, in 2004 the European Commission ordered the company to pay a fine of €497 million, to share its software code with competitors and to offer an unbundled version of the Windows operating system. Microsoft complied. Then, in 2005, the EU ruled that Microsoft would be fined $2.37 million per day if it did not improve the documentation supplied with the software code it provided to competitors. It is clear that if foreign companies want access to the EU market they must conduct business by EU rules.

The europeanization of business is often attributed to large multinational companies such as Microsoft, General Electric and Honeywell, and to large cross-border M&As in the financial sector, such as the takeover of ABN Amro by Fortis, RBS and Santander in 2007 (see table 2.5). However, the EU has also recognized the valuable role played by Small and Medium-sized Enterprises (SMEs) in the economy, not only as employers and contributors to production and employment, but also in respect of their ability to innovate and initiate technological change.

The European economic integration process has implications for business strategy and performance. Both large companies and SMEs often modify their strategies to take advantage of new opportunities in the enlarged European marketplace or to safeguard their positions against potential threats. The deepening, broadening and enlargement of the EU will have several implications for the enterprises doing business in this European marketplace, in terms of internationalization inside and outside the EU, rationalization of operations, harmonization of EU product standards and M&As.

2.6.1 Small and Medium-sized Enterprises: business benefits and costs

Most European SMEs, often family owned, have annual sales of less than €4 million, but thanks to flexibility, quality and service, low overheads, advanced production methods, innovation and a well-trained workforce, they are able to compete effectively and perform many functions more efficiently than larger companies. For example, some SMEs can offer their customers two-day delivery times. This enables their customers to keep a minimum inventory on hand, because the supplier will replenish the stock every other day. Since these SMEs are small operations that focus strongly on cost control and quality, their customers' success is crucial to their survival. The result is that SMEs, with their efficiency and flexibility, are proving to be the backbone of many industries.

In addition, a number of SMEs compete effectively against large companies in niche markets. Increasing consumer affluence is creating a growing demand for specialist products and services. For example, in the textile industry and other fashion/craft-based markets, in which economies of scale and scope and hence price considerations are of less relevance, goods and services are likely to be supplied by SMEs. Many SMEs have also prospered in the field of computer support and back-up.

To a certain extent, the economic recession of 2008/9 is proving beneficial to smaller businesses (e.g. makers of e-bikes) at the expense of larger ones (e.g. makers of cars). One branch of industry that has not been adversely affected by the credit crisis of 2007–09 is the bicycle trade, particularly the makers of new luxury e-bikes, electrically assisted pedal cycles. The bicycle manufacturer with the highest revenue in the EU, Accell, is well known in the Netherlands for its Batavus, Sparta and Koga-Miyata brands. Since the impact of the credit crisis on the European economies, sales of these bicycles have risen. The Dutch industry association Bovag expects a further rise in e-bike sales, as people choose to use a bike instead of a car due to the economic recession. Bovag is making efforts to encourage this trend even further by lobbying for tax advantages, since buying an e-bike, with its wide range of travel which can replace a car, is an environmentally friendly purchase.

Selling to a customer in another involves entering a completely different and unfamiliar market, which requires a strategy based on sound research. For SMEs in particular, this represents a substantial long-term investment of both time and money. It is less of an issue for large companies, which generally already have a marketing department to handle market research and strategy. SMEs, on the other hand, will have fewer opportunities to benefit from economies of scale and scope, and therefore their average costs are likely to be somewhat higher than those of their larger competitors in the market. This obviously limits their ability to compete on price. SMEs face many other problems as well. When it comes to selling and marketing, especially overseas, smaller enterprises are perceived by their customers to be less stable and reliable than their larger rivals. This lack of credibility is likely to hinder their ability to trade. Another difficulty for SMEs is the funding of R&D. Although the long-term survival of an SME may depend upon developing new products and processes in order to keep pace with changing market needs, their ability to attract finance is limited, as many SMEs have virtually no collateral (security or guarantee) and they are frequently perceived by banks as highly risky investments.

Case 2.4 Italian family firms

In Italy, more than ninety per cent of all SMEs and some of the largest enterprises are family owned. In the fashion industry, for example, Versace, Missoni and Benetton are family firms.

In addition, Italian families own important manufacturing companies and have operational control of some of Italy's major savings banks and transportation companies. The Fiat Group, for example, grosses more than €47.3 billion annually and employs more than 160,000 people. It does this as a conglomerate consisting of 777 companies with holdings in agriculture and construction equipment, automobiles, aviation, commercial vehicles, communications, insurance services, metallurgical products, manufacturing machinery and publishing.

Another large family-owned Italian business is Pirelli, whose annual revenue in recent years has been over US$6 billion and which employs about 28,000 people. Most of Pirelli's revenues are generated by its tyre and cable businesses. Along with Benetton, Pirelli has bought a controlling interest in Olivetti, the giant Italian computer and telecommunications corporation. Through Olimpia, Pirelli has an 18% stake in Telecom Italia, a telecommunications, information and communication technology company with an annual revenue of €32 billion and a workforce of around 83,000. This acquisition brought both Benetton and Pirelli into the wireless telecommunications business.

Fiat and Pirelli are typical examples of the ownership and influence of large Italian families in the country.

Through their vast holdings and political power, they have been able to maintain a tight rein on several sectors of the economy. In addition, these family firms are protected against foreign investment by a secretive banking system that is headed by the Milan bank Mediobanca. This bank has financed nearly all of the takeover deals in Italy during the last 35 years. The bank also holds positions on the boards of many of the country's conglomerates.

Seen from a global perspective, the Italian business system reflects the twin pressures of local family culture and the increasing demands of international business. Like their larger counterparts, the SME family businesses are now using their personal and business networks to create global enterprises that are branching out into the EU and elsewhere.

Alessandro Benetton

Bron: www.benetton.com

2.6.2 Internationalization by enterprises inside and outside the EU

Internationalization is the process by which an enterprise enters a foreign market (see section 2.1). An enterprise engaged in the internationalization process will regard foreign markets as risky, owing to the fact that it faces export marketing costs because these markets are unknown to it. To avoid such costs and risk, the usual strategy is to go abroad at a slow and cautious pace, often using the services of external specialists in international trade. When doing business abroad, there are several strategies for entry into foreign markets. In ascending order of depth of involvement in foreign markets, the following entry strategies or strategic concepts can be identified, with increasing levels of control, ownership and risk:
·   licensing and franchising (contractual agreements)
·   subcontracting
·   strategic alliances
·   joint ventures and consortia
·   using an agent or one's own sales representative
·   local packing and/or assembly
·   setting up a wholly owned subsidiary.

The choice of a particular entry strategy depends in part on the relative country-specific costs, such as labour costs. Section 5.6.3 elaborates further on these strategic concepts, and a description of the different entry strategies can be found in the glossary.

Initially, the EU integration process encourages enterprises to internationalize into neighbouring countries within the EU. The elimination of trade barriers also presents new opportunities to source input goods from foreign suppliers within the trading bloc. By venturing into other countries in the EU, the enterprise can generate new sales and increase profits. Internationalizing into familiar neighbouring countries also gives the enterprise the skills and confidence to internationalize further into markets outside the EU. The EU integration process leads to the creation of large multi-country European markets, which may be attractive to businesses from outside the EU. Such foreign enterprises tend to avoid exporting via an agent or sales representative as an entry strategy because trading blocs erect trade barriers against imports from outside the bloc. Accordingly, the most effective way for a foreign enterprise to enter the EU is to establish a physical presence there via FDI.

FDI represents the finance used either to purchase the assets to set up a new subsidiary abroad (or expand an existing one) or to acquire an existing business operation through M&A. In contrast to the entry strategy involved in exporting goods to a foreign market, in practice the FDI entry strategy usually involves the control and ownership, whole or partial, of a company in a foreign country. By building a production facility, marketing subsidiary or regional headquarters anywhere inside the EU, the outsider gains access to the entire EU and obtains advantages enjoyed by local enterprises based inside the trading bloc. For example, since the formation of the EU, the UK has become the largest recipient of FDI from the USA. US companies have chosen the UK as the beachhead to gain access to the massive EU market. In a similar way, European companies have established factories in Mexico to access NAFTA countries. Another common example of FDI is setting up a new overseas operation as either a joint venture or a wholly owned enterprise. For instance, the Japanese company Matsushita has positioned itself to become a major competitor in the European digital industry. It has entered into a joint venture with British Telecommunications for the purpose of developing multimedia wireless services and products.

Some EU countries are more successful at attracting FDI than others. For example, since its accession to the EU in 1986, Spain has spent EU funding allocations on improving its infrastructure. It has accompanied this expenditure with improvements in the business and investment environment. As a result, Spain has enjoyed success in attracting FDI and raising its GDP towards the EU-15 average. By contrast, Greece has also received EU funding allocations. Although these have been also spent on improving infrastructure, they have not been reinforced by reforms to the business and investment environment. Greece has therefore been considerably less successful at attracting FDI than Spain, and has made very little progress in pushing up its GDP.

During this process of internationalization, national managers may have to surrender some of their power and autonomy. For example, prior to EU unification, the Ford Motor Company maintained separate national headquarters in several EU countries. Following EU unification, Ford reassigned some decision-making power from its country heads to its European headquarters in Dagenham, England. The company centralized product design responsibility, brought pan-European design teams together in Dagenham and transferred financial control and reporting to its headquarters in the USA. Corporate restructuring can prove to difficult for managers like the head of Ford's subsidiary in Cologne, who chose to resign rather than lose status.

2.6.3 Rationalization of operations

Rationalization is the process of restructuring and consolidating an enterprise's operations that is often undertaken by management following regional integration. When an enterprise rationalizes, it creates redundancies with the aim of reducing costs and increasing the efficiency of its operations. For example, management may combine two or more factories into a single production facility that eliminates duplication and generates economies of scale and/or scope. Rationalization becomes an attractive option because, as barriers to trade and investment are lowered, a company that formerly operated separate factories in several countries can reap advantages by consolidating the factories into one or two central locations inside the trading bloc. For example, prior to the formation of the EU, many companies had factories in each of the many EU countries. After the launch of the EU, these companies merged their operations into plants in one or two European countries. Companies centralized their production in the EU locations that offered the lowest-cost facilities and other competitive advantages. Thus Caterpillar, the US manufacturer of earth-moving equipment, was one of many companies that shifted their focus from serving individual EU countries to serving the EU region. Caterpillar undertook a massive programme of modernization and rationalization at its EU plants to streamline production, reduce inventories, increase economies of scale and scope, and lower operating costs.

Companies can apply rationalization to other value-chain functions such as distribution, logistics, purchasing and R&D. For example, the elimination of trade barriers, customs checkpoints and country-specific transportation regulations that followed the formation of the EU allowed US enterprises to restructure their EU distribution channels, making them better suited to the enlarged EU marketplace. The creation of an enlarged EU eliminated the need to devise separate distribution strategies for individual countries. Instead, they were able to adopt a more global approach to the larger marketplace, generating economies of scale and scope in distribution.

2.6.4 Harmonization of EU product standards

To establish a common market that would permit the 'four freedoms', each EU member had to agree to change thousands of its national laws, regulations and product standards to ensure that they were compatible with those of other EU members. In practice, the Member State moved cautiously because of political pressures from domestic special-interest groups. As a result, conflicting national regulations, which affected nearly all goods and services purchased by Europeans, hindered trade and the completion of the common market. For example, Spain required that keyboards sold within its borders included a key with the 'tilde', an accent mark commonly used in the Spanish. No other country had such a regulation. Italy required pasta to be made of durum wheat, a requirement not made by other EU members.

The EU initially relied on a process of *harmonization* to eliminate such conflicts. The EU encouraged member countries to voluntarily adopt common EU-wide 'harmonized' regulations affecting intra-EU trade in goods and services and movement of resources. The harmonization process moved slowly, however, as domestic political forces resisted change. For example, to protect the purity of its language, Spain refused to yield on the tilde issue. EU producers spent huge amounts of money annually to comply with differing national regulations. These increased costs raised the prices paid by European consumers and reduced the global competitiveness of European manufacturers.

Progress towards eliminating conflicting product standards was so slow that some Eurosceptics believed the EU would disintegrate. However, the now famous Cassis de Dijon case was a good opportunity to create the concept of mutual recognition (see section 2.1). Adopting the principle of mutual recognition meant that the slow harmonization process could be bypassed and conflicting product standards would no longer serve as barriers to trade among EU members. Since then, the European integration process has focused more on encouraging enterprises to standardize their goods and services in order to push forward the competitiveness of European enterprises in world markets. Products exported to the EU must meet certain standards and technical regulations. Many of these regulations are common throughout the EU, but when they are not the product must meet the standards of the country to which it is exported. In many cases, products made in countries outside the EU have to be modified in order to gain EU entry. Enterprises prefer to offer relatively standardized merchandise in the various markets because it is easier and much less costly to make and sell a few models of a product than dozens of models. The formation of a more integrated EU has facilitated this streamlining and standardization of products and marketing activities: as conditions in the member countries become more similar, companies can increasingly standardize their products and marketing. For example, prior to EU unification, in order to comply with varying national regulations regarding the lighting, brakes and other specifications of tractors sold in Europe, J.I. Case, a manufacturer of agricultural machinery, produced numerous versions of the Magnum tractor. The harmonization of EU product standards enabled the company to standardize its tractor range, enabling it to produce just a handful of models that were nevertheless appropriate for the whole EU market. Standardization is not always possible, however, and local adjustment is still a must for successful marketing strategies.

As well as mutual recognition of each other's product standards and product norms being required by the single market, European Standards (ENs) have been defined for a number of products. A standard is a technical document that is used as a rule, guideline or definition. It is essentially a consensus-built and repeatable way of doing something. Standards are created by bringing together all interested parties, such as the manufacturers, consumers and regulators of a particular material, product, process or service. The European Committee for Standardization (CEN) has developed standards and other documents in an enormous number of areas. Formal European Standards from CEN have a unique status, since they also are national standards in every one of the EU's member countries. However, as mentioned by Hans Alting in the opening case study of chapter 1, European Standards are only applicable to a limited number of products. There are also many exceptions to the mutual recognition principle, and even when an agreement has been accepted for a specific group of products, countries are in many cases still allowed long transition periods before the arrangement comes into effect.

2.6.5 Mergers and acquisitions

The formation of the EU has also led to waves of M&A activity. In a merger, two enterprises of more or less equal size merge and form a larger company; in an acquisition, one larger enterprise buys (takes over) another smaller enterprise, in either a friendly or a hostile manner. An acquisition (or takeover) is considered to be 'hostile' if the board of directors of the target company rejects the offer, but the bidder continues to pursue it, or if the bidder makes the offer without informing the board beforehand. The process or result of a merger is sometimes called an amalgamation. M&As are related to rationalization, since the merger of two or more enterprises creates a new company which can produce a product on a much larger scale. For example, two engineering companies, Asea AB of Sweden and Brown, Boveri & Co. of Switzerland, merged to form Asea Brown Boveri (ABB). This merger enabled the new company ABB to increase its R&D activities and pool greater capital funding for major projects, such as construction, power plants and large-scale industrial equipment. In the pharmaceutical industry, the UK's Zeneca purchased Sweden's Astra to form AstraZeneca. This acquisition led to the development of blockbusters such as the ulcer drug Nexion and helped to transform the new company into a leader in the gastrointestinal, cardiovascular and respiratory fields. Another well-known example of a European M&A is Air France-KLM (in discussions with the Italian airline Alitalia in 2008/09). Since the Treaty of Maastricht fully established the free movement of capital in 1993 and the FSAP of 1999 provided the framework for an integrated market for financial services (see section 7.4), the EU has taken major steps to facilitate the europeanization of business. Table 2.5 shows that since the beginning of the century this has led to several significant cross-border M&A deals among Western European banks (see section 7.7 for more about the reasons for and different types of M&A activity).

As the impact of the financial crisis of 2007–09 continues to reverberate on both sides of the Atlantic, European M&As are at risk. The European M&A boom of 2004–2007, caused in part by the EU-25 and EU-27 enlargements in 2004 and 2007, could be the last wave of M&As. During the EU M&A boom many private equity firms purchased companies privately, without the use of shares traded publicly on the stock market. Private equity firms have a lot of cash and access to vast amounts of cheap debt. However, multibillion-dollar deals that once looked all but sewn up have been scrapped or delayed, and corporations and private equity players alike are reassessing their future takeover strategies in the wake of the downturn in the credit and equity markets.

Table 2.5 **Cross-border M&As among Western European banks (1998–2007)**

	Value (€ bn)	Year	Investor	Investor country	Target	Target country
1	71.8	2007	RBS, Fortis, Santander	UK, BE, ES	ABN Amro	NL
2	15.4	2005	Unicredit	IT	HVB	DE
3	13.9	2004	Santander	ES	Abbey	UK
4	11.2	2000	HSBC	UK	Crédit Commercial	FR
5	9.0	2006	BNP Paribas	FR	BNL	IT
6	7.2	2000	HVB	DE	Bank Austria	AT
7	5.9	2005	ABN Amro	NL	Antonveneta	IT
8	5.7	2007	Hypo Real Estate	DE	Depfe	IE
9	4.8	2000	MeritaNordbanken	SE	Unidanmark	DK
10	4.1	1998	ING	NL	BBL	BE

Conclusions

The overall objective of the European integration process is to create a market in which there are no economic barriers to trade between the Member States. When this is achieved, the EU will be the largest trading bloc in the world. The main drivers for further steps in the deepening and widening of European integration lie in the opportunity to achieve greater static and dynamic efficiency and to reap the benefits of economies of scale and scope. It is very difficult to evaluate the arguments of the proponents and opponents of European integration process, since the costs and benefits are partly political and partly economic and the effects could take a long time to materialize. Since the Treaty of Rome (1957), further steps towards economic integration have pushed forward first monetary and then political integration. Some common European policies follow the rationale of the common market and are market-driven in nature (e.g. competition policy), while others involve standardizing and harmonizing certain national policies among Member States (e.g. monetary policy), with the ECB as one of the supranational bodies. At different stages of the European integration process, 27 European countries have formed a common or single market, with common external tariffs and relatively free movement of goods, services, capital and persons, while 16 members have joined the euro zone, with a common monetary policy and exchange rate. There are still several barriers to creating an optimum currency area with full labour and capital mobility and common fiscal policies. Further steps in the direction of convergence of budget balances and harmonization of fiscal policies are necessary to create a politically integrated EU. The Treaty of Maastricht (1993) and the Growth and Stability Pact (1997) are agreements which lead in that direction.

From the viewpoint of individuals and businesses, the European integration process is a two-edged sword. Lowering tariff and non-tariff barriers within the trading bloc opens the markets of member countries to all individuals and businesses in those countries. Businesses can lower their average production, marketing, distribution and R&D costs by capturing economies of scale and scope as they expand their customer base within the trading bloc. Although businesses in EU Member States have gained improved access to a larger market, they also face increased competition in their home markets from businesses in other Member States, which threatens less efficient enterprises. A regional trading bloc such as the EU may also attract FDIs from non-member countries, as enterprises outside the bloc seek the benefits of insider status by establishing manufacturing facilities within the EU. Many aspects of strategy need to be considered when doing business in the EU, including an overall analysis of the macroeconomic environment, the feasibility of exporting, the rationalization of operations, harmonization of EU product standards and the value of internationalization in various forms, such as strategic alliances and mergers and acquisitions.

The costs and benefits of EU membership to the various Member States vary according to their particular economic circumstances. They will also depend on how completely the barriers to trade are removed, on the extent of monetary and economic union and on any further enlargements to the EU in the future.

Questions

2.1   What is the difference between *supranationalism* and *intergovernmentalism* in the context of the European integration process?

2.2 a   What are the advantages of setting up a business in Europe through a Foreign Direct Investment (FDI) compared to exporting goods and services?

2.2 b   What factors will determine whether a non-EU enterprise chooses to set up a business in the EU through export or through FDI?

2.3   What is the difference between 'negative' and 'positive' integration with regard to the European integration process? Give an example of both types of integration.

2.4   How is the opening up of trade and investment between Eastern and Western Europe likely to affect the location of industries within Europe that have (a) substantial economies of scale and scope; (b) little or no economies of scale and scope?

2.5   What are the benefits and costs of Economic and Monetary Union (EMU) from the perspective of the proponents (supporters) and opponents (critics) of the EMU project?

2.6   Name two essential differences between NAFTA and the EU.

2.7 a   How does *trade creation* differ from *trade diversion* in the EU?

2.7 b   Name two factors which will determine whether a country's joining a customs union will lead to *trade creation* or *trade diversion*.

2.8   What are the differences and similarities between Countervailing duty (CVD) and Anti-dumping (AD) measures?

2.9   How could the EU use non-tariff barriers (NTBs) to protect its markets from foreign competitors? What is the most important NTB? Give some other examples of NTBs.

2.10   What is meant by a *common procurement policy*? In which countries of the EU are such procurement policies most effective?

2.11   Why does the WTO appear to be so ineffective in resolving disputes between the EU and the USA?

The development of the European Union and its impact on business

3

Cleanair

Cleanair Limited (Ltd) was established in 1976 in Hounslow, England, as a company specializing in airport cleaning. Cleanair cleans everything in a modern airport, ranging from the interior of aeroplanes and the interior and exterior of buildings to office buildings and toilets. They have extended their business to the reselling of special cleaning products to other cleaning companies, and they also occasionally operate as an agent for workers in the cleaning business. The parent company is still located in Hounslow, but Cleanair has over 20 branches and subsidiaries inside and outside the European Union.

Cleanair has greatly benefited from all the new EU rules and regulations and has taken advantage of them to extend their business throughout Europe. First of all, because of the principle of the free movement of goods, Cleanair can now buy their cleaning products in large quantities from the cheapest supplier in Europe without having to pay any additional taxes. This has given them a cost advantage over their competitors.

A second advantage for Cleanair is the free movement of services. By providing cross-border cleaning services, Cleanair can now also compete in markets outside the UK. For instance, Cleanair will send a cleaning team to Brussels on the first flight of the day. The cleaning team will spend all day cleaning aeroplanes and at the end of the day will be flown back on the last flight to Heathrow.

Cleanair has also used the freedom of establishment principle to their advantage. Cleanair is established in the UK. Before the Treaty of Rome came into force, it was necessary to register and establish a company in every single country in which the company did business. Following a few remarkable court cases, it is now possible to establish a company in one country and do business through it in the entire European Union without having to re-register or re-establish the company . For Cleanair, which operates in all the major airports in Europe, this certainly brought a lot of opportunities. They could operate as a legally established company throughout the European Union, without having to invest a lot of money in establishing a legal entity in every country in which they operate.

Cleanair is considering whether it could also benefit from the freedom of establishment principle in yet another way. If a company can be set up anywhere in Europe, this can bring tax advantages. Corporation tax is payable in the country of registration and/or establishment. It is a fact that rates of corporation tax differ quite a lot across Europe. In Belgium, for instance, the rate is 34% while it is just 12.5% in Ireland. If Cleanair moved their headquarters from Hounslow, where corporation tax is 28%, to Dublin it would save them 15.5% in taxation on their profit. The relocation would produce a net benefit of £4.5 million.

This chapter describes the effect of a continuously changing Europe on companies and their workers. The move towards a more integrated Europe has taken place in several stages, and historically each stage has altered the way in which companies can conduct their business. This chapter analyses the impact of integration on the business environment at each of these stages. The illustrative case study above gives a clear example of how a particular industry has altered owing to changing circumstances in Europe. In the following text, the theoretical background and views about the influence of economical integration on business are discussed in detail.

3.1   From a European continent to the European Communities

This section describes the phase in which fear and insecurity gave way to greater economic stability in Europe. The effect of the Schuman Plan on postwar progress and prosperity was unprecedented. Although the integrative progress was at first limited to the coal and steel market, the effect on businesses throughout Europe was significant.

All the advantages of the European Community Treaty, from which the Cleanair Company benefited so greatly, did not come overnight. There has been a long but steady process leading to today's level of economic integration. This paragraph highlights some of the major steps on this European road to progress.

The idea of a unified Europe as we know it today was introduced in 1950 by the former French Foreign Minister, Robert Schuman. Before the so-called Schuman Plan, many historical efforts had been made to unite the European states. Most of them were rather unpleasant for European citizens: think of the campaigns of the Roman emperors, Genghis Khan, Alexander the Great, Napoleon and Hitler. More recently, friendlier but unsuccessful attempts were made to unite the states of Europe. In 1923 it was the Austrian Count Richard von Coudenhove-Kalergi who introduced the idea, and in 1946 Winston Churchill attempted to unite France and Germany in a United States of Europe.

Europe was not yet ready for such concepts as new state structures. Nationalist and colonialist attitudes stood in the way of this kind of progress and development. It was the Second World War and the collapse of Europe that led to a political vacuum which created a new political environment. In this new environment it was soon realized that:
· Europe was no longer the major concentration of superpowers and the centre of the world. The United States of America and the Soviet Union took over as the new superpowers, with greater military, political and economic power than all the European countries put together.
· The two world wars in Europe had decimated the population and hugely inhibited growth and progress.
· The people of Europe were tired of military conflict and were hoping and striving for a more stable, safe and beneficial international community.

These new ideas led to the establishment of a number of international organizations. Three different types can be recognized:

1 The European–Atlantic organizations that originated in the connections and relationships between the USA and Europe during and after the two world wars.

Examples are the Organisation for European Economic Co-operation (OEEC), a product of the Marshall Plan, which later led to the Organisation for Economic Co-operation and Development (OECD), and the North Atlantic Treaty Organization (NATO).

2 European intergovernmental organizations which readily accepted new member states. The members of these organizations were hesitant to sacrifice all or part of their sovereignty to a higher (supranational) organization.

An example is the Council of Europe. This organization has established a system of basic protection for the citizen: it has introduced the European Convention for the Protection of Human Rights and set up the European Court of Human Rights. All decisions are taken by unanimity and each member has the power of veto.

3 European organizations which aim for economic and/or political integration. These organizations are characterized by their supranational structure.

An example is the European Community. Subsections 3.1.1 to 3.1.9 trace the origins and history of the European Community as a supranational organization.

3.1.1   The Schuman Plan

Declaration of 9th May 1950

World peace cannot be safeguarded without the making of creative efforts proportionate to the dangers which threaten it [...]

[...] Europe will not be made all at once, or according to a single plan. It will be built through concrete achievements, which first create a de facto solidarity. The coming together of the nations of Europe requires the elimination of the age-old opposition of France and Germany [...]

In 1945 Jean Monnet was appointed Planning Commissioner in France, with responsibility for economic reconstruction. He began work on a scheme which he eventually proposed to Robert Schuman, the French foreign minister. On 9th May 1950 Jean Monnet and Robert Schuman introduced a plan that placed the: 'totality of German/French production of coal and steel as whole under a common High Authority, within the framework of an organization open to the participation of other countries of Europe'. The principal reason for this plan was the fear of another war. A practical solution to the threat of war was to share the raw materials of war production, such as steel and coal, which are essential to the manufacture of arms.

3.1.2   The Treaty of Paris

The Schuman Plan formed the basis of the European Coal and Steel Community (ECSC), which was established in 1952. The six countries (Belgium, France, Italy, Luxembourg, the Netherlands and West Germany) which signed the Treaty of Paris on 18th April 1951 agreed to pool their coal and steel resources for a period of 50 years, thereby creating the ECSC. The United Kingdom was invited to take part but declined to do so.

The ECSC was the real foundation of the European Union (EU) as we know it today. Particularly significant was the fact that a completely new entity was created, endowed with international legal personality and autonomous institutions. It was the first international body with supranational powers, because the member states shared their sovereignty for limited but defined purposes. Specifically, it was the High Authority within the ECSC that had control over the coal and steel production. The High Authority had supranational powers, since it could make binding decisions and recommendations.

3.1.3 The Treaties of Rome

Despite abortive attempts to set up a European defence community, the six founding states of the ECSC were still ready to take a further step towards integration. The Messina Conference of 1955 prepared the ground for further and broader economic ties. At this intergovernmental conference, the original six participants also agreed to co-operate in the fields of economics and atomic energy. This led to the two Treaties of Rome of 1957, which established two further communities, the European Economic Community (EEC) and the European Atomic Energy Community (Euratom). Both came into existence in 1958. The name of the European Economic Community has since been changed to European Community (EC).

Like the Treaty of Paris, the two new treaties were characterized by the creation of new entities endowed with international legal personality and supranational powers. In order for these entities to be effective, they required autonomous institutions possessing the power to develop new structures independent of the participating states.

3.1.3.1 The purpose of the European Community
The purpose of establishing the most important community, the EC, was and still is to ensure:
- political and economic stability in the region (peace)
- the welfare and wellbeing of all European citizens.

This is stated in both the preamble and Article 2 of the EC Treaty.

3.1.3.2 Measures for implementing EC goals
To achieve political stability, economic growth, and the welfare and wellbeing of all citizens, several measures must be carried out. These measures for implementing the goals of the EC can also be found in both the preamble and Articles 2 and 3 of the EC Treaty.

In Article 2, the measures mentioned are: 'establishing **a common market** and **an economic and monetary union**' and 'implementing **common policies or activities** referred to in Articles 3 and 4'.

In other words, the EC Treaty called for the establishment of:
1 a customs union
2 a common market
3 an economic and monetary union (EMU)
4 common policies.

The difference between these different stages in economic integration is explained in detail in 2.2.

3.1.4 Development of the EC Treaty

The EC Treaty itself has been amended over time by several other treaties. Significant alterations have been made owing to changes in the institutions and total structure of the organization, the introduction of the euro, the accession of new Member States and other influences. Figure 3.1 shows the successive treaties and their impact on the level of economic integration.

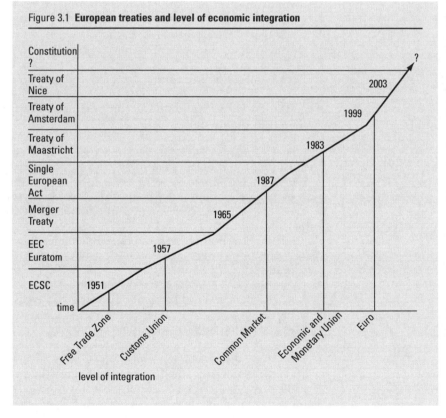

Figure 3.1 **European treaties and level of economic integration**

Currently, the EU as a whole is at the top right-hand corner of the chart. The question remains how the EU will progress further. Initiatives have been made to introduce a Constitution of Europe in the form of a treaty. Since the adoption of such a treaty involves intergovernmental decision making, every Member State has the power of veto, and the Netherlands and France did vote against the introduction of a European Constitution. After this failed attempt, the Member States attempted once again to take the EU to the next level by introducing the Treaty of Lisbon.

3.1.5 The Merger Treaty

Three separate treaties had respectively established the ECSC, EEC and Euratom. Each treaty had created an independent political institution, all of which retained their separate councils of ministers and executive bodies. The ECSC had a High Authority and the EEC and Euratom each had a Commission. On 8th April 1965 the Merger Treaty was signed, resulting in joint institutions for the three European Communities. Thereafter there was just one Council, one European Commission, one European Court of Justice and one Assembly (which was later renamed the European Parliament, EP).

3.1.6 The Single European Act (SEA)

The Single European Act (SEA) of 1987 was the first treaty that significantly changed the level of integration. The principal goal of the SEA was to remove all barriers to free movement between Member States. The SEA amended the three founding treaties (ECSC, EC and Euratom). Amendment was an absolute necessity, because Member States had growing concerns about consumer protection, employment protection and the degradation of the environment. Within the Member States, national legislation had set up entirely different national standards for goods and industrial protection. The result was that the growth of the economic market for goods and services was seriously threatened. Article 8a of the EC Treaty describes a way of tackling this problem: the creation of an internal market. The solution was to remove all legal, technical and physical obstacles to the free movement of goods, services, persons and capital.

The SEA also increased the powers of the European Parliament. In this new legislative system the Council was required to work together with the Parliament. A new co-decision procedure was introduced alongside the existing consultation procedure. Now the Parliament could propose amendments in four areas:
- prohibition of discrimination on the grounds of nationality (Article 12 of the EC Treaty)
- achievement of free movement of workers (Article 40)
- promotion of the right of establishment (Article 44)
- measures for implementation of the internal market (Article 95).

Due mainly to the extended character of Articles 12 and 95, and to a lesser degree that of the other two articles, the European Parliament has hugely enhanced its influence in Europe. The advantage of this is that the EC has become much more democratic, with the influence of the Member States through the Council being reduced and that of the directly elected Parliament increased.

© Council of the European Union

3.1.7 The Treaty of Maastricht

The Treaty of Maastricht is also called the Treaty on European Union (TEU) because this treaty established the EU as we know it today. The intention was to increase integration in areas other than the economic sphere. According to the SEA and the EC Treaty, it was never the intention for the common market to be the final destination. The intention was to create a union in which the Member States were united in economic, monetary, social and political areas. A federation like the United States of America was the ultimate goal of integration.

Article 1 of the TEU shows that even the EU is not the end point of the integration process, but a new stage: 'This Treaty marks a new stage in the process of creating an ever closer union among the peoples of Europe, in which decisions are taken as openly as possible and as closely as possible to the citizen'.

The Treaty of Maastricht introduced what is known as the 'three-pillar structure'. For a full understanding of this structure, an explanation of the words *sovereignty*, *supranational* and *intergovernmental* is necessary.

Sovereignty
Sovereignty is derived from the Latin phrase *suprema potestas* ('supreme power'), which implies that there is no higher authority. After the Peace of Westphalia in 1648 a system of sovereign states was developed, in which the kings and the pope no longer held supreme power. The states now embodied this highest power. Today, sovereignty can best be described as 'a supreme authority within a territory'. The establishment of the EC made it necessary for countries to give up part of their sovereignty to the newly formed organization, resulting in an organization with supranational powers.

Supranationalism

Supranationalism is a form of political decision making in which governments have jointly agreed to transfer part of their sovereignty to a higher organization. The concept of supranationalism is explained more fully in chapter 2.

Case study 3.1 Foot-and-mouth disease

In 2001 there was an outbreak of foot-and-mouth disease in the Netherlands. This is a serious viral disease affecting only cloven-hoofed animals. Domestic animals such as cattle, water buffalo, sheep, goats and pigs are susceptible, as well as antelope, deer, bison and other wild bovids. The policy of the Commission was to eradicate the disease by exterminating all cloven-hoofed animals within a certain radius of the source. This would mean the destruction of some extinct or near-extinct zoo animals if the disease should strike at a zoo. The government of the Netherlands considered using pre-emptive vaccination to counter the disease in such places as zoos, but according to the Commission this was not allowed at the time.

This example illustrates the fact that the Commission has higher powers over agricultural issues than the Member States. According to the Commission, the reason for not allowing vaccinations was that after being vaccinated an animal produces antibodies against the disease. To check whether meat had been infected with the disease, a sample would be tested for antibodies, but there was no way of telling whether the meat was contaminated due to the disease or due to vaccination.

An example of sovereignty which is not transferred to the EC is the drugs policy of the Netherlands. The Netherlands currently has a liberal attitude to marihuana products. Other Member States have disagreed with the policy of condoning so-called soft drugs. Although there is a lot of pressure on the Netherlands from other Member States to amend its drugs policy, the final power of decision is held by the Dutch authorities. No other country or institution can force any change in this policy.

Intergovernmentalism

This is a form of political decision making in which governments make cross-border agreements but retain their absolute sovereignty. The decision-making process often works on the basis of unanimity or consensus. The concept of intergovernmentalism is explained more fully in chapter 2.

3.1.8 The Treaty of Lisbon (ToL)

The Treaty of Lisbon (ToL) was signed on 13th December 2007. It has not yet been ratified by all Member States of the EU and will come into effect only after ratification. The intention of the ToL is to simplify the structure and organization of the EU. The main changes that it will introduce are the following:
- The ToL amends the TEU. After ratification of the ToL, the EU will continue to exist as a single combined entity. This means that the current pillar structure will disappear.
- An elected President of the European Council will replace the rotating presidency.
- Many changes will be made to the institutional framework, to make it more workable with 27 Member States.
- The EC Treaty will be renamed Treaty on the Functioning of the Union (TFU).
- The 'European Community' as such will disappear.
- The three-pillar system will be merged into one Union.

- The Charter of Fundamental Rights will be a separate legal document with the same legal status as the treaties.
- Qualified majority voting will be introduced in many additional areas within the EU.
- The Union will have legal personality, so it can accede to international treaties, for example.

3.1.9 Overview of the development of the European Union

Figure 3.2 **Development of the European Union**

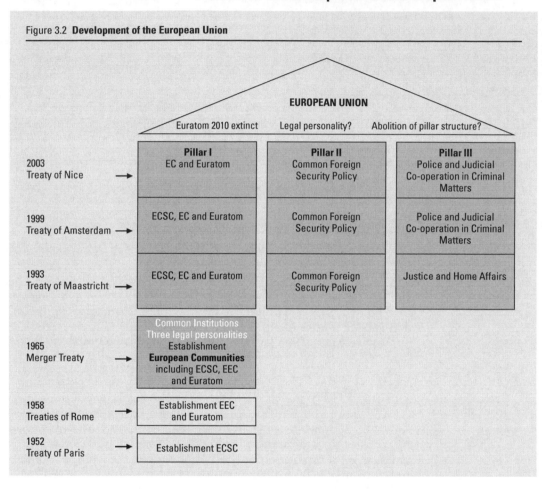

A good understanding of the three-pillar structure is essential to appreciating the effect on business practice of the Treaties which have jointly established the EU. Figure 3.2 shows the development of the European Union between 1952 and 2009. One of the major developments was the introduction of the three-pillar structure with the Treaty of Maastricht in 1993.

The three-pillar structure is explained in chapter 2, and chapter 4 explains the functioning and legislation of the institutions.

3.2 The effect of the Treaty of Rome on business

This paragraph describes the measure which had by far the greatest impact on European business life in the last millennium. This was the first and most fundamental step in moving from a mindset of coexistence to one of co-operation in the European economic arena. The introduction of a common market with the so-called 'four freedoms', above all, has had an enormous impact on European corporate structure.

The Treaty of Rome brought about change primarily through the formation of the internal market. The introduction of an internal market directly affected entrepreneurs through:
1 integration
2 free movement
3 competition rules.

3.2.1 Integration

Economic integration can take place by means of both *policy integration* and *market integration*. Policy integration, also called *positive integration*, is the integration of national policies into a European policy, whereby national rules are replaced by the European Standard. The directive is the primary European legal instrument for creating such standards.

Market integration, also called *negative integration*, is the integration of national markets, whereby national rules that restrict free trade are prohibited. The terms *positive* and *negative integration* are used to stress the difference in the way these forms of integration come into existence. In positive integration, a new norm is being created by focusing on rules that are permitted or are compatible with European rules. In negative integration, a new European Standard is being created in the opposite manner, by focusing on national rules that are not permitted or are incompatible with European rules. The key feature of market integration is that creating and maintaining restrictions on trade between Member States is prohibited. Policy integration, on the other hand, is a positive instruction to synchronize national policy. The EC institutions can assist in this.

Market integration and policy integration are strongly correlated. The more trade between Member States is integrated, the more the Member States must co-ordinate their national policies. For instance, moving from a free trade zone to a customs union involves the move to a common customs tariff and the adoption of a common trade policy in order for the customs union to be effective.

Positive integration is achieved mainly by means of harmonization. The starting point in harmonization is that the result after harmonization should be the application of one uniform rule to all Member States. Harmonization in fact replaces the differing rules of the Member States with a more or less uniform European rule. Qualified majority voting has gained importance in the European legislative process, and as a result it is now easier to pass legislation on minimum standards. Many decisions can now be taken with a majority of approximately two-thirds of the votes in the Council of Ministers, whereas with unanimous decision making a measure would very often be blocked by one Member State opposing it. The growth of qualified majority voting has therefore favoured minimum harmonization. There is at least a minimal uniform European rule, but Member States are allowed to maintain or introduce stricter rules than the European rule. An important qualification is that the Member State imposing a stricter rule can do so only for its own manufacturers, because enterprises from other Member States are protected by the minimal European Standard. Although the aim is to define one European Standard, the effect of minimum harmonization is that there can still be differences between national rules.

Harmonization primarily makes use of secondary EC law, in combination with judicial control, to integrate national policies. Primary EC law can be found in the treaties; secondary EC law is EC legislation coming from the Community institutions. According to Article 249 of the EC Treaty, the European legislature (generally the Council and the European Parliament acting together) has the power to pass laws of four types:
1 regulations
2 directives
3 decisions
4 recommendations.

For the purpose of harmonizing existing national legislation, the most effective legal instrument is the directive.

There is a profound distinction between regulations and directives. Regulations are addressed to EU citizens, are binding in their entirety, are directly applicable and have general application. This makes the regulation a very powerful instrument. Regulations work in exactly the same way for all citizens throughout the EU. Because of their direct applicability, EU citizens are entitled to exercise the rights resulting from regulations in their home countries. They can even enforce their rights in their national courts. The Member States have no right to influence, alter or change a regulation in any way, shape or form.

Unlike regulations, directives are addressed to the Member States, which are then obliged to amend their existing national legislation in accordance with the directive. They are allowed to adapt their national legislation in the way they think best, as long as it agrees with the directive. EU citizens cannot exercise any rights as a direct result of a directive, but only once it has been implemented in national legislation. The Member States must implement the directive within a prescribed timeframe.

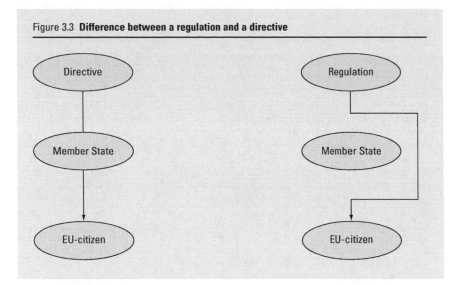

Figure 3.3 **Difference between a regulation and a directive**

Figure 3.3 clearly shows that the individual Member States cannot change regulations. However, Member States can implement directives. Because Member States have a lot of freedom in implementing the directive through their national legislation, directives are the favoured legal instrument when it comes to harmonization.

The advantage of harmonization for businesses is that every single enterprise in every country of the European Union has to follow the national rules which have been made in accordance with the directive. Although Member States do have the power to implement the directive in a way that suits them best, the result must be the same or nearly the same in all Member States. If the Netherlands, for instance, is a leader in the field of environmental protection, this creates an extra burden for Dutch businesses, since they have to comply with all sorts of legislation. This could give a disproportionate competitive advantage to enterprises in countries which do not have advanced environmental laws.

Another advantage for businesses is that products sold on the European market must comply with particular directives. As a result, businesses do not have to make specific products for specific countries and do not have to invest in parallel production lines in their factories. Electronic equipment, for instance, must meet several directives concerning the sale and production of electronic equipment. If a particular product is tested and found to be safe according to the directive, it can be sold throughout Europe without further testing in every single country.

Harmonization can have a positive effect on doing business. However, because businesses must observe a large number of European rules, harmonization is sometimes also seen as a burden.

Case study 3.2 KMD Panel Systems

KMD Panel Systems is a medium-sized Dutch company which produces fire safety sandwich panels. Fire safety sandwich panels are used in the construction industry to increase fire safety in buildings. KMD have been manufacturing their particular products since 1974, selling them only to the Dutch construction industry.

In 1998 KMD received a letter from BlitzBau GmbH, a German construction company. The German company was permitted under public procurement to start a vast construction project in several locations in Europe. BlitzBau was interested in sandwich panels with an extremely high safety rating. At that time, these were only produced in the Netherlands and in the USA, and it was obviously cheaper to buy the panels in the Netherlands than in the USA.

After several business meetings in both the Netherlands and Germany, the two parties were ready to draft a contract of sale. BlitzBau GmbH engaged a specialist German law firm to study and comment on the Dutch proposal. One of the issues raised by the German law firm was that of the user manual. According to German and European legislation, it was mandatory to provide a user manual in the language of the country where the products were to be sold. Article 1.7.4 of European Directive 98/37/EC states that the manual must be translated into the language of the country where the products are sold. The problem was that BlitzBau was unsure in which countries the panels would be used. The directive points out that, if it is unclear in which countries the product will be sold, the user manual must be translated into all the official languages of the European Union. After some negotiation it was agreed that the extra translation costs would be shared by both parties.

Another problem identified by the German law firm was the fact that all construction companies prefer to work only with quality controlled and certified materials. Two product certification marks were of particular importance. The German law firm said they required the GS mark (geprüfte Sicherheit) and in addition to that the CE mark. The Germans stated that it was mandatory under European law to have CE marking in order to sell the panels in Germany.

Now it was time for the Dutch company to start consulting European law specialists. They wanted to know if indeed the two certifications were necessary. They received their answer, which concluded: the GS mark is voluntary, but CE marking is indeed

mandatory on all products sold in Europe. By adding the CE mark, the manufacturer or person placing the product on the market or putting it into service affirms that the item meets all the essential requirements of the relevant European Directive(s). Examples of European Directives prescribing CE marking include those on toy safety, machinery and low-voltage equipment. There are about 25 directives that prescribe CE marking.

The next question was how to obtain such a CE mark for sandwich panels. After thorough investigation, KMD found that it was necessary to have the product tested by an independent testing facility and that there was no such facility in the Netherlands. After further investigation, it turned out that there was a testing facility in Antwerp, Belgium. The only problem was that there was no production line in this testing facility or anywhere else in Europe. To install such a production line would mean an additional investment of €650,000.

At that point, KMD Panel Systems wanted to tell all the parties involved that they could not fulfill the order due to the supplementary cost of testing. KMD thought they needed CE marking because they had initiated cross-border selling in Europe. The Dutch legal consultancy firm, however, told KMD that they had to continue their certification procedure. This was necessary because CE marking is mandatory for all products sold anywhere in The European Union, including products from the Netherlands sold within the Netherlands. Moreover, KMD was told that, if their products were involved in a fire, they could be sued for damages if the products were not CE certified. So it was mandatory to have the panels tested not only for new customers, but also for customers in the Netherlands.

KMD's export plans were turning into a disaster. The extra costs, amounting to more than half a million euros, placed a heavy burden on the company. European legislation was almost responsible for their insolvency, but KMD continued their certification process and was finally able to satisfy their new German client. The result of their CE-marking efforts was an increase in turnover of 64% in the first year. Even though European legislation had almost crushed the Dutch company, in the end it was the same legislation that made their remarkable export success possible.

This case is a clear example of how positive integration can impose the same rules on businesses throughout the European Union. On the one hand, the directives concerned were responsible for additional expenditure; on the other hand, they made expansion throughout the EU possible. The EC has produced a vast amount of secondary legis-lation in the form of regulations and directives. Smart business owners can use these new rules in their favour.

3.2.2 Barriers to free movement

In order to produce a product, a business needs four factors of production. The four factors are: goods, services, capital/payments and persons. A company always needs to obtain resources (goods), services, investment (capital) and workers (persons) from other companies. The services of an accountant, for instance, are needed in order to make a mandatory annual report. The common market can only be effective if these production factors can move freely around Europe without any kind of barrier, and exactly these freedoms are implemented in the EC Treaty. Further explanation of the working of the principle of free movement can be found in chapter 5.

In order for the single market to be effective, all barriers to trade between Member States must be removed. This is done by means of negative integration, which prohibits Member States from making rules that restrict intra-Community trade. The EC Treaty includes 16 Articles imposing prohibitions which are designed to prevent governments from raising barriers. These barriers may be of either a financial or a non-financial nature.

3.2.2.1 The effect on European business of the prohibitions in the EC Treaty

Table 3.1 **EC Treaty Articles imposing prohibitions**

Art. 12	Prohibition of discrimination by nationality	see example 3.1
Arts 25 & 26	Prohibition of import or export tariffs	see example 3.2
Arts 28 & 29	Prohibition of import or export restrictions	see example 3.3
Art. 31	Prohibition of discrimination by state monopolies of a commercial character	
Art. 39	Prohibition of discrimination between workers by nationality	see example 3.1
Art. 43	Prohibition of restrictions on freedom of establishment	see example 3.4
Art. 49	Prohibition of restrictions on free movement of services	
Art. 56	Prohibition of restrictions on free movement of capital and payments	
Art. 81	Prohibition of agreements between companies which restrict competition	
Art. 82	Prohibition of the abuse of a dominant position	
Arts 86–88	Prohibition of restrictions on competition by government corporations and prohibition of illegal financial support by governments	
Art. 90	Prohibition of discriminatory local taxes	see example 3.5

■ Example 3.1 Prohibition of discrimination by nationality

A Dutchman was born and educated in Belgium. He went to a Belgian law school and held a doctorate in Belgian law. Although a Belgian resident, he was excluded from legal practice in Belgium for the simple reason he did not have Belgian nationality. The European Court of Justice (ECJ) held that businesses and the self-employed should have access to activities in the Member States without hindrance, or direct or indirect discrimination. The court stressed that the right of establishment and the right to provide services are 'fundamental rights' and that Mr Reyners should be allowed to practise in Belgian courts of law (Reyners v. Belgian State, Case 2/74).

■ Example 3.2 Prohibition of import or export tariffs

The Dutch company Van Gend en Loos imported a chemical, urea-formaldehyde, from Germany into the Netherlands. The company was charged an import duty. Van Gend en Loos started court proceedings in the Netherlands to reclaim the duty, stating that it breached Article 25 of the EC Treaty on the free movement of goods. The question was whether or not a company could use this Article directly in their favour. The Dutch government claimed that the Article was addressed solely to the Member States. The Court, however, ruled that the Article had direct effect, meaning that companies could use the Article in their favour as if it were a national rule, before national courts. This was a landmark judgment which made it clear that European law had the power to overrule national law and could confer rights on individuals in the courts of their own state (Case 26/62).

■ Example 3.3 Prohibition of import or export restrictions

A huge amount of case law has grown up around Article 28 of the EC Treaty (mostly in combination with Article 30). This is because the Article gives businesses a direct means of contesting national laws that conflict with Community law. In 1977, for instance, the UK government prohibited the import of main-crop potatoes. A Dutch company that exported potatoes to the UK was financially disadvantaged by this legislation. The Dutch potato exporter disputed the measure in the UK High Court, stating that the import prohibition was a clear violation of Article 28. By virtue of a reference to Article 234 of the EC Treaty, the ECJ judged the ban was indeed illegal, since it was a clear obstruction to cross-border trade. This shows that an individual can challenge the national law of another Member State on the basis of European law (Meijer v. Department of Trade, Case 118/78).

■ Example 3.4 Prohibition of restrictions on freedom of establishment

Italy legislated to restrict access to various occupations in the field of tourism. They did so by allowing only Italian nationals to register as trainee journalists and regular contributors to publications, and by making reciprocity a condition for the inclusion of foreign journalists on the list of professional journalists. Italy also made laws that permitted only Italian nationals to compete for the award of licences to run pharmacies. The ECJ judged that Italy had failed to fulfill its obligations under Articles 39, 43 and 49 of the EC Treaty (Commission v. Italy, 15th October 1986, Case 168/85).

Further cases involving the prohibition of restrictions on freedom of establishment can be found in section 8.3.

© Noordhoff Uitgevers bv

■ **Example 3.5 Prohibition of discriminatory local taxes**
France introduced a road tax on a sliding scale: cars with engines over 16 horsepower (HP) were taxed at a significantly higher rate. At that time, however, French car manufacturers were not producing any cars over 16 HP. Foreign cars with more powerful engines were therefore taxed more heavily than domestically produced cars. A Frenchman who had imported a 36 HP German Mercedes went to court in France to demand repayment of the tax difference. The ECJ ruled that this particular French tax was incompatible with Article 90 of the EC Treaty (Humblot v. Directeur des Services Fiscaux, Case 112/84). After this judgment, the French government tried to remedy the discrimination found in the Humblot case by adding nine new categories to the sliding tax scale. The taxation rate still increased sharply at 16 HP, and the ECJ held that the discrimination had been reduced but not removed. French national law was still incompatible with Article 90 (Feldain v. Directeur des Services Fiscaux, Case 433/85).

These and several other cases affecting the car industry made it possible for businesses to find ways of selling their cars more easily to a wider market across Europe.

3.2.2.2 Competition law and its purpose in the EC

The common belief of economists is that, without public regulation, market power would be concentrated in the form of a *monopoly* or an *oligopoly*. In a monopoly, market power is held by a single company, and in an oligopoly, market power is held by a few players who react to each other's activities. The result, according to economists, is that the monopolist or oligopolist makes money at the expense of the consumer: the consumer's choice of products is restricted and there is less pressure to keep prices down. Another possible effect is that the monopolist limits output, which maximizes profit. For an internal market to function well, it is therefore absolutely essential to regulate competition in the EU.

It is claimed that EC competition rules exist for the sole purpose of maximizing consumer welfare, and that they provide for the most efficient allocation of resources and the minimizing of prices. This is only partly true. EU competition policy is not just aimed at the consumer but also focuses on:
- market integration: the establishment and maintenance of a single market, which benefits both consumers and producers
- fairness: the prevention of abuse of power by large producers and the making of illegal agreements between producers
- efficiency: keeping production and distribution efficient and economical and keeping producers up to date with technical progress.

The EC Treaty includes two principal categories of competition law. First, the EC controls cartels. A cartel is a group of comparable independent businesses which act together (*'concerted action'*) to control prices or to divide up the market, in order to make more profit. Each business can rely on its agreed market share. As a result they can control prices, they do not need to produce new products, and quality and service are now less important, since these businesses no longer have to

compete so hard. Usually, reduced competition means:
- higher prices (or sometimes lower prices, which can also be detrimental)
- lower quality
- poorer service
- less research & development.

Some types of agreement are very harmful to competition and these are almost always prohibited. Examples are secret cartels and other agreements in which competitors agree to fix prices, to limit production or to share markets or customers between them. Agreements between producers and distributors can be illegal if the resale prices are fixed. Not every agreement which limits competition is illegal: those that have more positive than negative effects are usually permitted. Agreements that are not made between competitors are more likely to be allowed.

Second, EC competition law addresses monopolies. It controls companies with a large market share which use their sheer size to make it difficult for other companies to trade on the market. The European Commission is the watchdog of European competition policy, using the powers invested in it by the EC Treaty.

EC competition law and policy are continuously changing, owing to changing values and social aims. European competition law derives from several sources. Its basis is set out in Articles 81–87 of the EC Treaty. Secondary legislation, consisting mostly of regulations and a few directives, is also an important source. Besides primary and secondary legislation, competition case law has been formed by a large number of cases before the European Commission and the ECJ. These cases are probably responsible for the greatest changes affecting businesses.

The legal framework of competition law, specifically Articles 81 and 82 of the EC Treaty, which deal with cartels and monopolies, is discussed further in chapter 5.

3.2.2.3 The effect of competition law on European business

■ **Example 3.6 The bread factory**
An example of concerted action can be found in the case of a new bread factory which started trading in Belgium. Four bread factories which were already trading jointly lowered their prices within one week of the new bread factory entering the market. Their prices were always exactly one cent below the newcomer's price. Although the existence of an agreement is difficult to prove, the behaviour of these companies clearly shows that they were acting together: it would be statistically impossible for them to react separately to the new factory's prices in this way. European competition laws have enabled new businesses to enter the bread market, because without regulation newcomers would have been forced out of the market.

■ **Example 3.7 Cheap flights**
Low-cost airlines have been able to set up operations and develop in Europe because the European Commission has opened up the airline industry to competition. The Commission monitors the airline industry closely, by checking on mergers, acquisitions and other possible infringements. This regulation has resulted in a greater range of destinations and lower prices, creating opportunities for new budget airlines and smaller but cheaper airports. Both business travellers and European consumers are already benefiting from a wider and more affordable range of services.

■ **Example 3.8 Fixed telephone costs**
On 1st January 1998 the European Commission opened up the telecommunications sector completely to competition. The result for business users and domestic customers was that they could save 23% and 13% respectively on national calls from fixed telephones in the period between mid 1998 and mid 2003. On international calls the reduction was even more dramatic: the average cost of calls to all European countries dropped by 45% for business users and 41% for domestic customers.

■ **Example 3.9 Vitamins cartels**
Eight pharmaceutical companies, including Hoffman-La Roche, have been fined by the European Commission for their participation in cartels designed to eliminate competition in the vitamins sector. These vitamins are used in a wide variety of products: vitamin supplements can found in cereals, biscuits, drinks, animal feed, pharmaceuticals and cosmetics. Since medicines and vitamins can have a very serious impact on consumers, the companies were fined over €800 million. They had been charging excessively high prices for over ten years, harming consumers and enabling the companies to make unlawful profits. The market for medicines, including vitamins, has become much more transparent since it has been under strict control.

■ **Example 3.10 Videogames**
Nintendo, a Japanese videogames manufacturer, and seven of its official distributors in Europe, entered into agreements to maintain artificially high price differences across the EU. Parallel trade (exports through unofficial distribution channels) was prevented by means of these agreements. Nintendo and its partners went to great lengths to discover the source of any such exports, and trading companies that permitted parallel trade were penalized by being given smaller shipments or sometimes boycotted completely. The result was that the prices of games consoles and videogames fluctuated widely between European countries. In the UK, for instance, they were 65% cheaper than in Germany and the Netherlands. The European Commission enforced a total fine of €168 million on Nintendo and its distributors. EC competition policy has contributed to the fact there is extensive parallel trading at present, creating endless opportunities to do business. The direct benefits of this trade to consumers include lower prices.

■ **Example 3.11 Car sales**
In 1998, the European Commission fined Volkswagen AG for prohibiting its Italian dealers from selling to German and Austrian customers, who were attracted by the lower prices in Italy. This is an example of parallel trading, as in the Nintendo case above, and it is illegal for car manufacturers to discourage parallel trading. Business customers and consumers can find the cheapest

pretax car prices in a six-monthly review published by the European Commission. Once again, EC competition policy is responsible for creating opportunities for businesses and possibly lower prices for consumers.

■ Example 3.12 Car sales multi-branding

Regulation 1400/2002 from the Commission stimulates competition in the car industry. The visible result today is that internet sales, multi-branding, cross-border purchases and advertisements throughout the single market have become commonplace. Car owners now have a wider choice of after-sales service providers, which can be either authorized service centres or fully independent workshops. No car workshop may be prevented from servicing any brand and they are longer obliged to operate a dealership as well.

One of the most important innovations introduced by this regulation is the multi-brand dealership. Since 1st October 2003, dealers are able to sell more than one brand within the same showroom. This 'multi-branding' strengthens dealers' commercial independence from their suppliers. Both businesses and consumers have benefited from these rules.

■ Example 3.13 Tyres

In 2001, Michelin was fined €20 million for abusing its dominant position. Michelin was active on the French market for replacement tyres for heavy goods vehicles in the 1990s. The company made over 50% of new replacement tyres for these vehicles and an even higher proportion of retread tyres. In fact, it had no real competitors. It was therefore difficult not to run up against Michelin in this business. Michelin used a cunning system of rebates and bonuses to make dealers dependent on its tyres and prevented them from choosing their suppliers freely. The judgment against Michelin made it possible for dealers to choose other tyre manufacturers.

■ Example 3.14 Microsoft

In 2004, Microsoft was fined half a billion euros for abusing its dominant position in the PC operating systems market between 1998 and 2004. At the time, Microsoft's Windows operating system held a 95% share of the market. Since the Commission's decisions and the ECJ's judgment were delivered, its market share has dropped to 88%. Microsoft was found to have withheld information which rival server software needed in order to connect properly with Windows-based PCs. In addition, Microsoft sold its operating system bundled with the Windows media player. This had the effect of placing the Windows media player on virtually all PCs and hence distorting competition by artificially driving content providers and applications developers to use the Windows media platform. It also gave the consumer less choice of media players, let alone operating systems.

■ Example 3.15 Partitioning the market

Consten was selling Grundig products in France under the GINT trademark. Consten and Grundig had agreed to make Consten the exclusive distributor of Grundig products under the Grundig and GINT trademarks, and Consten tried to prevent other companies from selling Grundig products in France. The Commission found that Grundig and Consten had artificially and illegally partitioned the market, with the result that all competition was eliminated. The ECJ judged that trademark rights do not prevent parallel imports. Since the prohibition of distribution agreements which eliminate competition, businesses have had many more opportunities for cross-border sales of goods.

3.3 The effect of the Treaty of Maastricht on business

The Treaty of Maastricht is also referred to as the Treaty on European Union (TEU). This treaty established the European Union in 1993.

The EU is an economic and political confederation of 27 European states. The TEU introduced the three-pillar structure, adding two pillars alongside the existing European Communities. The whole structure is called the European Union. The second pillar is the Common Foreign and Security Policy, which provides for joint foreign action and security action by the Member States. The third pillar is Police and Judicial Co-operation in Criminal Matters. It provides for co-operation in policy areas such as asylum, immigration, non EU-nationals, international crime and various forms of judicial co-operation.

3.3.1 Major changes effected by the Treaty of Maastricht

The TEU made other important changes in addition to the structural ones. The key features and concepts it introduced were:
- an economic and monetary union (EMU)
- the co-decision procedure (joint legislative action by the Council and Parliament)
- a defined role for the European Council (heads of state/government and President of the Commission)
- Union citizenship (see section 8.1.1)
- fundamental rights (human rights).

The most important change for businesses has been the establishment of EMU. This consists of two parts: a monetary union and an economic union. Both them have significantly influenced the business environment. With the introduction of the euro, all Member States participating in EMU have transferred their financial sovereignty to the European Central Bank (ECB). The ECB is completely independent in its co-ordination and implementation of monetary policy. The main objective of its monetary policy is to maintain price stability, which the ECB tries to achieve by keeping the inflation rate below or close to 2%. The national central banks also play a part in monetary policy through the European System of Central Banks (ESCB). Price stability concerns the internal value of the euro within the EU. It is defined as an annual increase of less than 2% in the harmonized consumer price index for the euro area. Inflation and deflation are strongly correlated with price stability.

3.3.2 The effect of the euro

Having a common currency brings benefits but also costs. Because the national currencies have disappeared, there are lower transaction costs involved in trade between Member States. These costs were formerly estimated at between 0.3% and 0.4% of the European gross national product. The common currency eliminates uncertainty over exchange rates between the national currencies of Member States and removes the negative influence of exchange rate risk on the internal market. Another benefit is the higher transparency of prices throughout Europe on the internal market, which is beneficial to consumers. Individual Member States have lost their control over the exchange rate mechanism, which reduces their influence on cross-border trade. Figure 3.4 shows the effect of EMU on intra-euro-zone trade and on euro-zone trade with others between 1992 and 2002, shortly after the introduction of the euro.

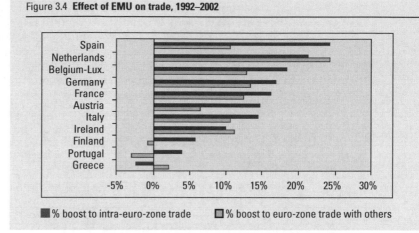

Figure 3.4 **Effect of EMU on trade, 1992–2002**

■ % boost to intra-euro-zone trade   ▢ % boost to euro-zone trade with others

Although an increase in trade can be measured after the introduction of the euro, it is very difficult to determine what has caused it. The increase may be attributable to lower (administrative) trading costs, price transparency, increased competition, reduced exchange-rate volatility, lower interest rates or a combination of any of the above. Economists have found it very difficult to establish a causal relationship between the common currency and export activity. A study by Baldwin and Taglioni (*Trade effects of the Euro*, 2004) seems to show that Small and Medium-sized Enterprises (SMEs) starting up new exports are mainly responsible for the increase in trade. They suggest that, as exchange rate risks are reduced, SMEs that were previously unable to protect themselves on financial markets have started exporting, resulting in the sudden increase in trade that followed the adoption of the euro.

3.3.3   Changes in legislative procedure

Before the Treaty of Maastricht, the European Council made legislation, consulting the EP. This was the co-operation procedure. The Treaty of Maastricht introduced the co-decision procedure under Article 251 of the EC Treaty. Under the new co-decision procedure, the Parliament and the Council jointly enact new legislation. As a result, the legislative procedure has become more democratic, through the requirement for EP involvement. The co-operation procedure for single-market legislation has been replaced by the co-decision procedure. Co-decision is now the primary procedure: there is a list of approximately 40 legal bases to which co-decision currently applies.

The Treaty of Maastricht and the Treaty of Nice (ToN) extended the co-decision procedure to legislative proposals in some areas of employment and industrial relations. The Treaty of Maastricht permitted qualified majority voting in Council in some of the areas listed in Article 137(1) of the EC Treaty, concerning for instance employment conditions, the work environment and equality. The co-decision procedure, combined with qualified majority voting in Council, is the method most likely to generate legislation in the field of employment and industrial relations.

In practice, the co-decision procedure not only affects the dynamics of the legislative process but also has a potential effect on the EU social dialogue. (This term refers to discussions and negotiations between the social partners, the representatives of employers and workers.) Coupled with qualified majority voting, the co-decision procedure makes it easier for the Parliament to promote or block legislation. This may provide an indirect incentive to the social partners to negotiate and conclude agreements within the social dialogue. An indirect effect of the introduction of the co-decision procedure could well be that business owners face more and stricter EU legislation in the field of employment and industrial relations.

3.3.4   Business example

■ **Example 3.16 Bayer Corporation**
Before the introduction of the euro, half of Bayer's sales and two-thirds of its profits came from European Community countries. Doing business in 1996 was unnecessarily costly and complicated owing to the large number of currencies within the European Community. Bayer was very much in favour of a common currency. They did not want to bear the expense of protecting themselves against exchange fluctuations.

After the introduction of the euro, the markets operated more transparently and pricing was simpler, with less variation across markets. In order to adapt to the euro, Bayer had to completely restructure the business and replace all of the internal accounting, warehousing, packaging, billing and payroll systems.

Bayer started to implement the restructuring process two years before the euro and needed more than 750 employees to work on the transition. All the back-office operations required consolidation. Before the euro, Bayer had at least one accounting centre to handle transactions for every single country in the EC. With the arrival of the euro, it harmonized its entire operation by opening one shared service centre for the whole of Europe. Bayer located this facility in Spain, which was then the most advantageous from a cost and operational perspective.

By combining all its European back-office activities and opening a combined service centre in Barcelona, Bayer had reduced its overall costs. In addition, it created a centrally planned marketing organization with new business and development strategies. In the new situation, this organization would decide which products would be produced in which plants for which customers throughout the EU. The arrival of the euro made it easy for Bayer to compare prices from suppliers all over Europe and to implement a uniform pricing strategy right across Europe.

The company's success was in fact due to the existence of one currency, one bank, one European and one global strategy. This outcome can therefore be attributed in large measure to the implementation of the Treaty of Maastricht.

3.4 The effect of EU enlargement on business

3.4.1 The EU enlargement process

The enlargement process has emerged as an outstanding success for the EU and its citizens, accomplishing one of the original purposes of European integration. The accession of twelve new Member States since 2004 has created a win-win situation for both new and old Member States and for the EU as a whole.

Enlargement has brought measurably greater economic prosperity for all EU citizens and has made Europe stronger in the world economy. According to the European Commission, the EU is currently the largest integrated economic area in the world. It accounts for more than 30% of the world's GDP and more than 17% of world trade (excluding intra-EU trade).

3.4.1.1 From six to 27

In 1951, six countries established the first European Community. Since then, there have been five further enlargements:

1951 Belgium, France, West Germany, Italy, Luxembourg and the Netherlands
1973 Denmark, Ireland and the United Kingdom
1981 Greece
1986 Portugal and Spain
1995 Austria, Finland and Sweden
2004 Cyprus, the Czech Republic, Estonia, Hungary, Latvia, Lithuania, Malta, Poland, Slovakia and Slovenia
2007 Bulgaria and Romania

The official candidate countries are currently Turkey, Macedonia and Croatia. There are also potential candidate countries: Albania, Bosnia and Herzegovina, Kosovo (under UN Security Council Resolution 1244), Montenegro and Serbia. None of these countries can simply join the Union when and if they feel like it: they have to meet the 'Copenhagen criteria'. According to these criteria, candidate countries are required to:
· uphold democracy, the rule of law, human rights, and respect for and protection of minorities
· have a functioning market economy, as well as the ability to cope with the pressure of competition and the market forces at work inside the Union
· be able to assume the obligations of membership, in particular adherence to the objectives of political, economic and monetary union
· adopt the *acquis communautaire* (the total body of EU law accumulated up to the present time).

3.4.2 The impact of enlargement

A distinction needs to be made between the impact of enlargement on the European Union as a whole, on the old Member States and on the new Member States.

3.4.2.1 The European Union as a whole

One of the most important changes for the Union is that democratic regimes with market economies have been established following the end of communism, with the result that security and stability have been strengthened throughout the Union. This has had the direct effect of increasing trade integration. Increased trade integration in the EU enables Member States to benefit from the economic law of *comparative advantage*. According to this theory, each country can gain by specializing in the goods in which it has a comparative advantage, and thus the growth potential of the entire EU is strengthened.

Enlargement has improved the competitiveness and resilience of the European economy by prompting improvements in the legal, regulatory and institutional environments and creating a more efficient division of labour. The EU as a whole has gained in terms of globalization by becoming more competitive in the world arena. A bigger EU is also a more important economic and political player in the world, with greater influence over issues of global importance, such as climate change and the international financial crisis.

3.4.2.2 The 15 'old' Member States

In the old Member States, export-oriented business owners realized that the new situation offered vast opportunities, created by increased trade flows, the elimination of trade barriers and access to cheap labour.

Investors from the old Member States swiftly grasped these new opportunities, bringing an enormous inflow of private capital into the new Member States. The result was an increase in income per capita in the new states from 40% of the old Member States' average in 1999 to 52% in 2008. The old states now send 7.5% of their exports to the new Member States, compared with just 4.75% a decade ago. The introduction of the euro has been partly responsible for this development.

Those old Member States which increased their trade with and investment in the new Member States have benefited most. New markets for exports and foreign investment have been opened up for businesses from the old states. These businesses have succeeded in strengthening competitiveness and maintaining employment in their own countries. In fact, investment in the new Member States, in such areas as machinery, furniture, medical instruments, chemicals and timber, has gone hand in hand with growing employment in the old states.

3.4.2.3 The 12 'new' Member States

The economies of the new Member States have been rapidly modernized. With their newly developed market economies, they were able to cope with the competitive pressures and market forces of the single market. Enlargement has considerably boosted these economies, with the effect of improving living standards in the new states. They have experienced rapid productivity growth, declining unemployment and a steep rise in income. Cyprus, Malta, Slovakia and Slovenia, which joined the euro area, have benefited even more, as they have abolished exchange rate risk, reduced transaction costs and gained access to capital at lower interest rates.

It is above all foreign investment in the new Member States which is responsible for economic restructuring and the growth in productivity and employment. Foreign investment has been particularly high in the financial sector, resulting in foreign-owned banks being established in many new Member States. The banks in Estonia and Slovakia are 100% foreign owned, compared to about 30% foreign ownership in Slovenia. The euro area has on average 20% foreign ownership. Not only the banking industry, but also foreign insurance groups from the old Member States have acquired a strong presence in the new Member States. This means that strict co-operation and control on the European scale is necessary in these sectors.

The ten new members experienced a total average growth in GDP of 4.9% between 2000 and 2008. They have also benefited from solid growth in employment, at a rate of about 1.5% per annum since 2004. This has been in conjunction with a steady increase in employment in the old Member States of about 1% per year since enlargement. Investments from old Member States have been primarily responsible for economic transformation in the new Member States.

On the other hand, it is important to emphasize that not all Member States have benefited equally from the enlargement. Some have experienced a strong economic downturn since the enlargement. Latvia and Hungary, for instance, have both been on the brink of bankruptcy. Latvia had to make drastic cuts in its budget (500 million lats, equivalent to €683 million) by July 2009 in order to receive the next instalment of its bailout loans from the International Monetary Fund (IMF), the EU and other lenders. The country agreed to a loan package of €7.5 billion in December 2008, which is conditional on cutting its budget deficit. Latvia's currency is linked to the euro, but the country has been hit so hard by the recession that many analysts believe it will have to devalue its currency. Latvia has promised to ensure that its deficit does not exceed 5% of GDP, but its finance minister, Einar Repse, has warned that the public deficit could still rise as high as 11.6%, despite the fresh cuts.

The situation in Hungary is not much better. Hungary is also on the edge of bankruptcy, while its citizens are struggling to pay off their mortgages and personal loans, mostly taken out in foreign currency. The Hungarian currency, the forint, has tumbled, while unemployment has rocketed, creating a tremendous debt trap. This also puts a great strain on banks backed by Western European taxpayers, particularly those of Switzerland and Austria.

The problem originated when forint interest rates were extremely high compared to lower-rate loans in Swiss francs and euros. The foreign rates gave Hungarian consumers extra purchasing power: more than 60% of Hungarian mortgages and car loans were taken out in a foreign currency. In October 2007, foreign-currency loans made up 93% of all lending in Hungary. The Hungarian government wants to guarantee that everyone who loses their job will be able to make their mortgage payments. The country has already been receiving IMF assistance and as a consequence has had to make big budget cuts.

It is not only Latvia and Hungary that have been and still are suffering; other Eastern and Central European countries have also been hit heavily by the crisis. Austria has therefore demanded that the EU set up a €150 billion (£134 billion) fund to bail out Eastern and Central Europe. Switzerland has promised to provide all the Swiss francs the Hungarian government needs to meet its repayment demands.

Despite the fact that some Eastern and Central European countries are going through a very difficult time economically, it can be said that the fifth enlargement has led to a larger, more integrated internal market and has created the conditions for the EU to become stronger, more dynamic and better equipped to face increased global competition.

3.4.2.4 Business examples

■ **Example 3.17 Faurecia**
Faurecia is a company that manufactures car seat mechanisms and frames, acoustic systems, door panels and dashboards. Faurecia has four production sites in Poland and employs more than 3000 people. To date, its investment in the country has been in excess of €200 million, and it exports more than 80% of its production. The factory at Grójec manufactures seat frames and mechanisms, which are transported for assembly into finished seats at factories close to customers' production sites. Faurecia has only one other factory in Europe (located in France) making the same components as Grójec. The company's representatives stress the high productivity of the plant – the most productive in Europe – and the high quality of the Polish workforce. In addition, wage costs have been considerably lower in Poland than in the traditional car-manufacturing regions of Western Europe.
(Source: http://ec.europa.eu/)

■ **Example 3.18 Fiat**
Fiat has invested heavily in Poland: since 1992 it has invested over €1.5 billion. Since the privatization of the formerly state-owned FSM factory, Fiat has had a production facility in Tychy, in southern Poland. There is also an engine plant in Bielsko-Biala, managed jointly by Fiat and General Motors. Roughly 80% of the Fiat cars produced in Poland are for export. The plant in Tychy is one of the most productive in Europe, and Fiat emphasizes the high quality of the Polish labour force.

Polish car production has been highly unstable, varying from as many as 632,000 cars manufactured in 1999 to just 303,000 cars in 2002, when Poland was in recession. Fiat's market share in Poland has therefore fluctuated quite a lot. In 2003 its share of the car market was 16.5% and it manufactured over 203,000 cars in Poland. The annual figure had risen much higher than that before the mortgage crisis struck, but in the first quarter of 2009 Fiat pro duced only 140,360 cars. That is equivalent to roughly 560,000 cars manufactured per annum, which is fewer than it produced in 1999. This fall is most probably due to the mortgage crisis which began in 2007.

The Polish Fiat company currently has around 3000 employees (750 workers were laid off in the first quarter of 2009). The quantity of local purchasing has gradually increased: purchasing in Poland outside the Fiat Group increased from 55% in 1992 to 85.7% in 2004. At the same time, the number of suppliers has more than halved, resulting in local consolidation.
(Source: http://ec.europa.eu/)

■ Example 3.19 The Netherlands

Highest benefits from EU enlargement in last 5 years

The Netherlands has benefited the most from EU enlargement during the last five years, a statement from the Ministry of Foreign Affairs has stated. Since 2004, the Dutch economy has grown by an extra 1.8 per cent on top of normally projected growth: in other words, by an extra 11 billion Euro, some 650 Euro per Dutch resident. Translated into tangible benefits, this is equal to a free skiing holiday each year for everyone in the Netherlands, showed a European Commission study of the economic impact of EU enlargement. The accession of new member states to the European Union in 2004 has led to extra economic growth in all 27 member states, and its impact has been especially favorable in the Netherlands. The Netherlands has also scored well in terms of trade. In the past five years, trade in the Netherlands has grown by 40 per cent, more than in any other member state. In September 2008, the Netherlands Bureau for Economic Policy Analysis also concluded that the EU's internal market has made the Netherlands four to six per cent richer. In money terms, this amounts to an extra month's salary per year for everyone. The study "Five Years of an Enlarged EU" shows that much of this extra wealth is due to the EU's eastward enlargement.

Source: *New Europe* (www.neurope.eu/), based on the European Commission publication *Five Years of an Enlarged EU*

The case described in example 3.19 suggests that there are several reasons why the Netherlands has benefited more than other countries. One is the fact that the Netherlands has switched from industry to services. In addition, the best performing Member States have built the most overlapping production chains, and these frequently involve partners from the new Member States. France, for instance, has lost market share in certain products because it failed to adopt proactive competition policies at the micro level and did not make a decisive shift to services.

3.5   The Treaty of Lisbon

In December 2001 the Convention on the Future of Europe was set up. The Member States required further action to extend supranationalism, simplify the existing treaties and clarify the role of national and regional parliaments in relation to the EU. In July 2003 the Treaty establishing a Constitution for Europe (or Constitutional Treaty) was drawn up. All the Member States signed the treaty, but ratification failed because in 2005 France and the Netherlands voted against it. After the failure of the Constitutional Treaty, European leaders decided at an intergovernmental conference in 2007 that a new treaty was essential for further progress. The most urgent needs were for greater efficiency in decision making, increased democracy through a greater role for the European Parliament and national parliaments, and also greater harmony with regard to common external policy. To date, only 23 of the 27 Member States have ratified the treaty. If the Treaty of Lisbon is ratified, it will introduce significant changes to the structure and organization of the European Union. However, these changes will probably have less direct effect on doing business in Europe than the Treaty of Rome and the Treaty of Maastricht.

3.5.1   Summary of key changes

The Treaty of Lisbon (ToL) will amend the TEU and the EC Treaty without replacing them. It will provide the Union with the legal framework and the tools to meet future challenges and to respond to its citizens' demands. The ToL will affect four main areas:
1 democracy
2 efficiency
3 fundamental rights
4 external relations.

3.5.1.1   Democracy
- The European Parliament will gain power in relation to EU legislation, the EU budget and international agreements. Of particular importance is the increased use of the co-decision procedure in policy making.
- National parliaments will become more involved through the application of the principle of subsidiarity (i.e. that the Union acts only where results can be attained more effectively at EU level).
- Citizens will be able to submit policy proposals to the Commission after raising one million votes across the Union.
- The categorization of competences in the ToL (a summary of which institutions have which powers) will clarify who is responsible for doing what.
- The ToL explicitly recognizes for the first time the possibility of a Member State withdrawing from the Union.

3.5.1.2   Efficiency
- In the Council, qualified majority voting will be extended to new policy areas, to make decision making faster and more efficient. From 2014, the qualified majority system will be based on a 'double majority': the majority of Member States and the majority of the population of the Union. This dual legitimacy will be achieved when a decision is taken by 55% of the Member States representing at least 65% of the Union's population.
- There will be a new post of President of the European Council, who will be elected for two and a half years.
- The EU's ability to act will be enhanced in such policy areas as combating terrorism and crime, energy policy, public health, civil protection, climate change, services of general interest (i.e. public services), research, space, territorial cohesion, commercial policy, humanitarian aid, sport, tourism and administrative co-operation.

3.5.1.3   Fundamental rights

With the incorporation of the legally binding Charter of Fundamental Rights into European primary law, European citizens are guaranteed more civil, political, economic and social rights. Other issues covered in the ToL include greater solidarity between Member States (leading to more effective enforcement of rights) and the increased capacity of the EU to act on freedom, security and justice.

3.5.1.4   External relations

- The EU will acquire legal personality, which will strengthen its negotiating power and effectiveness on the world stage.
- The ToL will give Europe a clear voice on the international playing field.
- There will be a new High Representative of the Union in foreign affairs and security policy.
- The new European External Action Service will provide back-up and support to the High Representative.

3.5.2   The influence of the key changes on business

The tendency of the ToL is that the new structure will enhance the powers of both the EU itself and its citizens. As an organization, the EU will gain more control over its functioning and its external relations. Citizens will gain power in the fields of democracy and fundamental rights.

European businesses may also notice the effects of the ToL in such areas as energy policy, commercial policy, climate change, services of general interest, research, space, territorial cohesion, sport, tourism and administrative co-operation. To what extent and in what way these changes will affect individual business owners is hard to evaluate, because the ToL's treatment of these areas is very general in nature. Its effects will only be measurable once the treaty has come into force and secondary legislation has been passed, and when judicial decisions have been made on the basis of it.

The ToL is not officially in force at the time of writing (September 2009). This will happen only when all Member States have ratified the treaty. Ratification means that the legislative body of the Member State has fully approved the treaty through its regular law-making process. Ratification is currently in progress in the Czech Republic; in Poland the president has yet to sign the instrument of ratification and in Ireland the people voted against the ToL in a referendum held in June 2008. It is planned to hold a second referendum in the second half of 2009. In Germany, the federal president has signed the law on ratification, but he will not sign the instrument of ratification until the Federal Constitutional Court rules on the compatibility of the treaty with the German constitution. Once these four Member States have officially ratified the Treaty, it will automatically enter into force.

If the ToL does not enter into force due to lack of support from Member States, most of the workings of the EU will remain unchanged. However, there will be a few changes: for instance, the composition of the

Commission needs to be altered. At the moment, according to the ToN, where there are 27 Member States the number of Commissioners must be less than that number. Because there are currently 27 Member States, if the ToL is not ratified the next Commission must have fewer than 27 members. The current rules provide that the Council must decide unanimously how many Commissioners there will be and how those posts will be rotated fairly between the Member States. If all Member States do ratify the treaty, it will mark a major step forward in the integration of Europe.

Conclusions

This chapter has shown how the introduction of a European Community and a European Union has dramatically changed the business landscape. The first major stage in this transformation was the establishment of the European Community through the EC Treaty. The aim of the EC Treaty was economic and political stability throughout Europe. Stability is achieved through the economic integration of its Member States. Integration is effected by establishing an internal market and later an economic and monetary union (EMU). Both the internal market and EMU have been very successful. The internal market is shaped around certain Articles in the EC Treaty which impose prohibitions. These Articles are directed to the Member States and to businesses, to prevent them obstructing or hindering trade and competition in Europe. They are of vital importance to the business owner, who has the right to enforce them before a national court. As a result, intra-Community trade barriers have largely been eliminated. Other trade barriers arise as a result of disparities between taxes and legislation in Member States. These can be eradicated by means of harmonization, which has made remarkable progress in the fields of trade in goods and services and capital movement. It has also made good progress in improving the free movement of persons: in continental Europe, for instance, there have been no internal border controls since 2008.

EMU has been operational since 1999. The introduction of a common currency is a major improvement for European businesses. This is due in large part to the elimination of exchange rate risk in trade within the European Union. The fact that economic policy is now made largely in Brussels instead of in the Member States has also contributed to economic integration and stability. The EC with a fully operational internal market is the effective heart of the Union.

This Union has been considerably enlarged since 2004. Enlargement has also created many new opportunities for business in Europe. Statistical data confirms that both the introduction of a common currency and the enlargement have been very beneficial to the European Union as a whole and especially to European businesses. It is possible that the Treaty of Lisbon will have the same or an even greater influence on European business than its predecessors. However, not all the Member States have so far ratified it, so the question remains whether European business owners will ever have the opportunity to benefit from the treaty's implementation.

Questions

3.1   Explain the difference between the European Union and the European Community.

3.2   What is the relationship between *sovereignty, supranationalism* and *intergovernmentalism*?

3.3   Which law-making procedure is best suited to the harmonization of legislation in the European Union?

3.4   What are the direct benefits to businesses of the introduction of the euro?

3.5   Give two examples of how businesses have benefited from the introduction of the internal market.

3.6   Explain why strict enforcement of European competition rules is essential to the optimal functioning of the internal market.

3.7   Businesses can break European competition law by forming cartels and by abusing a dominant position. Explain the similarities and differences between these two infringements.

3.8   Explain the difference in integration between a free trade zone, a customs union, an internal market and an economic and monetary union.

Case studies

3.9   A Dutch business owner receives a letter from the government. The letter states that the business must pay tax because it has exported tulip bulbs from the Netherlands to Canada. Obviously, the Dutch exporter is not happy with the decision.

Give the exporter advice on the options available and which is the best option in this situation.

3.10   A Dutch producer of in-car satellite navigation devices appoints an exclusive reseller for every province in the Netherlands and Belgium. Its agreements with these resellers include the following clauses:
1   The resellers are not allowed to sell the satellite navigation devices to purchasers from other provinces
2   The resellers are instructed not to sell the goods to their customers below a particular price.

Explain separately for both conditions 1 and 2 whether they are permitted under European law.

3.11   The agricultural industry in the UK produces a large amount of meat. Unfortunately, there have been many outbreaks of animal diseases in Europe, and particularly in the UK, including BSE (bovine spongiform encephalopathy or mad cow disease), foot-and-mouth disease and bird flu. France is one of the main buyers of British meat, but in 1996, after the BSE outbreak (180,000 cases in the UK and 900 in France), France called for an immediate ban on imports of British meat. France and the UK settled the matter in court.

Explain whether the French import ban was permitted under European legislation. Detail the points of view of both the UK and France.

The organization of the European Union

4

The long and winding road to banning tobacco advertising in the EU

It took 14 years for the EU ban on tobacco advertising to come into being. Besides the debates in the legislative branch of the EU, there were court proceedings in the judiciary branch challenging the legal basis of the directive. This case study follows the long and winding road to getting the legislation adopted and details the challenges brought by Germany and the Commission against some EU Member States.

The Commission sent its first draft legislation on this issue to the European Parliament (EP) in April 1989. The Parliament wanted a complete ban on the advertising of tobacco products. The Commission was willing to comply with some changes but did not support a complete ban. The amended draft was sent to the Council at the end of 1990, but there was not enough support for the proposal as it was then formulated. The Commission had to come up with a new draft.

In 1991 a new proposal was sent to the legislature and the European Parliament asked for a couple of amendments to the draft. The amended proposal failed to achieve the qualified majority vote it needed in Council in 1995, just as it had in 1990.

In 1997 the Commission finally came up with the amendments necessary to win over the majority of the Council, and it was now up to the Parliament to agree to the latest version of the proposal. Before Parliament finally agreed, there were extended discussions over serious doubts about the legal basis of the directive. Nevertheless, both the EP and the Council, with the exceptions of Germany and Austria, agreed to the proposal in its latest version, and as a result the directive came into force on 30th June 1998.

The Member States were granted three years to implement the directive in their national legislation. Germany, however, did not accept the legal basis of the directive and immediately challenged it before the European Court of Justice (ECJ). Germany took the position that the legal basis given for the legislation, the operation of the internal market, was insufficient. According to Germany, the directive should have been based on the Articles of the EC Treaty concerning public health, which required the unanimous consent of all EU Member States; in its opinion, the directive was therefore null and void.

Germany was not alone in opposing the directive. UK tobacco companies challenged the directive in the British courts, which referred the case to the ECJ.

In October 2000 the court agreed with Germany and the tobacco companies that the directive hindered the free movement of goods. Therefore the Article concerning the operation of internal market, which was included in the EC Treaty to encourage the free movement of goods and services, could not serve as the legal basis of the directive. The legislation was null and void and it was up to the Commission to propose a new solution.

The final version of the directive was agreed to by the European legislature in 2003. Although this version of the Tobacco Advertising Directive 2003/33/EC was again challenged by Germany, this time the European Court of Justice did not throw out the directive.

The Member States had to transpose Directive 2003/33/EC into national law by the end of July 2005. The Member States were also supposed to communicate the national legislative measures implementing the directive to the Commission by that date.

Supported by public opinion, it was now the Commission's turn to take a strong position on the matter. In October 2006 the Commission sent several 'letters of Formal Notice' to Spain, Italy, Hungary and the Czech Republic for non-compliance with the Tobacco Advertising Directive. The Commission was also starting infringement procedures against Germany and Luxembourg for failing to communicate the national legislative measures taken to implement the directive.

If the Member States fail to bring their legislation into line with the Tobacco Advertising Directive, the Commission will take the next step in the infringement procedure: it will send 'Reasoned Opinions' to the Member States concerned, giving a period of time within which the infringement must be remedied. If the Member States fail to meet the conditions of the 'Reasoned Opinions', the Commission may open proceedings before the European Court of Justice.

In this chapter the organization and institutions of the European Union (EU) are explained. The opening case study shows that the separate institutions have different roles in enacting and upholding EU legislation.

Section 4.1 makes some general observations on the organization of the EU. In section 4.2 the separation of powers within the EU is explained, and sections 4.3 to 4.5 go into more detail on the three branches of power and the different roles of the institutions. Finally, in section 4.6 some organizational changes proposed in the EU Constitution and the Treaty of Lisbon (ToL) are discussed.

By the end of the chapter, all the procedures involved in the chapter's opening case study will have been clarified.

4.1 Introduction to the organization

This section explains the special nature of the Treaty establishing a European Community (the EC Treaty) and the distinction between the European Community (EC) and the EU. It makes clear under what circumstances the Commission and the other institutions can exercise the powers described in the opening case study about the Tobacco Advertising Directive. To explain the uniqueness of the EU, the normal mode of collaboration between countries, intergovernmental co-operation, is described first. The difference between intergovernmental co-operation and supranational collaboration between countries is explained in chapters 2 and 3; this section describes the effect of these phenomena on the legislative powers of the Member States.

4.1.1 Intergovernmental co-operation

When countries decide to collaborate on an issue, they usually set out the results of their negotiations in a treaty, also known as a convention or an international agreement. A *bilateral convention* is an agreement between two countries; a *multilateral convention* is a treaty between more than two countries.

Most conventions are of an *intergovernmental* nature. In this type of co-operation, the countries remain in control of all political and legal decisions. A country's position cannot be overruled by the decision of one or more other countries, because decisions require *unanimous consent*. In other words, the countries do not give up their sovereignty by signing a treaty and neither do they give up their right to veto a proposal. It is up to the countries themselves to decide whether they choose to work together with the others or not.

In an intergovernmental context, a treaty does not create any higher institution than the countries involved themselves. This means that, once the treaty has entered into force, if one of the countries fails to perform in accordance with it, all the other countries can do is remind their counterpart to act in the agreed manner. One way of issuing a serious warning to a country is to withdraw one's ambassador from the country concerned or to expel that country's ambassador. The ultimate sanction against a country's failure to adhere to a treaty is to wage war.

Figure 4.1 illustrates the intergovernmental mode of co-operation between six countries.

Figure 4.1 **Intergovernmental co-operation**

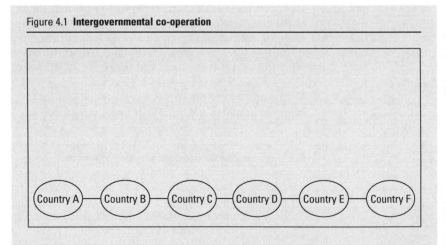

Examples of intergovernmental co-operation are the General Agreement on Tariffs and Trade (GATT), the treaty establishing the World Trade Organization (WTO), the North American Free Trade Agreement (NAFTA) and the North Atlantic Treaty Organization (NATO). The United Nations also functions largely in an intergovernmental manner, although the Security Council has the power to overrule the wishes of a particular country, apart from those of its permanent members.

Within the EU, areas such as a common foreign and security policy and co-operation in the fields of justice and home affairs remain intergovernmental. The Member States themselves decide to what extent they wish to co-operate on these intergovernmental issues.

■ **Example 4.1**
When the United States of America (USA) decided to invade Iraq in 2003, the EU was eager to come out with a unanimous statement on the issue. The UK supported the invasion, unlike France and Germany, which were opposed to it. As a result, it was not possible to make a joint EU statement.

■ **Example 4.2**
During the 1990s, France complained on several occasions about the Dutch policy on soft drugs. The Netherlands, however, could not be forced to change its policy, because it is a home affairs matter, which is an intergovernmental issue within the EU. The Netherlands retains full sovereignty over its soft drugs policy and cannot be overruled by any other country or institution in the world.

4.1.2   Supranational collaboration

There are only a few examples of supranational collaboration in the world. The most important one is the EC, which is part of the EU. In this mode of co-operation, a country's opinion can be overruled by a *majority* vote. The Member States have given up their right of veto. Within the EC, the institutions of the Commission, the Council of Ministers, the European Parliament and the European Court of Justice are superior to their national counterparts, so there is a higher legislature, a higher executive and a higher judicial branch. Figure 4.2 illustrates the supranational mode of co-operation between the six countries (Belgium, France, West Germany, Italy, Luxembourg and the Netherlands) which founded the European Economic Community (EEC) with the treaty of 1957.

Figure 4.2 shows how the Member States have given up their sovereignty over economic issues and handed authority in this area over to the EC institutions. The distinction made within the EU between intergovernmental and supranational issues explains why, in the opening case study, Germany contested the legal basis of the Tobacco Advertising Directive. Germany was of the opinion that banning tobacco advertising was an intergovernmental issue, whereas the Commission and the legislative institutions judged that it was admissible to introduce it on a supranational basis. Germany and Austria were overruled within the Council of Ministers, so the only way to defeat the directive was to bring a case before the European Court of Justice. At the time, health

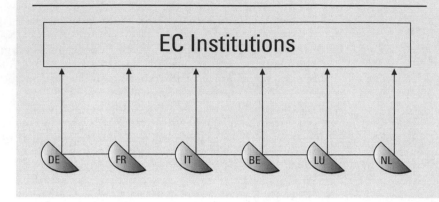

Figure 4.2 **Supranational co-operation after the Second World War**

EC Institutions

DE FR IT BE LU NL

issues came into the area of home affairs, and for that reason the court agreed with the German point of view. The directive should not have come into being because it required unanimous consent in the Council of Ministers. As a result, Germany had the right of veto on the issue and the directive was not valid.

Unlike the health issue involved in the Tobacco Advertising Directive, EC laws on the common market are of a supranational nature. In this area of law, a country's position can be outvoted in the Council of Ministers. Even though a country may not agree with the final text of the legislation, the national authorities still have to act in conformity with it. Only the European Court of Justice has the power to declare EU legislation null and void.

4.1.3 The European Union versus the European Community

Section 4.1.2 made it clear that different issues are dealt with in the EU through different forms of international co-operation. Decisions on a common foreign and security policy or co-operation in the fields of justice and home affairs will be made in an intergovernmental manner, by unanimous consent in the Council of Ministers, whereas economic issues will be decided in a supranational manner, which may result in a country's opinion being outvoted in Council.

Figure 4.3 shows the structure established by the Maastricht Treaty of 1993 in relation to the different modes of co-operation and legislation that came into being as a result. The EU's three-pillar structure is examined in chapters 2 and 3. Although some home affairs and justice matters related to the common market moved from the third pillar to the first one as a result of the Treaty of Amsterdam, the concept behind the pillars remains the same as it was in 1993.

Figure 4.3 shows that the EC is part of the EU. The EC pillar is of a supranational nature, whereas in the second and third pillar decisions have to be made by unanimous consent. So, depending on the issue, the ministers in Council decide either by majority vote or by unanimous consent.

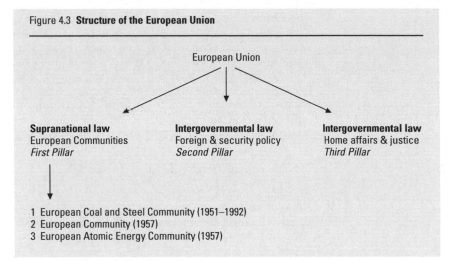

Figure 4.3 **Structure of the European Union**

European Union

Supranational law	Intergovernmental law	Intergovernmental law
European Communities	Foreign & security policy	Home affairs & justice
First Pillar	*Second Pillar*	*Third Pillar*

1 European Coal and Steel Community (1951–1992)
2 European Community (1957)
3 European Atomic Energy Community (1957)

This book focuses on international trade within the common market and therefore on matters relating to the first pillar of the EU. The law of the second and third pillars is not discussed and the principal institution of the EU, the European Council, is not studied. Although the meetings of the European Council, the heads of state and their foreign ministers are an important factor in European integration, their work focuses mainly on matters relating to the second and third pillars of the EU and therefore fall outside the scope of this book.

4.2 The separation of powers in the EU

This section explains the general organization of the EC by examining the different roles of the institutions within the Community. Their roles in creating, implementing and enforcing the law are explained in general terms. These three essential functions are exercised not only in the EU but also in every state in the world. This section gives an overview of the European separation of powers (or *trias politica*).

The EC's legislature is responsible for making law, the executive implements the law, and last but not least the judiciary is responsible for enforcing the law. The work of these institutions is discussed in greater detail in sections 4.3 to 4.5.

The three functions of making, implementing and upholding the law were named the *trias politica* by the French scholar Montesquieu (1689–1755), who studied the political organization of several countries in the eighteenth century. His conclusion was that, the more these branches were separated, the better the state behaved towards its citizens. A state works best when the governmental powers are divided between separate state bodies which, as a result, cannot abuse their powers so easily.

Such a separation of powers is also present in the EU. The institutions mentioned in Article 7 of the EC Treaty are the European Parliament, the Council (of Ministers), the Commission, the Court of Justice and (the least well known) the Court of Auditors. These institutions do not have unlimited power. On the contrary, Article 7 prescribes that they can only act within the limits of the powers prescribed in the EC Treaty. This principle, known as the *attribution principle*, means that the European institutions are only allowed to act in accordance with the Articles of the EC Treaty. It was because of these limits on the institutions' authority that the difference of opinion between Germany and the European legislature emerged in the tobacco advertising ban case.

4.2.1 Legislative power

As in the Member States, the most important act in the EU is that of creating law. The branch responsible for making laws is called the *legislature*. The legislative branch in the EU consists of two institutions: the European Parliament (EP) and the Council of Ministers.

The European Parliament

The European Parliament consists of the representatives of the citizens of all Member States. The rules governing the European Parliament are set out in the first section of Part V of the EC Treaty, which is concerned with provisions on the institutions. According to Articles 189 and 190, the members of the European Parliament are selected through general elections. The involvement of Parliament ensures that legislation is created in a democratic manner, because the people's opinion is heard.

Alongside the European Parliament, the EU legislature includes the Council of Ministers. The ministers look after the national interests of the Member States during the legislative process. The Council's main tasks are described in Article 202 of the EC Treaty: The Council is responsible for setting out the economic policies which will eventually result in legislative decisions. Article 203 prescribes that each state shall have one representative at a ministerial level, who has the authority to bind the Member State.

The European Parliament and the Council of Ministers are responsible for the bulk of EU legislation. However, the legislature may decide to let the Commission draw up the legislative detail for a particular European law.

4.2.2 Executive power

In every country in the world, legislation requires authorities to implement the law in practice. These authorities belong to the executive branch. In the EU, all the government authorities in the Member States co-operate with the EU's highest executive body, the Commission. It is not possible to implement EU law without the involvement of the national executive authorities.

The Commission is the most prominent executive institution of the EU. Its executive role is prescribed in Article 211 of the EC Treaty, the first Article in this section of the treaty that is specifically dedicated to the Commission's work of supporting the goals of the common market. Although each Member State has representatives on the Commission, its goals are truly European. The Commission focuses on ensuring that the Common Market operates in the best possible manner and makes proposals for achieving the most favourable results for Europe. As opposed to the Council of Ministers, in which the various national interests predominate in discussions, the Commission supports the best outcome for the European internal market as a whole.

Although the Commission's work has many aspects, its executive activities can be divided into three main functions:
1 The Commission drafts the proposals for EU legislation.
   Although laws are actually passed by two institutions other than the Commission, having the authority to produce the drafts gives it a huge influence over the content of legislation.

2 The Commission ensures that EU law is properly applied by the Member States.

This aspect of the Commission's work is mentioned as its first task in Article 211 of the EC Treaty. Because of its involvement in the various stages of EU legislation, the Commission has extensive knowledge of the content of the laws and how they should be implemented in the Member States. The Commission is the highest-ranking executive body in the EU, above the national executives. Member States are obliged to inform the Commission about how they actually implement EU law in their national legislation. The Commission is the guardian of EU law and has the authority to initiate proceedings against a Member State which fails to apply the law properly.

3 The Commission executes EU law.
   In large-scale competition and merger cases, the Commission is the only body which has the authority to execute EU law. In other cases, the national competition authorities have the authority to execute EU competition law, and the Commission checks whether they are executing the law correctly. This enables the Commission to focus on the most important cases in the single market, while the national competition authorities keep track of minor deviations from EU competition law.

The second and third of these functions are explained in greater detail in section 4.4.

The Court of Auditors is also related to the executive because it checks the financial accounts of the EU. It operates as an external financial auditing agency. Although its name suggests otherwise, the Court of Auditors has no judicial authority. Articles 246–8 of the EC Treaty cover this body, which gained the status of an institution when the EU Treaty came into force.

The Court of Auditors not only monitors the EU's own expenditure, but also audits the money that is spent in the Member States. Almost 80% of EU finances are destined for the EU Member States. When malpractice is discovered, this money has to be reimbursed. Irregularities are sometimes found in the financial management of the institutions themselves. The biggest upset caused by the Court of Auditors' work is described in case study 4.1.

Although the work of the Court of Auditors is very important in ensuring that EU money is properly spent within the Union, the institution does has no direct influence on the common market. It is therefore not discussed any further in this chapter.

1999: A bad year for Brussels

The European Commission has had a controversial year. The European Union suffered the worst crisis in its history in March with the unprecedented mass resignation of the European Commission. It followed complaints by the European Court of Auditors and the European Parliament over several years about wrongdoing in EU institutions.

The scandal was set in motion last autumn, when the European Parliament refused to discharge the 1996 commission budget and filed a motion of censure against the commission. Two months later an EC auditor, Paul van Buitenen, passed dossiers giving evidence of fraud and mismanagement to the European Parliament Green group and to the European Court of Auditors. He was suspended on half pay several days later.

In January, the European Parliament narrowly voted against passing the motion of censure against the entire commission. Instead, it established a committee of independent experts to examine specific allegations of wrongdoing against certain commissioners and in certain commission services.

In agreeing not to sack the commission, MEPs also extracted a promise from Jacques Santer, who was then the president of the commission, that he would accept and act on any recommendations by the committee.

The committee's report was published on 15 March and set in motion the resignation of all 20 commissioners. The report criticised commissioners for not being aware of malpractice within the services that they were supposed to be running.

It said: "This loss of control implies at the outset a heavy responsibility for both the commissioners individually and the commission as a whole."

The commissioner for education and research, Edith Cresson, was singled out for nepotism after she allegedly employed a long-standing dentist friend, Dr Rene Berthelot, in a fictitious post on a contract investigators called "manifestly irregular".

Monika Wulf-Mathies of Germany and Joao de Deus Pinheiro of Portugal were also criticised for putting their friends or relatives on the EU payroll.

By midnight the entire European Commission had resigned.

Mr Santer claimed he was "entirely exonerated" by the report and had "no guilt whatsoever" about the crisis. He was replaced as the commission president later this year by the Italian former prime minister Romano Prodi.

In a twist of fate, Mr Santer has now joined the body which brought about his downfall from the commission, after being elected as a member of the European Parliament in June.

As for the whistleblower, Paul Van Buitenen was reinstated to a new job. He is now employed in the personnel department, making decisions about replacing carpets and lampshades in the commission's buildings. [...]

Source: BBC news, Wednesday 25th August 1999, published at 11:13 GMT 12:13 UK

4.2.3   Judicial power

Although the Commission is seen as the guardian of European law, the institution which actually has the authority to uphold the law is the Court of Justice of the European Communities, generally referred to as the European Court of Justice or EC Court of Justice (ECJ). Section 4 of Part V of the EC Treaty includes articles on the judicial institution. In fact, as Article 220 of the Treaty explains, the European Court of Justice comprises two courts, the Court of Justice itself and the Court of First Instance. Both courts, each within its own jurisdiction, ensure that the law is observed in the interpretation and application of the EC Treaty.

In this branch of the *trias politica* there is co-operation between the EU institutions on the one hand and the national courts on the other. For the majority of citizens and commercial bodies in the EU, the national courts of law in the Member States provide the protection they need against breaches of European law. In fact, it is the national courts which ensure that European law is observed in the Member States. The obligation on national authorities to implement European law also has another effect: the national authorities may fine an enterprise for breaking European law. If the enterprise does not agree with the fine, it must bring the case before a national court of law instead of lodging a case in Luxembourg with the ECJ. If the judges in the national court are of the opinion that the ruling in European law is unclear, they may ask the ECJ for clarification. The ECJ therefore helps national courts by clarifying European law in cases where its application is unclear.

Only in very limited cases do private persons or companies have an opportunity to lodge a case with the ECJ. More detail about the different types of cases which come before the European Courts of Justice is given in chapter 5.

4.3 The legislative branch

This section explains the sources of European law and the way legislation comes into existence. The sources of European law can be divided into two: that of primary European law in the Treaties, and that of secondary European law, which is made by the European legislature.

4.3.1 European treaties

As shown in section 3.1, which traces the history of the EU, a long succession of treaties has led to the current version of the EC Treaty. It all started after the Second World War with the establishment of the European Coal and Steel Community(ECSC) in 1952. The first Treaty, setting up the European Economic Community (EEC), was signed in 1957 and has since been amended several times. When new states become members of the EC, they also enter into conventions within the EU.

What all EU conventions have in common is that they can only come into being when every Member State gives its consent. The EC Treaty has direct effect in every Member State and the legislation embodied in the treaty is the supreme law, even higher than the national constitutions.

The treaty that gives most information about the common market is the EC Treaty, which was published in its most recent consolidated form in 2006. Attempts to change the organization by introducing a Treaty for a European Constitution have failed, and there was not much hope for the Treaty of Lisbon either, since Ireland had voted against adopting that version of the EC Treaty in the first referendum.

4.3.2 The EC Treaty

The EC Treaty gives details of the common market and its principles and it allocates authority to all the EC institutions to ensure the operation of the market. Part I of the EC Treaty sets out the goals and principles of the EC, after which the four principles of free movement are listed. The free movement of goods is the basis of the common market idea, with a common customs tariff applied to trade with states outside the EU. The other three freedoms, the free movement of persons, services and capital, are explained in Part II of the treaty. Part III presents topics related to the common market, after which the rules governing the institutions are set out.

Some of the rules in the treaty apply directly to the Member States and others are directed to the institutions; for instance, when the institutions are allowed to make laws on a particular subject, it sets out the procedures which must be followed.

4.3.3 Regulations and directives

Two forms of legislation exist in the European Union: the *regulation* and the *directive*. Article 249 of the EC Treaty gives the following definition of a regulation: 'A regulation shall have general application. It shall be binding in its entirety and directly applicable in every Member State.'

Regulations are most like the national legislation that people are used to. As soon as a regulation comes into force, it applies in all Member States. An example of a regulation is the EC Regulation on Jurisdiction and Enforcement of Judgments, also called Brussels I. This regulation defines the court(s) that have jurisdiction in the case of an enterprise having a dispute over an international contract or some other problem with another enterprise in the EU.

Directives, on the other hand, are not to be compared with the workings of national laws. The EC Treaty gives the following definition in the third paragraph of Article 249: 'A directive shall be binding, as to the result to be achieved, upon every Member State to which it is addressed, but shall leave to the authorities the choice of form and methods.'

In other words, a directive does not have direct effect. The intended effect of a European directive has to be achieved through implementation by the national legislatures in the Member States. The goal of the directive is binding, but the way a country chooses to implement it is up to the national authorities, as long as its effect is incorporated into binding national regulations. A directive aims to achieve the same result through the laws of all the Member States. Case study 4.2 gives an example of the way a directive operates in the Member States.

Case study 4.2 **Daylight saving time directive**

This case study presents both the directive and its implementation in national legislation in the UK, where the existing national legislation had to be adjusted.

Directive 2000/84/EC of the European Parliament and of the Council of 19 January 2001 on summer-time arrangements

THE EUROPEAN PARLIAMENT AND THE COUNCIL OF THE EUROPEAN UNION,

Having regard to the Treaty establishing the European Community, and in particular Article 95 thereof,

Having regard to the proposal from the Commission(1),
Having regard to the opinion of the Economic and Social Committee(2),
Acting in accordance with the procedure laid down in Article 251 of the Treaty(3),

Whereas:

(1) The eighth Directive, 97/44/EC, of the European Parliament and of the Council of 22 July 1997 on summer-time arrangements(4) introduced a common date and time in all Member States, for the beginning and end of summer time in 1998, 1999, 2000 and 2001.

(2) Given that the Member States apply summer-time arrangements, it is important for the functioning of the internal market that a common date and time for the beginning and end of the summer-time period be fixed throughout the Community.

(3) Since the summer-time period considered most appropriate by the Member States runs from the end of March to the end of October, it is appropriate that that period therefore be maintained.

(4) The proper functioning of certain sectors, not only transport and communications, but also other sectors of industry, requires stable, long-term planning. Provisions concerning summer time should therefore be laid down for an unspecified period. Article 4 of Directive 97/44/EC provides, in that respect, that the European Parliament and the Council are to adopt, by 1 January 2001, the arrangements to apply from 2002 onwards.

(5) For reasons of clarity and accuracy of information, a timetable for the implementation of the summer-time period for the following five years should be published every five years.

(6) Implementation of this Directive should, moreover, be monitored by means of a report, to be presented by the Commission to the European Parliament, the Council and the Economic and Social Committee, on the impact of these provisions in all of the areas concerned. That report should be based on the information made available to the Commission by the Member States in sufficient time to enable the report to be presented at the specified time.

(7) Given that the complete harmonisation of the timetable for the summer-time period with a view to facilitating transport and communications cannot be sufficiently achieved by the Member States and can therefore be better achieved at Community level, the Community may take measures, in accordance with the principle of subsidiarity as set out in Article 5 of the Treaty. This Directive does not go beyond what is necessary to achieve those objectives.

(8) For geographical reasons, the common summer-time arrangements should not apply to the overseas territories of the Member States,

HAVE ADOPTED THIS DIRECTIVE:

Article 1
For the purposes of this Directive "summer-time period" shall mean the period of the year during which clocks are put forward by 60 minutes compared with the rest of the year.

Article 2
From 2002 onwards, the summer-time period shall begin, in every Member State, at 1.00 a.m., Greenwich Mean Time, on the last Sunday in March.

Article 3
From 2002 onwards, the summer-time period shall end, in every Member State, at 1.00 a.m., Greenwich Mean Time, on the last Sunday in October.

Article 4
The Commission shall publish a communication in the Official Journal of the European Communities(5), for the first time on the occasion of the publication of this Directive, and every five years thereafter, containing the timetable showing the dates on which the summer-time period will begin and end for the following five years.

Article 5
The Commission shall report to the European Parliament, the Council and the Economic and Social Committee on the impact of the provisions of this Directive on the sectors concerned by 31 December 2007 at the latest.

That report shall be drawn up on the basis of the information made available to the Commission by each Member State by 30 April 2007 at the latest.

The Commission shall, if necessary and following the conclusions of the report, make appropriate proposals.

Article 6
This Directive shall not apply to the overseas territories of the Member States.

Article 7
Member States shall bring into force the laws, regulations and administrative provisions necessary to comply with this Directive by 31 December 2001 at the latest. They shall forthwith inform the Commission thereof.

When Member States adopt those measures, they shall contain a reference to this Directive or be accompanied by such a reference on the occasion of their official publication. Member States shall determine how such reference is to be made.

Article 8
This Directive shall enter into force on the day of its publication in the Official Journal of the European Communities.

Article 9
This Directive is addressed to the Member States.

Done at Brussels, 19 January 2001.

For the European Parliament,	For the Council,
The President	The President
N. Fontaine	B. Ringholm

The directive requires that the legislation in all the Member States should be adapted. The following amendments were made to the national law of the United Kingdom:

STATUTORY INSTRUMENTS 2002 No. 262

SUMMER TIME
The Summer Time Order 2002

Made 12th February 2002
Laid before Parliament 18th February 2002
Coming into force 11th March 2002

At the Court, at Buckingham Palace, the 12th day of February 2002

Present,

The Queen's Most Excellent Majesty in Council

Her Majesty, in exercise of the powers conferred on Her by section 2(2) of the European Communities Act 1972 and all other powers enabling Her in that behalf, is pleased, by and with the advice of Her Privy Council, to order, and it is hereby ordered, as follows:

Citation, commencement and extent
1 – (1) This Order may be cited as the Summer Time Order 2002 and shall come into force on 11th March 2002.

(2) This Order shall have effect in Great Britain and Northern Ireland.

Amendments to the Summer Time Act 1972
2 – (1) The Summer Time Act 1972[2] shall be amended as follows.

(2) In section 1 (advance of time during period of summer time) –
(a) omit "Subject to section 2 below," in subsection (1), and

(b) for subsection (2) substitute the following –

"(2) The period of summer time for the purposes of this Act is the period beginning at one o'clock, Greenwich mean time, in the morning of the last Sunday in March and ending at one o'clock, Greenwich mean time, in the morning of the last Sunday in October."

(3) Omit section 2 (extension of period, and double summer time).

(4) In section 3 (interpretation of references), omit "or under" in subsection (1).

A. K. Galloway,
Clerk of the Privy Council

In the example presented in case study 4.2, the Member States had eleven months to transpose the law of the directive into national legislation. It took the UK a little longer than that. Unlike the subject of this chapter's opening case study, the issue of summer time was not under dispute in the EU. In the case of the ban on tobacco advertising, however, the Commission had to submit several drafts before the directive was successfully introduced.

In case study 4.2, it was Article 95 of the EC Treaty that gave the European legislature the authority to legislate. The articles of the EC Treaty that give the Council and European Parliament the authority to legislate also prescribe the conditions under which the law-making process may take place.

The EC Treaty refers to three possible procedures through which draft legislation may become either a regulation or a directive. All three start with the Commission submitting a draft, but the involvement of the European Parliament in the law-making process is different for each procedure. These are:
· the co-decision procedure
· the co-operation procedure
· the consultation procedure.

In the *co-decision procedure*, currently the most common legislative procedure, the European Parliament can be seen as a full co-legislature. The Council of Ministers does not have the power to adopt the legislation without Parliament's consent. The complicated procedure is described in Article 251 of the EC Treaty. In outline, if the Parliament and the Council are unable to agree with the proposal (even after having suggested several amendments), a Conciliation Committee consisting of members of both institutions will try to agree on a text that is acceptable to both institutions. If the committee succeeds in reconciling the opposing views, the regulation or directive comes into existence. If not, the Commission has to start the legislative procedure all over again, as the Commission did several times during the fourteen years it took to get the final draft of the tobacco advertising ban (opening case study) approved by both institutions.

Where the daylight saving time directive was concerned (case study 4.2), the EU law-making procedure was completed very quickly and without any difference of opinion between the institutions involved.

The *co-operation procedure* can also be complicated and lengthy. The ins and outs of the process are described in Article 252 of the EC Treaty. Under this procedure the Council of Ministers, with unanimous consent, has the power to overrule the Parliament's position on a draft. Now that the co-decision procedure has become the one most frequently prescribed, the co-operation procedure applies only in a few legislative situations, such as that described in Article 102 of the EC Treaty.

The *consultation procedure* is used only where the Treaty confers the authority to legislate on a subject which has a direct impact on the Member States' financial situation, such as taxation. In the consultation procedure, the Council of Ministers acts without needing the consent of the European Parliament. The Parliament has only the right to give its opinion to the Council of Ministers. When the subject of legislation is related to the second or third pillar, the Council of Ministers decides unanimously using this law-making procedure, as in the situation described in example 4.3.

■ **Example 4.3**
When the Commission produces draft legislation on harmonizing Value Added Tax between the Member States, the procedure prescribed by Article 93 of the EC Treaty has to be followed. Unlike the previously explained procedures, the consultation procedure is described in Article 93 itself: 'The Council shall, acting unanimously on a proposal of the Commission and after consulting the European Parliament [...], adopt provisions for the harmonization of legislation concerning turnover taxes, excise duties and other forms of indirect taxation [...]'

Now that the EC Treaty prescribes the co-decision procedure as its standard law-making procedure, the EP has become a proper co-legislature as a result. EU legislation is now enacted in a more democratic manner than it was at the time of the original EC Treaty of 1957, when the consultation procedure was the most common way of bringing legislation into being.

4.4 The executive branch

In this section the executive tasks of the Commission are explained. The Commission's executive work consists largely of two principal tasks: actually execution of EC law on the one hand and monitoring the executive work of the other authorities responsible for executing EC law. In major competition cases, the Commission itself executes the provisions of the EC Treaty. Chapter 5 explains more about this side of the Commission's work. The other principal executive task is carried out after European legislation has been enacted, and it is this work that is explained in this section.

The Commission monitors all the executive work that has to be carried out in the EU. To make the Commission's work possible, the national authorities have to give the Commission information about how EU law is implemented in their particular Member State. In the opening case study on the tobacco advertising ban, the Commission was unhappy about the way in which some countries implemented the directive. Germany and Austria provided no information about the implemented legislation at all. According to the directive, the Member States had to provide a national framework which made it possible to monitor and regulate tobacco advertising. One of the Commission's most important tasks, therefore, is to check whether all EU legislation is implemented properly and in a timely manner. The EC Treaty gives the Commission special powers to encourage the Member States to act in accordance with EU legislation.

Article 226 procedure: the infringement procedure

The basis of this aspect of the executive work is laid down in Article 226 of the EC Treaty. Although the Article forms part of the provisions for the European Court of Justice, the task of taking action against Member States who have not performed according European law is granted to the Commission. Case study 4.3 describes an example of an infringement procedure in accordance with Article 226.

Case study 4.3 **Energy Performance of Buildings: Commission launches Court proceedings against Belgium and the UK**

28 February 2008

The European Commission today launched court proceedings against Belgium and the United Kingdom for failure to notify adequate national implementing measures as required by the 2002 Energy Performance of Buildings Directive. The goal of the Directive is to reduce energy consumption in buildings and it thus forms an important part of EU legislation aimed at improving overall energy efficiency.

The Commission already sent both Member States a letter of Formal Notice in February 2006, and a Reasoned Opinion in October 2006, requesting them to notify urgently the transposition measures required by the Directive. However, Belgium and the UK have failed to provide information to demonstrate convincingly that they have fully implemented the necessary measures. In particular,

the Commission has not received official notification of measures for the implementation by Belgium of:
1 completely specified energy performance requirements for buildings and for inspection requirements for boilers and air conditioning systems (from the Walloon Region); and
2 a methodology to calculate the energy performance of non-residential buildings and the complete specification of minimum energy performance requirements for existing buildings which undergo major renovations (from the Brussels Capital Region).

For the UK the information is lacking of:
1 implementation of the Directive in Gibraltar; and
2 provisions related to energy performance certificates, and on the inspection of boilers and air conditioning systems in Northern Ireland.

Source: www.eumonitor.net/modules.php?op=modload&name=News&file=article&sid=95378

Case study 4.3 shows how the Commission executes its monitoring tasks under Article 226 of the EC Treaty. The procedure involves several stages before the case may be referred to the European Court of Justice. In this chapter's opening case study, too, the Commission initiated the infringement procedure against several Member States.

There are six separate stages in this procedure:
1 The complaint is filed and assessed by the Commission.
2 The Commission takes the first official step in the Article 226 procedure by sending a *Letter of Formal Notice* to the Member State.
3 The Member State is allowed to react to the Formal Notice.
4 The Commission may then send a *Reasoned Opinion* to the Member State.
5 The Commission starts litigation in the European Court of Justice.
6 The court delivers a judgment stating whether or not EU law has been infringed.

Stage 1

The procedure is initiated when the Commission learns that national legislation of a Member State does not comply with EU law. Citizens and companies may file complaints with the European Commission when they are disadvantaged by national law, or by the act or omission of a national authority. A complaint can be made by anyone who considers that EU law is breached by an authority in a Member State. There is a special complaint form available in all EU languages which may be sent to the Commission in Brussels or to the Commission's national agencies. The form can be found at the following internet address: http://ec.europa.eu/community_law/your_rights/your_rights_forms_en.htm.

In 2006 the number of complaints made was 1049. This figure was slightly lower than in 2005, when the Commission registered 1154 complaints. In around 70% of complaints, the problem is resolved before the Commission has to take the next step in the procedure (stage 2).

In other cases, a Member State may not yet have communicated the measures for implementing the EU law to the Commission according to the schedule laid down in the directive, as happened in both the opening case study and case study 4.3. Or, when a Member State has provided information on its national legislation, the Commission may decide that those measures do not conform to the requirements set out in the EU legislation. In 2006 the Commission initiated the infringement procedure in 565 cases as a result of its own investigations. The remaining 40% of cases dealt with by the Commission were registered in the year 2005.

Stages 2 and 3

Once the Commission has decided that an infringement of EU law is taking place, it moves on to the second stage of the procedure by sending the Member State a *Letter of Formal Notice*. In this notice the Commission explains its position on the breach of EU law. The notice grants the Member State a period of time to comply with the law and an opportunity to submit its observations, which is the third stage in the procedure. The Commission may have misinterpreted the national legislation, in which case the Member State will clarify the matter. If a Member State is not able to convince the Commission that it has fulfilled its obligations under the EC Treaty, the Commission will take the procedure one step further.

Stages 4 and 5

In the fourth stage, the Commission sends a *Reasoned Opinion* to the Member State, which specifies a period of time within the Member State has to rectify its breach of EU law. If the Member State still fails to comply with the law, the Commission may bring the case before the European Court of Justice, which is the fifth stage of the procedure. With this referral to the ECJ, the Commission's executive work comes to an end and the judicial branch of the EU steps in. These first five stages are therefore referred to as the administrative stages of the Article 226 procedure. The rest of the procedure is discussed in section 4.5, which deals with the European Court of Justice.

Between 1999 and 2005, the average time taken by the administrative stages of the Article 226 procedure was 20.5 months from registering the case to filing the court case with the ECJ. When the Commission had to initiate an investigation as a result of a complaint being made, the proceedings took an average of 28 months, whereas in cases registered as a result of failure to inform the Commission about national measures to implement a directive the average duration of the procedure from registration to filing the court case was 14.5 months.

In 2001, the number of the Letters of Formal Notice which led to Reasoned Opinions and to court referrals was recorded. Table 4.1 shows all the actions taken by the Commission in 2001 at each stage, in relation to each of the 15 Member States.

Table 4.1 **Infringement actions in 2001 by stage of administrative procedure and by Member State**

Member State	Formal Notice	Reasoned Opinion	Referral to ECJ
Belgium	87	44	13
Denmark	38	10	2
Germany	73	39	12
Greece	83	71	16
Spain	65	37	14
France	74	50	22
Ireland	80	50	13
Italy	96	53	22
Luxembourg	50	33	10
Netherlands	53	25	5
Austria	80	44	7
Portugal	73	38	7
Finland	61	16	2
Sweden	58	14	3
United Kingdom	79	45	14
Total	1050	569	162

Source: European Navigator (www.ena.lu/)

The table shows how much enforcement work is done by the Commission before the case is brought before the European Court of Justice. The investigative work that has to be done before the Commission decides to send a Letter of Formal Notice is much greater. In around

70% of cases initiated by complaints, the Commission decides not to send a letter. If the Commission decides to pursue the case and refers it to the ECJ, the case will be known as 'Commission v. [Member State]'.

When a complaint is made by a Member State, a similar procedure to that of Article 226 is initiated. Article 227 of the EC Treaty confers the same sort of powers on the Commission as Article 226. These cases are rare, however. The Commission's own investigations and complaints from other stakeholders are usually sufficient to bring the case to the Commission's attention. The few such cases that go all the way to a judgment of the ECJ are known as '[Member State] v. [Member State]'.

Even after the European Court of Justice has decided that there has indeed been a breach of EU law, the executive work of the Commission continues. The Commission then has to monitor whether or not the Member State complies with the judgment. If a Member State is unwilling or unable to rectify the infringement and comply with the EC Treaty and the judgment, the Commission is authorized to start another administrative procedure under Article 228 of the EC Treaty. The only difference between the Article 226 and Article 228 procedures is that the Commission is allowed to claim a lump sum or penalty payment when it refers the case to the ECJ for a second time. Before the Commission does so, a second letter of Formal Notice will be sent, after which the Member State is given the opportunity to make its observations. If the information from the Member State does not convince the Commission, it will send a second Reasoned Opinion, which gives the final deadline for compliance with the judgment. If the Member State still fails to comply, the Commission will refer the case to the ECJ, together with a claim for a lump sum or penalty payment.

4.5 The judicial branch

This section discusses the most important activities of the judicial branch of the EU. It begins by giving general information about the European Court of Justice and then explains the most frequently used procedures, including the preliminary ruling, the infringement procedure and the annulment procedure. The fact that the national courts in the Member States are in fact the first courts to apply EU law is also made clear. This information serves to clarify which procedures were involved in the opening case study on the Tobacco Advertising Directive.

Article 220 of the EC Treaty confers the judicial power in the EU on the Court of Justice and the Court of First Instance, both of which have their seats in Luxembourg.

These courts ensure that the law is observed in the interpretation and application of the EC Treaty. Although the Court of Justice is the highest judicial institution in the EU, most cases in which European law is applied are heard in national courts. In fact, the national courts in the Member States are indispensable to the European separation of powers. They deal from first to last instance with questions of European law, and only in cases where the application or interpretation of European law is unclear may the national courts ask the European Court of Justice for clarification of the law in question. This procedure is called the *preliminary ruling* procedure and is described in Article 234 of the EC Treaty. Other important procedures are the *infringement procedure* and the *annulment procedure*. The majority of cases brought before the European Court of Justice are preliminary rulings. In 2007, the court registered 580 new cases. Of these, 265 were referrals by national courts for a preliminary ruling; the rest consisted predominantly of infringement procedures.

4.5.1   Article 234 procedure: the preliminary ruling procedure

Article 234 of the EC Treaty authorizes the European Court of Justice to hear preliminary cases. The procedure is 'preliminary' because the court's judgment is an answer to a question posed by a national court in a Member State. The national court will ultimately render the decision.

As already stated, it is the national courts in the Member States that hear European cases. In the opening case study in this chapter, the UK tobacco companies lodged a case before a British court in their attempt to overturn the Tobacco Advertising Directive. Article 234 provides that, if a question concerning the interpretation of the EC Treaty or the annulment of a secondary law is raised before a national court, that court may decide to refer the question to the Court of Justice. The national court case will be suspended for the duration of the proceedings before the European Court of Justice. The ECJ answers the question from the court concerned by giving the correct interpretation of EU law or by giving a ruling stating that the secondary law should be annulled. The ECJ publishes its judgment to inform the national courts of how the European law in question should be interpreted or which secondary law is annulled. The national court which raised the question then completes the national proceedings. The decision that is binding on European citizens is the national judgment which complies with the ECJ's preliminary ruling.

The most famous judgment made by the European Court of Justice was a preliminary ruling concerning the soccer player Jean-Marc Bosman.

Case study 4.4 The Bosman case

Jean-Marc Bosman was a professional football player for the first-division team Royal Football Club Liège, in Belgium, between 1988 and 1990. A new contract was offered to him reducing his salary from Bfr120,000 to Bfr30,000 per calendar month. Mr Bosman refused to sign it and was put on the transfer list at the age of 25.

During his search for a new team in France, Belgium and the Netherlands, Bosman felt that both the football club RFC Liège and the football regulations set up by the national and international football associations were preventing him from finding a new position. For instance, Bosman had already accepted an offer of employment from a French second-division club, within the scope of Article 39(3)(a) of the EC Treaty. RFC Liège, however did not co-operate with the transfer.

In order to get the necessary co-operation for the 1990–1991 season, Bosman lodged several cases with the court of first instance in Liège, against RFC Liège and the Belgian Soccer Association and also against the European and World Football Associa-

---

tions, UEFA and FIFA. During the more than five years of court proceedings he played for third- and fourth-division football clubs, not earning enough to support his family. Because he could no longer afford a house of his own, he had to move in with his parents.

The appeal court in Liège referred the question to the European Court of Justice. The court was not sure whether the transfer money claimed by RFC Liège at the end of a contract breached the freedom of movement for workers laid down by Article 39 of the EC Treaty. Later in the national proceedings, the problem of the number of foreign players was also referred to the ECJ, because, according to Bosman, the regulation in question prevented him from being employed by football clubs in France and elsewhere in Europe.

RFC Liège and the football associations contended that football clubs were entitled to take a different position from ordinary employers. The ECJ disagreed with this position in its ruling of 15th December 1995, judging that the associations and football clubs could not apply rules that restricted the rights of individuals under the EC Treaty.

Addressing the nationality rules, the court ruled that Article 39(2) of the EC Treaty expressly grants freedom of movement to workers. It entails the abolition of any discrimination based on nationality between workers of the Member States, as regards employment, remuneration or conditions of work and employment.

Because of the problems that could have arisen as a result of this ruling, the ECJ decided that the direct effect of Article 39 of the Treaty could not be relied upon in cases arising before the date of the judgment, except by those who had brought court proceedings or raised an equivalent claim under the applicable national law before the date of judgment.

Following the preliminary ruling in December 1995, the national court case was able to continue in 1996. The Belgian court of appeal decided the amount of damages to be paid to Bosman, of which he has lived ever since. The final payment of the settlement was made in 1998, eight years after the first emergence of the dispute.

Sources: Case C-415/93, 15th December 1995, ECR 1995 page I-04921, and interviews with Bosman in the Observer and Sporta Magazine.

A preliminary ruling helps the national courts to make the final decision on whether a claim is justified by European law. In case study 4.4, against all the odds, Bosman was able to defeat the all powerful stakeholders. Unfortunately, at the age of 31, he was no longer in a position to take advantage of the new freedom of movement for football players.

In the opening case study, a national court case challenging the Tobacco Advertising Directive was pending. Whether or not the UK court had already decided to refer the case to the European Court of Justice is not known. It is known, however, that the tobacco industry was also challenging another tobacco directive at the time.

If a company, as in the tobacco advertising case, or a citizen, like Bosman in case study 4.4, has a complaint about the application of European law, the company or citizen has two options:
1 to make a complaint to the Commission, and/or
2 to lodge a case with a national court of law.

The first option does not give the company or citizen any certainty as to whether the Commission will actually warn the Member State in its executive role as guardian of European law (explained in section 4.4). In Bosman's case, the infringement proceedings would not give the football player either the rights he was entitled to or damages for the infringement of the free movement of workers by his football club and the football associations. Bosman could have made a complaint to the Commission, but for the infringement procedure of Article 226 of the EC Treaty to be invoked, a government authority in a Member State must have breached European law. In the Bosman case, it was RFC Liège and the football associations which were at fault.

In Bosman's case, lodging a court case in Belgium claiming free access to another football club in France was the best option. In the tobacco advertising case, the Commission was already active in its executive role as guardian of European law, so a complaint by a company or citizen was not necessary.

4.5.2 Article 226 procedure: the infringement procedure

Of the 221 direct actions before the European Court of Justice in 2007, 212 were referrals by the Commission based on Article 226 of the EC Treaty. Most of the procedure is executed by the Commission in its executive role as the guardian of European law, as explained in section 4.4: first the Commission learns of the infringement through a stakeholder's complaint or its own investigations. Then the Commission sends a Letter of First Notice, describing the alleged infringement and allowing the Member State in question to submit its observations. If the Commission decides that an infringement still exists, it sends a Reasoned Opinion, giving the Member State a period of time to comply. If the Member State does not succeed in rectifying the infringement, the Commission will bring the matter before the ECJ.

In the tobacco advertising case, the Commission did threaten to refer some cases of infringement to the ECJ. On 28th June 2006 the following press release was issued.

■ **Example 4.4 European Commission press release**

IP/06/868

Brussels, 28 June 2006

Commission refers Germany to the European Court of Justice on tobacco advertising

The European Commission has today decided to refer Germany to the European Court of Justice (ECJ) for non-transposition of the Tobacco Advertising Directive 2003/33/EC. The Court referral follows the letter of formal notice sent in October 2005 and a reasoned opinion sent in February 2006. The referral to the ECJ is the next step in the infringement procedure.

European Health and Consumer Protection Commissioner Markos Kyprianou said: "Tobacco advertising and sponsorship glamorises tobacco and incites children and young adults to start smoking. I am determined to hold all Member States to account for their implementation of this key piece of EU legislation, and if this means referring the matter to the Court, so be it."

The Tobacco Advertising Directive
The Tobacco Advertising Directive 2003/33/EC bans tobacco advertising in printed media, on radio and over the internet. It also prohibits tobacco sponsorship of cross-border events or activities, such as Formula One races. It applies only to advertising and sponsorship with a cross-border dimension. Advertising in cinemas and on billboards or using merchandising (e.g. ash trays or parasols) therefore falls outside its scope, although these can still be banned under national law – a path chosen by several EU Member States.

Tobacco advertising on television has been banned in the EU since the early 1990s, and is governed by the TV Without Frontiers Directive. The Tobacco Advertising Directive was agreed by the European Parliament and Council in 2003 and had to be transposed into national legislation by 31 July 2005. By this date, Member States should have adopted national transposition measures and communicated them to the Commission.

Other cases
The Commission has also sent a reasoned opinion for non-transposition to Luxembourg on 7 February 2006. On 4 April, Luxembourg replied that the government had changed its policy in terms of tobacco control and that it had thus withdrawn its support for Germany's application for the annulment of the Directive before the ECJ. It also announced its intention to transpose the Tobacco Advertising Directive by July 2006. The Commission welcomes these steps and will ensure that they are properly followed up in the committed time frame.

In April 2006, the Commission also sent "letters of formal notice" to the Czech Republic, Italy, Hungary and Spain for wrong transposition of the same Directive as they allow exemptions from the sponsorship ban which is a core aspect of this legislation. These cases will be examined by the Commission in July.

Source: http://europa.eu/rapid/pressReleasesAction.do?reference=IP/06/868

When a case is brought before the European Court of Justice, the Commission will explain in what way the Member State failed to comply with the EU law. The Member State will be heard, and other Member States are also allowed to give their observations. Before the ECJ rules on the matter, an Advocate General gives an opinion. The Advocates General can be described as the advisers of the ECJ, and the court usually follows their recommendations.

After all the parties have been heard, the court decides whether or not it agrees with the Commission's view on the matter. If it does, the court orders a Member State to take measures to bring its national law or its actions into line with EU law. The judgment is known as 'Commission v. [Member State]'.

The referral of Germany's case to the ECJ did not result in a judgment 'Commission v. Germany', because Germany gave up its resistance to the directive after the Advocate General's opinion was published in the course of the proceedings. Germany declared publicly that it would not continue to object to the directive and promised to implement it by the end of 2006. According to the Commission's report on the implementation of the Tobacco Advertising Directive, published in May 2008, all the Member States had correctly implemented the directive. There was no longer any need for an infringement procedure under Article 226 of the EC Treaty.

4.5.3   Article 230 procedure: the annulment procedure

In the annulment procedure, the European Court of Justice examines the legality of acts by the EC's institutions. Every institution or other body of the EC is obliged to operate within the framework of the treaties, but mistakes can be made in legislative or executive work. In the case of the Tobacco Advertising Directive, Germany started annulment proceedings twice in order to overturn the directive. The first time, Germany was successful and the directive became null and void as a result. This section shows that Member States are not the only parties having the right to lodge such cases. It also explains what acts the ECJ has the power to review.

The acts that can be reviewed by the ECJ include legislation by the Council of Ministers and the European Parliament, as well as legislation or decisions of the executive branch which are delegated to the Council or the Commission. It is up to the Member States, the Commission or the European Parliament to lodge a case with the ECJ if they are of the opinion that a legislative or executive measure breaches any Articles of the EC Treaty. The court case must be lodged within two months of the measure's publication.

In the tobacco advertising case, Germany was successful in the first annulment procedure against Directive 98/43, and as a result the Commission had to present a new proposal to the European legislature. The new Directive 2003/33/EC was also challenged by Germany in 2003. The European Court of Justice reviewed the directive and analysed in 161 paragraphs whether Article 95 of the EC Treaty could legally serve as the legal basis of the new directive.

Case study 4.5 **Germany v. European Parliament and Council of the European Union**

JUDGMENT OF THE COURT

12 December 2006

Action for annulment – Approximation of laws – Directive 2003/33/EC – Advertising and sponsorship in respect of tobacco products – Annulment of Articles 3 and 4 – Choice of legal basis – Articles 95 EC and 152 EC – Principle of proportionality

In Case C-380/03,

ACTION for annulment under Article 230 EC, brought on 9 September 2003,

[...]
69 It remains to determine whether, in the fields covered by Articles 3 and 4 of the Directive, those articles are in fact designed to eliminate or prevent obstacles to the free movement of goods or the freedom to provide services or to remove distortions of competition.

[...]
71 The adoption of such a prohibition, which is designed to apply uniformly throughout the Community, is intended to prevent intra-Community trade in press products from being impeded by the national rules of one or other Member State.

72 It should be pointed out that Article 3(1) of the Directive expressly permits the insertion of advertis-

ing for tobacco products in certain publications, in particular in those which are intended exclusively for professionals in the tobacco trade.

73 Furthermore, unlike Directive 98/43, Article 8 of the Directive provides that the Member States are not to prohibit or restrict the free movement of products which comply with the Directive. This article consequently precludes Member States from impeding the movement within the Community of publications intended exclusively for professionals in the tobacco trade, inter alia by means of more restrictive provisions which they consider necessary in order to protect human health with regard to advertising or sponsorship for tobacco products.

74 In preventing the Member States in this way from opposing the provision of advertising space in publications intended exclusively for professionals in the tobacco trade, Article 8 of the Directive gives expression to the objective laid down in Article 1(2) of improving the conditions for the functioning of the internal market.

75 The same finding must be made with regard to the freedom to provide services, which is also covered by Article 8 of the Directive. Under this article, the Member States cannot prohibit or restrict that freedom where services comply with the Directive.

[...]

81 Accordingly, it must be held that, as has been stated in paragraph 78 of the present judgment, Articles 3 and 4 of the Directive are intended to improve the conditions for the functioning of the internal market.

82 It should be pointed out that the limits of the field of application of the prohibition set out in Articles 3 and 4 of the Directive are far from random and uncertain.

83 In defining the field of application of the prohibition laid down in Article 3 of the Directive, the German version alone uses the term 'printed products' ('Druckerzeugnisse') in the heading of that article, whereas the other language versions use the term 'printed media', thereby showing the will of the Community legislature not to include every type of publication in the field of application of that prohibition.
[...]

87 In addition, the prohibition laid down in Articles 3 and 4 of the Directive is limited to various forms of advertising and sponsorship and, contrary to the provisions of Directive 98/43, does not amount to a general ban.

88 It follows from the foregoing that Article 95 EC constitutes an appropriate legal basis for Articles 3 and 4 of the Directive.
[...]

Source: Germany v. EP and Council, Case C-380/03, ECR 2006 Page I-11573

Germany had already promised to comply with the directive when it learned that Advocate General Léger had advised the Court on 13 June 2006 to dismiss the action for annulment. When the actual judgment was made in December 2006, Germany had already implemented the directive correctly.

Besides the Member States and the institutions of the EC, both the Court of Auditors and the European Central Bank (ECB) may also lodge a court case if they feel that their rights have been infringed. Cases between the institutions, other bodies and Member States are heard before the European Court of Justice in one instance.

The fourth paragraph of Article 230 of the EC Treaty provides for direct action by natural and legal persons against the decisions of Community institutions. This is the only procedure in which a natural or legal person is allowed to initiate a direct action before the European Court of Justice, in this case in the Court of First Instance. Usually these cases concern a decision by the Commission which a citizen disagrees with, often in major competition cases, where the Commission imposes very large fines. The court case must be initiated within two months of the publication of the measure. The most famous annulment case was Microsoft's appeal against the Commission's (at the time) highest-ever fine of €497 million.

Case study 4.6 EU court confirms the 497 million euro fine against Microsoft

26 September, 2007
Microsoft has lost the appeal made to the Court of First Instance against the European Commission's (EC) ruling of monopoly abuse that obliged Microsoft to grant competitors access to its server protocols and to unbundle its Media Player software from its Windows operating system.

The case has a long history; following a complaint in 2003 from Novell that accused Microsoft of making server protocol information unavailable, the European Commission gave a preliminary ruling ordering Microsoft to unbundled Windows Media Player from Windows and to give information to competitors to ensure compatibility with Windows servers. Considering Microsoft had not complied with that ruling, in March 2004, the European Commission fined Microsoft with the highest fine in the EU history – 497 million euro.

Microsoft paid the fine but made an appeal to the Court of First Instance which, on 17 September 2007, rejected this appeal with the exception of a small part related to the appointment by the EC of a monitoring trustee "with the power to have access, independently of the Commission, to Microsoft's assistance, information, documents, premises and employees and to the source code of the relevant Microsoft products". The costs related to the trustee were to be supported by Microsoft.

"The Court finds that the Commission did not err in assessing the gravity and duration of the infringement and did not err in setting the amount of the fine. Since the abuse of a dominant position is confirmed by the Court, the amount of the fine remains unchanged at EUR 497 million" said the official press release of the Court.

Following the decision, José Manuel Barroso, President of the European Commission stated: "This judgement confirms the objectivity and the credibility of the Commission's competition policy. This policy protects the European consumer interest and ensures fair competition between businesses in the Internal Market."

The decision was considered by Competition Commissioner Neelie Kroes as a great victory: "That decision set an important precedent in terms of the obligations of dominant-companies to allow competition, in particular in high tech industries. The Court ruling shows that the Commission was right to take its decision. Microsoft must now comply fully with its legal obligations to desist from engaging in anti-competitive conduct. The Commission will do its utmost to ensure that Microsoft complies swiftly."

The court's decision was largely welcomed by several organisations. "Microsoft can consider itself above the law no longer. Through tactics that successfully derailed antitrust processes in other parts of the world, including the United States, Microsoft has managed to postpone this day for almost a decade. But thanks to the perseverance and excellent work of the European Commission, these tactics have now failed in Europe" said Georg Greve, president of the Free Software Foundation Europe. Open Forum Europe also stated: "Open Forum Europe welcomes this decision, and looks to the whole ICT industry to respond by taking positive steps to increase competitive choice."

The reaction of the US Department of Justice was, not surprisingly, a critical one to the decision of the Court of First Instance and Thomas O. Barnett, the assistant attorney general for antitrust, declared on 17 September that the decision would have "the unfortunate consequence of harming consumers by chilling innovation and discouraging competition."

In response to this statement, Neelie Kroes considered the US officials' judgement as totally unacceptable: "The European Commission does not pass judgement on rulings by US courts and we expect the same degree of respect from US authorities on rulings by EU courts," she said.

Microsoft's top lawyer said that the first priority of the company was to comply with EU competition law and that the company has not yet taken any decision related to the next legal steps. Microsoft has two months to appeal the decision to the European Court of Justice.

Source: www.edri.org/edrigram/number5.18/microsoft-decision-tpi

---

The stakeholders' initial reactions to the decision can also be seen on YouTube at www.youtube.com/watch, under the heading 'Microsoft loses EU antitrust appeal'.

The ruling made by the Court of First Instance is subject to an appeal within two months to the Court of Justice. Microsoft did not appeal against the court's decision and promised to comply with the Commission's instructions. However, it took Microsoft almost three years to do so. As a result, the Commission decided on 27th February 2008 to levy a record fine of €899 million for non-compliance with the 2004 decision during that period.

More about this decision can be seen on YouTube under the title 'European Commission Fines Microsoft $1.3B'. A case against this decision of the Commission is pending with the Court of First Instance.

4.6 Organizational changes

This section explains the need for changes to the organization of the EU. Although the EU's history is covered in greater detail in chapter 3, some background information is given here before describing the current situation.

In 1957 the EEC was founded with six members: the Benelux countries, France, West Germany and the country in which the Treaty was signed, Italy. In the 50 years since then, the number of Member States has grown to 27. As a result, almost every institution comprises 27 members. The institutional provisions of the present Treaty were designed for a union of 15 countries rather than the current situation of 27 Member States.

4.6.1 The EU Constitution

The first attempt to bring about the necessary changes was made by the Treaty establishing a Constitution for Europe, signed in 2004. This treaty envisaged replacing all the existing EC and EU treaties, and introducing new institutions, new forms of legislation, a flag and a hymn. But the combination of enlarging the EU by 10 new Member States and a introducing a European Constitution amounted to too much change for many EU citizens. Both the Netherlands and France rejected the Treaty in referenda. As a result, preparations were made to introduce what became the Treaty of Lisbon.

4.6.2 The Treaty of Lisbon (ToL)

The ToL was signed on 13th December 2007, but the process of ratifying the new treaty is still in progress. All the Member States have to adopt it, either by the consent of parliament or by a referendum. The ToL is designed to make EU institutions more efficient and to 'streamline' decision making in the enlarged EU of 27 nations. This streamlining has been implemented in two ways: by amending the pillar structure and by altering the organization of the institutions.

Instead of the current three pillars, the EU will in future consist of two. The first (EC) pillar and the third pillar (home affairs and justice) will merge into one EU pillar. The area of Foreign Affairs will remain a matter for intergovernmental co-operation between the Member States, even when meetings are presided over by a High Representative of Foreign Affairs and Security Policy, who also becomes the Vice-President of the Commission. The fact that the Union becomes a single legal personality under the new treaty will strengthen the Union's negotiating power in the world, but it does not change the mode of intergovernmental co-operation between the countries.

The streamlining of the organization of the institutions has brought about the following key changes. In the legislative branch of the EU, the merger of the two pillars gives the European Parliament greater influence, as the co-decision procedure (renamed 'ordinary legislative procedure') becomes the standard mode of legislation. The co-operation procedure will be abolished in this branch. The consultation procedure remains in force in the more sensitive (financial) areas.

Two innovations introduced by the Treaty establishing a Constitution of Europe are also included in the ToL. These are a structural *involvement of national parliaments* and the *Citizens' Initiative*. Under the Citizens' Initiative, one million citizens from a number of Member States will be entitled to bring forward new policy proposals for the Commission's attention.

The structural involvement of national parliaments includes a procedure whereby the national parliaments have the right to force the Commission to re-examine a proposal. If the Commission decides to pursue the proposal, it has to explain why it did not take account of the national parliaments' objections. It is then up to the EU legislature to decide whether it agrees with the Commission's proposal or with the position of the national parliaments.

In the Council of Ministers, from 2014 on, the calculation of the qualified majority will be based on a 'double majority': the majority of Member States and the majority of the population of the Union. A double majority will be achieved when a decision is taken by 55% of the Member States representing at least 65% of the Union's population. This voting procedure was already proposed in the European Constitutional Treaty of 2004 and was reintroduced under the ToL.

In the executive branch, the number of representatives in the Commission will be reduced from the current 27 to 18. This means that, from 2014 on, only two-thirds of Member States will have a Commissioner. The posts will rotate among all the Member States.

The number of institutions will increase from five under the current EC Treaty to seven under the ToL. Alongside the Court of Auditors, which is already an institution under the current treaty, the European Central Bank (ECB) will also become an institution. The European Council is the other new institution under the ToL. The European Council is the forum in which the heads of states decide on new policies. It does not have legislative power.

In the judicial branch of the EU no major organizational changes are planned. However, because of the merger of the current first and third pillars, the European Court of Justice will have jurisdiction over more cases than in the current situation.

The Irish people voted against the ToL in a referendum held in June 2008. If a further referendum in Ireland does not approve the Treaty, the ToL will not enter into force. At the time of writing, all the other Member States had voted in favour of the ToL and a second Irish Referendum was scheduled for Friday 2nd October 2009.

Conclusions

The opening case study of this chapter introduced the sometimes lengthy and difficult manner in which European legislation is adopted. The nature of European law and the different roles played by the European institutions in the European separation of powers were then explained. The European Community pillar of the EU is supranational, which means that the Member States have given up their sovereignty in particular economic areas. In these fields European law is at the top of the hierarchy of legislation and the EU institutions are the highest-ranking authorities. In the other pillars of the EU, the Member States remain sovereign, and as a result they cannot be bound against their will.

The internal or common market is an EC matter, on which the European legislature has the authority to make legislation. In the law-making process, the Commission makes the proposals and the Council of Ministers and the European Parliament have to select the appropriate legislative procedure to enact the proposal. The opening case study made it clear that in some areas it may not be easy to introduce legislation. The first Tobacco Advertising Directive was successfully challenged by Germany before the European Court of Justice, the EU's highest court, using the annulment procedure. The second attempt to produce European legislation on a tobacco advertising ban was again challenged by Germany, but this time it was upheld by the court. Section 4.5 on the judicial branch of the EU also detailed the other two main procedures used in EU law: preliminary rulings and the infringement procedure.

As soon as Directive 2003/33/EC on tobacco advertising came into force, the Commission took action as the guardian of European law. As the highest-ranking executive body, the Commission initiated the administrative stages of the infringement procedure, which however did not result in a ruling 'Commission v. Germany'. By the end of 2006, all the Member States fulfilled their obligations under the EC Treaty and the directive.

Last but certainly not least, this chapter explained how the organization of the EU needs to change to accommodate today's large number of Member States. The Treaty establishing a Constitution for Europe did not enter into force and we were still waiting to see whether the organizational changes of the Treaty of Lisbon will be approved by all 27 Member States. In november 2009 all member states did so.

Questions

4.1   Explain in your own words the difference between the European Union and the European Community.

4.2   Explain why it is important to apply the concept of the separation of powers in the European Union.

4.3   Explain what types of European legislation can be enacted.

4.4   Which EU authority has the power to draft European legislation?

4.5   Which European institutions belong to the legislative branch of the EU? Explain the relationships between these institutions.

4.6   Which institutions belong to the executive branch of the EU? Explain the relationships between these institutions.

4.7   Which institutions belong to the judicial branch of the EU? Explain the relationship between these institutions.

4.8   Please explain in which situations the different proceedings before the European Court of Justice take place.

Case studies

4.9   The EU Member States wish to legislate on a common asylum procedure for refugees entering the EU.
    a   Explain whether asylum is an intergovernmental issue or a supranational issue within the EU.
    b   Explain why this makes a difference to the legislative procedure.
    c   By which European authority/ies should the legislation be drafted? Which Article of the EC Treaty prescribes this?
    d   Describe the rest of the legislative process according to the Article(s) of the EC Treaty that allocate(s) the powers involved.

4.10   A directive on the safety of consumer products was adopted on 1st July 2003. The directive set the deadline for transposition of the directive into national law as 31st March 2005. Belgium and Hungary were unable to pass the laws necessary to implement the directive in time.
    a   Which European authorities are involved in the process of adopting such a directive?
    b   What would have been the difference if a regulation had been adopted on the subject?

A manufacturer of toys in Hungary is fined by the Hungarian authorities because the companies did not produce the toys in accordance with Hungarian legislation. The manufacturer, however, had conformed to the standards set out in the EU directive of 1st July 2003.

c   Which authority has the power to hear the case between the Hungarian manufacturer and the Hungarian executive authority?

d   Which procedure can be used by which authority to clarify the provisions of the directive? Explain the proceedings in detail.

e   Which European authority has the power to initiate a case against Hungary and Belgium for not implementing the directive in time? Describe the procedure in detail.

f   Explain what happens if Hungary and Belgium are still not able to implement the legislation correctly after having been found guilty of infringement by the European Court of Justice.

The single market and international business strategy

2

The free movement of goods and international business strategy

5

Exporting to Italy, France or Spain?

Grün GmbH produces magnetic parts for the automotive and medical instruments industries. The parts are made in China and the half-finished products are assembled and/or adjusted in Hamburg, Germany, where Grün GmbH is based.

As a result of its success in the German market, Grün's management was eager to export the company's hi-tech products to other countries in Europe. When a number of foreign customers started to make requests for information through Grün's new website, the management decided it was time to develop a proper export strategy.

One of the management team's first decisions was that they needed to select a destination country. A survey showed that Italy, France and Spain were the best countries to start exporting to. Then the team decided to develop a marketing strategy and sent the directors and middle managers involved on export training courses.

In the meantime, information on Grün's products was sent to a potential customer in Italy and one in France. After several weeks of exchanging information on products and prices, a deal was made with the Italian customer, who was located in Udine. A full containerload of magnetic parts was to be sent to Italy in two months' time under a Delivered Duty Paid (DDP) condition.

The lead time for the parts from production in China to arrival at Grün's location in Hamburg was six weeks. Then the goods would have to be adjusted and packaged for the Italian customer. After these stages of the delivery had been completed, Grün would have one week left to transport the goods to Udine by the delivery date of 24th November.

The company had to overcome several problems before the actual export to Italy could take place. First, a problem arose over the importation of the magnetic parts into the European Union (EU). Second, the management needed to know whether the company would have to pay the charges levied by the German Association for Technical Co-operation.

A third problem concerned an obligatory assessment of the products which was required by Italian law even though an assessment report by the German Institute of Technology was already available. These assessments cost over €100,000. Would Grün now have to have another assessment made?

Last but not least, there appeared to be a sudden prohibition on heavy lorries using the A2 motorway in Austria. Austria wanted to implement this measure within two months, in order to protect the environment. Grün had already booked the shipment with a haulage company and now faced extra charges for the miles that would have to be spent on making a detour.

Grün's management had not realized that so many things could go wrong in an export situation. Now that the contract had already been concluded with the Italian company, the problems needed to be solved as soon as possible, otherwise they could expect further legal problems from an unhappy Italian customer.

This chapter presents two important approaches to the single market for goods. The first part (sections 5.1 to 5.3) focuses on the legal approach to doing business in the market. The second (sections 5.4 to 5.6) deals with the economic and marketing aspects of the manufacturing industry.

In section 5.1 the common or single market and the free movement of goods are examined. Section 5.2 explains how business is usually done between enterprises around the world as well as within the European Community. The most important contractual requirements, such as the delivery terms 'Incoterms 2000' and the main payment options, are discussed.

In section 5.3 it becomes clear that national laws may, deliberately or otherwise, hinder the free movement of goods. Both financial and physical infringements by national authorities and the remedies available under European law are explained. This section also clarifies the key aspects of European competition law.

Section 5.4 discusses the significance of the manufacturing industry in Europe, its strengths and its weaknesses, while section 5.5 deals with its international trading relationships. Finally, in section 5.6 the most important aspects of marketing goods in Europe are examined.

5.1   The common or single market and the free movement of goods

In 1957, the countries of the European Community (EC) agreed to create one common, single or internal market, replacing the separate markets of the individual Member States. The basic principles of the single market are set out in Article 3 of the EC Treaty and cover two major areas:
1 the four fundamental freedoms within the market:
   - free movement of goods
   - free movement of persons
   - free movement of services
   - free movement of capital
2 the principle of fair competition between businesses in the common market.

This section explains the most important ideas behind the single market and the free movement of goods.

The single market has been established largely through legislation and financial measures designed to secure a strong internal market. The main features of the common market are set out in the Convention establishing a European Community (the EC Treaty). The EC Treaty makes the following tools available to achieve the goals set out in its first Article:
1 the treaty provisions
2 secondary European law in directives and regulations
3 common policies.

5.1.1 Treaty provisions

One of the most important tools that the EC Treaty makes available to businesses in Europe is its instruction to the national authorities not to infringe the free movement provisions. Article 3, for instance, instructs the Member States to abolish all obstacles to the freedoms of movement. The main obstacles used by states to protect their national industries are:

- import and/or export licences, demanding government approval before the goods may be exported or imported
- quotas for goods, meaning that the government of a country decides on the quantity of goods that may be imported
- tariffs for goods, meaning that a sum of money needs to be paid to the government before the goods are allowed to enter the national market, which makes the imported goods more expensive than their domestic equivalents.

Case study 5.1 shows how trade barriers work and what their consequences can be.

Case study 5.1 Disagreement over US imports of Chinese textiles

China assails U.S. textile quotas

BEIJING: China responded angrily on Sunday to the new limits that the United States placed on its clothing exports, and manufacturers here called for tit-for-tat restrictions. The reactions followed the announcement on Friday by the U.S. Department of Commerce that it would impose new quotas on Chinese-made garments. In addition, the European Commission, under pressure from national capitals, is considering similar action.

The U.S. quotas, which would limit increases in Chinese imports of the affected garments to 7.5 per cent a year, were a "betrayal of the fundamental spirit of trade liberalization espoused by the WTO" and would "seriously damage the confidence of Chinese businesses and people in the international trade environment since China joined WTO," Chong Quan, a spokesman for the Commerce Ministry in China, said in response to Washington's decision, referring to the World Trade Organization.

"The Chinese government reserves the right to adopt further measures under the WTO framework," Chong added, in a statement that was published in the country's state-run press on Sunday.

The U.S. commerce secretary, Carlos Gutierrez, announced quotas on Chinese-made cotton trousers, shirts and underwear. He cited a rise of up to 1,500 per cent in Chinese garment exports since early January, when the United States and Europe abolished a system of quotas that limited imports.

This latest looming trade fight between Beijing and Washington comes at a brittle time in their economic relations. The U.S. trade deficit with China, the biggest exporter to the U.S. market, rose to $21 billion in the first four months of this year, compared with $11 billion for the first four months of last year.

U.S. manufacturers and Bush administration officials complain that Beijing has kept its currency exchange rate low to encourage exports of cheap Chinese goods, and U.S. textile makers claim that they have lost up to 6,000 domestic jobs because of Chinese goods.
[...]
1 As of Jan. 1 2005, decades-old import quotas that had restricted flows of garment imports were abolished worldwide, giving all WTO members unrestricted access to global markets. Since then, China's share of garment exports to the United States and Europe has grown rapidly. Chinese exports of cotton trousers to the United States have grown 1,500 per cent since the start of the year, according to U.S. Customs figures.

The measures Washington announced Friday were "safeguard measures" that WTO rules allow for when a country's domestic market is "disrupted" by an import surge. The European Union is considering similar restrictions.
[...]

Source: Chris Buckley, in the *International Herald Tribune*, 16th May 2005

In the EC context, Articles 23 to 31 of the EC Treaty contain most of the 'prohibitions' promoting the free movement of goods and combating trade barriers such as the quotas mentioned in case study 5.1. In the opening case study, Grün GmbH also came up against problems when importing technical products from China into the EU. Such problems may either be the result of an EU trade barrier against products from China or be due to a mistake on the part of the exporter or importer.

Before the European Community came into being, similar trade barriers existed between the European countries. The EC Treaty's prohibition of trade barriers gives European businesses the opportunity to sue national authorities if EC rules are being violated by the authorities of a Member State. Section 5.3 gives more information about how the treaty helps businesses to deal with trade barriers affecting day-to-day business in Europe.

5.1.2 Secondary European law in directives and regulations

In addition to these 'prohibition' Articles, the treaty also includes provisions giving the EU legislature the authority to legislate in order to create a single market.

Countless directives designed to harmonize differing national laws and regulations have been issued during the last 50 and more years. As well as aiming for standardization of goods across the EU, directives and regulations also aim to set higher standards for products and consumer safety.

From 1985 on, the 'New Approach' to harmonization moved away from the idea of putting all the standards themselves into directives. The new approach resulted in the secondary legislation laying down levels of safety rather than technical rules. In other words, the legislation is restricted to what is necessary to guarantee a high level of protection.

The New Approach Directives often require that products be certified by third parties, such as laboratories and inspection and certification bodies, which are referred to as the 'Notified Bodies'. The Member States are allowed to nominate these bodies, which are independent of government.

In the chapter's opening case study, Grün GmbH was hit by Italian legislation granting the Italian Survey Institute the right to assess the magnetic parts. How Grün should tackle this problem is set out in section 5.3.

The majority of the products produced in the EU are covered by New Approach Directives. This harmonization affects over 20 different sectors of industry, including electrotechnical products, machinery, radio/telecoms equipment, toys, medical devices and construction products. A list of directives and standards can be found at www.newapproach. org/Directives/DirectiveList.asp.

Some people wonder whether the single market will ever be completed. In fact, the common market, just like national markets, will never be perfectly regulated. The most important reason for this is that there will always be new goods and issues that national legislators would like to regulate. In the opening case study, for instance, Grün GmbH was puzzled by the Italian law on the obligatory assessment of technical parts because the products had already been approved by the German Institute of Technology. In other words, the Italian mandatory legislation on this subject hindered Grün GmbH from doing business with its Italian customer. Grün GmbH faced serious risks if it decided to go ahead with the deal without having the required assessment done, even though there was also German legislation on the subject.

National legislators can create new laws with enormous speed, unlike the European legislature. The Council of Ministers and the European Parliament (EP) first have to wait for the Commission to come up with a proposal on the issue. Then, the directive or regulation can come into existence only after the approval of the majority of ministers and members of the EP has been obtained. Once all these steps have been completed, legislation in the Member States has to be harmonized.

The legislative solution may be too slow to help Grün GmbH when faced with trade barriers. For Grün, a better solution would be if the Italian requirements were found to violate a prohibition in the EC Treaty. In that case, the Italian legislation could not be applied to the company. Grün GmbH would then not have to fear punishment by the Italian authorities and would not have to wait for a directive on the subject to harmonize the rules on technical product assessments in more detail and for this to be implemented in the national laws of the EU Member States.

5.1.3 Common policies

In some areas there is hardly any room left for a national policy, because EU policies have overruled the national ones, creating a common EU policy. A common market policy only exists in a few economic areas, however. The best-known examples are the common agriculture and fisheries policy and the EU customs laws. Case study 5.2 is an example of the influence of a common policy on businesses in the EU. The companies in this example deal directly with the European executive authority, the Commission.

As case study 5.2 shows, the common policy and the legislative and executive measures on fisheries replace all national law on the subject. This is also the case in the area of customs law: all imports into the common market are regulated by EU law, in accordance with the common policy and legislation on the subject. The national customs authorities execute the EU legislation and ensure that the customs rules are implemented correctly.

In areas where no such comprehensive common policy exists, national laws and their European counterparts exist side by side. However, European legislation ranks higher in the hierarchy than the corresponding laws of Member States.

In other words, the single market will always need new European legislation in one form or another, just as the national markets do. In the European context, primary legislation in the form of the prohibitions embodied in the treaty, secondary legislation and common policies are all needed in order to ensure that businesses can overcome problems in cross-border trade in the internal market. Before we look more closely at how the EC Treaty provisions may be able to help Grün GmbH, the way businesses regulate their relationships with each other is examined in section 5.2.

5.2 Private law aspects of doing business in the common market

This section focuses on the contractual aspect of doing business in Europe, by explaining the most important features of the international sale of goods for Grün GmbH. To do this it is necessary to examine the private law of doing business in the internal market and to explain the difference between private and public law.

5.2.1 The difference between private and public law in the EU

In order to make clear how law influences the day-to-day conduct of business, it is essential to understand the difference between *public law* and *private law*.

Public law is the area of the law in which government authorities are granted certain legal powers which ordinary citizens do not have. For example, only certain government bodies have the authority to levy taxes, to arrest citizens or to issue licenses (such as a building permit for extending a house or factory). Unfortunately, we as ordinary citizens do not have these powers.

In public law, one of the parties will be a government body deciding on a particular issue. Public law consists largely of *mandatory law*, which means that citizens, companies and other government bodies are not allowed to deviate from the law. The EC Treaty is an example of legislation in the public law area: the Member States have to obey the provisions which create rights for citizens and obligations for the Member States. The articles on competition law (Articles 81ff) are mandatory for citizens and companies.

In *private law* it does not matter who the parties involved in the legal relationship are. Private law focuses on certain legal areas, such as contracts and issues of ownership, and may consist of either mandatory or *permissive law*. Most contract law is permissive law, which means that the parties involved in a contractual relationship may reach a different solution to a legal problem than the one prescribed by private law.

Sometimes, however, the national or European legislature wishes to protect the weaker party by using mandatory law. In such cases, the parties are not allowed to deviate from the mandatory law, whether public or private.

Contracts, public law and private law

Contracts are influenced by public law. If a company wants to import weapons, it must apply for a special licence because there is no free movement of goods in this area. Selling women and children is also prohibited by public law and qualified as a criminal act in most countries in the world. Such a contract would therefore be *null and void*, which means that the contract does not legally exist.

In Grün GmbH's case, Italian and Austrian public law also influences the way business can be conducted. Grün will have to find out whether another assessment is necessary and whether the trucks carrying the goods will have to take a different route through Austria.

If a problem arises between contracting parties, they have to examine whether their contract is in accordance with the requirements of both public and mandatory private law. If the contract is valid according to those rules, the parties will have to look for a solution to the problem in the provisions of the contract itself. If the contract does not provide the solution, the applicable permissive law can be consulted for an answer to the problem. Figure 5.1 shows the relationship between the different areas of law applicable to a contract.

Figure 5.1 **The influence of public law and private law on contracts**

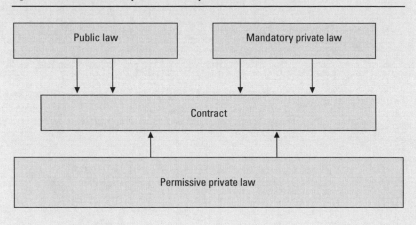

European law is most influential in the area of the public law of Member States. Most of its provisions regulate the public legal activities of a Member State. Bearing in mind the information given in section 5.1, figure 5.1 illustrates how European legislation aims at giving businesses as much room as possible to do business without trade barriers.

The EU has also created a lot of legislation in the area of private law, however. In some cases, the EU legislature's intention is to protect a weaker party or the environment by enacting private legislation on a subject. Businesses checking the conditions that regulate cross-border trade therefore have to examine both national and European sources of mandatory legislation in the areas of private as well as public law.

Private law systems in the Common Market
Except in the British Isles, most private law in the Member States is set out in their civil codes, such as Germany's 'Bürgerliches Gesetzbuch' and Italy's 'Codice Civile'. The legislation in these codes is presented in a orderly way in several volumes, describing the obligations of the parties in general terms. If a problem occurs, lawyers and perhaps eventually judges will look for the applicable articles in the code to resolve it. The Scandinavian countries do not have a formal civil code system like that of the continental EU Member States.

England, Wales and Ireland have a different form of law called *common law*. Common law is not codified in any way, but is established by judges. In order to find the law on a certain problem, lawyers have to examine court judgments. The written legislation enacted by Parliament has the function of supplementing or replacing common law. These written laws have to be very precise in their provisions, because if any aspect is omitted the ruling of common law on that aspect will be applied rather than the newly enacted legislation.

In fact, every Member State in the EU has its own private law, whether it is codified after the example of the French 'Code Civil' introduced by

Napoleon or after the example of the other most influential code, the German one. For businesses involved in cross-border trade, the existence of these different legal codes can be quite confusing. Most businesspeople expect there to be a European Civil Code and, despite the fact that the Member States will not be agreeing to a European Code in the near future, academics have already come up with a suggestion for one: the 'Principles of European Contract Law' (PECL).

In the meantime, businesses have to turn to the national private law codes and the United Nations (UN) Convention on Contracts for the International Sale of Goods (CISG) to resolve their private law problems.

5.2.2   The international contract of sale and the CISG

As far the free movement of goods in the EU is concerned, the most important contract for businesses involved in cross-border trade is a contract for the international sale of goods. The UN's Convention on Contracts for the International Sale of Goods (CISG) applies to international sales contracts for movable goods between commercial parties.

The text of the CISG was agreed in 1980, and between that year and July 2009 74 countries around the world signed up to the convention, creating an international private law code for sales contracts between companies. The number of contracting states to the CISG is still steadily growing. The world's largest economic nations are contracting states, including China, the USA, Japan, Germany and France. However, some important trading nations, including India and Brazil, have not yet joined the CISG. The appendix at the end of chapter 5 lists the CISG states.

Most EU Member States have joined the CISG, but Ireland, Malta, Portugal and the UK have not signed up. In cross-border trade within the EU, the CISG applies to sales contracts when the seller or both parties are from a contracting state. In the chapter's opening case study, both Grün GmbH and the Italian buyer belonged to a CISG state, so the CISG does apply to their contract, as it does to Grün's contract with its Chinese supplier.

The parties to a contract, however, may exclude the application of the CISG to the contract either as a whole or in part. In other words, the CISG constitutes permissive law rather than mandatory law.

The CISG comprises 101 articles and it is not capable of solving all the legal problems that may arise between a seller and a buyer. The national law of the seller's country fills the gaps that are not covered by the contract, the contracting parties' general conditions or the CISG. National private law is therefore also known as 'gapfilling law'.

The parties to a contract, lawyers and judges have to check several sources of law in order to find out the legal position on any issues. For instance, if Grün GmbH has a disagreement with its Italian customer over the sales contract, the parties should check the provisions of at least the following documents:
1 the contract between Grün GmbH and the Italian company
2 the general conditions of either seller or buyer, depending on which party last issued its general conditions; or, according to the highest German judge, those provisions of both sets of general conditions which do not conflict
3 the provisions of the CISG if the convention applies to the contract
4 the national law of (usually) the seller, unless the contract or general conditions prescribe the law of the buyer's country.

These four sources of law are explained in more detail in subsections 5.2.2.1–4.

5.2.2.1 The international contract of sale
This subsection explains the most important aspects of an international sales contract, giving information about contract conditions and explaining the 'Incoterms 2000' delivery terms and payment terms.

An international contract of sale may be concluded orally or in writing. The CISG allows oral contracts, as do most European codes. If there is a written contract it usually includes conditions relating to:
· the parties and the places of business
· the goods that are being sold and contract price
· the delivery terms (see 'Incoterms 2000' below) and delivery date
· the payment method and date
· any warranties that may be given, obliging the party concerned to meet the stated specifications
· information on the penalties that apply if one party breaks its obligations
· a *force majeure* clause exempting one or both parties from fulfilling their obligations under the contract
· the national law (e.g. German or Italian law) that applies to the contract

- provisions for dispute resolution, such as litigation in a particular court or arbitration before a special tribunal, e.g. that of the International Chamber of Commerce (ICC).

When the contract is concluded, its conditions become law between the parties. The contract will be respected by judges and arbitrators throughout the world.

Of these conditions, the Incoterms 2000 delivery terms and the payment terms are the most important in an international sales contract and are explained in more detail below.

Incoterms 2000

Incoterms 2000 is a set of standard definitions of terms, drawn up by the ICC and published in its most recent version in 2000. It codifies common practice in the international sales trade and defines 13 delivery terms which specify the obligations of seller and buyer in the execution of a contract of sale.

The aim of Incoterms 2000 is to avoid misunderstandings between sellers and buyers around the world. The Incoterms provide the contracting parties with answers to the following questions:
1 Who is responsible for which aspects of the transportation of the goods?
2 Where does the risk transfer from seller to buyer?
3 Where does the legal delivery take place?
4 Who is responsible for which customs duties and tariffs?
5 Is either party under an obligation to insure the goods?

In the contracts of sale that Grün GmbH concluded with its Chinese supplier and its Italian customer, the use of Incoterms 2000 could have clarified which party was responsible for resolving the problem with EU Customs and the problem of the prohibition of heavy trucks on the A2 in Austria.

The ICC divides the 13 Incoterms into four groups. The E-group consists of just one term, Ex Works (EXW). It represents the fewest obligations on the seller in the execution of the sales contract. If this Incoterm is applied to the sales contract between the Chinese seller and Grün GmbH, the seller's only obligation is to package the goods and make them ready for transportation at his own premises in China. The seller's location is also the place where the risk transfers to the buyer (even before the goods are loaded onto a truck) and where the legal delivery takes place. Grün has to pay all the costs of transportation from the seller's location to his own and pay all customs duties. If the EXW Incoterm were included in the contract, Grün would have to resolve the problem with EU Customs. There is no insurance obligation on either party under an EXW condition, so Grün would run the risk of damage and loss during transportation and it would be up to the German company to decide whether to take out insurance to cover this.

If Grün GmbH had included the EXW Incoterm in its sales contract with the Italian customer, it would have been up to the buyer to resolve the problem over the A2 motorway in Austria.

The F-group consists of three Incoterms: Free Carrier (FCA), Free Alongside Ship (FAS) and Free On Board (FOB). The last two can be used when transportation by sea is involved. Under the FAS Incoterm, the Chinese seller would have to bring the goods to the port and place them alongside the ship. This is also the location where the delivery to the buyer takes place and where risk transfers from seller to buyer. The seller would clear the goods through Chinese Customs; Grün would be responsible for clearing EU Customs.

The FOB condition would take the Chinese seller's obligation a little further than the FAS condition: the seller would now also have to bear the cost of loading the ship. The risk of damage or loss would pass to Grün GmbH as soon as the goods passed the ship's rail. This is also the point where the delivery takes place. Nor the seller or the buyer are under any insurance obligation; this obligation is only present when the abbreviated Incoterm includes the letter 'I'.

The FCA Incoterm could be suitable for the contract with the Italian supplier. In that case, Grün would be responsible for delivering the goods to the named place, even though the risk would transfer to the Italian buyer when the goods are presented to the first carrier. This is also the point at which the legal delivery takes place. The customs obligations are the same for all the Incoterms in the F-group: the parties are each responsible for clearing their own customs.

The C-group consists of four Incoterms. The terms Carriage Paid To (CPT) and Carriage and Insurance Paid to (CIP) can be used for all modes of transportation. Cost and Freight (CFR) and its insurance variation, CIF, can only be used when transportation by sea is involved. The C-group is the most difficult group of Incoterms to fulfill in business cases. The obligations of the Chinese seller and Grün GmbH, for example, would be divided across two continents: some obligations resemble those of the F-group and apply in the seller's country or continent, whereas the transportation obligation could extend all the way to Hamburg.

The Chinese seller would have almost the same obligations under a CFR Hamburg, Germany, as under a FOB Shanghai, China. The only obligation that extends to the European continent is the obligation on the Chinese seller to pay for the sea transport. If a CIF Hamburg were included in the contract, the obligations on the seller would resemble a FOB Shanghai with two extra obligations: the cost of sea transport from Shanghai to Hamburg and insurance for this voyage.

The D-group is the largest group of Incoterms. In this group the obligations of the seller extend to the buyer's country or continent. The terms are Delivered At Frontier (DAF), Delivered Ex Ship (DES), Delivered Ex Quay (DEQ), Delivered Duty Unpaid (DDU) and Delivered Duty Paid (DDP). The DDP Incoterm imposes the most obligations on the seller. All these obligations extend to the named place, usually the buyer's premises.

The DAF Incoterm cannot be used when a frontier is being approached by sea. In the case of sea transportation, DES or DEQ are more appropriate. Under a DDU the buyer is responsible for the duties involved in importing the goods into the EU, and within Europe a DDU resembles a DDP Incoterm. As section 5.3 explains, within Europe no duties are permitted between EU Member States.

If a DDU were part of the contract with the Italian customer, the problem of the Austrian motorway ban on heavy trucks would be Grün's.

In order to find out who has to resolve the EU Customs problem, the contract of sale between Grün GmbH and its Chinese supplier must be checked. Whether it is Grün's problem or not, an excessive delay at customs will make Grün late with the delivery to its Italian customer and will breach the sales contract with the customer. In the latter legal relationship, the Incoterm specified in the contract (DDP) means that Grün has to deal with the Austrian motorway problem.

Payment conditions
The other vital provision in an international sales contract is the means of payment for the goods. The European legislature has been very active in providing a framework to ease financial transactions between Member States for European businesses.

The use of an International Bank Account Number (IBAN) and Bank Identifier Code (BIC) have been mandatory since 1st January 2007 when making transfers in euros between banks in the EU and the European Economic Area (EEA), which includes the EU Member States plus Iceland, Liechtenstein and Norway. The banks are not allowed to charge citizens or businesses more for a cross-border euro payment than for a domestic bank transfer.

The Directive on Payment Services (PSD) provides the legal basis for the creation of an EU-wide single market for payments. The aim of the directive is to make cross-border payments as easy, efficient and secure as domestic payments within a Member State. The directive also provides the legal foundation making the Single Euro Payments Area (SEPA) possible. In this area too, the EU provides the conditions for easy cross-border trade, but the businesses themselves have to make the actual deal by negotiating a contract.

Where movable goods are involved in a transaction, the types of payment available to the parties are different from those available, for instance, in a contract for services. The only options for the parties to a contract for services are 'payment on open account' and 'payment in advance' (and combinations of the two).

In the chapter 5 opening case study, the Chinese seller would probably want part of the contract price to be paid in advance. The most usual arrangement would be for this first instalment to be paid before the magnetic parts are actually produced and for the remainder to be due when the goods are placed on board a vessel in Shanghai. This is also the place where the Chinese seller would have to deliver the magnetic parts under the terms FOB Shanghai or CIF Hamburg, Germany, Incoterm 2000.

The process of having the goods loaded onto the vessel in exchange for payment of the price can also be specified in other modes of payment, such as *documentary collection* and *documentary credit*. These modes of payment can only be used for international sales.

If a documentary credit, also known as a Letter of Credit (L/C), were specified in the contract with the Chinese supplier, Grün GmbH would have to apply for credit at its bank. If the bank decided to give the credit, a Letter of Credit would be issued and sent via the Chinese bank to the seller.

When the Chinese bank authenticated the credit, the seller would start shipment of the goods. As soon as the goods had been loaded onto the ship, the sea carrier would issue a receipt known as a Bill of Lading (B/L). The B/L is also an document of title. The seller has to send the B/L and other documents needed by the buyer in order to import the goods into the EU to the buyer's bank. Grün's bank would examine the B/L and other documents before paying the Chinese seller.

Because of the involvement of the German bank in issuing credit for the transaction and examining the documents sent by the seller, a documentary credit is the most expensive payment option.

Documentary collection is a less expensive way of exchanging documents and payment through banks. If this were specified in the contract between Grün GmbH and the Chinese seller, a bank in Germany would collect the money for the Chinese seller. When Grün paid the contract price at the bank, the documents, including the Bill of Lading, would be handed over to Grün. With the Bill of Lading, the buyer can receive the goods from the carrier in Hamburg, whereas the other documents are used to clear the magnetic parts for import. The delay at EU Customs could have been caused by the seller sending an incorrect document.

5.2.2.2 The general conditions

For businesses engaged in international trade, having a set of general conditions is very important. The conditions are drawn up specially for the business that is using them. Using general conditions means that businesses do not have to negotiate every condition individually every time they enter into a contract. The conditions under which an enterprise prefers to do business with all its customers usually form part of the general conditions.

By using general conditions, an enterprise is able to do business under the best possible conditions. The general conditions of an enterprise that sells goods usually include provisions ensuring that a deal is made only when a confirmation of order has been sent, and that the seller remains the owner of the goods until they have been paid for in full. One also finds clauses specifying that the law of the seller's country will apply to the contract and that the courts of the seller's country have jurisdiction. In the contract of sale between the Chinese supplier and Grün GmbH, such conditions would not be in the German company's favour.

The general conditions apply to the contract as long as the enterprise informs the other party before the contract is actually concluded that business is being done under its conditions. Which set of general conditions applies to the contract also depends on the market position of seller and buyer. If the Chinese seller, for instance, is the stronger party, Grün GmbH will find it difficult to negotiate some of the conditions out of the Chinese company's general terms of delivery and into the main body of the contract. How the two contractual documents together make up the legal relationship between seller and buyer is shown in figure 5.2.

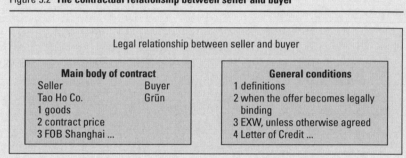

Figure 5.2 **The contractual relationship between seller and buyer**

In the main body of the contract, the specific conditions applying to negotiations with a particular customer are set out. If these provisions do not provide a solution to a problem that arises between the parties, the provisions of the applicable conditions can be examined. If the general conditions are also silent on the matter, the applicable law may give an answer to the problem.

5.2.2.3 The provisions of the CISG

Unless the parties to the contracts in the chapter's opening case study excluded the CISG in their contract or general conditions, the CISG will apply to both of Grün GmbH's contracts. The parties, their lawyers and, in the last resort, judges will examine whether the CISG provides solutions to any problem that arises.

The CISG provides rules and therefore solutions in the following areas:
- which cases the CISG applies to
- the offer and acceptance of the offer
- the seller's obligations and the buyer's sanctions against a non/ underperforming seller
- the buyer's obligations and the seller's sanctions against a non/ underperforming buyer
- actions available to both seller and buyer, such as claiming damages
- payment of interest and miscellaneous provisions.

The articles contained in the CISG represent permissive law. This means that the parties may exclude the whole, any part or just a single article of the CISG. For instance, when a DDP Incoterm 2000 is included in a contract, the parties may agree to a different procedure from what is prescribed in the CISG Articles on delivery.

In the opening case study, Grün GmbH may miss the deadline for delivery of the magnetic parts to its customer in Italy for two reasons: the delay at EU Customs and the delay caused by the Austrian truck ban. The delay at EU Customs is Grün's risk if the contract specifies FOB Shanghai or CIF Hamburg. If the delivery delay is also partly caused by the Austrian authorities, whether this failure to perform is excused will depend on the contract between Grün and its Italian customer. If the contract specifies DDP Udine, Italy, and does not include a *force majeure* condition, then according to Article 74 of the CISG the Italian buyer may claim damages if the delivery is late. Because the interest rate is not mentioned in Article 78 of the CISG, the national law applying to the case would have to be examined.

5.2.2.4   The national law and jurisdiction applying to the contract

This subsection explains the national law that applies to the contract and clarifies which court of law has jurisdiction in the case of a dispute that cannot be settled out of court.

A national body of law will only be examined if the contract, the general conditions and the CISG (if it applies) do not provide the answer to a legal question. Which national law applies is not easy to determine. In the case of Grün's European contract in the opening case study, it could either be German or Italian law. Within Europe, the Member States have made a treaty to solve this problem: the European Community Convention on the Law applicable to Contractual Obligations (Rome I, 1980) provides an answer to the question of which of the two national codes of private law applies. This convention will be replaced by a regulation as of 17th December 2009. According to Article 3 of Rome I, the parties are allowed to choose the applicable law in their contract. Where a choice is not made, according to Article 4 of Rome I and the regulation the seller's law applies. In Grün's case this means that the German Civil Code will apply to its contract with the Italian customer.

The European legislature has also been very active on the issue of deciding which court(s) will have jurisdiction in the event of a dispute between the parties which they are unable to settle out of court. According to Regulation 44/2001 on Jurisdiction and the Recognition and Enforcement of Judgments in Civil and Commercial Matters (Brussels I), the parties may choose to specify in their contract a particular court of law to settle their disputes. This condition is known as a 'choice of forum'. If the parties are unable to agree on this, the general rule is that the courts of the defendant's country have jurisdiction. In Grün's case, if the Italian customer decided to sue Grün for late delivery of the goods, a German court would have jurisdiction according to Article 2 of Brussels I. In the event that a DDP were included in the contract, an Italian court would also be allowed to hear the case, because according to Article 5 of Brussels I the Italian court would be the court of the place of delivery. In that case it would be up to the Italian claimant to decide in which country he wished to bring litigation.

Whatever the jurisdiction, the law that applies remains the same: the judges will look into the contract, the general conditions, the CISG and national law to decide the case.

European legislation has made many new procedures available to companies. One of the most recent EU instruments is the regulation on a European Payment Order, which makes court procedures redundant in the case of uncontested claims. Businesses can claim their money without the usual expenses of a court case, such as lawyers' fees.

As far as Grün GmbH is concerned, there are no private law problems to tackle yet. Its main problems are being caused by government authorities, and therefore we shall return to the solutions European law has to offer under the EC Treaty.

5.3 Infringements of the free movement of goods

When businesses decide to engage in cross-border trade within the European Union, they need to be aware of the fact that national authorities are not allowed to interfere in the process. As explained in section 5.1, national authorities have to respect the prohibitions imposed by the Articles of the EC Treaty. This section takes a closer look at these Articles, which give businesses legal protection against infringements of the free movement of goods.

Subsection 5.3.1 examines financial infringements and 5.3.2 considers physical infringements. Both subsections also offer solutions to Grün GmbH's problems with the government authorities. Finally, subsection 5.3.3 clarifies the EU's competition law.

5.3.1 Financial infringements

The provisions of the EC Treaty which aim to prevent financial barriers being imposed on businesses are contained in Articles 23 to 27 and Articles 90 to 93. The financial barriers can be divided into two categories: that of customs duties and all charges having equivalent effect and that of taxes. The first category of financial barriers is prohibited between Member States, whereas internal taxes may be levied as long as they meet the requirements of Article 90 of the treaty. In fact, businesses can save quite a lot of money by being aware of the distinction between a charge having an equivalent effect (which is prohibited by Article 25) and internal taxes (which states are allowed to levy according to Article 90).

5.3.1.1 Customs duties and charges having equivalent effect in the customs union

Article 23 of the EC Treaty describes the main rules governing the customs union, which is what the EC actually is. The customs union covers all trade in goods and involves the prohibition of customs duties on imports and exports between Member States and of all charges having equivalent effect. The customs union also involves a common customs tariff imposed on countries outside the EU. The EU's common policy on customs is described in section 5.1. EU legislation and policy have completely replaced national laws and policies in this area.

In this chapter's opening case study, customs duties may be applicable when the magnetic parts are imported into the EU. Article 24 of the EC Treaty ensures that, if all EU Customs requirements have been complied with, the products are allowed to circulate freely within the EU. In this case the magnetic parts will be able to circulate freely in Germany and the rest of the EU after all import formalities have been complied with and customs duties have been paid. From that moment on, Article 25 of the treaty also applies to these parts, which originated from China.

The prohibition of customs duties and charges having equivalent effect is repeated in Article 25. This prohibition is explained in example 5.1. It is not the name of the charge or duty that is relevant, but the act of charging money on goods crossing borders between Member States. Article 25 applies even if duties or charges are levied between regions of one Member State, because of the absolute nature of the prohibition of customs duties.

■ Example 5.1
In the event of an Italian authority imposing a charge just because Grün's magnetic parts cross the Italian border, these charges are considered to be customs duties or charges having equivalent effect. It does not matter what the charge is called in the particular Member State. The simple fact that money is being demanded for crossing an internal EU border is sufficient for the prohibition in Article 25 of the EC Treaty to apply.

These days, hardly any customs duties are levied between the Member States. However, businesses need to be more aware of all the kinds of charges that have an equivalent effect to customs duties. These are any pecuniary levies on the import and export of goods.

Article 25 does not present any exceptions to its rule: it is an absolute rule. Money can only be charged on the import and export of goods when a fee is paid to an enterprise for a particular service or where the protection of public health is involved. In both cases the service or inspection must be mandatory under European or other international rules. The service or inspection should also promote the free movement of goods. The service and charges must be applied in the same way to all goods and the fee must not exceed the actual costs involved.

In the case Commission v. Italy, Case 46/76, ECR 1969 page 193, the European Court of Justice did not agree with a fee for statistical services because the benefit to businesses was too indirect. In another case, a charge for compulsory veterinary and public health inspections carried out on the importation of raw cowhides could not be excepted from Article 25 prohibition because a general health inspection cannot be regarded as a service to the importing company and it was not a mandatory inspection under European or other international rules (Brescia v. Amministrazione delle Finanze, Case 87/75, ECR 1976 page 129).

The ECJ has ruled time and again that a charge imposed on goods crossing a frontier, however small and whatever its designation and mode of application, constitutes a charge that is prohibited by Article 25 of the EC Treaty.

5.3.1.2 Internal taxes

The other category of financial barrier arises when a Member State imposes an internal tax. The tax regime in the Member State of origin may be different from that in the Member State of destination of the goods, in which case the free movement of goods within the single market is hindered. The ideal situation for businesses in the EU would be for all Member States to impose the same level of taxes in the same manner on the same products. This, however, is not (yet) the situation. The Member States have sovereignty in the area of internal taxes, which means that they have the power to impose new taxes. As a result, differences between the tax systems of Member States arise, which hinder the free movement of goods.

These differences will have to be resolved through fiscal harmonization, an important aspect of which is Value Added Tax (VAT). Harmonization is more difficult in the area of internal taxes than in other areas because Article 93 of the EC Treaty prescribes that the Council has to act unanimously when adopting legislation on taxation. This explains why there is still not a single rate of VAT throughout the EU and why there are so many exceptions to the minimum rates set in the VAT directives. In this area of the law, it may be more accurate to speak of 'approximation' of laws than of 'harmonization'.

Although Member States have the power to introduce new tax laws, Article 90 of the EC Treaty states that no Member State shall impose, directly or indirectly, on the products of other Member States any internal taxation of any kind in excess of that imposed directly or indirectly on similar domestic products. It also states that no Member State shall impose on the products of other Member States any internal taxation of such a nature as to afford indirect protection to other products.

In other words, the same tax should be levied on the same kind of product, regardless of whether a product originates from another Member State. Example 5.2 illustrates how a trade barrier may arise if an internal tax is imposed on goods.

■ Example 5.2

If the Italian government announces a tax rise of 40% on all products made of steel, this tax must be levied not only on Grün's products but also on products made by its competitors operating in Italy. Whether the goods are made and sold in Italy or whether they are being imported to or exported from Italy, the tax will have to be paid.

The same tax should be imposed on the products of Italian manufacturers as on products originating from other Member States. If the tax levied on steel products originating from another Member State is higher than on similar Italian products, Italy will be in breach of Article 90 of the EC Treaty.

In summary, when imposing taxes Member States are not allowed to make any distinction according where the goods originally came from. Discrimination against products on the grounds of national origin is prohibited within the EU.

5.3.1.3 The difference for businesses between Article 25 and Article 90
Businesses operating in the single market can save a lot of money by being aware of the prohibitions set out in Articles 25 and 90 of the EC Treaty. This awareness can help them to make the right business decisions, as case study 5.3 shows.

Case study 5.3 **Strong beer tax levied in France**

Monks insist on high-alcohol beer

A French Government drive against alcoholism has incurred the wrath of Belgium's famous Trappist monks. Famous for vows of silence, the Trappist monks are also well known for brewing strong beers, including Chimay and Westmalle. But the French Government now wants to slap high taxes on any of those beers that contain more than 8.5% alcohol.

The Trappist brewers argue that this is against the spirit of the European free trade area, the single market. They also say the new tax will effectively double the cost of a bottle of beer to the consumer and dent their brewing revenues by 2.5m euros (£1.63m; $2.63m). The French Government's decision to tax high-alcohol beers is both unfair and illogical, according to Henroz Phillippe, a spokesman for Trappist brewers. And they have asked the European Commission to investigate.

Watered down
The new fiscal measures were announced unexpectedly at the end of last year in order to deter alcoholism. But French wine – which has a stronger alcoholic content than Trappist beer and is already taxed less than beer – is not being penalized in the same way. Most French wines have more than 10% alcohol content.

"If somebody wants to get drunk quickly, I guess they would go for a cheap wine rather than a specialist beer," Mr Phillippe told the BBC's World Business Report.

Some of Belgium's biggest brewers have already watered down their products in order to evade the new policy. And the tax will affect very few French brewers, who do not tend to brew beer of that strength.

Mr Phillippe says the real losers are the small brewers who are unable or unwilling to adapt their traditional products. He is confident that the European Commission will come to their rescue.

Source: BBC News, world edition, Friday 10th January 2003, 12:42 GMT

When a financial barrier has been announced, as in case study 5.3, it is important for a business to check what kind of financial barrier they are dealing with before making any important business decisions. There are two main courses of action available in such cases: one is to comply with the new legislation and adapt the product, and the other is to contest the measure, risking loss of profit due to lower exports.

Some Belgian and Dutch brewers chose to take the first course. They adapted their beer in such a way that its strong flavour was retained even though the alcohol content was reduced to below the 8.5% figure. Developing a new product involves an enormous financial investment. These brewers complied with the new financial barrier because they did not want the barrier to affect their export figures to France.

In case study 5.3 the Trappist brewers took the opposite course: they immediately filed a complaint with the European Commission. Chapter 4 explains the Commission's role as the guardian of European law: Article 226 of the EC Treaty allows the Commission to lodge a case with the ECJ if a Member State breaks European law after having been warned by a Reasoned Opinion on the subject.

The question here is which group of brewers made the right business decision. The issue boils down to whether or not the French authorities breached any of the articles of European law. The following subsection examines whether an infringement of either Article 25 or Article 90 has taken place and suggests how businesses can take action against infringements.

5.3.1.4 Actions by businesses against financial infringements

If the French tax were imposed on the import and export of strong beer only, Article 25 of the EC Treaty would apply. In that case the charges would not be payable because they are prohibited by Article 25. The appropriate action for the enterprises concerned may be to write to the French national authorities, either explaining why the enterprise is of the opinion that the charges are not payable or reclaiming charges already paid. In case study 5.3, however, the tax did not have to be paid only as a result of crossing a EU frontier, so Article 25 did not apply.

In cases where Member States do impose import or export duties or charges having equivalent effect, which are prohibited by Article 25, the enterprises concerned may also file a complaint with the European Commission. In the event of an enterprise reclaiming the charges paid, it is a good idea to enclose a copy of the complaint made to the Commission with the enterprise's note to the national authorities. When an official complaint is filed with the Commission, the national authorities tend to take such a claim more seriously. Sometimes simply mentioning the intention of making an official complaint is enough to make the authorities reconsider their decision. If they do not agree with the claim, the enterprise concerned should lodge a case with the national court in order to recover the money.

In case study 5.3 Article 25 did not apply, even though the Treaty states that the prohibition also applies to customs duties of a fiscal nature. The French legislative measure was in fact presented as a tax, suggesting that all strong beers would be affected, whether they were imported or exported or whether the beer were produced in France to be consumed by French customers. Under those circumstances, Article 90 of the EC Treaty applies. This Article has the effect of prohibiting the levying of a tax on a product that is rarely produced in France, resulting in French-produced goods not being taxed in the same way.

When a tax like the one featured in case study 5.3 is announced, the best action the businesses concerned can take is to write a note to the relevant national authorities. The businesses will have to explain why they are of the opinion that the tax is unlawful. It is also a good idea to file a complaint with the European Commission before the tax is imposed, as the Belgian brewers did.

The Commission sent a letter to the French authorities on 27th December 2002, drawing attention to the repercussions of taxing (in France) sales of beer from other Member States with an alcohol content above 8.5%. As a result of all these actions, the French authorities suspended the tax, so in the end neither action by the brewers in the national court nor a hearing before the ECJ was necessary to resolve the issue.

Case study 5.3 and many other cases demonstrate that it is very important for businesses to have a basic knowledge of European law. Enterprises that know which taxes and charges they must pay and which are prohibited by the EC Treaty's creation of a single market will be able to save a lot of money. Any prohibited charges and taxes that have been paid because they were already due can be reclaimed after the event.

Looking back on the decisions the businesses in the case study had to make when the strong beer tax was announced, the Trappist brewers who contested the tax were right in the end. Moreover, the brewers who developed new beers to meet the 8.5% maximum alcohol level made all that investment for nothing and were set back in comparison with their competitors who fought the taxation.

5.3.1.5 Financial barriers and the case of Grün GmbH

In the opening case study, a charge was levied by the German Association for Technical Co-operation for carrying out its assessment of Grün GmbH's product. The company's management would like to know whether it is liable to pay this charge. The information given in this section suggests that the charge should be more closely examined. If the association has government authority to levy the charge, three different situations are possible.

The first situation is that the charge could be characterized as a customs duty levied on products originating outside the EU. There is a common policy and EU legislation in this area. The common customs tariff is intended to achieve an equalization of customs charges levied at the Community's borders on products imported from non-EU countries, in order to avoid any distortion of free internal circulation or of competitive conditions. Both the unity of the Community's customs territory and the uniformity of the common commercial policy would be seriously undermined if the Member States were authorized to impose charges having equivalent effect to customs duties on imports from non-member countries. So this charge cannot be levied as a customs duty on the magnetic parts from China.

The second situation is that the charge could be payable because the magnetic parts are leaving German territory. This would be a charge equivalent to a customs duty, which is prohibited by Articles 23 and 25 of the EC Treaty.

The third situation is that the charge could be characterized as a German tax. In that case, the charges would be permitted, but Grün should check whether the same kind of tax is levied on the same kind of German product, as prescribed in Article 90 of the treaty. If the charge is non-discriminatory, it will have to be paid by Grün GmbH.

In situations 1 and 2, Grün GmbH does not have to pay the money due to the association. The best option for Grün's management is to write a note to the association explaining why the company is of the opinion that the charge is illegal. Grün can also choose to file a complaint with the European Commission. The Commission may decide to act on the complaint by sending a letter to the German government, and this could eventually lead to a Reasoned Opinion and possibly a court case before the ECJ.

If Grün GmbH has already paid the illegal charge, the company will have to reclaim the money from the association. If its claim is not successful, Grün may initiate proceedings in a German court in order to get its money back.

On the other hand, if the German Association for Technical Co-operation does not have government authority to levy the charge, because the charge arises out of an obligation based on private law, the association's activities should be checked against the Articles on competition law in the EC Treaty. Subsection 5.3.3 gives further information on competition law.

5.3.2   Physical infringements

National authorities may also enact legislation that restricts the free movement of goods in a non-financial manner. Infringements of this type are called physical infringements. This subsection explains the various types of physical barriers and the exceptions to the prohibitions of the EC Treaty. The case study for this chapter is followed up to see whether Grün GmbH is affected by physical barriers to free movement, and advice is offered to businesses on how to deal with infringements of this kind.

5.3.2.1   Quantitative restrictions and measures having equivalent effect

Before the European Community took effect in 1958, the Member States had a variety of legislation to protect their domestically produced goods. A traditional way of keeping foreign goods out of the domestic market is to use *quantitative restrictions*, which include:
- import bans
- import and export permits
- import and export quotas.

But other measures having an equivalent effect to quantitative restrictions (MEQRs) are also prohibited by Articles 28 and 29 of the EC Treaty. The ECJ ruled in the Dassonville case (case study 5.4) that 'all trading rules enacted by Member States which are capable of hindering, directly or indirectly, actually or potentially, intra-Community trade are to be considered as measures having an equivalent effect to quantitative restrictions'.

Case study 5.4 The Dassonville case

Gustave Dassonville, a wholesaler in business in France, and his son Benoît Dassonville, who managed a branch of his father's business in Belgium, imported into Belgium scotch whisky, under the brand names 'Johnnie Walker' and 'Vat 69', which Gustave Dassonville had purchased from the French importers and distributors of these two brands of whisky.

The Dassonvilles affixed to the bottles, with a view to their sale in Belgium, labels bearing among other things the printed words 'British Customs Certificate of Origin', followed by a handwritten note of the number and date of the French excise bond on the permit register. France does not require a certificate of origin for scotch whisky.

Although the goods were duly imported into Belgium on the basis of the French documents required, and cleared for customs purposes as 'Community goods', the Belgian authorities considered that these documents did not properly satisfy the objective described by Royal Decree No.57 of 1934. The public prosecutor was therefore

of the opinion that the Dassonvilles had committed the following criminal offences:
1 they committed forgeries or assisted therein and
2 they sold whisky without the proper documents.

The Belgian court in which the case was pending asked the European Court of Justice for a preliminary ruling on whether or not the Belgian legislation could be characterized as a measure having equivalent effect to quantitative restrictions (MEQR).

First, the ECJ defined a 'measure having equivalent effect to quantitative restrictions' in Article 28 of the latest version of the EC Treaty.

The Court ruled that when, in the absence of a Community system guaranteeing for consumers the authenticity of a product's designation of origin, a Member State takes measures to prevent unfair practices in this connection, it is subject to the condition that these measures should be reasonable and that the means of proof required should not act as a hindrance to trade between Member States and should be accessible to all Community nationals.

For the Dassonvilles, the ruling meant that they had not committed the criminal offences they had been charged with in Belgium. As a result, they were not convicted by the Belgian court.

As this case shows, the European Court of Justice has played a very important role in clarifying what type of legislation can be characterized as quantitative restrictions or measures having equivalent effect. In countless cases the ECJ ruled in favour of the free movement of goods and against any national legislation or other actions that hindered free trade. For instance, even if import permits are granted on request, such a measure involves bureaucracy that similar domestic products do not have to submit to. In the 'buy Irish' case (Case 249/81, ECR 1982 page 4005), the Irish government created a national campaign to promote Irish products which might hinder the importing of products from other Member States.

An important group of MEQRs is the *technical requirements* set unilaterally by Member States. Even though there are many directives aimed at standardizing these requirements, it is important to be aware that a national technical requirement may be illegal according to Articles 28 or 29 of the EC Treaty.

Other examples of MEQRs are:
- obligatory indication of origin
- obligatory quality inspections and inspections of documents that take an excessive amount of time

- legislation on when a particular generic name may be used, e.g. the name 'Sekt' (German sparkling white wine) could only be applied to wines made in a German-speaking country and containing at least 60% grapes producd in Germany. Foreign sparkling white wines were nog allowed to use the name 'Sekt' and consequently had a more difficult time on the German market.

The vast number of such cases shows that businesses need to be aware of quantitative restrictions, especially in the form of measures that have equivalent effect, in order to stand as good a chance in the market of a another Member State as they have in their home market.

5.3.2.2 Three exceptions to the prohibition of quantitative restrictions
There are three exceptions to the principle of the free movement of goods without quantitative restrictions. One exception is grounded in Article 30 of the EC Treaty, whereas the other two were permitted by the ECJ. The latter exceptions are known by the names of the cases concerned, 'Cassis de Dijon' and 'Keck'. These three exceptions to the free movement of goods are explained here in chronological order.

The Article 30 exception
Article 30 of the EC Treaty gives Member States the authority to restrict imports, exports or goods in transit when there is a justification that is permitted by the Article. The permitted justifications are on the grounds of:
a public morality, public policy or public security;
b the protection of the health and life of humans, animals or plants
c the protection of national treasures possessing artistic, historic or archaeological value
d the protection of industrial and commercial property.

These justifications are explained below by means of examples. Article 30 prescribes that such prohibitions or restrictions shall not constitute a means of arbitrary discrimination or a disguised restriction on trade between Member States. In other words, if a genuine justification of the physical trade barrier applies, the quantitative restriction must be such that it does not protect domestic production in the Member State and does not allow arbitrary discrimination.

Justification a   Public morality, public policy or public security
If a Member State prohibits the import of erotic sex toys, the quantitative restriction may be justified on grounds of public morality. The Member State is allowed to define public morality by its own standards. However, if the production of such materials is not forbidden in the Member State itself, the last sentence of Article 30 applies: the import restriction constitutes a means of arbitrary discrimination, as national law does not prohibit the domestic production of such goods.

Justification b   The protection of the health and life of humans, animals or plants
A famous example of a Member State attempting to justify its restriction of the free movement of goods on public health grounds is the 'Reinheitsgebot' case. Beer could only be marketed under the German name 'Bier' if it was brewed using the ingredients prescribed by German law. The German government defended its strict law on beer ingredients,

which excluded beer containing additives, before the European Court of Justice in the following way:

> Since beer is a foodstuff of which large quantities are consumed in Germany, the German government considers that it is particularly desirable to prohibit the use of any additives in its manufacture, especially in so far as the use of additives is not technologically necessary and can be avoided if only the ingredients laid down in the Biersteuergesetz are used. In those circumstances, the German rules on additives in beer are fully justified by the need of public health and do not infringe the principle of proportionality.

The German 'Reinheitsgebot' resulted in an import ban on beers which, although lawfully manufactured in other Member States, had not been brewed in conformity with the German rules. The ECJ (Case 178/84, ECR 1987 page 1227) considered that the German designation 'Bier' and its equivalents in the languages of other Member States could not be restricted to beers manufactured according to the German rules. The court held that the only measures allowed to restrict the free movement of goods are those that are actually necessary to protect public health. The German rules on beer, however, entail a general ban on additives. Their application to beers lawfully produced in and imported from other Member States is contrary to the principle of proportionality and is therefore not covered by the exception provided for in Article 30 of the EC Treaty.

The most important circumstances where a national measure is permitted despite representing a quantitative restriction is the prohibition on importing goods that are infected with a disease, such as beef during the outbreak of bovine spongiform encephalopathy (BSE), otherwise known as mad cow disease. This disease can cause Creuzfeldt-Jakob disease in humans, which claimed over 80 lives in the UK. An import ban on British beef was permitted under Article 30, and the Commission introduced a general import ban in 1996. France continued to enforce an embargo on British beef even after the European Commission lifted its ban in August 1999. This embargo, however, was not permitted under the last sentence of Article 30 because it constituted a measure of arbitrary discrimination, since the danger of contamination and therefore the danger to the health of humans and animals was over.

Justification c   The protection of national treasures possessing artistic, historic or archaeological value

Italy tried to justify an tax on archaeological goods designed to make their export less appealing. However, the justifications of Article 30 can only be invoked for quantitative restrictions of cross-border trade in goods, and not on financial barriers between Member States.

The European legislature meanwhile introduced measures to make national legislation imposing quantitative restrictions on these grounds unnecessary. One of these measures is a regulation that imposes uniform border controls on the export of protected goods to non-member countries.

Justification d   The protection of industrial and commercial property

Examples of industrial and commercial property are intellectual property rights, such as patents, trademarks, design rights and copyright. If the owner of a registered design for a handbag in the Netherlands tries to prevent the importation of an identical bag made in France without the consent of the Dutch owner of the intellectual property, this justification under Article 30 applies. However, if the goods were distributed lawfully in the market of another Member State with the consent of the owner of the intellectual property rights, preventing their importation is not allowed. This is an example of the principle of exhaustion of rights.

The Cassis de Dijon exception

The Cassis de Dijon exception was introduced by the European Court of Justice. Article 30 of the EC Treaty does not mention such justifications as consumer or environmental protection by Member States. In the Cassis de Dijon case, the ECJ permitted these extra justifications under strict conditions.

Case study 5.5 **Cassis de Dijon**

West German law prescribed that only drinks with an alcohol level of at least 25% could be sold as fruit liqueurs in Germany. A German supermarket chain, Rewe-Zentral AG, was prohibited from importing Cassis de Dijon, a French liqueur with an alcohol level of 15% to 20%, on the grounds that the alcohol level was too low. The German court that heard Rewe's case applied for a preliminary ruling to find out whether the German law breached Article 28 of the EC Treaty or whether quantitative restriction was justified on the grounds of consumer protection.

The West German government contended that the legislation was non-discriminatory and that there was as yet no European legislation harmonizing the different laws of the Member States on this matter. Until such legislation was passed, the Member States should be free to protect their consumers against unfair practices.

The ECJ did not accept this line of argument. The court agreed that consumers may be protected against unfair commercial transactions, but considered that the means chosen by the West German government breached Article 28. The court introduced the principle of mutual recognition (known as the 'Cassis de Dijon principle'), whereby a product manufactured in accordance with regulations and permitted in one EU Member State must be permitted in other EU Member States. The protection of consumers against weak spirits had already been taken care of by the French legislature. The mandatory fixing of minimum alcohol content by West German law hindered the free movement of goods and could not be justified. As the liqueur met French standards, it had to be permitted on the German market.

The ECJ also decided that the problem of consumer protection could be solved by less restrictive measures such as printing the alcohol content and an indication of the origin on the label.

Source: Rewe-Zentral AG v. Bundesmonopolverwaltung für Branntwein, 20th February 1979, Case 120/78, ECR 1979 page 649.

In this case the European Court of Justice decided that, in the absence of EU legislation on the issue, other grounds than those mentioned in Article 30 of the EC Treaty could be used to justify restrictions on the free movement of goods. Although consumer protection against unfair commercial transactions was allowed, the court ruled that the exception should be applied under strict conditions. Where the consumer is already protected by the law of the exporting country, the imposition of protective laws by the importing country is unnecessary and hinders the free movement of goods, which is prohibited by Article 28 EC.

The ECJ also reminded Member States that, when seeking to protect the consumer, they should consider the least restrictive legislation, such as the requirement for information to be given on the packaging of goods. In the Cassis de Dijon case, the German legislation promoted beverages with a high alcohol content and excluded from the German market products from other Member States which did not conform to that description. That effect of the legislation constituted an unjustifiable obstacle to the free movement of goods.

So, although this case introduced a new exception to the free movement of goods, as a result of the application of strict conditions it did not allow the German legislation to be applied to goods imported from other Member States where similar legislation existed.

Case study 5.6 The Keck case

The French government prohibited the resale of goods at a loss in order to protect the small shops against unfair competition from large supermarket chains. Breaking this law was a criminal offence. Keck and Mithouard were prosecuted for violating the legislation and the French judge hearing the case asked the European Court of Justice for a preliminary ruling on whether the protective legislation was a quantitative restriction or measure having equivalent effect according to Article 28 of the EC Treaty. If that were the case, Keck and Mithouard should not be convicted unless an exception to Article 28 applied.

The ECJ accepted another exception to Article 28 alongside the Article 30 and Cassis de Dijon exceptions because of the broad Dassonville definition of a measure having equivalent effect to a quantitative restriction. The ECJ had decided in the Dassonville case that any measure introduced or funded by a government authority that might hinder cross-border trade was a measure having equivalent effect to a quantitative restriction. In the Keck case, the court considered it necessary to re-examine and clarify its case law because of the increasing tendency for traders to invoke Article 28 of the EC Treaty. Businesses were challenging any rules that limited their commercial freedom, even where such rules were not aimed at products from other Member States. For this reason the ECJ drew a distinction between a genuine quantitative restriction and a measure designed to regulate certain selling arrangements that does not prevent access to the market and does not discriminate in its effect on the market between goods of different origins. The provisions must apply to all relevant traders operating within the national territory and must affect in the same manner, in law and in fact, the marketing of domestic products and of those from other Member States.

Source: Keck and Mithouard, Joined Cases C-267/91 and C-268/91, ECR 1993 page I-6097 (www.ena.lu/)

The Keck exception
This exception to the basic rule of not allowing any physical restrictions on the free movement of goods is applied in a different way from

the exceptions described above. In cases where Article 30 or the Cassis de Dijon exception applies, there is a real restriction of cross-border trade that is however justified on the specific grounds given in Article 30 EC or on the conditions of the Cassis de Dijon exception. Where the Keck exception applies, there is no real quantitative restriction or any measure having equivalent effect.

The ECJ decided that selling arrangements by a Member State that do not actually hinder the free movement of goods and are applied to all products in the same way may be excepted because they do not fall under the prohibition of Article 28 of the EC Treaty. Examples of such legislation on selling arrangements are rules about shop closing times and regulations on clearance sales.

5.3.2.3 Actions by businesses against physical infringements
If a business is hindered by physical infringements of Article 28 of the EC Treaty, affecting imports, and Article 29, affecting exports, its first step is to find out whether the infringement is justified by Article 30 or by the Cassis de Dijon or Keck exceptions. If the infringement is not justified, the business is allowed to continue its export or import activities and ignore the national legislation that infringes the EC Treaty.

The risk that a business takes when it persists in its cross-border trade is a fine by the Member State concerned or seizure of the goods because the activity is considered a criminal offence. If the Member State in question decides to fine the company, the management should explain why its cross-border activities are not criminal offences, referring to Articles 28 and 29. If goods are seized, the business should immediately bring a court case for the release of the goods.

5.3.2.4 Physical barriers and the case of Grün GmbH
Grün GmbH has to overcome two problems that may relate to physical infringements by Member States. The first problem is the Italian government's requirement of a technical assessment. The intention behind the legislation is to ensure the quality and safety of products on the Italian market, but where an export transaction like the one between Grün and its Italian customer is involved, the legislation hinders cross border trade. The Italian requirement is a technical barrier that constitutes a measure having the same effect as a quantitative restriction, which is prohibited by Article 28 of the EC Treaty.

The requirement may be justified on the grounds given in Article 30 of the EC Treaty. The justification that may be relevant is that the health of persons and animals may be at risk. However, if the magnetic parts have already been examined by the German Association for Technical Co-operation, applying the Italian legislation would be disproportionate and therefore not permitted.

The same reasoning can be used to check whether the Cassis de Dijon exception applies to the case. Although the Italian legislation may protect consumers against unsatisfactory products, the consumers are already protected by similar German legislation. Because the Italian requirement does not involve selling arrangements, the Keck exception does not apply.

The conclusion therefore has to be that the Italian legislation on the technical assessment is in breach of Article 28 of the EC Treaty. Grün can export the magnetic parts, using the German assessment to demonstrate the safety of the goods. Grün's management needs to be aware, however, that the Italian government may fine the company for breaching its legal requirements. Grün will not have to pay the fine because, if the Italian government applies this law against Grün, Italy will be breaking European law as set out in Articles 28 and 29 of the EC Treaty. If it is fined, Grün should send a note to the Italian authority concerned, which can be backed up with a complaint to the European Commission. If its goods are seized, Grün will have to bring a court case in Italy for the release of the goods.

5.3.3 Resolving problems with competitors

This section gives a brief explanation of EU competition law. The provisions of the EC Treaty described so far in this chapter are directed at the Member States, in order to ensure the proper functioning of the common market. In Articles 81 and 82, on the other hand, the EC Treaty forbids businesses to distort competition. The most important aspects of Article 81 are discussed in subsection 5.3.3.1; subsection 5.3.3.2 contains information on Article 82.

The chapter's opening case study does not involve any competition problems, but the German company's competitors could well take actions that are prohibited under Articles 81 and 82. Those actions are also discussed below.

5.3.3.1 Competition rules under Article 81 of the EC Treaty
Almost every country in the world has legislation to ensure fair competition within its territory. The legislation for the EU's single market is based on Articles 81 to 86 of the EC Treaty. The most important aspects of Article 81 are explained here, as well as the actions which businesses can take against distortions of competition.

Paragraph 1 of Article 81 declares a number of actions incompatible with the common market if they affect trade between the Member States and result in the prevention, restriction or distortion of competition within the common market. Such actions can be agreements between businesses, but also decisions taken by trading associations and even concerted practices that prevent fair competition on the single market. If businesses or associations were allowed to make the agreements prohibited by Article 81, consumers would ultimately have to pay higher prices for the products or services. The EC Treaty aims to prevent these distortions in the common market by disallowing agreements and other actions by businesses that create unfair competition.

In some cases it is not individual businesses themselves that create unfair competition in the market, but rather associations in which businesses co-operate with one another. An example of this kind of distortion is given in example 5.3.

■ Example 5.3

Suppose that the German Association for Technical Co-operation, mentioned in this chapter's opening case study, decides in its annual meeting that raw materials and part-completed products must be purchased from other members of the German organization. The association also agrees to impose fines on members that do not follow the new purchasing rules. These actions would definitely distort competition within the Common Market. Associations in certain lines of business have levied fees on members that decide to leave the association.

Example 5.3 shows that not only may individual businesses engage in activities that distort competition, but associations may be tempted to make decisions that are good for the members of that particular organization but distort fair competition in the single market and result in higher prices for the end users of the goods and services.

There does not even need to be an actual agreement between businesses or decision by an association. Article 81 of the EC Treaty also prohibits *concerted practice* by enterprises, such as copying each other's pricing policies, even if they have not actually met and agreed to distorting actions of this kind.

■ Example 5.4

In the 1990s the Commission examined the pricing policies of the ferry operators involved in routes between the European continent and the British Isles. The companies had decided to adopt a common pricing strategy without reaching an actual agreement. Their pricing policies could not be explained by normal economic factors and were therefore considered to be concerted practice, which is prohibited by Article 81. In the end the companies admitted to having held meetings of a prohibited nature. Their meetings resulted in prices that hardly differed from one another and that distorted the competition.
Source: Commission Decision 97/84/EC, 30th October 1996, Official Journal L 26, 29/01/1999 pages 23–34

Besides pricing policies, Article 81(1) also gives examples of other prohibited actions, including the limitation or control of production and markets, which place other businesses at a disadvantage. All such actions are automatically void, which means that the prohibited agreements and decisions by associations do not legally exist. The problem, however, is that the parties may still act according to these unfair agreements, thereby disadvantaging other businesses and the end users of the products and services.

Exceptions

The EC Treaty allows the Commission to permit some prohibited actions as long as the conditions of Article 81(3) are met. In order for an exception to the competition rules to apply, an agreement, decision or practice that is in principal unfair must meet three major conditions:
1 it must contribute to improving the production of goods or promoting technical or economic progress
2 it must be beneficial to consumers
3 it must not restrict other businesses or competition in the market in a disproportionate manner.

Competition must remain reasonably fair despite the exempted agreements, decisions or practices. The Commission is allowed to decide in individual cases that they constitute such an exceptional case, but most cases are covered by one of the regulations defining the conditions under which the Article 81(3) exceptions apply. An example of such a regulation is Regulation 2790/1999 on 'vertical agreements', which allows sole and exclusive distribution agreements when the conditions prescribed in the regulation are met. The existence of such an exception does not mean that a company can exclude all competition in the market, as case study 5.7 explains. This case also shows how the competition rules work in practice and how difficult it is for businesses to fight against unfair competition.

Case study 5.7 Distribution of sound systems in the common market

An American company selling professional sound systems for theatres and open air concerts set up a distribution network in the single market. Each distributor operated in an exclusive territory, and the territories coincided with the countries of the EU, except for Belgium and Luxembourg, where a single distributor was engaged. The Dutch distributor, a limited company located in a city close to the German and Belgian borders, developed a very good relationship with the American manufacturer. The fact that the Dutch company always sold the equipment at below the recommended price was never a problem for the American company. The German and Belgian distributors, however, were not pleased with their Dutch counterpart's competitive pricing. They saw more and more customers buying equipment from the Dutch distributor instead of from them.

Complaints by the German and Belgian distributors were ignored by the American manufacturer until its board of directors decided to sell the company. The new American management disagreed with the Dutch distributor attracting customers from the German and Belgian territories and it therefore ended the distributor's contract. However, the letter that was sent to confirm the termination of the distribution agreement did not mention the real reason. Instead, the US management declared in the letter that it had decided that in future there should be just one distributor for the Benelux countries and that the distributor for the new territory would be the current distributor for Belgium and Luxembourg. The Dutch company, which had always been a financially sound organization, now had to file for bankruptcy, leaving the almost 30 employees and management to look for other jobs in the industry.

Case study 5.7 illustrates several aspects of EU competition law. The first aspect is the question of whether EU competition rules also affect an American company operating within the single market. The positive answer to this question is known as the 'extra-territorial effect' of EU competition law.

Another aspect illustrated by case study 5.7 is that forcing the Dutch company to engage a certain price is prohibited by Article 81(1)(a). The American company's division of the common market into several territories is also prohibited by Article 81(1)(c). However, Regulation 2790/1999 on vertical agreements exempts the division of markets if the distribution network meets the requirements of the regulation. This regulation allows the American company to have distributors operating in exclusive territories, but it prohibits the distributors involved from completely closing the market to cross-border activities. Vertical agreements are allowed to contain a condition that businesses refrain from advertising for customers in territories other than their own. However, the conditions of the distributor contract and the parties' activities may not prohibit businesses from selling to customers from other distributors' territories. In case study 5.7 the Dutch distributor did not actively advertise in other territories. However, due to its competitive pricing German and Belgian customers decided to buy their equipment abroad. These activities must be allowed under EU competition rules. Unfortunately, the American manufacturer ended the distributor agreement instead.

Even though the American company had broken EU competition law, it was hard to prove that the real reason behind its termination of the distributor contract was unlawful. The American manufacturer never repeated the reason they initially gave to the Dutch distributor. Without the necessary evidence, the Dutch company could not bring a court case in the Netherlands. As explained in chapter 4, the judicial protection of EU law is provided first and foremost by the national courts.

The Dutch company was not able to make a complaint to the Commission either, because the amount of money involved in the cross-border trade was not great enough. In its 'announcement on agreements of minor importance' (de minimis) of 2001 the Commission declared that the Commission would not start any investigations in cases having little impact on the common market.

The national competition authorities also apply a certain impact level before they will start investigations against businesses involved in unfair competition. So, without the hard evidence of the real reason behind the termination of the contract, the distributor could not engage in any litigation against the American manufacturer, nor could it involve the European Commission or a national competition authority.

An example of a more successful unfair competition case was the litigation against Microsoft. This case, which led to a trial before the ECJ and the court's imposition of its highest penalty so far, is examined in chapter 4.

5.3.3.2   Competition rules according under Article 82 of the EC Treaty
This subsection explains the most important aspects of Article 82 of the EC Treaty. Article 82 prohibits any abuse by one or more businesses of a dominant position in the common market or a substantial part of it. Like Article 81, Article 82 also gives examples of how a dominant position may be abused.

First, the business or businesses must have a dominant position in the relevant market. It is only then that a business is able to abuse its position and distort fair competition.

Dominant position
According to the Commission, a business has a dominant position when it has such economic strength that it is able to prevent effective competition. Economic strength is measured in market share compared to that of the competitors.

A dominant position exists if the market share is over 70%. In many cases, however, the Commission has concluded that a dominant position existed with a market share of over 45%. Sometimes businesses have a dominant position if they have a significant role in the control of production and distribution. The conduct and performance of a business or ready access to the international capital market can also lead to a dominant position. In most cases, however, it is the market share that is decisive.

Market

In determining the relevant market, it is essential to establish the specific market to which the business sells. A manufacturer will wish to define the market as widely as possible, since this will reduce the likelihood of dominance. According to the Commission, however, markets should be defined as precisely as possible. The Commission distinguishes between product markets and geographic markets. The product market covers goods which are identical or which are looked upon by customers as interchangeable or substitutable by reason of the products' characteristics, their prices and their intended uses.

■ **Example 5.5**

United Brands is a distributor of bananas with a market share of over 45% in this particular market. United Brands claimed to be active on the fresh fruit market, where their market share was significantly lower.

The Commission stated that United Brands was active in the banana market, because a banana cannot be replaced with any other fruit (substitutability). For them to be active on the fruit market, as claimed by United Brands, a banana would have to be easily swapped for an orange. Obviously, that was not the case.

Companies may operate not only in a very specific product market, but also in a specific geographic market. The geographic market is an area in which the conditions of competition are homogeneous and which can be distinguished from neighbouring areas. Thus it may be the entire area of all Member States of the European Union, or it may be much smaller and coincide with a single national territory. In the Ice Cream case, a Dutch company supplied retailers in Ireland with freezer cabinets, either free or at a nominal charge, under the condition that they were used exclusively for the Dutch company's products. The Commission found that these exclusive dealing agreements were an abuse of a dominant position, because competitors were prevented access to the specific Irish market.

Mergers

The market share of companies that either merge or engage in a takeover will increase. If the new market share is substantial, the Commission may classify this as a dominant position. In doing so, the Commission recognizes the effect of *concentration*. A concentration is an increase in control on a lasting basis resulting from either a merger or an acquisition.

There is a major difference between a dominant position as such and a dominant position resulting from a merger or acquisition. In the Continental Can case, it was decided that mergers that eliminate competition automatically infringe Article 82 of the EC Treaty, without the necessity of proving a causal link between dominance and abuse. In other words, if two companies merge they may acquire a dominant position, and as a result they may infringe Article 82 even without abusing their dominant position.

The main question is whether the concentration will impede effective competition. If effective competition is restricted, the concentration will be declared incompatible with the common market.

Case study 5.8 is a classic example of how a company can abuse its dominant position in the relevant market.

Case study 5.8 **AKZO and the UK peroxide market**

AKZO held a dominant position in the UK peroxide market. When a new company attempted to enter the same market, AKZO would reduce its prices to below the cost of making the product. As a large international company, AKZO had no difficulty in surviving despite this pricing policy. AKZO's competitors, however, were unable to match it and were forced to abandon the UK market. In this way, AKZO was able to eliminate new competitors from the market and raised its prices as soon as the threat of competition was removed.

Source: AKZO Chemie BV v. Commission, Case C-62/86, ECR 1991 page I-3359

This case shows that abuse of a dominant position can result in the elimination of competitors from the market, eventually leading to higher prices. AKZO's low prices were intended only to rule out the competition, not to maintain a good price over a longer period of time. In AKZO's appeal against the Commission's decision, the ECJ upheld the Commission's fine.

In Grün GmbH's case there are no immediate competition problems, but the other case studies and examples show that problems may arise in the future or if a merger with another large company is announced.

Conclusions: legal aspects of the single market (sections 5.1 to 5.3)

Businesses involved in cross-border trade will meet all kinds of problems that they will have to resolve. Companies enter into contracts and use general conditions. In so doing, they cannot use a European civil code because there is no common European private law: each Member State has its own private law, which complicates cross-border trade. The EU has mainly been active in enabling cross border payments and providing new legal procedures for uncontested claims.

In Grün GmbH's case, the company encountered difficulties when importing goods from China and exporting products to Italy, due to problems in the area of public law. The company faced both financial and physical barriers erected by Member States, which are not permitted under the EC Treaty. Concerning the financial barriers, there are no exceptions to the rules of Article 25 of the EC Treaty. However, the Member States do have the power to levy taxes, and these are permitted as long as they are not discriminatory according Article 90. Concerning the physical barriers, even though the free movement of goods is enshrined in the EC Treaty, there are three exceptions to the rules of Articles 28 and 29.

Sections 5.1 to 5.3 also discussed the best way for Grün GmbH to react to the national authorities' infringements of European law. If a business that is active in the Common Market is aware of the legal implications, it may be able to save a lot of money and avoid being driven out of a market when faced with national legislation that breaches European law.

Another important aspect of the free movement of goods and services is the promotion of healthy competition in Articles 81 and 82 of the EC Treaty. Now that Grün GmbH is aware of the legal aspects of doing business in the single market, the company must pay serious attention to developing a marketing strategy and concentrating on how best to run the business in the longer as well as the shorter term. Marketing strategies are discussed in section 5.6, but the position of European manufacturing industry and its international trading relations are first explored in sections 5.4 and 5.5.

5.4 Manufacturing in Europe

With Europe as an integrated single market, one would expect to see specialization and economies of scale in manufacturing, leading to more intense competition, higher productivity and a greater supply of products at lower prices. More than 50 years after the Treaty of Rome, what are the effects of this integration?

The Dutch Central Planning Bureau (P Dekker et al, *Marktplaats Europa*, Sociaal en Cultureel Planbureau, Den Haag, 2007) estimated that intra-EU-trade was 30% to 60% higher than it would have been if the then fifteen Member States had not been members of the EU. As a result of this extra trade, the average European was earning around 10% more. However, increased market integration is not the consequence of EU policy alone, but also of a reduction in trading costs due to other factors, including technological progress. In addition, the growth of market integration can be attributed to a significant extent to integration with non-EU countries under the General Agreement on Tariffs and Trade (GATT).

Today, European manufacturing industry, comprising 2,280,000 enterprises, directly contributes around 22% of EU gross domestic product (GDP). However, it is estimated that each job in manufacturing is linked to two jobs in manufacturing-related services, so that an estimated 75% of EU GDP and 70% of jobs depend on the manufacturing sector.

How important manufacturing is for Europe and which sectors are of particular interest is examined in subsection 5.4.1. The threats faced by Europe in the international business environment are identified and discussed in 5.4.2 and, finally, some possible responses to those threats are suggested in 5.4.3.

5.4.1 How important is manufacturing for the EU?

European manufacturing is an important part of its economy and accounts for 2,280,000 enterprises, €6,930 billion turnover, €1,800 billion added value and almost 37.5 million employees in EU-27. Table 5.1 lists the principal products of European manufacturing businesses in 2006. It shows that over €260 billion of added value (approx. 4% of total added value) was contributed by the manufacturers of motor vehicles (of all types). However, the number of enterprises is declining. This is not only because of business closures, but also due to mergers, takeovers, split-offs and break-ups.

Table 5.1 **Principal products of European manufacturing companies (2006)[1]**

	Value (€ million)
Motor vehicles with a petrol engine > cm³ (including motor caravans of a capacity > 3000 cm³)	119 405
Motor with a diesel or semi-diesel engine > 1500 cm³ but <= 2500 cm³	96 646
Beer made from malt (excluding non-alcoholic beer, beer containing <= 0,5% by volume of alcohol, alcohol duty)	29 320
Radio transmission apparatus with reception apparatus	26 906
Fresh bread containing by weight in the dry matter state <= 5% of sugars and <= 5% of fat	23 219
Ready-mixed concrete	22 686
Grated: powdered; blue-veined and other non-processed cheese (excluding fresh cheese; whey cheese and curd)	21 623
Cartons; boxes and cases of corrugated paper or paperboard	18 809
Cake and pastry products; other baker's wares with added sweetening matter	18 201
Sausages not of liver	17 686
Good vehicles with a diesel or semi-diesel engine, of a gross vehicle weight <= 5 tonnes (excluding dumpers for off-highway use)	16 850
Motor vehicles with a diesel or semi-diesel engine	16 241
Grey Portland cement (including blended cement)	15226
Hot rolled flat products in coil (wide strip) of a width of 600 mm or more (of steel other than of stainless steel of of high speed steel)	14 801
Vehicles compression-iginition internal combustion piston engines (diesel or semi-diesel) (excluding for railway or tramway rolling stock)	14 712
Prefabricated structural components for building of cement	13 448
Cigarettes containing tobacco of mixtures of tobacco substitutes (excluding tobacco duty)	13 198
Vehicle reciprocating piston engines of a cylinder capacity > 1000 m³	12 581
Motor vehicles with a diesel or semi-diesel engine > 2500 m³	14 489
Fresh or chilled cuts of beef and veal	12 442

1   Excluding products of generic nature (other), sales of services such as repair, maintenance and installation; estimates.

Source: Eurostat (PRODCOM)

Globalization has had a considerable impact on the location of production. Many enterprises have extended their operations beyond national borders with the aim of (amongst other things) getting closer to their customers, circumventing trade barriers, reducing costs (of labour, transportation or source materials), guaranteeing the supply of source materials or avoiding regulation. Groups of (predominantly large) enterprises are at the core of the globalization process and can be seen as agents of cross-border transactions, as they control decisions, information flows and strategies across a range of countries.

Throughout Europe, the proportion of foreign-controlled enterprises in each of the 27 Member States is less than 6% of the total number of enterprises (with the exception of Estonia: 19.6%). However, given their relatively large average size, these enterprises often make a significant economic impact. Figure 5.3 shows that foreign-controlled enterprises generated 30% of the manufacturing sector's total value added in 2004 in the ten Member States for which data are available.

Figure 5.3 **Share of value added and employment generated by foreign-controlled enterprises, average for available Member States, 2004**

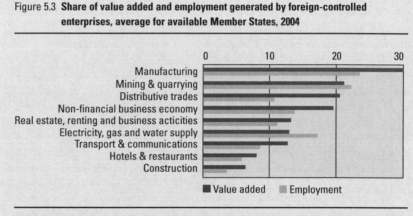

1 Weighted average based on data available from Bulgaria, the Czech Republic, Estonia, Spain, Cyprus, Latvia, Lithuania, Hungary, Austria (2003), Portugal, Romania and Slovakia.

■ **Example 5.6 Importance of the food, beverages and tobacco industry**
Food, beverages and tobacco manufacturing is a key sector for employment, employing 4.8 million people in 2004 (a 3.8% share of employment in the non-financial business economy of the EU-27). In addition, nearly three-quarters (74.6%) by value of the exports of food, beverages and tobacco products by EU-27 Member States were to other EU Member States, the highest proportion in any sector of industry.

Across the EU-27, the 296,000 enterprises in the food, beverages and tobacco manufacturing sector in 2004 generated]200 billion of value added, contributing 3.9% of the value added of the non-financial business economy. (This includes Manufacturing, Construction, Wholesale and retail, Hotels and restaurants, Transport, storage and communication, and Real estate, renting and business activities).
The food, beverages and tobacco manufacturing sector is also one of the key sectors in employment terms.

© Noordhoff Uitgevers bv

5.4.1.1 Energy consumption

A breakdown of industrial purchases of energy gives an indication of their importance in the cost structures of different activities. Averages derived from available data for 2004 show that, among industrial activities, the largest purchasers of industrial energy were the manufacturing sectors Chemicals, rubber and plastics (22.9%) and Metals and metal products (20.8%).

5.4.1.2 Shift of the manufacturing sector to low-wage countries

As detailed in subsection 5.5.2, the more developed countries of the EU have been losing ground – with respect to manufacturing their own products – to Eastern European countries and emerging economies such as the BRIC countries (Brazil, Russia, India and China).

For countries such as Germany, France and the UK to maintain a manufacturing industry, they need to adapt to manufacturing products which these low-wage countries cannot offer (or can only offer to a limited extent). The (ever-)higher standards of living, infrastructure, free enterprise and education enjoyed by the Western European countries are strengths that provide the basis for focusing on hi-tech and advanced production technologies.

Maintaining and generating more efficient channels from manufacturing plant to customers in the Western European economies may also help to prevent a shift to low-wage countries, and production improvements made possible by computer aided design (CAD), computer aided manufacturing (CAM), quality assurance/control (QA) and innovative materials handling may give the more developed countries within the EU an edge over the less developed ones.

In the chapter's opening case study, Grün GmbH outsources the manufacture of parts to a company in China, but the parts are assembled in Germany. One reason for this procedure may be that patent protection is less rigorous in China, so in order to avoid patent infringements separate parts may be manufactured at different locations. In this way the patent owner retains control of the commercialization of its products and prevents illegal selling of the end product.

5.4.1.3 Branding and promotion

Europe also hosts manufacturing facilities for multinationals from other economic blocs, such as Asia and the USA. These companies have their products manufactured in Europe for branding and promotional reasons. Their investment also needs to meet given targets for economic performance (e.g. the ability to produce a net contribution, possibly thanks to lower tariffs and quotas), market share, understanding of the foreign market and so on.

Manufacturing subsidiaries of the Japanese car makers Nissan and Toyota, for instance, are established in the UK and export from there to the rest of Europe. Many governments are happy to attract these manufacturing subsidiaries, which can become significant contributors to local economies.

In order to maintain a competitive edge, European enterprises need to engage in continuous innovation, including innovation in manufacturing. In the 2007 European Survey, 90% of management in all sectors responded that the best way to face increasing competition in the near future was by means of product innovation.

However, there were constraints on innovation, and the main ones are shown in Figure 5.4.

Figure 5.4 **Main constraints on innovation for SMEs**

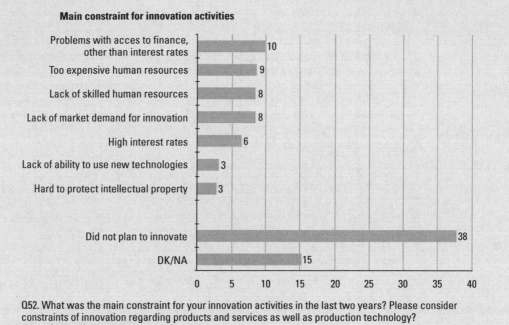

Main constraint for innovation activities

Q52. What was the main constraint for your innovation activities in the last two years? Please consider constraints of innovation regarding products and services as well as production technology?
Base: SMEs, %, EU-27

Source: The European Survey 2007

Obtaining finance for innovation in manufacturing is a problem which seems to impair growth in this sector in particular (cited by 18% of manufacturing respondents compared with 10% across all sectors). The lack of trust this implies may be due to the fact that many SMEs are run by owners/managers who know how to produce goods but are inexperienced or lack skills in negotiating finance for R&D and innovation. Another cause may be the size of the investment that is necessary, which makes risk assessment (especially in complex production technology) difficult. Examples are state-of-the-art colour printers, which may cost several hundred thousand euros, or highly advanced imaging devices for the healthcare industry, which may even cost millions of euros. Investors (including banks) may therefore be very reluctant to come forward.

The OECD (Organisation for Economic Co-operation and Development) taxonomy categorizes manufacturing according to the level of complexity of the technology involved. Table 5.2 lists the manufacturing sectors according to these levels.

Table 5.2 **OECD taxonomy based on technological complexity of manufacturing industries**

High-technology industries

353	Aircraft and spacecraft
2423	Pharmaceuticals
30	Office, accounting and computing machinery
32	Radio, television and communication equipment
33	Medical, precision and optical instruments, watches and clocks (instrument engineering)

Medium-high-technology industries

31	Electrical machinery and apparatus, n.e.c.
34	Motor vehicles, trailers and semi-trailers
24–2423	Chemicals excluding pharmaceuticals
352+359	Railroad equipment and transport equipment n.e.c.
29	Machinery and equipment, n.e.c.

Medium-low-technology industries

351	Building and repairing of ships and boats
25	Rubber and plastics products
23	Coke, refined petroleum products and nuclear fuel
26	Other non-metallic mineral products
27+28	Basic metals and fabricated metal products

Low-technology industries

36+37	Manufacturing n.e.c.; Recycling
20+21+22	Wood, paper, printing, publishing
15+16	Food products, beverages and tobacco
17+18+19	Textiles, textile products, leather and footwear

n.e.c.= not elsewhere classified)

Source: www.oecd.org/ (2003)

Many analysts believe that, if Europe is to become the world's most competitive knowledge-based economy in the near future, a strong and competitive manufacturing sector is indispensable. A European economy based on service industries alone cannot survive in the long term, but there is a clear need to transform manufacturing from a resource-intensive to a knowledge-intensive and innovative sector. This requires a competitive research & development (R&D) environment, which in turn depends on favourable EU framework programme conditions and the adaptation of education and training schemes.

While European manufacturing displays a number of strengths, such as the availability of leading-edge research capabilities in a number of Member States and the introduction of principles of sustainable development, it also has two key weaknesses: low productivity growth, particularly compared with the USA, and insufficient innovation.

5.4.2 What are the threats to the manufacturing sector?

The share of manufacturing in OECD economies is declining and this trend is likely to continue. In addition, the distinction between manufacturing and services is becoming increasingly blurred, as more and more businesses are finding out when positioning their products. Furthermore, manufacturing is becoming ever more integrated at the global level. However, although manufacturing production is declining in OECD countries, innovation in this sector continues to be dominated by OECD countries.

The Western European manufacturing sector faces growing competition from Asia and India, both of which are starting to offer lower-cost and higher-quality products by exploiting the competitive edge gained from access to new technologies. Sector-level figures show a decline in the relative importance of intra-EU-15 trade in most manufacturing sectors between 1988 and 2005. An extreme case was the textiles, clothing, leather and footwear sector, in which the importance of intra-EU-15 imports declined dramatically.

China is playing an ever increasing role in EU trade alongside the EU's traditionally strong partners: the USA, Japan and Switzerland. China currently accounts for almost 7% of manufacturing imports into the EU-15, whereas in 1988 its share was less than 1%.
The new Member States in Central and Eastern Europe are also continuing to gain strength and threaten established neighbouring markets.

Because of this increased competition, enterprises are having difficulty in maintaining their market share and therefore their revenues. Moreover, high energy prices, high labour costs and the rising cost of many half-fabricates and raw materials are reducing the profitability of the European manufacturing sector. Competition from countries that benefit from cheap labour and lower peripheral costs (e.g. in logistics and through direct access to natural resources) is making life difficult for mature European manufacturers.

Another threat and inhibitor of growth is that individual countries are reluctant to give up their quality control systems in favour of a European Standard. The single market entails, among other things, mutual recognition of each other's standards and product norms, and European Standards have been defined for a number of products (CE marking). In reality, there are many exceptions to the mutual recognition principle, however. And where an agreement has already been accepted for a specific group of products, countries are in many cases still allowed long transition periods before the arrangement comes into effect. For example, office chairs manufactured in the Netherlands may not satisfy German ergonomic standards and hence could not be sold in that country. European Standards are only applicable to a limited number of products. Harmonization and standardization of product norms will not be easily achieved. (Source: interview with Frans Alting, Team leader for international trade, North Netherlands Chamber of Commerce, 19th January 2009, ConnectEurope Convention 35)

5.4.3   What responses to these threats are available to the EU?

Despite the challenges, a revival of Western Europe's declining manufacturing sector is possible, provided that many enterprises change their culture and focus on adapting to a continuously changing economic reality. Some promising responses to the threats are:

- focusing on hi-tech and advanced production technologies. The driving force must come from business, facilitated by the EU.
- the expansion of a skilled workforce (training and education) in Europe.

5.4.3.1   Focusing on hi-tech and advanced production technologies

Change is inevitable: manufacturers must expect changes to jobs, salaries, benefits, standards of living, the economy and government policies, and must adapt the way they conduct business to these changes. If enterprises are to compete in the global manufacturing arena, they must make a determined drive towards price reduction and focus on best practice in order to minimize overheads and maximize profit.

Mature manufacturers are refining their supply chains and adapting their procurement operations, but this is not enough. Consideration must also be given to the manufacturing process. Enterprises must rethink the types and diversity of products they manufacture.

Although the European Union needs to facilitate change, by passing legislation and allocating funds to stimulate adaptation and innovation, the responsibility for change lies with businesses themselves. As we have seen, it is becoming extremely difficult for European businesses to compete on price, particularly for manufacturers of small components that can be easily shipped around the world and are not dependent on short lead times. Low-tech self-assembly products and mass-produced items are almost impossible to undercut. To survive – and indeed thrive – in this highly competitive marketplace, manufacturers must utilize their expertise and hone it to their advantage.

European manufacturers need to focus on improving throughput and reducing inventory, by manufacturing to order rather than stockpiling, especially in sectors affected by cyclical demand. They also need to strive for zero-defect manufacturing, to retain their global reputation for quality. A commitment to continuous improvement in this field is imperative. Further, they must automate a high proportion of their labour-intensive manual operations, to reduce the monthly wage bill. A firm commitment is needed to upgrade or replace underperforming equipment and facilities. Low-tech components and products should be outsourced to manufacturers in low-cost countries.

Change in the manufacturing sector will not be driven by a major leap forward. Gradual progress is far more likely, and enterprises cannot wait. They must look at their own businesses and begin to make the changes that can give them a competitive advantage in the future. The sooner these enterprises adapt to today's global manufacturing market, the better for countries with mature economies.

■ Example 5.7 Unilever

Paul Polman, CEO of the Dutch–British food and body-care giant Unilever, has stated that the company can still grow in Europe (Interview in *NRC Handelsblad*, May 2009). This, he believes, will be accomplished by an efficient supply structure and more tailored marketing in the various countries. Growth will also be accomplished by means of product innovation; examples are pyramid-shaped tea bags, small Magnum ice sticks and hair-minimizing deodorant.

The EU must continue to:
- invest in research and innovation in order to encourage the development of technologies that the rest of the world desires but cannot necessarily develop for itself
- protect discoveries and intellectual property as an incentive to innovators
- develop framework programme conditions to stimulate innovation and entrepreneurship.

In 2000, the EU launched the Lisbon Programme, with the aim of becoming the world's most advanced knowledge-based economy by 2010. It proposed spending 3% of GDP on research (approximately €4 billion annually) by 2010. The European Research Council uses funding allocated by Lisbon to attract researchers from all over the world in fields including health, nanotechnologies, the environment and energy. EU research funding also aims to increase co-operation between Member States by prioritizing projects that bring together research centres, enterprises and universities from different countries.

The Commission has grouped the Lisbon Programme initiatives under eight 'key measures with a high European value-added' to focus policy making. The eight key measures are:
- supporting knowledge and innovation
- reform of state aid policy
- simplification of the regulatory framework
- completion of the internal market for services
- global agreement on the Doha Round (The Doha Development Round or Doha Development Agenda is the current round of global trade negotiations by the World Trade Organization (WTO), which commenced in November 2001. Its objective is to lower trade barriers around the world, enabling countries to increase global trade.)
- removal of obstacles to physical, labour and academic mobility
- developing a common approach to economic integration
- supporting efforts to deal with the social effects of economic restructuring (e.g. job losses).

Unfortunately, the results are not guaranteed. Factors limiting the effectiveness of the programme include ageing populations, especially in the major European markets, and a decline in productivity growth due to falling labour quality and slowing investment growth. Also, investment in Europe in general is falling behind.

In order to benefit from EU policies and investment, the manufacturing sector needs to change in a number of ways. First, change should have the desired effect of moving the sector from a resource-based to a low-carbon, knowledge-based model. For example, the sector should capitalize on the availability of leading-edge research capabilities in a number of Member States and introduce principles of sustainable development. Second, industry will have to move from mono-disciplinarity to a model based on multi-competence and multi-disciplinary innovation, in which the added value will be achieved through collaboration across sectors and national borders. This means that processes of innovation centred on the strengths within an industry will give way to processes that exploit the strengths of other industries or sectors. In the medium term, added value will come primarily from the increasing convergence of the three most revolutionary industries: microelectronics, nanotechnology and biotechnology. Third, production will move from the macro scale to the micro and nano scales (in applications such as medicine, electronics and energy production).

In the current EU environment, the hi-tech manufacturers have the best potential for growth. The hi-tech sectors are:
1 Aircraft and spacecraft
2 Pharmaceuticals
3 Office, accounting and computing machinery
4 Radio, television and communication equipment
5 Medical, precision and optical instruments, watches and clocks

The following subsections briefly discuss some key data (number companies, turnover, number of employees) on the high potential sectors and propose one or more possible solutions to strengthen and increase its competitiveness.

Aircraft and spacecraft
In 2004, the EU-27's aerospace equipment manufacturing sector consisted of 2,200 enterprises, which created € 25 billion of value added, 14.1% of the transport equipment manufacturing total. This share of value added was considerably higher than the sector's 11.9% contribution to the EU-27's transport equipment manufacturing workforce, implying high labour productivity.

The aerospace equipment manufacturing sector is highly concentrated within the EU and the USA, and within a few large manufacturers with a pyramidal supply chain: manufacturers of aircraft, missiles, space equipment and engines are at the top of the pyramid, above a second tier of suppliers making systems and medium-sized enterprises producing structural elements and components, and a final tier of SMEs contributing materials, software and services (note that these may be excluded from data on this sector, as their principal activity may not be the manufacture of aerospace equipment). There are two main market segments for the aerospace sector, military and civilian, with the former dependent on government defence spending plans and the latter cyclical.

Aerospace equipment manufacturing is one of the most important manufacturing sectors in terms of research & development (R&D). Table 5.3 shows the level of intramural R&D expenditure by this sector in seven of the Member States (which collectively accounted for over

80% of EU-27 value added in this sector). In these Member States alone, intramural R&D expenditure by this sector exceeded]6.5 billion. The sector's contribution to manufacturing R&D was particularly significant in France and the UK, the two EU-27 Member States most specialized in this sector.

Table 5.3 **Manufacture of aircraft and spacecraft (NACE Group 35.3): Intramural R&D expenditure in selected Member States, 2004**

	R&D expenditure (€ million)	Share of manufacturing R&D expenditure (%)
DE	1 327.7	3.2
FR	2 603.1	16.7
AT	3.9	0.2
PT	0.3	2.5
RO	0.2	3.2
SE	220.9	3.7
UK[1]	2 400.2	19.1

1 Share of manufacturing R&D expenditure, 2003.

Pharmaceuticals

In 2004, the pharmaceuticals manufacturing sector of the EU-27 consisted of approximately 4,400 enterprises which generated €59.5 billion of added-value, almost a quarter (23.8%) of the value added contributed by chemicals, rubber and plastics manufacturing as a whole. A huge proportion (90.2%) of the value added generated by the pharmaceuticals sector came from the pharmaceutical preparations manufacturing subsector, the remainder coming from the manufacture of basic pharmaceutical products (see table 5.4).

Table 5.4 **Manufacture of pharmaceuticals, medicinal chemicals and botanical products (NACE Group 24.4): Structural profile, EU-27, 2004**

	No. of enterprises (thousands)	Turnover (€ million)	Value added (€ million)	Employment (thousands)
Pharmaceuticals, medicinal chemicals and botanical products	4.4	180 171	59 541	589.8
Basic pharmaceutical products[1]	0.8	16 500	5 840	70.0
Pharmaceutical preparations[1]	3.5	164 000	53 700	520.0

1 Rounded estimate based on non-confidential data.

New marketable medicines are usually the result of years of painstaking R&D, and according to the European Federation of Pharmaceutical Industries (EFPIA) only three in ten new products will produce revenues that more than cover their R&D costs. The importance of R&D in this sector is underlined by the fact than on average around 10% of all manufacturing R&D expenditure in 2003 was made by pharmaceutical enterprises.

The profitability of the pharmaceuticals manufacturing sector in the EU-27, as measured by the gross operating rate (the percentage of total production capacity being utilized), was notably higher than for chemicals, rubber and plastics manufacturing as a whole, with a rate of 15.9% in pharmaceuticals manufacturing compared to 12.0% overall. The highest gross operating rates in this sector were recorded in Ireland (46.8%, 2003), Sweden (41.7%), Slovenia, Hungary and Belgium (each a little over 30%).

Progress in this sector is likely to be achieved in the following areas: closer collaboration with centres of excellence; increasing R&D efficiency, with input from academics and EU and government bodies, resulting in reduced time to market; improving business models to serve smaller markets.

Office, accounting and computing machinery

The electrical and optical equipment manufacturing sector generated]189.7 billion of value added in 2004, contributing 3.7% of the value added created across the EU-27's non-financial business economy. The 196,400 enterprises active in the sector employed 3.6 million people across the EU-27, accounting for 2.9% of the non-financial business economy workforce. The sector includes 161,400 people employed by 9,700 enterprises in computer and office equipment manufacturing (see table 5.5).

Table 5.5 **Manufacture of computers and office equipment (NACE Division 30): Structural profile, EU-27, 2004[1]**

	No. of enterprises (thousands)	Turnover (€ million)	Value added (€ million)	Employment (thousands)
Computers an office equipment	9.7	59 500	11 500	161.4
Office machinery	1.0	5 500	1 800	31.8
Computers and other information processing equipment	8.7	54 000	9 710	130.0

1 Rounded estimate based on non-confidential data.

This sector operates within an established legislative framework that covers issues such as product safety, energy labelling, minimum efficiency requirements, eco-design and waste. The best options for dealing with future challenges seem to be continuous implementation of innovative technologies and building on the experience and expertise available in the countries that are currently strong in this sector (including Germany, Hungary, Ireland and the UK).

Radio, television and communication equipment

The radio, television and communication equipment sector employs 812 400 people in 28,500 enterprises. Two subsectors, engaged in the manufacture of electronic valves and tubes and other electrical components and the manufacture of television and radio transmitters and apparatus for line telephony and line telegraphy, each employed about 300,000 people across the EU-27 in 2004, with the remainder of the sector's workforce (185,000 or 22.8%) employed in the manufacture of television and radio receivers, sound or video recording and reproducing apparatus (see table 5.6).

Table 5.6 **Manufacture of radio, television and communication equipment (NACE Division 32): Structural profile, EU-27, 2004**

	No. of enterprises (thousands)	Turnover (€ million)	Value added (€ million)	Employment (thousands)
Radio, TV & communication equipment	28.59.7	201 024	51 057	812.4
Electronic valves and tubes and other electronic components[1]	9.0	60 000	16 554	310.0
Television and radio transmitters and apparatus for line telephony and line telegraphy[2]	14.2	92 000	:	300.0
Television and radio receivers, sound or video recording or reproducing apparatus and associated goods[2]	5.7	48 809	9 197	185.2

1 Rounded estimates based on non-confidential data; value added, 2003.
2 Rounded estimates based on non-confidential data.

Technological innovation in radio, television and communication equipment has lead to miniaturization, digitization and convergence into multifunctional products (such as third-generation mobile phones incorporating high-speed internet access and video telephony). Competition and short product lifecycles are drivers for European manufacturers to innovate. In this context, the EU Framework Programmes on research & development may provide platforms for sharing ideas and innovating. The energy efficiency of products is an area of change, and innovation in this area, in combination with sustainable production, could generate added value in this sector.

The EU Framework Programmes are notorious for their administrative complexity when it comes to handling applications for programmes or projects and requests for R&D subsidies; simplification and transparency would help SMEs, especially, to make greater use of this EU resource.

Medical, precision and optical instruments, watches and clocks (instrument engineering)

The manufacture of medical, precision and optical instruments, watches and clocks and activities related to the manufacture of these products are collectively referred to here as 'instrument engineering'. One million people were employed by 92,700 enterprises in the instrument engineering sector in 2004, accounting for 28.3% of the electrical machinery and optical equipment manufacturing workforce (see table 5.7).

Table 5.7 **Instrument engineering (NACE Division 33): Structural profile, EU-27, 2004**

	No. of enterprises (thousands)	Turnover (€ million)	Value added (€ million)	Employment (thousands)
Instrument engineering[1]	92.7	127 680	51 376	1 020.0
Medical and surgical equipment and orthopaedic appliances	59.3	46 821	19 614	434.2
Instr. and appl. for measuring, checking, testing, navigating and other purp.[1]	16.9	52 963	21 062	360.0
Industrial process control equipment	7.4	11 560	4 175	91.9
Optical instruments and photographic equipment[1]	8.0	15 000	6 000	120.0
Watches and clocks[1]	1.2	1 500	540	13.0

1 Rounded estimates based on non-confidential data.

An important characteristic of this sector is the close link between the instrument manufacturers and the users, who are often universities, research organizations and the R&D departments of industrial enterprises. Key drivers for the development of the instrument sector are the research system (universities, research organizations, funding system, incentives, etc.) and the industry's willingness to use new technologies. The key strengths of this sector are the workforce's high level of education and qualifications and the quality of production. Assembly, automation and engineering are also strengths in the global context.

The general weakness of Europe's instrument engineering sector is seen in the marketing and commercialization of new technologies, entrepreneurship and time to market. More effort should be put into the commercialization of R&D activity in this sector. The area of nanotechnology seems especially promising for manufacturing. The sector may also gain a competitive edge by capitalizing on the general trend towards sustainable development.

This sector is relatively labour intensive and countries that are currently strong in this sector, such as Germany, Slovenia and Sweden, are primary candidates to strengthen the sector in Europe.

5.4.3.2 Expansion of a skilled workforce in Europe: training and education

In 1987, the European Commission set up a unique arena for stimulating innovation in the EU. Erasmus, the EU's flagship education and training programme, enables 200,000 students to study and work abroad each year, as well as supporting co-operative ventures between higher education institutions across Europe. Around 90% of European university-level institutions take part in Erasmus and 1.9 million students have participated since it started. More than 3,100 higher education institutions in 31 countries participate, and even more are waiting to join. The annual budget is in excess of €400 million.

The overall aims of Erasmus are to create a European Higher Education Area and foster innovation throughout Europe. Its actions include supporting enterprises by means of student placements and visits from foreign lecturers and by enabling co-operation between universities.

The European Commission has integrated its various educational and training initiatives (including Erasmus) under a single umbrella, the Lifelong Learning Programme, with a significant budget of nearly €7 billion for 2007–2013. By helping European citizens to acquire new skills, knowledge and qualifications, the programme also aims to bolster the competitiveness of the European labour market.

5.5 The import and export of European goods

The formation of a single EU market has made trade much easier than it was before integration. However, exporting to another EU country can still be difficult and costly for an enterprise, owing to the often substantial economic and socio-cultural differences, of which language is only one.

Europe is lagging behind other economically developed areas, and therefore success and failure factors are identified and discussed in subsection 5.5.1. Subsection 5.5.2 examines macroeconomic information on the importance of trade for Europe and, finally, subsection 5.5.3 suggests strategies for improving trade (especially for SMEs).

5.5.1   What are the success and failure factors for exporting?

Irrespective of the entry strategy selected by an enterprise, the road to successful exporting presents many challenges. Based on the experiences of the many enterprises that have tackled these challenges, six important factors can be identified for successful exporting. These are:

- commitment by the company's management
- an exporting approach founded on a strong skills base
- a good marketing and information communication system
- production capacity and capability, product superiority, competitive pricing
- effective market research
- an effective national export policy.

It is obvious that management must be committed to its export strategy, but it is often less obvious that, when an enterprise starts exporting, it is embarking on a 'learning curve' and it may not reap the benefits of its export strategy for many years. Management also has to assess which skills are needed and whether these are present within the company or must be hired on a temporary or permanent basis or outsourced. SMEs usually start by outsourcing expertise and gradually integrate these skills into the company on a more permanent basis.

Marketing, communication and market research are discussed in some detail in section 5.6.

Figure 5.5 summarizes the main constraints businesses encounter when exporting their products. The figures are from SMEs exporting within and/or outside the EU; overall, seven out of ten enterprises export to countries within the EU.

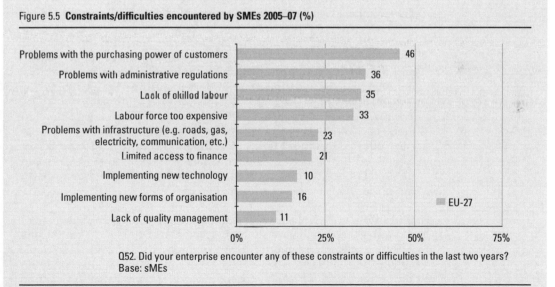

Figure 5.5 **Constraints/difficulties encountered by SMEs 2005–07 (%)**

Constraint	%
Problems with the purchasing power of customers	46
Problems with administrative regulations	36
Lack of skilled labour	35
Labour force too expensive	33
Problems with infrastructure (e.g. roads, gas, electricity, communication, etc.)	23
Limited access to finance	21
Implementing new technology	10
Implementing new forms of organisation	16
Lack of quality management	11

■ EU-27

Q52. Did your enterprise encounter any of these constraints or difficulties in the last two years?
Base: sMEs

Source: The European Survey 2007

Besides the problem of finding a customer base able to afford the products offered (46%), two problem areas emerge as affecting most European businesses: the problem of stringent administrative regulations (36% of SMEs claim to have faced difficulties in this area) and the issues of the availability (35% report problems) and cost of appropriate human resources (33%).

The largest European enterprises are the least concerned about the issue that most troubles European SMEs: the purchasing power of customers. According to managers of SMEs in most industry sectors, this is their most important problem. Only 29% of LSEs (Large-Scale Enterprises, employing at least 250 workers) encountered problems with the purchasing power of their customers, while 46% of SMEs were affected by this difficulty. LSEs are most concerned about administrative regulations (38% as against 36% of SMEs) and the lack of skilled labour (42% as against 35% of SMEs).

The case of Grün GmbH perfectly illustrates the administrative regulations an enterprise may encounter in its export activities. In Germany and Italy, 8–10% more SMEs than in other EU countries reported difficulties over administrative regulations in 2005–07 (the EU-17 average was 36%). Apparently, when it comes to actually doing business in the single European market, the stimulation of cross-border trade aimed at by the EU is not yet working very well in these two countries.

Grün identified three export destinations of interest: Italy, France and Spain. If the constraints of administrative regulations are considered alone, Spain would have been the most attractive: only 11% of the enterprises surveyed mentioned this factor as being a burden for their business with Spain. For Italy and France the response was 45% and 37% respectively.

5.5.2 How important is exporting for European companies?

The number of exporting SMEs in the EU increased from 64,500 in 2000 to 72,870 in 2007, an increase of 13%. However, in the European Survey 2007 fewer than one in ten SMEs (8%) reported any turnover from exports, which is significantly lower than the corresponding proportion of large enterprises (28%). This indicates that in general international trade is more important to large enterprises than to SMEs.

The main export obstacle for SMEs is their lack of knowledge of foreign markets (13% of exporting SMEs mentioned this as their prime obstacle), followed by import tariffs in destination countries and the lack of capital (both 9%). Ways of coping with lack of knowledge are discussed in subsection 5.5.3.and section 5.6. Where to look for solutions to import tariff obstacles is also suggested in 5.5.3.

Within the EU, involvement in export varies greatly: some small, open economies report a relatively high involvement in exports (in Estonia 23% of SMEs have some turnover from exports, in Slovenia 21%, in Finland 19%, in Denmark 17%, etc.) and some of the small economies are quite closed, with a low proportion of SMEs involved in exports (Cyprus 3%, Bulgaria 4%, Malta 6%). SMEs in some of the largest EU countries have little involvement in cross-border trade, most notably in Spain (3% have turnover from exports) and France (6%). In Germany, exporting SMEs amount to 9%, in Italy 7% and in the UK 9%.

Distance plays an important role in trade: in general, the greater the distance between countries, the more limited trade between them will be. (This may be one reason why the management of Grün GmbH decided to start by exporting to Italy rather than Spain.)

Figure 5.6 shows the main export destinations of enterprises in the EU. As might be expected, the most popular destinations are within the EU: of the 8% of EU SMEs that export their products, 82% export within the EU and only 12% to the rest of the world.

Figure 5.6 **Main export destinations of enterprises in the European Union**

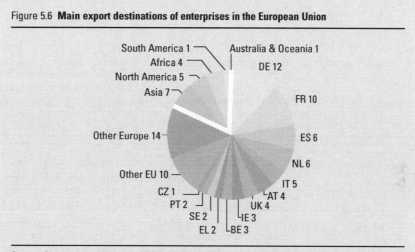

Source: *Observatory of European SMEs, Analytical report of fieldwork November 2006–January 2007,* Flash Eurobarometer 196, The Gallup Organization

The favourite export destinations – the UK, Germany and France, Spain, the Netherlands, Austria and Italy – also belong to what could be called the 'inner circle' of EU trade.

Looked at on the global scale, EU trade with the rest of the world in 2007 amounted to €2.7 trillion. Table 5.8 summarizes EU trade with its five main partners worldwide. Trade with the emerging market China has increased very rapidly during the first decade of the twenty-first century.
Trade with India, another major emerging market, is still modest: it occupies ninth place with 2.1%.

Table 5.8 **EU trade in goods with the top five partners in 2007**

The major import partners				The major export partners				The major trade partners			
Partners	€ millions	%		Partners	€ millions	%		Partners	€ millions	%
World	1,426,008	100.0		World	1,239,919	100.0		World	2,665,926	100.0
1 China	231,516	16.2	1	USA	261,463	21.1	1	USA	442,567	16.6
2 USA	181,104	12.7	2	Switzerland	92,787	7.5	2	China	303,273	11.4
3 Russia	143,880	10.1	3	Russia	89,100	7.2	3	Russia	232,980	8.7
4 Japan	78,104	5.5	4	China	71,757	5.8	4	Switzerland	169,487	6.4
5 Norway	76,841	5.4	5	Turkey	52,641	4.2	5	Japan	121,861	4.6
	Total	49.9			Total	45.8			Total	48.7

Source: http://trade.ec.europa.eu/doclib/docs/2006/september/tradoc_113366.pdf

5.5.3 Purchasing

Enterprises not only sell their products in global markets, but also purchase significant amounts of their inputs (raw materials, energy, capital, etc.) on foreign markets. The average EU SME purchases 12% of its inputs abroad, excluding labour (4% of workers come from abroad).

The percentage of inputs purchased abroad is the highest in Europe's smallest and most open economies: Malta (46%), Luxembourg (40%), Ireland (35%), Estonia (31%), Iceland (27%) and Cyprus (27%). By contrast, some of the largest European countries are the least reliant on foreign resources, especially France (6%), Italy (8%), Germany (9%) and Spain (10%), but also the Czech Republic (9%) and Norway (10%).

It seems that it is the size of the host economy rather than the size of the enterprise that most affects the proportion of inputs purchased abroad. The negative correlation between the size of economies and the proportion of inputs purchased abroad is relatively strong: the smaller the economy, the higher the percentage of inputs purchased abroad. Of course, this is hardly surprising; the bigger the national economy, the higher the chance that a company will find its resources within the country.

Section 5.4.3 reviewed the importance of the five hi-tech industry sectors and discussed ways in which they could remain competitive. The following subjections give import and export figures for these sectors.

Aircraft and spacecraft
In 2006, the total trade in aerospace equipment by the EU-27 states was fairly evenly split between intra-EU and extra-EU trade. Extra-EU exports were valued at €39.2 billion, some 51.5% of total exports, and extra-EU imports were valued at €29.5 billion, equivalent to 49.9% of total imports. Some 22.3% of the EU-27's exports of transport equipment to non-member countries in 2006 were accounted for by aerospace equipment, while these products' share of transport equipment

imports was 28.9%. France, Germany and the UK dominated trade in aerospace equipment, accounting together for 84.1% of exports by EU-27 states and 78.5% of imports.

Pharmaceuticals
A higher proportion of pharmaceutical products was exported by EU-27 states to non-member countries in 2006 than the average for chemicals, rubber and plastic products as a whole (39.0% as against 32.6%). The trade was dominated by intra-EU exports. The value of extra-EU exports of pharmaceuticals was €69.8 billion (a 6.4% share of industrial exports), and the main markets for these exports were the USA (35.1% of extra-EU exports) and Switzerland (13.1%). Although the value of EU-27 imports of pharmaceutical products increased to €39.9 billion in 2006 (3.2% of industrial imports), the trade surplus widened to €29.8 billion. As well as being the main markets for exports of pharmaceutical products, the USA and Switzerland were the sources of the overwhelming majority of pharmaceuticals products imported from outside the EU 27 (a joint share of 78.8% split fairly evenly between them).

Germany and Belgium were the principal exporters of pharmaceutical products, accounting for 20.2% and 18.1% respectively of (intra- and extra-EU) exports by the EU-27 states.

Office, accounting and computing machinery
The EU-27 had a trade deficit of €51.2 billion for office machinery and computers in 2006, which represented a substantial widening of the deficit recorded in 2005 (€42.3 billion) and an acceleration of the trend noted since 2001. The trade deficit in 2006 was a result of EU-27 imports valued at €80.1 billion (almost two fifths of which came from China) and exports of €28.9 billion. Computers and other information processing equipment represented 89.8% of total exports and 92.5% of total imports in 2006.

Among the Member States, the Netherlands was the largest trader, exporting (intra- and extra-EU) €39.2 billion worth of office machinery and computers and importing €39.5 billion worth of these products.

Radio, television and communication equipment
The EU-27 had a trade deficit in radio, television and communication equipment of €36.0 billion in 2006. Imports of radio, television and communication equipment from non-member countries into the EU-27 were valued at €99.5 billion in 2006, the majority of these goods coming from countries in the Far East, including China (32.6%), South Korea (12.6%) and Japan (10.8%). Overall, intra-EU imports accounted for a slightly more than half (54.4%) of the total value of radio, television and communication equipment imports by the EU-27 states, underlining the importance of the internal market for these goods. The UK and Germany were the main traders in radio, television and communication equipment, with a combined share of 41.6% of the value of EU-27 states' (intra- and extra-EU) exports and 37.6% of their imports.

Medical, precision and optical instruments, watches and clocks (instrument engineering)

In 2006, the EU-27 recorded a trade surplus with non-member countries of €6.9 billion in medical, precision and optical instruments, watches and clocks, resulting from exports valued at €54.1 billion (a little over a quarter of the total value of electrical machinery and optical equipment exports) and imports valued at €47.2 billion. Exports of medical, precision and optical instruments, watches and clocks to non-member countries were almost as valuable as trade in these goods between Member States, accounting for 47.9% of all exports by EU-27 states. Germany, Ireland and the Netherlands were the main traders in this sector.

5.5.4 How can the export of goods be increased?

This subsection presents ways in which exporting by European companies might be increased. To achieve this requires both changes on the part of European enterprises and facilitating a more favourable European environment on the part of the European Commission.

Innovation

When an enterprise exports for the first time, this constitutes innovation for that enterprise. But a business making (specialized) innovative products often has to go abroad, because of the small size of the domestic market (e.g. the Netherlands). And if an enterprise is active abroad, it may be confronted with new competitors, new ideas and other challenges. These could be incentives to innovate still further, in order to stay ahead of the competition. So in fact the circle closes, where innovation leads to exporting and exporting to innovation.

This is the main reason why the Chamber of Commerce of the Netherlands has opted for an integral and comprehensive approach in its consulting practice, in its organization and in its co-operation with external partners. This organization believes that it is no longer possible to isolate international trade from a business's other core activities.

Communication skills

Enterprises (especially SMEs) should set a higher priority on language skills in order to successfully export their products. One of the key findings of a study commissioned by the Directorate General for Education and Culture of the European Commission in December 2005 on the use of language skills by SMEs and their impact on business performance was that a significant amount of business is being lost to European enterprises as a result of a lack of language skills. It was estimated that 11% of exporting European SMEs (945,000 enterprises) may be losing business because of communication barriers. The survey identified a clear link between languages and export success.

Four elements of language management, which can be combined in different ways, were found to be associated with successful export performance: taking a strategic approach to multilingual communication, appointing native speakers, recruiting staff with language skills and using translators or interpreters. An SME investing in one or more of these four elements was calculated to achieve export sales 44.5% higher than one that failed to invest in them.

For large companies, the highest priority is to communicate in global languages other than their own, such as Spanish, Mandarin and Russian. Russian (along with German and Polish) is extensively used in Eastern Europe, French is used to trade in areas of Africa and Spanish is used similarly in Latin America. Longer-term business partnerships depend upon relationship building and relationship management. To achieve this, knowledge of the target country culture and language is essential.

Simplification and harmonization of regulations
9% of European companies reported import tariffs in destination countries as a major obstacle to exporting. Table 5.9 shows which instruments, already provided in the 1957 Treaty of Rome, are available to combat barriers to exports.

Table 5.9 **Specific measures in the Treaty of Rome in respect of the free movement of goods**

obstacles	instruments
mutual tariff barriers to trade	elimination of mutual import tariffs (1958-1968)
quantitative import and export restrictions	reduction of quotas
national interventions in agricultural markets	common agricultural policy
non-tariff barriers	policy harmonization

The instruments established by the are not yet fully benefiting businesses. National regulations can still interfere; for instance, the time it takes to export a product to Greece and Portugal is three times the average for exports to Austria, Finland and Sweden. Even within the customs union, with a common external tariff and internal free movement, the differences between Member States are significant. Simplification of import and export regulations by individual Member States may reduce those differences and make it easier to trade with and within the EU.

Differences in technical standards also continue to constitute an important obstacle to the free movement of goods, because the principle of mutual recognition is not always properly applied and harmonization is often slow in coming. A new proposal from the European Commission may reduce these obstacles. In addition, improved foreign access to public tenders for government projects may promote the integration of the goods markets.

Grün GmbH, faced with the obligatory assessment of its magnetic components prescribed by Italian law, would certainly benefit if such harmonization were already in place between Germany and Italy.

5.6 The marketing of goods in Europe

The job of a European marketer is a challenging one. When this role is compared with that of his or her American, Indian or Chinese counterpart, it becomes clear that in order to serve a market of comparable size the European has to shift from domestic to international marketing activities. Consequently, the European marketer has to deal with importing and exporting, and with such issues as cross-cultural considerations and the adaptation of product positioning.

The diversity of the EU market is enormous. Many EU countries have small populations: 15 of the EU-27 countries have a population of less than 10 million. Successful companies originating from these countries will very soon have to consider exporting their products. At the other end of the scale, Germany is the biggest national market in Europe (82 million), followed by France (64 million), the UK (61 million), Italy (58 million) and Spain (40 million). These countries are quite often the first foreign markets to be targeted by exporters.

In the non-financial business economy, there were almost 20 million enterprises active within the EU-27 in 2005. The overwhelming majority of these (99.8%) were SMEs, employing fewer than 250 people. Their relative importance was, however, lower in terms of their contribution to employment and wealth creation: only 67.1% of the non-financial business economy workforce was employed by an SME, while 57.6% of the non-financial business economy's value added was generated by SMEs.

Subsection 5.6.1 describes some features of the European internal market which may be important to commercial managers. Some aspects of practical relevance to conducting market research within Europe are discussed in 5.6.2, and 5.6.3 examines aspects relevant to international strategy and factors to be taken into consideration when introducing products and/or maintaining market share in existing markets. Finally, 5.6.4 describes the impact that the internet has had and continues to have on European business.

5.6.1 The EU internal marketplace

The first advantage of market integration and of creating an EU internal marketplace is that countries can specialize in the production of goods in which they have a relative advantage. For consumers, this implies an ample supply of goods at a low price. The second advantage is that businesses are able to produce on a larger scale and hence more cheaply. Development costs can be spread over a large number of products, so the price remains low and innovation is encouraged. Swedish furniture is a good example of this: with extensive supplies of wood, Sweden has been able to specialize in wooden furniture, and because of the large sales market, prices have remained low and innovation has proved profitable.

The third advantage of a large integrated market is the spreading of risk. For consumers, for instance, this means that they are more likely to be able to obtain a product if they can source it from several countries. The fourth advantage is that information is exchanged more freely and, as a consequence, innovation will take place at a faster pace.

The EU offers several opportunities intended to reduce the constraints on businesses operating in the common European marketplace (see also section 2.6). When asked about the relative importance of the major features of the internal market, over a third of European managers commented that these opportunities were not relevant to them, either because they only operate domestically or for some other reason. In particular, micro-enterprises and those active in the construction sector tended to respond that the question was irrelevant in their case.

The majority of SMEs in the EU consider the fact that several Member States share the same currency to be the most important feature of the internal market from their enterprise's point of view. The proportion is not significantly higher within the euro zone, which indicates that SMEs inside and outside the euro area benefit approximately equally from the common European currency. The larger an enterprise, the more likely it is to consider the euro an important opportunity: 57% of LSEs regard the common currency as very or rather important, while 'only' 25% of micro-enterprises regard it as very or rather important from their own perspective.

SMEs in the EU – at least, those who do not dismiss the idea of doing business in the internal market – also acknowledge the importance of EU-wide harmonized standards: the proportion of managers who think this is a very or rather important feature of the internal market (39%) is significantly larger than those who think it is not at all or not very important for them (24%).
The responses reveal a significant difference between SMEs (30% see benefits in EU standards replacing national ones, 53% do not) and LSEs (38% as against 46%). Despite this variation, the majority of managers in all industry sectors and sizes of enterprise see no benefit in EU standards replacing national ones.

From a customs point of view, only selling goods to non-EU countries is considered as exporting. Nevertheless, from the perspective of the businesses concerned, selling to other EU countries is still definitely exporting. Foreign markets – including foreign EU markets – are very different from the home market. Differences in culture, language, consumer preferences and distribution channels all play very important roles in this perception. However, the euro has made international operations easier and less risky.

This book is concerned with the multi-faceted business environment within Europe. However, to put this in perspective it is helpful for a marketer – just for a moment – to consider how globally operating companies (for example, multinationals such as Unilever, Microsoft and Shell) perceive the EU. How attractive would this economic entity seem to them, either as a market or as a supplier? Table 5.10 presents a SWOT (strengths, weaknesses, opportunities, threats) analysis of the EU, listing a few of the major factors that may be relevant to decision making.

Table 5.10 **SWOT analysis of the EU as a single market compared with other global economic blocs (not comprehensive)**

Strengths	Weaknesses
• Advanced infrastructure (roads, air, waterways) • Innovative force due to cultural and economic diversity • Diversity in businesses (risk spreading) • Proximity (over land) of huge market area (e.g. Russia) • Long history and experience of international trade • High standard of living across the EU • High coverage of internet users	• Scattered knowledge and experts • Cultural and language barriers • Lack of energy sources and therefore dependency on non-EU suppliers (e.g. Russia) • Fragmentation, both institutional and regulatory • Taxation differences • Paucity of hi-tech SMEs • Complex legal and regulatory environments for enterprises developing intellectual property • Too many programmes providing different levels of financial support for different reasons
Opportunities	**Threats**
• Globalization • Emerging markets • Economic growth of developing countries generating new markets for hi-tech products	• Economic recession • Emerging growing economies (e.g. India, China) offering cheaper products and labour

Note that many features could be identified which are strengths in a historical perspective (e.g. harmonization, EU constitution, single currency) but do not offer added value in the current situation when considering the EU's attractiveness as a single economic entity compared with other global economies.

5.6.2 Market research within Europe

It is beyond the scope of this book to discuss the various market research methods available to underpin strategic and operational decisions, and there are many excellent textbooks on this subject. It suffices here to mention a few specifically European factors that need special attention when collecting data to inform decisions on market-entry strategies and operational marketing.

European (international) market research plays an important role in developing a framework for making important strategic marketing decisions about a business's international operations. The business needs to gather information that is accurate, timely and relevant, in the face of the cultural, economic and/or legal constraints that may exist in another country. Data collection techniques used in the domestic market cannot necessarily be replicated internationally, and the data collected internationally cannot be interpreted in the same manner as it is domestically.

The key marketing decisions that need to be made relate to the marketing mix:
- Which market, how and when to enter
- Whether to enter, leave or expand activities
- Whether to add, delete or modify products in the international market
- How to determine the appropriateness of promotional activities
- How to assess the relationship between price and demand
- How to secure distribution channels and the logistics of getting products to consumers.

An enterprise that needs to carry out market research within Europe can choose to work either with an international market research organization with experience in Europe or with a market research organization in the target country. Business research organizations are located in many areas of Europe. An important selection criterion is the experience an organization has in the enterprise's industry, sector or specific products.

It is important to consider whether online or face-to-face market research is the best method of collecting responses to the research questions. Web-based services can prove a convenient alternative to person-to-person research methods, which are more time-consuming and often more costly. Many research organizations provide online options alongside their face-to-face services. Data can be collected by means of:
1 focus groups
2 surveys
3 panels
4 studies
5 interviews
6 data collection.

There are hundreds of market research organizations in Europe. Reed Business Information and Ezilon provide information on a large number of these, giving the marketer a wide choice of organizations from which to choose. The EUbusiness website (www.eubusiness.com/) is the leading independent online business information service about the European Union. Founded in Luxembourg in 1997, the site is owned and managed by EUbusiness Ltd in the United Kingdom. It provides news and information for business professionals, updated daily, about EU policy, legislation, economic data and opportunities.

A few market research organizations are mentioned here; a sensible first step is to check their websites to establish the relevancy of their services to one's own business. In Europe, market research companies include AC Nielsen BASES (with offices in many European countries), Desk-Research Nederland (a Dutch company), Veraart Research (serving all European countries), Experience Solutions (a UK-based company) and Intelace (serving Poland and Eastern Europe). UK-based Infiniti Research provides Web-based B2B (business-to-business) research and other research services. Harte-Hanks, a European company with offices in the UK, Germany, France, Spain and Belgium (and other locations) offers online focus groups and Web surveys. Zoomerang, which has an office in the UK, offers online panels and other market research services. PMR Research, serving Poland and Eastern Europe, offers self-administered online surveys and other research options. UK-based Syclick offers survey design software, which enables the user to create Web- or email-based surveys.

Even defining one's research objectives carefully and selecting the best qualified market research organization does not always guarantee a successful outcome. The collection of and analysis of primary data in European countries may encounter several obstacles. Some problems associated with primary data are:

- Ability to communicate opinion: the existence of 27 different cultures, governments and educational systems may complicate questioning and objective interpretation of surveys. The self-reference criterion (tendency to evaluate the international situation in terms of one's own domestic culture) in commercial managers may influence interpretation in relation to ethical and moral issues.
- Willingness to respond: open and closed societies may have a different impact on response rates.
- Sampling: variations in population density and between rural and urban areas may complicate comparable sampling between countries.
- Language and comprehension: translation and interpretation costs can be very high.
- Respondent bias: cultural differences may shape answers according to social status or taboos existing in certain countries.
- Non-response bias: the reason for non-response may differ between countries and therefore interpretation of (similar) results may be different. Extrapolating the findings to reach conclusions for the total population may therefore not be justified.

5.6.3   European marketing strategy and operations

This section systematically discusses some key aspects of the challenging world of the European marketer, starting with strategic information and ending with how a European marketer can use the tools available in the marketing mix. First, the reasons why enterprises want to internationalize are briefly discussed. Then the various options for entering a foreign market are reviewed, including some pros and cons when selecting an entry strategy. Competition within Europe and how EU legislation and harmonization may help or hinder European marketing are dealt with next. Finally, features of operational marketing in Europe are explained in terms of using the marketing mix.

5.6.3.1 Why do companies internationalize?

First, it is important to know why a (successful) company takes the risk of starting to do business abroad. The reasons will most probably influence the entry strategy adopted and management's commitment to embarking on this internationalization adventure. In general, there are seven reasons:

1. opportunity development
2. leveraging key success factors abroad
3. following customers abroad
4. pursuing diversification
5. taking advantage of economies' different growth rates
6. exploiting differences in product life cycle
7. internationalizing for defensive reasons.

In order to establish the chances for success, management needs to determine the attractiveness of the industry (macro-level), the sector (meso-level) and the enterprise (micro-level). This information is most probably available for the domestic market, but the data should also be collected and evaluated for each targeted foreign market.

In the opening case study of this chapter, reasons 1 to 3 in the list above were the predominant drivers for change for Grün GmbH. This means that Grün GmbH must establish the attractiveness of its industry (magnetic parts) and of two sectors (automotive and medical instruments) for France, Italy and Spain by focusing its marketing communication on aspects of those three drivers. Tools for determining this attractiveness include DESTEP analysis (of demographic, economic, social, technological, ecological and political factors) and Porter's Five Forces model.

5.6.3.2 Which market-entry strategies can be used?

The simplest and quickest way to enter a foreign market is by exporting. An enterprise may use this option, for instance, to sell its overcapacity due to a saturated domestic market. The downside of this option is that the enterprise will gain limited knowledge of the foreign market and will be very dependent on the demand of the foreign buyer (retailers, wholesalers, etc.). For long-term strategic reasons a more sustainable entry strategy is advisable. Table 5.11 gives an overview of the main strategies and options for entering a foreign market.

The single market has made it easier to conduct international business in the EU, and therefore the choice of entry strategy is determined more by cost efficiency (e.g. locating production in low-wage Eastern European countries) and by commercial factors related to interesting foreign target markets than it is by entry barriers. Another effect of the EU is that the harmonization process has largely eliminated import restrictions, and therefore there is now less need for companies to invest directly in a foreign market (FDI) within the 27 Member States.

It is important to note that the choice of any strategy involves a trade-off between several factors: investment (costs), knowledge of the foreign market, profitability, (quality) control of the marketing and sales activities, and short- versus long-term commitment. Figure 5.7 illustrates how these factors relate to the various strategies.

Table 5.11 **Market-entry strategies**

Strategy	Options	Comments
Export-based entry	• Indirect exporting • Direct exporting • Sales office in the foreign market • Licensing • Franchising	The most common way for SMEs to export is by appointing an agent or distributor (direct exporting). The advantage over indirect exporting (through export merchants) is more control over the marketing mix.
Manufacturing-based entry (FDI)	• Joint venture • Acquisition • Merger • Greenfield operation (building one's own manufacturing plant)	This strategy is initially very expensive due to asset and management costs. There have been many mergers in the pharmaceutical industry, especially in the last three decades. The merger of Hoechst (German) and Rhone-Poulenc Rorer (French) to form Aventis is considered one of the most successful. (See section 7.7 for a detailed discussion of the pros and cons of mergers.)
Relationship-based entry	• Contract manufacturing • Strategic alliance • Countertrade	A prerequisite for success with this entry strategy is to build and maintain a long-term relationship.

Figure 5.7 **Alternative market-entry strategies**

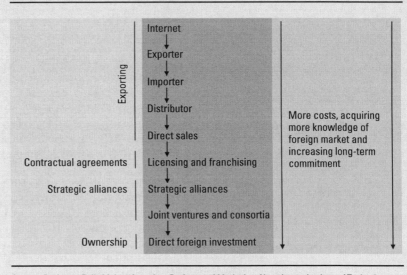

Source: Professor Rajiv Mehta, Associate Professor of Marketing, New Jersey Institute of Technology, Newark, N.J. © 2005 The McGraw-Hill Companies, Inc. (adapted)

The impact on an enterprise's management of setting up a foreign subsidiary or starting a joint venture is high, as figure 5.7 shows. However, there are many reasons for accepting the high risks involved. Figure 5.8 shows what the main drivers are for European SMEs.

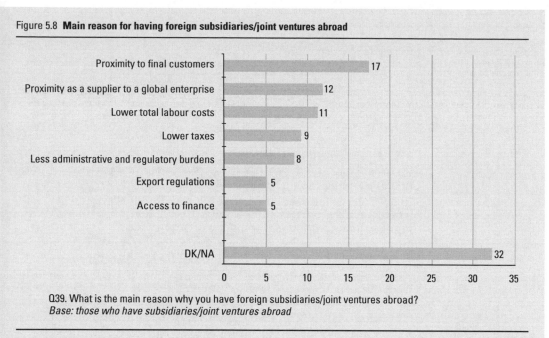

Figure 5.8 Main reason for having foreign subsidiaries/joint ventures abroad

Proximity to final customers	17
Proximity as a supplier to a global enterprise	12
Lower total labour costs	11
Lower taxes	9
Less administrative and regulatory burdens	8
Export regulations	5
Access to finance	5
DK/NA	32

Q39. What is the main reason why you have foreign subsidiaries/joint ventures abroad?
Base: those who have subsidiaries/joint ventures abroad

Source: The European Survey 2007

The motivations for setting up a foreign business are markedly different for different sizes of business. LSEs create partnerships to get closer to their final customers, whereas SMEs and micro-enterprises are more likely to indicate the proximity of the corporation(s) of which they are suppliers.

The foreign business partners of EU SMEs are primarily located in the EU itself: 77% of the locations of all joint ventures and foreign subsidiaries mentioned by EU SMEs are in other EU-27 states. Partnerships outside the EU are in the expected regions: Asia, North and Latin America and Africa.

The contribution of such partnerships to the income of enterprises ranges from only 7% (large-scale European enterprises) to 2% (SMEs).

Case study 5.9 **Berg Toys BV**

Berg Toys BV is a well-known Dutch company. It is the world market leader in manufacturing, selling and exporting pedal go-karts, trampolines and tricycles, and its products have a reputation for excellent quality, sustainability and strength. Three-quarters of Berg's revenue derives from foreign markets. It supplies 3,000 dealers in 26 countries, consumers, schools and crèches, and is active in the area of recreational products. All Berg products have CE certification and are tested for safety by the inspection bodies TÜV and SGS. The trampolines are tested and approved by the TÜV and AIB-Vinçotte.

When it first started exporting to France, Berg Toys used a direct export strategy. However, cultural differences, communication problems and the distance involved were reasons for changing to an indirect export strategy. Berg Toys now exports to France via third parties.

The company's first step before entering the French market was to consider every stage with the aid of a checklist. These stages included visiting potential clients, starting a collaboration based on a few years' experience and – in individual cases – intensifying the collaboration. The limiting factors for France were also considered: high commission payments and difficulty of access to import certificates.

The distributor network in France can supply several target markets. Distributors are identified through consumer fairs and business-to-business fairs. In Berg's indirect export strategy, every product group has its own exclusive distributor.

The head office of Berg Toys handles all the export activities for the Benelux countries and Germany. For these countries a direct entry strategy was used, and this has proved successful because of cultural overlap and easier communication.

5.6.3.3 Competition within Europe

Increased trade produces increased competition, which reduces profit margins and pushes prices down. This leads to higher production by a smaller number of businesses, after the least productive businesses have left the market. Average productivity per employee therefore rises as a result of increased competition due to trade.

An empirical fact underlying this effect of trade is that the productivity of businesses (and their workers) varies. One business produces efficiently, at low cost, and is profitable. Another produces much less efficiently and is barely able to avoid bankruptcy. The increased competition that results from opening up markets leads to a reduction in profit margins, so that the more productive businesses survive.

The majority of European enterprises perceive an increase in competition, and this perception is common to all sectors. The response to this intensification of competition is to put more effort into their products (quality and differentiation) and marketing.

The question arises: how have the changes brought about by a single European market affected the competitiveness of businesses? Figure 5.9 shows how important some of these changes are considered to be. The majority of EU enterprises consider having the same currency in most Member States to be the most important feature of the internal market from their enterprise's point of view.

One would expect large corporations to be more strongly in favour of harmonized technical standards than small companies. There is also a difference in attitude between the various sectors: the manufacturing and trade sectors do see benefits in EU standards replacing national ones, but in the healthcare, personal services and hospitality sectors most managers are pessimistic about the possible gains from the substitution of EU standards for national ones.

5.6.3.4 Single European market legislation and harmonized technical standards

This topic is also discussed in section 5.1. One of the objectives of the EU is to realize an internal, single market in which products can be traded freely without any trade restrictions. The adoption of harmonized European product legislation and CE marking offers manufacturers and exporters great advantages by eliminating the differing national product regulations imposed by Member States of the EU and the states of the European Economic Area (EEA). This should benefit and stimulate international trade within the EU.

Figure 5.9 **Opportunities offered by the EU internal market, % EU-27**

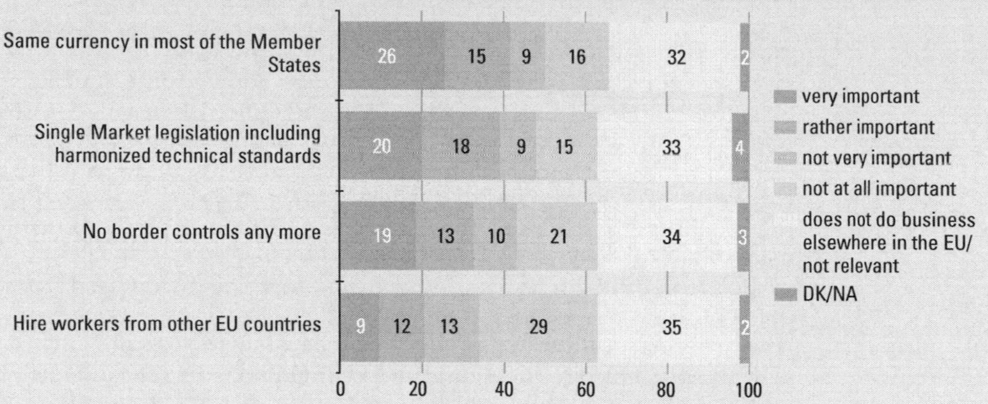

	very important	rather important	not very important	not at all important	does not do business elsewhere in the EU/ not relevant	DK/NA
Same currency in most of the Member States	26	15	9	16	32	2
Single Market legislation including harmonized technical standards	20	18	9	15	33	4
No border controls any more	19	13	10	21	34	3
Hire workers from other EU countries	9	12	13	29	35	2

Q26. The following question is related to the possibilities that the internal market of the European Union offers. Please tell me how important each of the following possibilities is for your enterprise's ability to do business in the European Union.

Source: The European Survey 2007

This new European legislation has far-reaching consequences for industry, both within and outside the EEA. Manufacturers and exporters are now confronted by new health and safety requirements for their products. They must comply with mandatory EU regulations, carry out associated procedures and develop systems for complying with health & safety and documentation requirements.

■ **Example 5.8 REACH for trade in chemicals**
On 29th October 2003 the European Commission adopted a proposal for a new EU regulatory framework for chemicals, COM (2003) 644 (updated in 2006). Under the new system, named REACH (Registration, Evaluation, Authorisation and restriction of CHemical substances), enterprises that manufacture or import more than one tonne of a chemical substance per year are required to register it in a central database. The aims of the new regulation are to improve the protection of human health and the environment while maintaining the competitiveness and enhancing the innovative capability of the EU chemicals industry. REACH also gives greater responsibility to industry to manage the risks from chemicals and to provide safety information on the substances. This information is passed down the chain of production. Since the introduction of REACH, delays and costs have been substantially reduced in the chemicals trade.

CE marking is proof of conformity to European standards and enables manufacturers and exporters to circulate products freely within the EU. It indicates that the manufacturer has satisfied all the assessment procedures specified by law for that product. Although consumers may perceive the CE marking as a quality mark, it is not. It addresses itself primarily to the national surveillance authorities of the Member States, and its use simplifies their task. Just looking at the CE marking will not tell the surveillance authorities with which directive a given product complies; it is the 'declaration of conformity' that contains the details of the directive(s) with which the product complies and the standards that were relied upon in ensuring compliance.

The New Legislative Framework, the modernization of the New Approach for the marketing of products, was adopted in Council on 23rd June 2008 and finally published in the Official Journal on 13th August 2008. According to the Enterprise and Industry Directorate General (http://ec.europa.eu/enterprise/newapproach/index_en.htm), this broad package of measures, which has the objective of removing the remaining obstacles to free circulation of products, represents a major boost for trade in goods between EU Member States. It will bring particular benefits for SMEs, who will no longer be discouraged from doing business outside their domestic markets. Existing market surveillance systems for industrial products will be strengthened and aligned with import controls. These measures will reinforce the role and credibility of CE marking. In addition, trade in goods which do not fall under EU legislation will be improved. From now on, a Member State that intends to refuse market access will have a duty to talk to the enterprise and to give detailed objective reasons for any refusal, making life easier for businesses.

This package of measures will have an impact on a large number of industrial sectors, representing a market volume of around €1500 billion a year. The objective of the package is to facilitate the functioning of the internal market for goods and to strengthen and modernize the conditions for placing a wide range of industrial products on the EU market. The package builds on existing systems to introduce clear Community policies which will strengthen the application and enforcement of internal market legislation.

The Enterprise and Industry Directorate General (DG) works to ensure that EU policies contribute to the sustainable competitiveness of EU enterprises and facilitate job creation and sustainable economic growth. It plays a major role in implementing the Lisbon strategy. The DG pays particular interest to the needs of manufacturing industry and SMEs. The DG is responsible for the management of a large volume of legislation on the internal market. This accumulated body of law covers the provisions on industrial policy and SMEs, and legislation in the field of industrial products, including over 482 directives. It provides a valuable information tool known as the 'Pink Book', which is a structured list of the legislation for which the DG is responsible. The 'Pink Book' is a valuable resource for those working in the area, providing a comprehensive listing per sector of the applicable legislation which is updated twice a year to take account of legislative developments.

5.6.3.5 Aspects of operational marketing

Once a target country has been selected, a strategic and operational marketing plan must be written. A practical and efficient way of producing such a plan is by summarizing the external (market) and internal (company) factors in a SWOT analysis and creating a SWOT matrix. This matrix enables management to compare different strategy options and decide which one(s) they feel most comfortable with. The option chosen will most likely differ for each target country. For SMEs, the driver for entering a foreign market is very often a combination of the quality of management and serendipity (opportunity for development). There are no recipes for successful internationalization other than total management commitment, thorough analysis and careful planning.

Once a decision has been made, data must be collected and a marketing plan produced for the selected country. It is important to give the strategy time to succeed: perseverance is required and there is no such thing in international business as 'instant success'. SMEs especially should bear in mind that costs precede benefits and make a conservative estimate of the time it will take to achieve a return on their investment.

Both qualitative and quantitative analysis are necessary for the implementation of the marketing plan. Fortunately, a number of excellent websites can be consulted for benchmarking, industry and country analysis in Europe.

In the EU, the marketing budgets of private companies range from 2.6% to 5% of annual revenues. However, the economic downturn and more intense competition will probably cause this percentage to rise in the near future. In response to fiercer competition, the primary strategy of SMEs is to enhance product quality and intensify their marketing efforts. Increasing working hours, looking for new markets abroad and especially cutting production are seen as last-resort strategies.

Case study 5.10 A European marketing strategy for ECCO, a Danish shoe manufacturer

ECCO was founded in 1963 and is today a global shoe brand. ECCO is a vertically integrated company, spanning the globe: it has fully owned tanneries in Indonesia, Thailand, China and the Netherlands, production facilities in Denmark, Portugal, Slovakia and India, and sales subsidiaries in most European countries as well as in Asia and in North and South America. An important element in the development of ECCO's position is an accelerating process of making the ECCO brand visible among retailers, and the number of new stores opened is growing year by year. In 2008, the number of ECCO stores increased by 135, in line with ECCO's ambitious growth strategy, which aims at increasing the number of ECCO stores to 1,500 by the end of 2013. Today (2009) ECCO has more than 800 stores and shop-in-shops in 91 countries around the world.

The New Member state countries, especially Poland, Hungary and the Baltic states, are all considered very important growth markets by ECCO. ECCO has chosen to be a first mover in many of these markets, as well as in Ukraine and Russia, in order to establish the ECCO brand. Distribution and sales are organized through long-term contracts with local

retailers and chains on a cash basis, thus involving low investment and minimum risk for ECCO. If needed, ECCO is prepared to consider forming joint ventures with local agents or establishing fully owned ECCO shops in order to satisfy increasing demand, as it has done in many Western countries.

The accession of new Member States will stabilize the ECCO strategy to continue production and expand sales in the region, and if need be to contribute by making direct investments in retail structures. More important for the ECCO strategy are the prospect of long-term, high economic growth to ensure increased sales and the establishment of predictable legal structures to safeguard against fraud and arbitrary infringements of contracts.

Although most of the new EU countries produce shoes locally, ECCO does not regard the competition as very serious. One reason for this is that production costs in these countries – especially wages, which are very important in shoe production – are likely to increase quite rapidly, in line with the general rise in the standard of living, following membership of the EU. Therefore the main competition in the coming years is more likely to derive from China, a major shoe producer whose exports will no longer be limited owing to its WTO membership.

5.6.3.6 The marketing mix

The marketer's proven formula for marketing and selling products is the 4 Ps: Product, Price, Place and Promotion – the 'marketing mix'. Using the marketing mix most effectively is challenging, especially in Europe. When drawing up a positioning strategy for a product in another European country, one needs to find out for each P how it may be affected by national and EU regulations. Each P is discussed separately below in the European context.

Product

A business's product is its offering to the market in exchange for payment, which in turn determines profit. Careful product planning in an international context is therefore critical to a company's success in European markets. The European marketer is faced with a number of important product-related decisions. These include branding strategies, brand-name strategies, degree of adaptation or standardization, packaging and labelling. An inexperienced European enterprise will usually make these decisions in the domestic market prior to any export activity. Product decisions for European markets must always be made with careful consideration of their impact on the other elements of the enterprise's international marketing mix.

An excellent way of examining all aspects of a product is to use the Product Component Model. Figure 5.10 illustrates all the components a marketer has to assess and evaluate in order to bring a product to the market. The single EU market has not (fortunately) eliminated the range of cultures and the differences in needs and wishes for products across Europe, and therefore many components of B2C (business-to-consumer) as well as B2B products may have to be adjusted to foreign markets.

Modifications may involve aspects of all three layers illustrated in figure 5.10: the core components (e.g. technical issues and performance standards), the packaging components (e.g. branding) and the support services components (e.g. warranty and servicing issues). The relevance of some of these components in the European context is discussed below.

Product branding

Brand names are an important component of product marketing in the international context: the marketer must decide whether to use a single European brand name, regional brand names, a different brand name in each country or the company name as a brand name. Language differences between the domestic and target countries will influence these branding decisions.

Trademarks

Registration of trademarks in other European countries may be necessary to protect against intellectual piracy and may necessitate modification of the product, together with its branding and packaging.

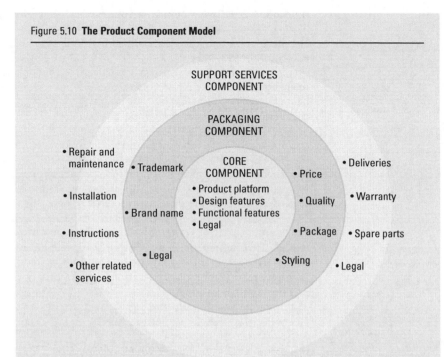

Figure 5.10 **The Product Component Model**

SUPPORT SERVICES
COMPONENT

PACKAGING
COMPONENT

CORE
COMPONENT
• Product platform
• Design features
• Functional features
• Legal

• Repair and maintenance
• Trademark
• Price
• Deliveries
• Installation
• Quality
• Warranty
• Brand name
• Instructions
• Package
• Spare parts
• Legal
• Other related services
• Styling
• Legal

Warranty and servicing issues
European marketers need to ascertain what the minimum warranty and guarantee periods are for their product line in each country. Who is to be responsible for repairing faulty goods during the warranty and guarantee periods (an intermediary or the manufacturer) must be determined early in the European product planning process. The company should also research customer expectations on warranty and servicing periods early in the process.

Legal components
There may be European legal requirements affecting international product decisions in all three layers of the model (see 5.6.3.4 above). The factors determining whether a similar product can be marketed in different European markets and whether modifications are necessary include:
· cultural similarities/differences between Member States
· national directives or guidelines in each Member State relating to minimum product standards
· differing consumer attitudes towards the product within each Member State
· whether consumers in each Member State can afford the product
· the strength and activities of competitors.

■ **Example 5.9 Does modification of a medical device for the French market
pay off?**

The medical and surgical equipment and orthopaedic appliances sector in the
EU comprises 593,000 enterprises with 434,200 employees. In France, however, health insurance funds are facing deficits, leading to cost pressures on
manufacturers. There are also rigid control systems regulating a number of
high-cost devices, including medical devices. As a result, a number of high-
cost devices are restricted throughout the country.

Lengthy bureaucratic procedures and low reimbursement levels further reduce
the attractiveness of this major European market. And, although the reuse of
medical devices is banned, making it more attractive to export to France, the
tight national regulations will most probably require too many modifications
to medical devices for foreign manufacturers to enter the French market.

The standardization versus adaptation dilemma involves both internal
factors (the competencies and resources of the enterprise) and external
factors (DESTEP). Factors that encourage product standardization include:
1 high costs of adaptation
2 nature of the product
3 convergence of conditions between countries
4 economies of scale in manufacture
5 economies in marketing
6 economies in research & development
7 economic integration between countries
8 variation in consumer needs and tastes
9 competition.

Factors that support product adaptation include:
1 legal requirements
2 differing conditions of use
3 variations in purchasing power
4 government influence
5 different consumer tastes and behaviours
6 different physical environments
7 lack of adequate support systems.

EU integration can be said to have had a positive effect on product
branding. Marketers in Europe increasingly have to consider national
branding versus EU branding, and a shift can be seen from national
product positioning (and branding) to EU branding. Examples of companies with pan-European branding are IKEA and LEGO (see also case
study 5.10.).

In general, EU integration has had a favourable effect on products. It
has stimulated competition and therefore led to more rapid innovation. This has increased product diversity and availability. The increase
in pan-European competition has also had a positive effect on the
product quality.

The Ecodesign Directive provides consistent EU-wide rules for improving the environmental performance of energy-using products (EuPs) through ecodesign. It prevents disparate national legislation on the environmental performance of these products from becoming an obstacle to intra-EU trade. This should benefit both businesses and consumers, by facilitating the free movement of goods across the EU and by enhancing product quality and environmental protection.

EuPs are products which use, generate, transfer or measure energy (from electricity, gas or other sources). This includes not only consumer goods such as boilers, water heaters, computers, televisions, but also industrial products such as transformers, industrial fans and industrial furnaces. EuPs account for a large proportion of the energy consumption in the EU.

On 16th July 2008, the Commission proposed to extend the Ecodesign Directive to a wider range of products in order to cover all energy-related products (ErPs). In addition to EuPs, ErPs include other products which do not consume energy, but which impact on energy consumption. For example, windows, insulation materials and water-using devices (e.g. shower heads and taps) do not consume energy but can contribute to saving energy.

The Commission proposes to amend only the scope of the Ecodesign Directive: the basic principles and the decision-making process of the current directive should remain unaltered, in order not to disrupt its ongoing implementation.

Promotion

The role played by promotion in European marketing is the same as its role in domestic marketing; that is, communicating with audiences to achieve desired outcomes. The international marketer has a number of communication tools for reaching the intended audience. These tools are advertising, sales promotion, personal selling and public relations.

To make clear how promotion can be made effective in the European market, a widely used communication theory is first illustrated (see figure 5.11) and briefly explained.

Figure 5.11 **Basic communication theory**

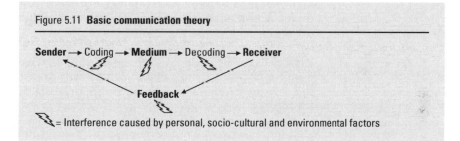

Sender → Coding → **Medium** → Decoding → **Receiver**

Feedback

= Interference caused by personal, socio-cultural and environmental factors

First, the Sender (a person, business or brand) wants to convey a message. Before the sender sends the message, the communication is encoded so that is suitable for the Medium to be used. This medium should be appropriate for the product and the (foreign) environment. It is important to know how much a given medium (e.g. TV, internet, radio) is used in the targeted market, because the penetration of different media varies from country to country. For example, newspapers have maintained their lead in Central and Northern European countries (Denmark, Finland, Germany, Sweden, etc.), but television is the leader in advertising investment in Mediterranean countries (France, Greece, Italy, Portugal and Spain).

How the Receiver receives (decodes) the message will depend on factors such as whether the content is interesting, the message is clear, the translation of the language is accurate, and the words, actions, pictures or sounds are appropriate. Feedback enables an assessment of whether the communication's objectives are being achieved. The timing of the feedback (immediate or delayed) is dependent on the type of communication strategy employed.

Interference distorts the message and disrupts the communication between sender and receiver. Technical and external factors may contribute to interference: competitive activity is a major source of 'noise', but so is poor-quality reproduction or transmission of printed, audio or visual material. Interference can also be caused by erroneous interpretation of social norms, local tastes and preferences, as well as by the religious and moral standards that prevail in a given country.

One reason for misinterpretation of the potential European customer by the marketer is the country-of-origin effect (COE). This refers to any influence that the country of manufacture (i.e. the exporter's domestic market/country) has on a consumer's positive or negative perception of a product. The COE affects brand image and becomes a more complex issue when a product is being promoted in multiple European countries.

The time element in promoting a product is analysed with the aid of the AIDA model: Attention, Interest, Desire, Action. ('Action' refers to buying the product and is the most difficult stage to communicate effectively.) The model assumes that, in order to reach the last A (Action), customers will always have to go through the first three phases. This fixed sequence implies that communication must address the appropriate phase according to the product's life cycle. For instance, McDonalds' communication strategy in Europe is focused exclusively on the Action phase of the AIDA model, but introducing any new product means first generating Attention.

Parallel to the decision on product adaptation versus standardization, European marketers must make an important strategic decision regarding their promotional campaigns in international markets. Key issues for this decision include:
· Is consumers' desire for the product local or European?
· Is differentiation required(because of language differences, availability of media outlets, government controls and competitors' activities) and, if so, how much?
· Do all aspects of the promotional mix require differentiation? If not, which do, and how much differentiation of each one?
· What is the availability of intermediaries (e.g. media buyers, advertising agencies) and what is their role in the promotional effort?

The trend to increased standardization of European advertising is due to three factors: the convergence of consumer behaviours, the internationalization of the media, which enables the delivery of transnational campaigns, and the legislative framework of harmonization due to internal market integration. Two benefits of standardization are particularly clear: the opportunity to exploit the same brand image across Europe and the possibility of obtaining economies of scale in campaign productions. More and more businesses are recognizing the convenience of a pan-European marketing and communication strategy. However, in European promotion two levels of activity have to be considered: objectives, targeting and campaign production tend to be more standardized, while media planning and buying tend to be more adapted to local markets.

The EU has an important role in ensuring the appropriate usage of promotion by businesses across Europe. The European policy for the 27 Member States has three main objectives:
· to create an open and unified European market
· to have the 'right' amount of competition in that market
· to encourage fair competition unhampered by market abuse and restrictive practices.

These objectives should benefit the efficient promotion of products throughout Europe. However, harmonization of product promotion (marketing communication in general) across the EU Member States turns out be more difficult than expected. European legislators need to find a balance in order to develop directives acceptable to all the EU Member States, who are individually responsible for their consumer protection. Examples of 'problem area's are:
· marketing to children and other vulnerable groups
· marketers and animal welfare and other environmental concerns
· the use of 'shock' advertising
· the promotion of greed and excessive behaviour
· the sale and promotion of potentially dangerous products (e.g. alcohol, tobacco, pharmaceuticals, fireworks).

Moreover, the governments of the EU Member States regulate the use of media for promotion in the interest of protecting their citizens from undesirable influences. Such regulations relate to:
· the product that can be promoted
· the content of what is said
· by whom it is said
· how it is said
· the time at which it is said
· the medium used.

In transnational advertising campaigns, marketers need to consider not only the national laws, self-regulatory rules and systems in all the EU countries, but also the European Advertising Standards Alliance (EASA). EASA was created in 1992 and promotes responsible advertising by providing detailed guidance on how to go about self-regulation in advertising across the single market for the benefit of consumers and businesses. EASA has helped to set up several self-regulatory systems in Europe over the years and still continues to promote self-regulation at both national and European level, by informing the European institutions of the benefits of advertising self-regulation. Especially at the European level, EASA has been successful in promoting self-regulation as an alternative to detailed legislation.

In 2004 the advertising industry signed the EASA Advertising Self-Regulation Charter, in which the advertisers, the agencies and the media pledged to make self-regulatory systems across the whole of Europe stronger and more effective. This involved setting up systems in some of the new EU countries, which did not yet have a self-regulatory system, and strengthening the already existing systems. Building on the charter, EASA secured a number of commitments and reported back to the European institutions by the end of 2007. The report found that, although further improvements could be made, many of the self-regulatory organizations (SROs) had met or were on their way to meeting the commitments put in place.

One of the ways in which EASA strengthens and consolidates self-regulation is by providing SROs with 'best practice recommendations'. EASA currently has best practice recommendations in the following areas:
- code drafting and consultation
- communications and awareness
- complaint handling
- confidentiality
- copy advice
- jury composition
- monitoring of advertising
- publication of decisions
- substantiation.

EASA's cross-border complaints system has been in operation since 1992. It was set up in response to the forthcoming single market and the need to address problems arising from advertising circulating in one EU Member State but carried in media originating in another. It provides a complainant with the same redress available to consumers in the country of origin of the media in which the advertisement appears.

There are two basic principles behind the cross-border system. The first is 'country of origin', a concept enshrined in EU law to facilitate the growth of the single market. In the case of the cross-border complaints system, an advertisement must comply with the rules of the country where the promotional medium is based (or, in the case of direct mail advertising, the country where the consumer is based). The second principle is 'mutual recognition', meaning that EASA members agree to accept advertisements which comply with the self-regulatory rules in the country of origin of the media, even if those rules are not identical to their own.

In 2008 EASA co-ordinated the handling of 120 cross-border complaints (in 2007 the number was 92, in 2006 128 and in 2005 116). Sixty cases related to 'rogue trading' (involving either bogus directory publishers or other types of scams). Of these 60 complaints, 35 were transferred to the appropriate authorities for further action. The remaining cases could not be pursued because the operators could not be identified or located (for example, because they were operating from PO boxes).

Finally, EASA has been involved in several research projects, including the monitoring of advertisements in more controversial areas such as food and alcohol to check whether they adhere to the code. Not only does EASA provide information to members of the public and researchers interested in the advertising self-regulatory issue, it also actively informs policymakers and the advertising industry of the newest developments.

In addition to EASA, there are several trade associations (such as the Institute of Sales Promotion (ISP), Institute of Practitioners of Advertising (IPA), Institute of Public Relations (IPR) and Direct Marketing Association (DMA)) which help marketers to avoid making major mistakes when promoting their products.

The European marketer will always have to deal with a dynamic EU that offers many opportunities and threats. However, the greater the marketer's understanding of the EU, the better equipped he or she will be to interpret the challenges correctly and translate them into a winning and profitable pan-European business strategy.

■ **Example 5.10 If these products were promoted in another country, would they sell?**
- *Alu-Fanny*: French foil wrap
- *Crapsy Fruit*: French cereal
- *Kum Onit*: German pencil sharpeners
- *Plopp*: Scandinavian chocolate
- *Pschitt*: French lemonade
- *Atum Bom*: Portuguese tuna
- *Kack*: Danish sweets
- *Mukk*: Italian yogurt
- *Pocari Sweat*: Japanese sport drink
- *Poo*: Argentinian curry powder

Place (Distribution)
Experts estimate that more than half of all world trade is handled through agents and distributors. Given this estimate, the selection of the right agent and/or distributor is critical.

The choice of how to distribute is based on the costs an enterprise is willing to incur and how much control it wishes to have over the process (see the discussion of export strategy in subsection 5.5.3). The distribution function in European marketing is a crucial exercise, because if it is not well executed, a manufacturer's product cannot be sold, regardless of how good that product is. The manufacturer and its intermediaries must have a clear, common objective to ensure a long-term win–win situation for all parties.

European marketing organizations typically spend some time recruiting, motivating and nurturing their international distribution channels to ensure that an appropriate level of market coverage and customer service is achieved. The marketing organization must make important decisions about the roles that the channel members will play in the European market and how they will be compensated for their efforts.

European distribution is different from domestic distribution for the following reasons:
- Distances travelled in international distribution are (usually) greater than those in domestic distribution.
- There are usually more channel members associated with European distribution.
- National factors such as culture, laws and business ethics make European distribution more challenging.
- The level of customer service provided in international markets tends to be lower than in the domestic market. Relevant characteristics of the final consumer in the target country are: expectations of service, place of purchase (e.g. supermarket versus other retail outlets) and expectations of after-sales service (if applicable).
- The reputation of proposed channel members with final consumers is important.
- The distance consumers in the target country are prepared to travel to buy the product is a limiting factor.
- European distribution involves intermediaries not usually required in domestic distribution (e.g. freight forwarders, export merchants).
- European distribution requires the exporting manufacturer to rethink its product's packaging in order to factor in differences in climate and the distance the product must travel.

Intra-European distribution is different from extra-European distribution (e.g. in the USA, China, Japan or Latin America) for the following reasons:
- Distances travelled in extra-EU distribution are even greater than those in intra-EU distribution.
- National factors in the extra-EU context may even be more challenging than intra-EU differences.
- In extra-EU distribution the use of intermediaries may be more complex.
- In extra-EU distribution taxes, tariffs and administration may be different and costs may be higher.
- Extra-EU distribution may be complicated by import barriers.

The advantages of an enterprise managing its own distribution in a European market are:
- more control over the distribution function in the European market
- easier expansion of the distribution function (if required)
- a greater presence/visibility for the business in the international market
- long-term economies of scale are possible (especially if the market for the product expands)
- possible cost savings in the long term (once initial set-up costs have been absorbed) since there are no ongoing payments to channel members.

To increase the efficiency of the distribution channel, a business may manufacture and/or store its products in another country. Motives for manufacturing abroad include reduction of transportation costs, but also elimination of duties (in the EU), access to raw materials and cheap labour, demonstration of strong commitment to a local market and avoidance of restrictions on imports.

The advantages for a business of locating warehousing and storage in the foreign market are:
- greater control over the distribution function
- relative freedom to locate the facilities anywhere in the international environment
- freedom to determine the size, shape and layout of the storage facility
- opportunity to defray part of the set-up and running costs of the facilities by subcontracting storage space to other businesses.

The disadvantages of locating warehousing and storage in the foreign market are:
- the facilities may be costly to establish and to maintain
- permission may be withheld by the foreign government
- the location and size of the facilities may be determined by the foreign government (and may therefore be unsuitable).

Distribution channels for industrial goods are likely to differ from distribution channels for consumer goods. Typical differences include the following:
- Industrial products usually have shorter distribution channels.
- There is a greater reliance on international distributors of industrial goods to perform installation, servicing and maintenance of the products sold.
- There are (usually) fewer distributors of industrial products than of consumer goods, hence there is often less choice of distributor.
- International distributors of industrial products are often required to have been trained in the technical performance of the product.

The EU single-market policy has to a large extent eliminated or at least reduced the problems associated with transportation delays and customs clearance. However, a problem that has grown because of the free movement of goods in Europe is the existence of *grey markets*. A grey market involves unauthorized distributors circumventing authorized channel arrangements by buying the company's products in low-price countries and selling them in high-price countries at prices that undercut the competition. An example is the parallel import of medicines.

Price
The questions that generally need to be considered when developing a pricing strategy are:
- Which European market segments should the enterprise concentrate on?
- Who are its major European competitors?
- What are the competitive strengths of the European competitors?
- Why and how do European consumers buy?
- Which are the major segments in the European market for the product/service?

How consumers buy has changed particularly dramatically in the past two decades. It has become common practice to make cross-national comparisons when buying convenience and speciality goods. This price transparency in the European market is growing, and its key drivers are the single currency and the internet. Globalization and online shopping are force towards cross-national standardized pricing, and the euro also makes the comparison of purchase prices easier for potential customers.

When calculating sales prices, the balancing cost of transport, the volume of sales and the competition in the foreign market must be allowed for. Government regulations, export inspection costs and local taxes must also be taken into account. The government of a country can dictate to the international supplier what prices can be charged in the market. It does this because its main responsibility is to its citizens, not to the supplier.

Although Europe is a well developed economic region, there are differences (between Eastern and Western and to a lesser extent Northern and Southern EU countries) in standards of living and average incomes per capita, so a centralized EU pricing strategy is inadvisable for many products. Companies are relatively free to set a different price for their products in each country, but the absence of import taxes within the EU prevents prices from differing too much between (neighbouring) countries, because of the danger of parallel importing (as in the case of medicines). Finally, whether price differences are maintained will also depending on the complexity of the product and the service requirements.

Another factor that needs mentioning in connection with price setting is *transfer pricing*. A transfer price is the price at which goods (or services) are sold between divisions or subsidiaries of a company. Transfer pricing can be used to reduce the price of goods shipped from a subsidiary in a high-tax country to a subsidiary in a low-tax country, so that little profit is earned in the high-tax country. Transfer pricing does not occur in the context of simple exporting, but rather in international investment, when a company has divisions operating in other countries. Multinationals are able to exert a huge influence on the global economy.

A direct consequence of strong competition is that the prices of tradable goods will converge. Has the internal market indeed led to price convergence? The consumer price index (CPI) is often used to measure price trends. This index comprises both tradable and non-tradable goods and services. R.P. Faber and A.C.J. Stokman ('Price convergence in Europe from a macro-perspective: Product categories and reliability', DNB Working Paper no. 34, 2005) have shown that the CPI spread between eleven EU countries halved between 1965 and 2003. The factual openness of the EU countries has contributed significantly to this.

As already mentioned, a narrowing of price differences can also be expected because of the euro, since a single currency makes it much easier to compare prices between countries. However, this effect cannot yet be demonstrated irrefutably in empirical terms, partly because the time that has elapsed since the introduction of the euro is too short. Price differences within the euro zone are certainly comparatively small, but this was already the case before the introduction of the euro. Partly because a number of European countries had strongly linked their currency to the Deutsche Mark, price differences were small even before 1999.

A recent study by J. Crespo Cuaresma, B. Égert and M.A. Silgoner ('Price Level Convergence in Europe: Did the Introduction of the Euro Matter?' *Monetary Policy & the Economy* Q1/07) empirically investigated price convergence. The researchers compared the euro-area countries with a group of control countries between 1990 and 2006, using price-level data on over 160 products and services in 27 European cities. The study's conclusions confirm that price convergence took place at the beginning of the 1990s. There is, however, little evidence that the introduction of the single currency has led to a further narrowing of price differentials. In fact, price dispersion has remained remarkably stable in the EU in recent years, whereas it has increased slightly since 2003 in the control group.

5.6.4 Electronic commerce in European marketing

Since Tim Berners-Lee invented the World Wide Web in 1989, modern life has changed enormously, both privately and professionally. It is hard to imagine any profession in which the internet does not play a role. It is also considered one of the main drivers of globalization.

In the internet, European marketers have gained another medium for their marketing communication strategy. It is not equally important for all industries, but email and websites are common goods. Related technologies such as SMS, Wireless Application Protocol (WAP) and third-generation mobile phones increase international communication options yet further. Their usage depends on the business model and business strategy an enterprise pursues.

Comparing the EU's internet penetration (60% of the population) with that of the rest of the world (19%) shows that Europe has a distinct advantage. The ten largest internet markets in Europe at the end of 2003 comprised 79% of all European internet users, numbering 165.1 million. Germany is the largest market in Europe, followed by the UK, which now has over 30 million internet users. Three countries outside Western Europe, Poland, Russia and Turkey, are in the top 10. Poland is the fifth-largest internet market in Europe, ahead of Spain, which has a population of similar size.

The use of English predominates on the internet. This implies that non-English speakers have access to a much more limited range of information. There are no filters on accessing internet information, and thus there is greater scope for misinterpretation and miscommunication of messages on the internet. As 'word of mouse' replaces 'word of mouth', it is much more difficult to assess the objectivity or bias of information.

An important decision for many European businesses is not whether to use information technology to improve their international business practice, but rather how best to use information technology to stream-line their operation. K.L. Page-Thomas, in 'Electronic Marketing: The Bigger Picture' (*Marketing Review, 5/3* (Autumn 2005), 243-262), out-lines five core activities for which electronic resources are used:
1   to acquire data and information from stakeholders
2   to provide data and information to stakeholders
3   to communicate one-to-one with stakeholders
4   to manage and conduct stakeholders' transactions
5   to manage or distribute the product offer to stakeholders.

European organizations are constantly striving to offer their interna-tional and domestic consumers easier access to the company and its products through the use of the internet. Increasingly, companies will embrace the internet in more facets of their business, as it not only reduces (in many cases) the cost of doing international business, but it exposes the company to many more consumers in a single European market than could have been thought possible ten years ago.

Conclusions: business aspects of the single market (sections 5.4 to 5.6)

The free movement of goods within a single European market is gener-ally considered to be a blessing for modern businesses. It not only strengthens the internal market, but it also enhances the competitive strength of the EU in relation to other global economic blocs (such as the USA, Japan, China and India). Careful planning and profound knowledge of the target countries, especially with respect to their socio-cultural characteristics and language, are key factors for success in other countries.

Section 5.4 discussed the position of European manufacturing and its strengths and weaknesses. The EU needs to strengthen the hi-tech sectors in particular. In order to encourage and fully benefit from innovation, the European educational systems (research universities and technical universities) should collaborate more intensively with businesses.

Challenges are also posed by the protective measures taken by individual countries and their reluctance to give up some of their national regulations to promote increased competition between the 27 Member States. Simplification of EU regulations and harmonization of national regulations are necessary in order to improve competitiveness within the EU (section 5.5).

Finally, the complexity of the single European market remains a challenge for the European marketer (section 5.6). EU integration has had some favourable effects on products and on the effectiveness of EU-wide product branding. The single market has stimulated competition, leading to more rapid innovation. This in turn increases product diversification and availability. Moreover, more intense pan-European competition has also had a favourable effect on product quality.

Harmonization of the promotion of products (marketing communication in general) across the EU Member States, however, has turned out be more difficult than expected. European lawmakers need to develop directives acceptable to all the EU Member States, who are individually responsible for consumer protection.

The distribution function in European marketing is complex, but there are multiple options available to make it cost effective. The EU single-market policy has to a large extent eliminated or at least reduced the communication problems and delays.

An integrated market will promote competition and therefore prices will to a certain extent converge within the EU. However, differences in standards of living and average incomes per capita make centralized EU price setting for many products not advisable.
In general, the diversity of entry strategies available and the opportunities for creative utilization of the marketing mix, combined with the new openings offered by e-commerce, enable companies to successfully generate business within and outside Europe.

Questions

Legal aspects of the single market (sections 5.1 to 5.3)

5.1   Name the five most important aspects of the single market.

5.2   How can the EC Treaty provisions on the single or internal market be used by businesses against national authorities?

5.3   Explain the benefits of the New Approach to harmonization for the free movement of goods in the common market.

5.4 What are the most important elements in an international sales contract of goods?

5.5 Does European law have any influence on the concepts of common law and civil law?

5.6 What are the most important competition rules for companies operating in the internal market?

Case studies (sections 5.1 to 5.3)

5.7 The German authorities have decided that a tax should be levied for using the German 'Autobahn' (motorway). A Latvian company is now faced with much higher costs for exporting its products to France. It decides not to pay the tax.
a Is the Autobahn tax permitted under European law?
b In which cases is such a tax prohibited under the EC Treaty?
c Are there any exceptions to these EC rules?
d Where does a company have to bring litigation if it does not agree with the amount of tax that is being levied?

5.8 France decides that all raw potato chips should be examined before they can be sold in the French supermarkets and other outlets. The reason for the legislation is that some diseases may develop after the potatoes have been peeled and cut into chips. A Belgian producer of raw chips asks you for advice on this new French legislation.
a Is the French legislation permitted under the EC Treaty?
b Which exceptions may be relevant in this case?
c Does any of the exceptions apply in this case?
d What advice would you give the Belgian company: to stop exporting to France because of the new requirement or to continue exporting to France despite the new legislation? Explain your advice.
e What problems may occur as a result of exporting the Belgian chips to France in defiance of the new French legislation? Are there any solutions to these problems?

5.9 Read the Microsoft case study in chapter 4 (case study 4.6) and answer the following questions.
a Which competition rules were breached by Microsoft? Explain why the article(s) of the EC Treaty apply.
b Does EU competition law apply to a US-based company?
c Which procedure in which court of law did Microsoft appeal to?

Business aspects of the single market (sections 5.4 to 5.6)

5.10 Mention at least three threats to European manufacturing and identify two possible solutions.

5.11 What needs to be improved in order to stimulate exporting by European enterprises?

Case studies (sections 5.4 to 5.6)

5.12   Based on the ways that are suggested in this chapter of improving the single European market and looking at Porter's Value Chain, identify any adaptations of its primary and secondary activities that a European enterprise may have to make in order to remain competitive within Europe in the near future (3–5 years). Describe these adaptations for an enterprise of your choice.

5.13   Suppose you are the marketing director of a European electric car manufacturer. What steps would you take to export your product to one of the other 27 EU Member States?

5.14   Select two European countries and describe the requirements a business in one country needs to take into account in order to position a food product in the other European country. Use a concrete example, e.g. meat, dairy products, vegetables, ice cream.

5.15   Identify one sector on which the EU should focus in order to stimulate its pan-European performance. Give at least three reasons why this sector must be targeted.

July 2009, 74 state 5

State	Signature	Ratification, Accession, Approval, Acceptance or Succession	Entry into force
Albania		13th May 2009	1st June 2010
Argentina		19th July 1983	1st January 1988
Armenia		2nd December 2008	1st January 2010
Australia		17th March 1988	1st April 1989
Austria	11th April 1980	29th December 1987	1st January 1989
Belarus		9th October 1989	1st November 1990
Belgium		31st October 1996	1st November 1997
Bosnia and Herzegovina		12th January 1994	6th March 1992
Bulgaria		9th July 1990	1st August 1991
Burundi		4th September 1998	1st October 1999
Canada		23rd April 1991	1st May 1992
Chile	11th April 1980	7th February 1990	1st March 1991
China	30th September 1981	11th December 1986	1st January 1988
Colombia		10th July 2001	1st August 2002
Croatia		8th June 1998	8th October 1991
Cuba		2nd November 1994	1st December 1995
Cyprus		7th March 2005	1st April 2006
Czech Republic		30th September 1993	1st January 1993
Denmark	26th May 1981	14th February 1989	1st March 1990
Ecuador		27th January 1992	1st February 1993
Egypt		6th December 1982	1st January 1988
El Salvador		27th November 2006	1st December 2007
Estonia		20th September 1993	1st October 1994
Finland	26th May 1981	15th December 1987	1st January 1989
France	27th August 1981	6th August 1982	1st January 1988
Gabon		15th December 2004	1st January 2006
Georgia		16th August 1994	1st September 1995
Germany	26th May 1981	21st December 1989	1st January 1991
Ghana	11th April 1980		
Greece		12th January 1998	1st February 1999

State	Signature	Ratification, Accession, Approval, Acceptance or Succession	Entry into force
Guinea		23rd January 1991	1st February 1992
Honduras		10th October 2002	1st November 2003
Hungary	11th April 1980	16th June 1983	1st January 1988
Iceland		10th May 2001	1st June 2002
Iraq		5th March 1990	1st April 1991
Israel		22nd January 2002	1st February 2003
Italy	30th September 1981	11th December 1986	1st January 1988
Japan		1st July 2008	1st August 2009
Kyrgyzstan		11th May 1999	1st June 2000
Latvia		31st July 1997	1st August 1998
Lebanon		21st November 2008	1st December 2009
Lesotho	18th June 1981	18th June 1981	1st January 1988
Liberia		16th September 2005	1st October 2006
Lithuania		18th January 1995	1st February 1996
Luxembourg		30th January 1997	1st February 1998
Mauritania		20th August 1999	1st September 2000
Mexico		29th December 1987	1st January 1989
Moldova		13th October 1994	1st November 1995
Mongolia		31st December 1997	1st January 1999
Montenegro		23rd October 2006	3rd June 2006
Netherlands	29th May 1981	13th December 1990	1st January 1992
New Zealand		22nd September 1994	1st October 1995
Norway	26th May 1981	20th July 1988	1st August 1989
Paraguay		13th January 2006	1st February 2007
Peru		25th March 1999	1st April 2000
Poland	28th September 1981	19th May 1995	1st June 1996
Republic of Korea		17th February 2004	1st March 2005
Romania		22nd May 1991	1st June 1992
Russian Federation		16th August 1990	1st September 1991
Saint Vincent and the Grenadines		12th September 2000	1st October 2001
Serbia		12th March 2001	27th April 1992
Singapore	11th April 1980	16th February 1995	1st March 1996
Slovakia		28th May 1993	1st January 1993
Slovenia		7th January 1994	25th June 1991
Spain		24th July 1990	1st August 1991
Sweden	26th May 1981	15th December 1987	1st January 1989

State	Signature	Ratification, Accession, Approval, Acceptance or Succession	Entry into force
Switzerland		21st February 1990	1st March 1991
Syrian Arab Republic		19th October 1982	1st January 1988
The former Yugoslav Republic of Macedonia		22nd November 2006	17th November 1991
Uganda		12th February 1992	1st March 1993
Ukraine		3rd January 1990	1st February 1991
United States of America	31st August 1981	11th December 1986	1st January 1988
Uruguay		25th January 1999	1st February 2000
Uzbekistan		27th November 1996	1st December 1997
Venezuela (Bolivarian Republic of)	28th September 1981		
Zambia		6th June 1986	1st January 1988

The free movement of services and international business strategy

TFS Trial Form Support International AB operating in the single market

Company

TFS Trial Form Support International AB is a clinical contract research organization (CRO). Its function is to provide clinical trial services in all phases to the life science industry in Europe, the USA and Asia.

TFS Trial Form Support started in Sweden in 1996.

Currently it has 450 employees and 19 offices spread throughout Europe, Asia and the USA.
In order to analyse the factors affecting commercial success or failure it is important to understand the process of a clinical trial (without necessarily going into exhaustive detail).

Services

Innovative pharmaceutical companies spend roughly fifteen to twenty per cent of their turnover on R&D in their quest for new medicines. These R&D activities can be divided into a discovery, a preclinical and a clinical phase. The clinical phase includes testing the experimental medicines on healthy humans and patients with the targeted disease. In the marketing of a new medicine an extensive and transparent R&D trajectory is mandatory, in which every step of the R&D process showing benefit from the new treatment will be scrutinized by national and international regulatory bodies (e.g. the EMEA in Europe and the FDA in the USA). For this case study it is sufficient to know that R&D activities are to a large extent outsourced to CROs.

The added value of a CRO is based on different aspects and may include:
- Extensive network of hospitals and clinicians in order to recruit patients for a clinical trial
- Knowledge of the targeted disease (therapeutic area)
- Knowledge of regulatory requirements and procedures in a particular country in order to obtain approval for recruiting patients
- Efficient data management
- High-quality analysis and reporting.

Expansion in Europe (and globally) of CROs is driven by the need of their global clients to carry out their R&D processes as internationally as possible. It is related to the need for efficiency in obtaining international marketing approval of a medicine to launch it globally.

The market is attractive and growing

Competition is intense and the challenge is how to compete in a marketplace where the five global players hold 45% of the total market. However, the total CRO market is expected to reach US$24 billion by 2010 as biopharma businesses' spending on outsourcing services continues to soar, new research reveals.

As a result, the reliance on service providers and in particular CROs has rocketed in the past few years and the total CRO market is now estimated at US$14 billion, and expected to grow at an annual rate of 14–16%, according to market research firm Business Insights.

The report, entitled 'The CRO Market Outlook: Emerging Markets, Leading Players and Future Trends', stated that CROs provide substantial global reach to drug developers and have become critical contributors to clinical activity.

Quintiles is the industry's biggest player with 14% of the global market, followed by Covance and PPD, holding 10% each.

According to the Chairman and CEO of Covance, Joe Herring, in the company's Annual Report of 2007:

> In 2007, we continued to benefit from strong market dynamics favouring contract research organizations (CROs) such as Covance. Today, approximately 25% of all biopharmaceutical drug development spending is outsourced, which represents a CRO market greater than US$15 billion. Over the next five years, industry analysts expect the level of outsourcing to increase to 35% and the CRO market to double to US$30 billion.

Internationalization strategy of TFS

TFS's strategy is to create a pan-European CRO with operations and services corresponding to clients' needs.

The growth of TFS is based on two strategic choices: the establishment of sales offices in foreign countries and the acquisition of (smaller) CROs or complementary service providers in the life science industry.

A historic overview of major international expansion activities is given in table 6.1. The table illustrates how important it is for a European company to have free movement of services and how various European requirements and constraints affect international business strategy.

Table 6.1 **Internationalization activities of TFS**

Year	Activity	Objectives & expected effect
1996	Foundation in Sweden	To be recognized by our clients as the top quality provider of clinical trial services in Europe and by our consultants as an attractive employer.
2005	Acquisition of its competitor, CDC Clinical Data Care (CDC)	Operations in Sweden, Spain and Japan. 250 employees in all of the Nordic countries, the UK, Spain, Italy, Portugal, Russia, the Baltic States and Japan. The two companies, TFS and CDC, will complement each other's operations on many levels.
2006	Moving its headquarters from Helsingborg, Sweden, to the southern university city of Lund, Sweden	Establishment in the heart of Medicon Valley, one of the leading biotechnology clusters in Europe, and close to some of the company's largest clients in the south of Sweden and in northern Denmark. The region is one of the strongest pharmaceutical and biotech clusters in Europe and comprises a large number of universities, hospitals and more than 300 life science companies.

Year	Activity	Objectives & expected effect
2006	Expansion of its current representation in Lisbon, Portugal	Portugal is an important market with high potential in clinical trials and we need to put more focus in that region.
2006	Opening of a business support office in the centre of Tokyo, Japan	Co-ordination of the increasing number of clinical development projects in Europe managed by TFS for its clients based in Japan.
2007	Launching courses and a three-month global trainee programme	The courses and trainee programme are designed for professionals working on clinical trials of both pharmaceutical products and medical devices. To secure the need for well trained professionals in the clinical trial area. Also, branding of TFS, cross-selling and networking.
2007	Receipt of French tax credit approval	This means TFS is an approved organization carrying out R&D activities for the account of French private life science organizations. Any French company involved in R&D activities working with TFS on clinical development can be refunded (by the French government) part of the cost of clinical trial services provided by TFS.
2008	Establishment of its first office in the United States, in Cambridge (Massachusetts)	To serve the growing number of US-based midsized and small life science entities seeking clinical development support from TFS. To consolidate this important market segment (close to 25% of our global net revenue comes out of the USA).
2008	Acquisition of IMRO TRAMARKO Holding BV, an independent CRO based in the Netherlands	The acquisition will expand TFS's operational reach to the Benelux region and Germany.
2008	Introduction of global trainee programme in Finland	Securing the need for well trained professionals in the clinical trial area.
2008	Establishment of regional headquarters for Central and Eastern Europe (CEE) in Budapest, Hungary	Expansion of clinical operations in CEE by means of establishing a number of new legal entities and clinical operational teams in the CEE countries.

In this chapter various aspects of providing services in Europe and forming a European business strategy are illustrated with the aid of the chapter's opening case study. In the first section the principles of free movement are explained and the current state of the single market for services is outlined.

In the second section the protection afforded by European legislation to the free movement of services is explained. The main rules and their exceptions are explained. There is also information on what businesses can do when they are hindered in the movement of services.

The last two sections examine the import and export of services from a marketing point of view as well as marketing strategies in general and the particular strategy adopted by TFS, the subject of the chapter's opening case study.

6.1 The single market for services

In this section the current state of the single market for services is explained. The explanation includes the basis of the concept of free movement in the EC Treaty, as well as the sort of services to which the European concept of free movement applies. The section makes clear that it will not always be easy for TFS to benefit from the advantages of the single market for services.

6.1.1 The Treaty provisions on the free movement of services

The idea of a common market extends to other ways of doing business than delivering goods (which resulted in the clause regarding the free movement of goods in the EC Treaty). Services are crucial to the European internal market. The free movement of services constitutes the engine of economic growth and accounts for 70% of GDP and employment in most Member States. Individuals who are self employed and wish to provide services in another Member State may rely on the provisions of the EC Treaty that are dedicated to this subject. Article 49 of the Treaty prescribes that restrictions on *freedom to provide services* within the Community are prohibited in respect of nationals of Member States who are established in a State of the Community other than that of the person for whom the services are intended. In the chapter's opening case study the research services of TFS were initially provided out of Sweden across the single market and beyond. Later, the management decided to establish strategic subsidiaries in other Member States, such as Portugal and Hungary.

If a service provider, such as TFS, wants to start a business in the same State as the party receiving the service, there is another freedom involved, *the freedom of establishment* prescribed by Article 43. These two freedoms, the free movement of services and the freedom of establishment, often coincide and therefore the EC Treaty provisions have a similar structure. Chapter 8 explains the freedom of establishment in more detail.

Article 50 of the EC Treaty explains which kinds of service enjoy free movement within the EU. First the Article makes clear that only services provided for reward enjoy free movement under the EC Treaty. Second, qualifying services exclude activities that fall under other free movements, such as free movement of goods, people and capital. Examples of services included in Article 50 of the EC Treaty are:
- activities of an industrial character
- activities of a commercial character
- activities of craftsmen
- activities of the professions.

In the chapter's opening case study, TFS offers research expertise throughout the EU and it also uses research companies in other Member States to carry out specific research for TFS. These activities can be characterized as of industrial and commercial character and therefore fall within the scope of the free movement of services of Articles 49 and 50 of the EC Treaty. Examples of activities of craftsmen and the professions are cross-border services of carpenters, plumbers, builders, doctors, nurses and lawyers and so on.

Generally speaking, Article 50 of the EC Treaty allows for three types of cross-border activity:
1 The service provider crosses the border with another Member State. This situation is present for instance when a Polish builder offers his services elsewhere in the EU.
2 The recipient of the service crosses the border with another Member State. This situation occurs when a patient wants to have an opera-

tion in a hospital of a Member State other than his State of residence.

3 The service itself crosses the border with another Member State. This situation occurs for instance when television programmes are sent over a border.

In the chapter's opening case study all three situations may occur. TFS offers research services to other companies around the EU and is therefore the provider of the services. The research may be done in Sweden, the home state of TFS, while the recipient remains domiciled in its own Member State. TFS probably travels to the recipient at different stages of the research project, after which the final result will be sent in a report to the customer.

TFS also uses specialized companies to help with its research. In this situation TFS is the recipient of the service. As a result TFS may be travelling to the specialized research company in order to get the research done. Most likely the research is done at the premises where all the specialized equipment is present.

The third situation mainly occurs with radio, television and internet services that are able to cross borders by themselves. In the chapter's opening case study, this situation may occur when TFS sends the final result of a particular research project to the client or when a report is sent to TFS as the recipient of a specialized research service.

There are also some *activities excluded* from the free movement of services. These activities, which are described in Article 51 of the EC Treaty, are services in the field of transport and activities in the field of insurances and banking that involve movements of capital. The latter activities are covered by the free movement of capital. In this book, chapter 7 is dedicated to that subject.

As far as transportation is concerned, the EC Treaty includes provisions for a common policy on the subject. The principle of free movement of services is present in this area as well but there are complications, which are dealt with in a separate part in the EC Treaty. Secondary EU law, via regulations and directives, take a more prominent role here. This book does not provide any specific information on the common transport policy set out in Article 70 of the EC Treaty.

6.1.2 The exceptions to the free movement of services based on the EC provisions

In this subsection the most important exceptions to Articles 49 and 50 of the EC Treaty are discussed. There is also a reference to the chapter's opening case study and an assessment of whether an exception may be expected for TFS.

The EC Treaty stipulates several exceptions to the free movement of services. Article 55 lists exceptions to Articles 45 to 48 on the freedom of establishment. The exceptions can be summarized as *justifications in the public interest*.

Article 45 allows a Member State to take measures to protect the exercise of an official authority. For this reason the free movement of services offered by lawyers is better assured than that of the services of public notaries, whose activities may include various official functions. But it does not mean that Member States may hinder the free movement of services or the freedom of establishment by setting a nationality requirement, as case study 6.1 explains.

Case study 6.1 **Requirements of nationality and the protection of official authority**

On 12th October 2006 the Commission released the following press report:

Nationality requirements for notaries: Commission acts to ensure correct implementation of EU law in 16 Member States

[...]
The Commission has decided to send reasoned opinions to Germany, Austria, Belgium, France, Greece, Luxembourg and the Netherlands on the grounds that these Member States allow only nationals of their own country to qualify and practise as notaries.

In the view of the Commission, this nationality condition is contrary to the freedom of establishment provided for in Article 43 of the EC Treaty and cannot be justified by reference to Article 45, which exempts activities related to the exercise of official authority.

The Court of Justice has ruled that such participation must be direct and specific. However, the Commission considers that this does not apply in the case of notaries, as they cannot impose a decision against the will of one of the parties they are advising. In other words, notaries do not take decisions with regard to State authority and therefore cannot be deemed to exercise such authority.

As regards the high level of qualifications required to become a notary, there is a less restrictive method of ensuring that this level is maintained, namely by applying Directive 89/48/EEC on the general system for the recognition of diplomas, which makes it possible to check by means of an aptitude test (or probationary period) whether candidates possess the necessary level of knowledge of national law.

The failure to transpose this Directive is the second grievance stated in the reasoned opinion relating to the Member States mentioned above, with the exception of France, which has transposed it.

Spain, Italy and Portugal have abolished the nationality condition previously in force for notaries. The elimination of this condition does not imply a change in the status of notaries, particularly in respect of certain activities being reserved for this profession. Moreover, these infringement procedures do not affect the powers of the Member States to regulate the profession of notary, particularly in terms of laying down measures to ensure the quality of notary services, including examinations.

Portugal has still not transposed Directive 89/48/EEC for the profession of notary. That is why the Commission has decided to send it too a reasoned opinion.

Since the same nationality condition appears to exist in the Czech Republic, Estonia, Hungary, Latvia, Lithuania, Malta, Poland, Slovakia and Slovenia, the Commission has also decided to send these countries requests for information in the form of letters of formal notice. The letters of formal notice, which are the first stage in the procedure laid down in Article 226, also relate to the refusal to transpose Directive 89/48/EEC on the general system for the recognition of diplomas.

Source: Rapid Press Release Europe, IP/06/1385, 12/10/2006

In previous cases the European Court of Justice (ECJ) had decided that a genuine official authority should be involved and that the restrictions to the free movement of services should be explained in definitive terms. The Commission therefore took action against 16 Member States that had not been applying the EC Treaty articles providing for free movement or applying the Treaty's exceptions inappropriately. Other States had not transposed the directive for notaries and therefore breached European law. Information on the way the Commission is allowed to initiate legal proceedings against Member States can be found in chapter 4 of this book.

Article 46 of the EC Treaty lists exceptions admissible in national regulations in order to protect public policy, public security or public health. There is a lot of case law involving architects, dentists, doctors, lawyers and even tour guides in which the European Court of Justice makes clear that requirements of service providers may not be discriminatory or disproportionate when a Member State is trying to safeguard the public interest involved. Case study 6.2 explains how Member States may protect the public interest and how the ECJ assesses the admissibility of national regulations.

Case study 6.2 Are gambling regulations in a Member State justified?

Stanley is one of Stanley Leisure's operational conduits outside the United Kingdom. It is authorized to operate as a bookmaker in the United Kingdom, having been licensed by the City of Liverpool. It is subject to controls by the British authorities in the interests of public order and safety. Stanley operates in Italy through more than 200 agencies, commonly called 'data transmission centres' (DTCs). The DTCs supply their services via premises open to the public in which a data transmission link is placed at the disposal of gamblers so that they can access the server of Stanley's host computer in the United Kingdom. The DTCs are run by independent operators who have contractual links to Stanley. Mr Placanica, Mr Palazzese and Mr Sorricchio, the defendants in the main Italian proceedings, are all DTC operators linked to Stanley.

Italy had been pursuing a policy of expansion in the betting and gaming sector with the aim of increasing tax revenue. Therefore the Italian legislation could not be justified by reference to the aim of protecting consumers or of limiting their propensity to gamble or of limiting the availability of games of chance. The purpose of the Italian legislation was a desire to channel betting and gaming activities into systems that were controllable, with the objective of preventing their exploitation for criminal purposes. That is why the Italian legislation provided for the control and supervision of the persons who operate betting and tipster contests through a licensing system. There was also police authorization of the premises where the betting takes place.

In the hope of obtaining licences for at least 100 betting outlets in Italy, Stanley investigated the possibility of taking part in the tendering procedures in 1999. Stanley realized that it could not meet the Italian conditions concerning the transparency of share ownership because it formed part of a group quoted on the regulated markets. Accordingly, it did not participate in the tendering procedure and holds no licence for betting operations.

As DTC operators for Stanley, Mr Placanica and others had pursued the organized activity of collecting bets without the required police authorization. The Public Prosecutor brought criminal proceedings against him before the Tribunale di Larino (Italy). The Italian court decided it needed more information on whether the Italian legislation breached Articles 49 and 50 of the EC Treaty and, if so, whether an exception in accordance with Articles 45 to 48 applied in this case.

The European Court of Justice ruled that the prohibition imposed on intermediaries such as the defendants in the Italian proceedings constituted a breach of the free movement of services, even if the intermediaries were established in the same Member State as the recipients of the services.

In this case, the court ruled it necessary to consider whether the restrictions imposed by the Italian government may be recognized as exceptional measures, as expressly provided for in Articles 45 and 46 of the EC Treaty, or justified in accordance with the case law of the court, for reasons of overriding general interest.

Restrictive measures imposed should therefore be examined in order to determine in each case whether they are suitable for achieving the objective or objectives invoked by the Member State. The court also ruled that the measures may not go beyond what is necessary in order to achieve those objectives. In any case, those restrictions must be applied without discrimination.

In the absence of a procedure for obtaining licences open to operators who had been unlawfully barred from obtaining a licence under a previous tender procedure, the European Court of Justice held that a lack of a licence could not be a ground for sanctions against such operators. Contrary to Community law, Italy made the grant of police authorizations subject to possession of a licence at the time of the last tender procedure and had refused to award licences to businesses quoted on the regulated markets. In consequence, Italy cannot apply criminal penalties to persons such as the defendants Placanica and others in the main proceedings.

In other words, even when exceptions to the principal rule of free movement of services apply, Member States must be very careful not to be too strict in applying legislation that protects the general interest. The measures should be suitable for protecting the general interest and not in any way discriminatory. In the Placanica case the discrimination took place at a time when authorizations were issued only to businesses based in Italy.

As long as there is no Community legislation on the topic, Member States are allowed to have national policies to protect consumers, public order and the general interest. However, case study 6.2 shows that Member States are restricted in taking protective measures by Community law. The restrictions have to be tested for effectiveness and appropriateness.

With regard to the chapter's opening case study the exceptions may provide a threat to the services TFS is providing or receiving when the public interest or public health is concerned. Especially in the area of public health, services related to research in medicines may be highly regulated by the Member States. TFS may be faced with criminal charges on the one hand and with double protective measures on the other: those of the State of establishment and those of the State where the service is delivered. Consequently TFS will certainly benefit from unimpeded free movement of services in the single market.

6.1.3 The current state of the single market for services

In the previous section it became clear that Member States still apply national legislation that may hinder the free movement of services within the EU. The EC Treaty allows Member States to protect consumers and topics of general interest such as public order and public health.

In this section the current state of the single market for services is assessed. Community law on the topic is explained and the most important legislative measure, the Services Directive, clarified. Finally, the influence of the current situation on the company in the chapter's opening case study, TFS, is assessed.

In 2002 the Commission examined the state of the free movement of services. It declared that internal market barriers affected the movement of services more than the movement of goods. In addition, the *service provider* is subject to the qualification standards of a Member State.

Member States tend to be most protective in the *business-to-consumer services sector* by setting qualification standards. In fact the threats to the free movement of services can be divided into three main areas:
1 the requirement for certain standards of education
2 the requirement to use certain materials
3 the fulfilment of certain procedures before the service can be provided.

In Case study 6.3 the Commission warned Germany to stop hindering manual therapists in providing their services by setting certain professional qualifications.

This case study shows that even though there are directives to ensure the free movement of services within the EU, infringements still take place. It shows that despite Article 49 of the EC Treaty and the existence of such directives, businesses still need to beware of requirements that breach the primary law laid down in the EC Treaty and secondary laws as formulated in directives and regulations.

Secondary European law on free movement of services
There are two distinct groups of secondary European law on the free movement of services.

The first group consists of directives on *professional requirements*. The European legislature issued quite a few directives concerning the qualifications of certain professions such as doctors, dentists, nurses, midwives, veterinarians, architects and pharmacists. These directives lead not only to a system of mutual recognition of professional qualifications but also to automatic recognition on the basis of harmonization of minimum training conditions. Member States have to respect degrees and other diplomas obtained in another Member State.

For other groups of professions, Directive 1999/42/EC Member States gives a service provider the opportunity to demonstrate that he has acquired the knowledge and skills which were lacking. In this case, the host Member State shall give the applicant the right to choose between an adaptation period and an aptitude test by analogy with Directives 89/48/EEC and 92/51/EEC. In 2005 these directives were partly replaced by Directive 2005/36/EC, which should have been implemented in 2007. The directive prescribes a general system of dealing with professional requirements. The Member States should take account of the qualifications obtained in other Member States and assess whether they correspond with their own qualifications. The directive prescribes that certain levels of training must be respected by all Member States. The directive also gives some additional rules for the professions for which an automatic recognition of qualifications exists, such as doctors and nurses.

Case study 6.3 **Manual therapists providing services in Germany**

On 14th April 2009 the Commission released the following press report:

Professional qualifications: Commission sends formal request to Germany concerning manual therapists

The European Commission has formally requested Germany to amend its legislation on the recognition of manual therapists' qualifications. This request takes the form of a "reasoned opinion", the second stage of the infringement procedure laid down in Article 226 of the EC Treaty. If there is no satisfactory reply within two months, the Commission may refer the matter to the European Court of Justice.

The Commission has decided to send a reasoned opinion to Germany regarding the non-conformity of its legislation on the mutual recognition of manual therapists' qualifications. According to the German framework recommendations issued on the basis of the Sozialgesetzbuch V, all physiotherapists who provide manual therapy services for patients insured by the health insurance funds have to complete a post-graduate training course in manual therapy if they want their patients to receive reimbursement of the fees for those services from the health insurance funds. On this basis, the German authorities refuse to recognise manual therapists' qualifications obtained by EU citizens in other Member States because their training is different from the German training requirements.

In the Commission's view, such refusal contradicts the principle of mutual recognition established by Directive 2005/36/EC on the recognition of professional qualifications. The fact that the reimbursement of the corresponding fees by the health insurance funds is dependent on the possession of a given qualification by the professional concerned constitutes a form of regulation of the activity or profession concerned, which then falls under Directive 2005/36/EC. This implies that Germany has to implement the general system of recognition of diplomas for the activity/profession concerned, in order to allow EU citizens trained in other Member States to have access to the activity concerned under the same conditions as its own nationals.

Germany may make the recognition of a qualification obtained in another Member State subject to passing an aptitude test or fulfilling a supervised adaptation period if the training requirements in the other Member State are substantially different from its own training requirements. However, it cannot refuse recognition [by] stating that the two training courses are not comparable. The Commission believes that the current German legislation relating to the profession of manual therapists seriously compromises the system of mutual recognition of professional qualifications and deprives manual therapists who obtained their qualifications in a Member State other than Germany of the possibility of exercising their profession in Germany.

Source: Rapid Press Release Europe, IP/06/1385, 12/10/2006

The other group of secondary European law is the more *general legislation* on services. The most important and recent example of this group is the Services Directive (Directive 2006/123/EC of 12th December 2006). The directive has a general scope and covers services such as construction and crafts, retail, most of the regulated professions, business-related services and tourism. It came into being after a report by the Commission on the state of services in the single market in 2002. The Commission drew up an extensive inventory of barriers which were preventing or slowing down the development of services between Member States, in particular those provided by SMEs. The report, 'The State of the Internal Market for Services', concluded that a decade after the envisaged completion of the internal market, there was still a huge gap between the vision of an integrated European Union economy and the reality as experienced by European citizens and providers. The barriers affected a wide variety of service activities across all stages of the provider's activity and had a number of common features, including administrative burdens for service providers, the legal uncertainty associated with cross-border activity and the lack of mutual trust between Member States. Because the movement of services constituted the engine of economic growth and accounted for 70% of GDP and employment in most Member States, this fragmentation of the internal market had a negative impact on the entire European economy. Freedom of movement of services, unfortunately, was not as developed as the free movement of goods.

The Services Directive aimed to cope with these problems and set out *three major tasks* for Member States in order to establish genuine freedom of movement of services in the single market.

1 The first task was a thorough review and adaptation of existing national legislation. The Member States must simplify their authorization schemes and get rid of the economic needs tests and nationality or residence requirements imposed on the provider or his staff. The aim was to simplify national legislation and reduce the administrative burden and legal research and compliance costs for businesses.

2 The second task the directive set out was the obligation to set up 'Points of Single Contact'. Service providers should be able to easily obtain all information and complete all necessary procedures at one point instead of having to contact a number of administrative or professional bodies. All procedures through Points of Single Contact must be available at a distance and by electronic means. The concept of eGoverning was to be introduced as a result.

3 The third main task for Member States was to set up a network of *administrative co-operation* between the national authorities of the Member States. The Commission developed an Internal Market Information system which allowed the exchange of information on legislation in each Member State. The system is now operational for the Professional Qualifications Directive discussed above and can be found at http://ec.europa.eu/internal_market/qualifications/index_en.htm/ under 'database on regulated professions'. The directive's implementation period ends on 28th December 2009.

The adoption and implementation of directives, however, does not mean that there are no longer any infringements on the free movement of services. On 16th October 2008 the Commission decided to take six Member States to the European Court of Justice for failure to implement or to give notice of national laws instituted to transpose Directive 2005/36/EC on the recognition of professional qualifications and five other Member States for not implementing a directive on reinsurance.

The current situation regarding the free movement of services in the single market holds very important information for TFS, the company in the chapter's opening case study. The company needs to be aware that the EC Treaty provides all kinds of legislation facilitating the provision of services to other Member States and the obtaining of R&D services from other EU States. The company must take into consideration, however, that several exceptions to the principle of free movement of services may be allowed. Also there may be national provisions that are unnecessary or disproportionate and therefore not allowed. For example, in one Member State medical laboratories were allowed to analyse only specimens collected at least 60km away. The Commission reported this and many other impediments to the free movement of services at all stages of service provision. The EU legislature subsequently issued several directives on professional qualifications as well as the Services Directive, which was adopted in 2006. The latter directive is designed to remove remaining impediments and put an end to unnecessary administrative procedures involving the provision of cross-border services. Even though TFS may be using the Single Point of Contact system and using eGovernment facilities, the company still needs to beware of infringements of EU law.

6.2 European protection of the free movement of services

Section 6.1 explained that despite primary and secondary EU law, companies such as TFS may still need protection. In this section the way companies may seek protection against infringements of the free movement of services is explained. Businesses must realize that the protection will have effect in a long term but that there is also protection available for the short term.

This section also explains the decisions service-providing businesses must make when they are confronted with infringements by Member States. Should they continue to provide cross-border services or stop providing the services because of the effects of the infringements? Cases and examples are included to explain the business decisions and the effects of those decisions in general and for TFS in particular.

6.2.1 Long-term protection of EU law

As explained in chapter 4, the Commission is the main upholder of European law. This section summarizes the procedures and explains that the Commission's protection may offer companies long-term protection.

The role of upholder of EU law is awarded to the Commission in Article 226 of the EC Treaty. The Commission first asks Member States which are infringing the law to explain their legislation to the Commission. If the Commission is still of the opinion that European law is being breached, it will issue a reasoned opinion. The Member State in question is usually given two months to put an end to the infringement. If they are not able or willing to do so, the Commission may decide to bring the case before the European Court of Justice. If the ECJ agrees with the Commission's allegations, it will order the Member State to end its breach of European law. Case study 6.4 illustrates the role of the Commission and the proceedings of the ECJ in a research & development case.

On 18th March 1999, following a complaint by a German laboratory regarding the French rules on bio-medical analysis laboratories, the Commission sent a letter requesting information from the French authorities, who replied on 21st September 1999. By letter giving formal notice of 1st February 2000, the Commission informed the French government that, in its view, certain provisions of the French rules in question raised problems of compatibility with the right of establishment and the freedom to provide services provided for in Articles 43 and 49 of the EC Treaty. The French authorities failed to reply to that letter and as a result the Commission sent the French Republic a reasoned opinion on 24th January 2001, requesting it to take the measures necessary to comply therewith within two months of its notification. The French authorities replied to the reasoned opinion by letter of 6th June 2001, rejecting the Commission's complaints. As the Commission was not satisfied with that reply, it lodged a case against France with the European Court of Justice on 21st December 2001. The Commission was of the opinion that France had infringed Articles 43 and 49 of the EC Treaty by requiring that bio-medical analysis laboratories established in other Member States have a place of business in France in order to obtain the requisite operating authorization. France also precluded any reimbursement of the costs of bio-medical analyses carried out by a bio-medical analysis laboratory established in another Member State.

The ECJ ruled that Article 49 of the EC Treaty may only be derogated from in accordance with articles laid down in the EC Treaty and with the case law of the court. The court ruled that it is permissible under Article 46 to maintain the quality of medical services not only by ensuring that the directors and staff of bio-medical analysis laboratories hold the necessary qualifications but also by checking, by periodic inspection, that analyses are at all times carried out in accordance with the rules laid down by the French legislature and the French authorities and, in particular, with the required authorization. However, according to settled case law, where measures taken are justified on the basis of an exception provided for in the Treaty, it must be established that those measures do not go beyond what is objectively necessary for the aim to be achieved. The requirement that bio-medical analysis laboratories have a place of business in France goes beyond what is necessary to achieve the aim of protecting public health.

The court also ruled that the refusal by sickness insurance funds to reimburse the costs of analyses carried out by laboratories with their place of business in another Member State is unnecessary in order to maintain the high level of public health protection.

The French legislation on both issues breached Article 49 of the EC Treaty.

Source: European Court of Justice, Commission v. France, Case C-496/01, 11th March 2004, ECR 2004 page I-02351

This case shows that a German laboratory filed a complaint with the Commission before the year 1999. The ECJ's ruling was delivered on 11th March 2004, so it took more than five years before a complaint resulted in a ruling by the ECJ. Article 228 paragraph 1 of the EC Treaty prescribes that after a ruling of the ECJ in which the court has found that the Member State has failed to fulfil an obligation under the EC Treaty or its secondary law, the State must take all necessary measures to comply with the judgment. The time between lodging a complaint with the Commission and the required compliance can therefore be even longer than the five years taken in case study 6.4.

In some cases the measures necessary to comply with the judgment are not (entirely) taken, as case study 6.5 on biotechnology legislation illustrates. In those cases the time span between the lodging of the complaint with the Commission and the correct action of the Member State can be even longer.

The Commission proposed fines against France for failure to adopt biotechnology legislation.

[...]
In spite of a judgement delivered by the European Court of Justice on 27 November 2003, France has failed to correctly and fully transpose the Directive on the contained use of genetically modified micro-organisms (GMMs) into national law. Following the judgement, the Commission has sent several letters to the French authorities reminding them of the need to ensure that a system for the safe use of GMMs is put into place. As foreseen under the EU Treaty, the Commission will ask the Court to impose a daily financial penalty on France. It proposes a daily sum of €168 800. The penalty would be finally set by the Court and would apply from the day France is condemned by the Court of Justice for a second time in this case.
[...]

Source: Rapid Press Releases, IP/06/109, 01/02/2006

Cases 6.4 and 6.5 show why companies such as TFS who file a complaint with the Commission should be aware of the fact that they may achieve the desired result only several years later. In most cases, however, the complaint will also have the effect that the national authorities no longer apply the national regulations that breach European law. For businesses such as TFS operating in the single market, that would be a desirable result.

6.2.2   Short-term protection of EU law

The question remaining is what short-term protection EU law offers TFS and other businesses against barriers to the free movement of services. When businesses decide to provide services in a market other than their own, they must carry out research on the requirements of the service in the other market. Cases 6.1 to 6.5 show that breaches of EU law take many forms. As soon as businesses have to comply with legislation other than they are used to in their home country, they should be aware of the fact that they may have stumbled on a trade barrier in the single market for services. As we have seen before, these barriers may take the form of qualifications for service providers, authorizations and inspections of the service, etc. These barriers are allowed when they are justified by one of the prescriptions of the EC Treaty, such as Articles 45 and 46. For TFS, for instance, the interest of public health is an important exception to the basic rule of the free movement of services.

The company must now assess whether the exception is allowed under Articles 45 or 46 EC. If the company in question has already complied with similar rules in its home country, extra measures in the country of service may be disproportionate. If a company like TFS is of the opinion that they already comply with safety rules in the home country, Sweden, the extra measures may be barriers forbidden by Article 49.

The TFS management and the managements of other companies now face an important decision. Does the company continue with the plans

to export or import the service or not? The answer to this question may also be influenced by the consequences of disregarding the national legislation of a different Member State. Most Member States have similar ways of enforcing legislation. There are two major effects to be expected when companies disregard the requirements of national law:
1 criminal charges and fines
2 administrative measures such as declining permits or other authorizations.

If the management decides to go on with providing or importing the service, the company has to be aware that they must convince the national authorities that their legislation breaches European law. If the national authorities are not convinced, they will probably bring criminal charges against the company or decide to decline authorization for the service. In both cases the companies will have to provide the same arguments to the national courts, similar to those in case study 6.2 concerning the criminal charges against Mr Placanica. In most cases the national courts are able to make a decision based on European law, without consulting the European Court of Justice.

When the national court has questions about the application of primary or secondary European law, that court may ask the ECJ for help in accordance with Article 234 of the EC Treaty. The ECJ will explain the European law in such a way that the national court is able to assess whether the national legislation is allowed or prohibited by EU law.

When the national court case is suspended for the preliminary ruling, the company in question has to wait a couple of years for the ECJ's final answer and then wait again for the final ruling of the national court. In this case the company is not provided with short-term protection against the breach of EU law.

For short-term protection, business must assess the national requirements of the service and convince the other Member State's authorities that their legislation breaches EU law when applied to a cross-border service in the single market. At this stage, the company may announce that it will file a complaint with the Commission on the matter. This may produce the desired result that the contested legislation will not be applied.

Usually businesses do not want to be caught up in legal proceedings and therefore often decide not to continue to provide their service in another Member State. That is why the EC has implemented the Service Directive and the 'Single Points of Contact' in every Member Sate, where all the administrative procedures take place through eGoverning.

6.3 The import and export of services

Services were the main activity of 14.5 million enterprises in the EU-27 in 2005, which generated a turnover of €11,974 billion. (The services discussed in this chapter do not include financial and insurance services, unless otherwise specified; see table 6.2 for the classification of services.)

© Noordhoff Uitgevers bv

With an annual turnover of €2,991 billion and employing 76 million people, services accounted for almost sixty per cent of the non-financial business economy (including manufacturing, construction, wholesale and retail, hotels and restaurants, transport, storage and communication, and real estate, renting and business activities).

In terms of employment, it was the largest sector, well ahead of industry and construction, which had shares of 29% and 11% respectively. The United Kingdom, the Netherlands, Ireland and Greece were clearly the most specialized in terms of employment as the services sector made up more than seventy per cent of their non-financial business economies. In contrast, Romania and Slovakia were the least specialized with shares of 43.2% and 43.7% respectively.

Table 6.2 **Definition of services according to the Nomenclature générale des Activités économiques dans les Communautés européennes (NACE – General Industrial Classification of Economic Activities in the European Communities) Rev.1. classification**

70	Real estate services	
72.1–6	Computers	• Hardware consultancy • Software consultancy • Data processing • Database activities
73	Research & development	
74.11, 74.12, 74.14	Professional	• Legal activities • Accounting and tax consultancy • Management consulting
74.15, 74.13, 74.4	Holding companies	
	Marketing	• Market research • Advertising
74.2, 74.3	Technical	• Architectural activities • Engineering activities • Technical testing and analysis
71.1, 71.21–23, 71.31–33	Leasing and renting equipment	• Renting of transport and construction • Renting of office machinery incl. computers
74.5	Labour recruitement and provision of personnel	
74.6, 74.7	Operational	• Security activities • Industrial cleaning
74.81–84	Other	• Secretarial and translation activities • Packaging activities • Fairs and exhibitions

Looking at employment in the four main activities that make up the EU-27 services sector, 'Distributive trades' was the largest in 2005, making up 40.7% of the total. 'Real estate, renting and business activities' (including legal, accounting and management services and labour recruitment) was the second largest activity (32.2%). 'Transport and communications' ranked third while 'Hotels and restaurants' was the smallest activity in terms of employment. It is also important to point out that the services sector is a key employment sector for women in particular, and that they therefore stand to benefit greatly from new opportunities offered by the completion of the internal market for services.

Since services constitute the engine of economic growth and account for the better part of GDP and employment in most Member States, the importance of the service industry cannot be overestimated. However, the apparent fragmentation of the internal market has a negative impact on the entire European economy, in particular on the competitiveness of SMEs and the movement of workers, and prevents consumers from gaining access to a greater variety of competitively priced services.

(See 6.1 for a detailed discussion of how the EC Treaty aims to stimulate cross-border trade. Articles 49 and 50 are especially important for understanding cross-border trade and its relation with the national regulations.)

After this brief introduction to services in Europe, we first examine the success and failure factors for exporting services within the EU – as perceived by the companies involved (6.3.1). Section 6.3.2 discusses some macro-economic data on intra-EU and extra-EU trade. The section ends with some suggested solutions to the insufficient exploitation of trade opportunities within the EU (6.3.3).

6.3.1 What are the success and failure factors for exporting services?

Trade of services within the EU is not as widespread as it might be. Therefore it is important to know which factors companies identify as aiding or restricting them in exporting their services. On the demand side the issue is what problems/restrictions do companies encounter when they are considering buying a cross-border service.

First let us have a closer look at export barriers.

Of the barriers to exporting specified in figure 6.1, those cited as significant by the largest proportion of businesses were difficulties in identifying clients, and language and cultural barriers.

The top three barriers that companies identified – identifying clients, language and culture and commercial presence – are all related to marketing (communication) issues. How those barriers may be eliminated is discussed in 6.4.

On the demand side location was the main barrier when companies searched for services outside their country.

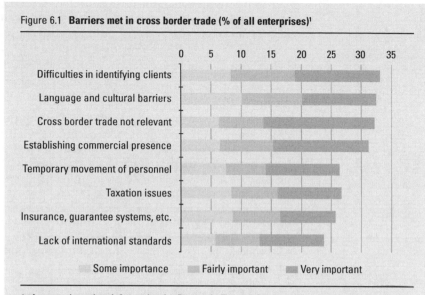

Figure 6.1 **Barriers met in cross border trade (% of all enterprises)[1]**

Difficulties in identifying clients
Language and cultural barriers
Cross border trade not relevant
Establishing commercial presence
Temporary movement of personnel
Taxation issues
Insurance, guarantee systems, etc.
Lack of international standards

Some importance Fairly important Very important

1 Average based on information for Denmark, Finland, Germany, Greece, Latvia, Lithuania, Poland, Romania, Slovenia, Slovakia, Spain, Sweden and the United Kingdom.

Source: Eurostat (SBS)

In Figure 6.2 only positive answers have been retained. This shows that location (40.3%) was confirmed as the main barrier to purchasing services across Member States. Otherwise, the results tended to show country-specific trends, language, for example, being a relatively important barrier in Finland and Sweden, cultural and trust barriers, as well as legal and regulatory barriers, being relatively important in Denmark, and economic barriers in Lithuania.

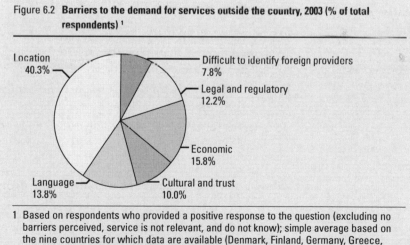

Figure 6.2 **Barriers to the demand for services outside the country, 2003 (% of total respondents) [1]**

Location 40.3%
Difficult to identify foreign providers 7.8%
Legal and regulatory 12.2%
Economic 15.8%
Cultural and trust 10.0%
Language 13.8%

1 Based on respondents who provided a positive response to the question (excluding no barriers perceived, service is not relevant, and do not know); simple average based on the nine countries for which data are available (Denmark, Finland, Germany, Greece, Latvia, Lithuania, Poland, Slovenia and Sweden).

Source: Eurostat, SBS

In hi-tech activities, manufacturing enterprises tended to be more likely than service providers to report that their main external service provider was from another country, although this was not the case for IT services, accounting and book-keeping, or financial services (where hi-tech service enterprises may seek information and expertise from abroad when no local knowledge is available).

The EU should recognize the special characteristics of services and design support programmes accordingly. Most of the EU internationalization support programmes focus on products either explicitly or by default. There is a definite lack of programmes focused specifically on service support. This can be partially explained by the lack of experience or expertise of most trade promotion agencies in the area of supporting the internationalization of services.

Differences in regulation form a significant obstacle for trade in services. The Services Directive represents a first step towards resolving this problem but is still far from enabling the optimization of economic potential in this area. (See also 6.4.3.)

Differences in political structure, legal systems and quality of governance can affect the volume of business transactions between two partner countries. In a political structure that devolves many responsibilities to local government – as Germany does to its *Länder* – a multiplicity of rules can arise that impede imports and direct foreign investment. Empirical research shows that differences in legal systems between countries can likewise lead to extra information costs and to extra costs for legal aid in business disputes. For both trade in services and foreign investments those costs can be a major impediment.

The quality of institutions in a Member State is also important for trade, investment and migration. For instance, countries with a reputation for good and transparent governance are more successful in the export of services.

Finally, diversity in culture and language factors can reduce the effectiveness of internal market policy.

6.3.2 How important is the import and export of services for Europe?

To date, the services sector is lagging behind the goods sector in terms of market integration. The ratio of intra-EU to extra-EU exports of services is around 1:3. For goods this ratio is much higher, at around 2:1. This means that, in the case of goods, EU integration has fostered intra-EU trade relative to trade with the rest of the world.

Another way to look at this is to see that services account for about 28% of total EU external trade (the remaining 72% being goods), while the corresponding proportions in the case of EU internal trade are 20% and 80%. The data thus suggests that the services sector is less open to international trade than the goods-producing sector and that EU market liberalization has not notably improved market integration, at least over the past few years.

International trade in services currently amounts to around 12% of the added value in services. This percentage is considerably lower than for goods.

In 2007, the EU Member States registered exports of services worth €1,160 billion, of which exports to other Member States amounted to €658.6 billion, while exports to countries outside the Union amounted to €501.4 billion. In other words, the internal market accounted for 56.8% of total exports. Figure 6.3 shows that intra-EU exports as a share of the total exports of all Member States have decreased continually in recent years, from 58.6% in 2004 to 56.8% in 2007. For imports, the shares are more stable.

Figure 6.3 **Share of Member States' intra-EU and extra-EU in trade in services**

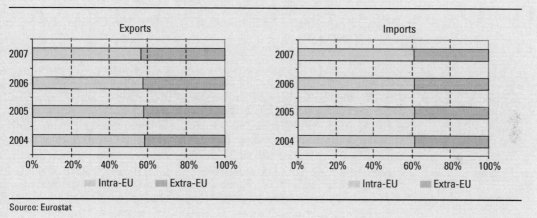

Source: Eurostat

Intra-EU trade

Intra-EU services are not equally distributed among the various sectors. Table 6.3 shows that, in 2007, the service categories with the highest share of intra-EU exports were travel and communication services, with 71% and 69% of total exports respectively. However, where travel accounts for about a quarter of total service exports; communication services, on the other hand, account for only about 3%.

It should be noted that the intra-EU share of insurance services has decreased significantly in recent years, from 68% in 2005 (above average) to 51% in 2007 (below average). A decrease was also observed in computer and construction services, signifying that exports outside the EU have increased at a higher rate than exports to the EU internal market in these service categories.

Table 6.3 **Intra-EU share of exports among service categories**

	Total exports from all MS (€ bn)		Share in total exports (in %)		Share of intra-EU exports in total exports (in %)	
	2005	2007	2005	2007	2005	2007
Services	**969.0**	**1160.0**	**100**	**100**	**58**	**57**
Transportation	211.2	244.6	22	21	51	52
Travel	236.7	267.1	24	23	72	71
Communication services	25.7	31.1	3	3	71	69
Construction services	23.6	28.6	2	2	48	44
Insurance services	19.3	29.3	2	3	68	51
Financial services	76.8	119.9	8	10	54	55
Computer and information services	49.8	58.6	5	5	65	60
Royalties and license fees	39.5	44.5	4	4	40	42
Other business services	251.3	304.2	26	26	53	51
Personal, cultural and recreational services	11.6	12.4	1	1	58	60
Government services, n.i.e.	16.8	16.8	2	1	53	54

Source: Eurostat

Note:
Other business services include merchandizing and other trade-related services, operational leasing services (rental) without operators, and miscellaneous business professional and technical services, which is again sub-divided into legal, accounting, management consulting, and public relations services, advertising, market research and public opinion polling services, research & development services, architectural, engineering and other technical services, agricultural, mining and on-site processing services, other miscellaneous business, professional and technical services, and services between affiliated enterprises.

■ **Example 6.1 Contribution of business services to European economic growth**
Kox and Rubalcaba (2007) analysed the contribution of business services to European economic growth.

They argued that:
- business services has had several positive external effects outside the industry itself, particularly in the areas of innovation and productivity development
- the sector makes its own, direct contribution to technological innovation, particularly in software and engineering
- it contributes directly, through non-technological innovations, to labour productivity development in client industries
- the business services sector contributes to the diffusion of production-frontier knowledge among client companies, with regard to many areas of competence and business development. As a result, business services contribute to the general speed of technological and non-technological innovation in the European economy.

The authors concluded that for the prosperous development of European business services, EU-wide policies that override what national governments do (or can do) to improve the market performance of national business services sectors are needed.

However, to deal with market failures in business services development, EU policies may need to be formulated with a co-operative eye to Member States' national policies. Such co-operation may pertain, for instance, to quality standards, recognition of professional qualifications, and business tax regulations. Some policy issues, such as employment policies for the business services industry, might perhaps more efficiently be left to the governments of EU Member States, although some Commission activities and policies could help to promote employment-related actions at regional and national level.

Figure 6.4 shows the share of total intra-EU trade in services (exports + imports) among individual Member States (MS) in 2007. Germany accounts for 15% of all intra-EU transactions in services (13% of all intra-EU exports and 18% of all intra-EU imports). It is followed by the UK (12%), Spain (9%), Italy (9%) and France (8%).

Figure 6.4 **Member States' share of total intra-EU trade in services, 2007**

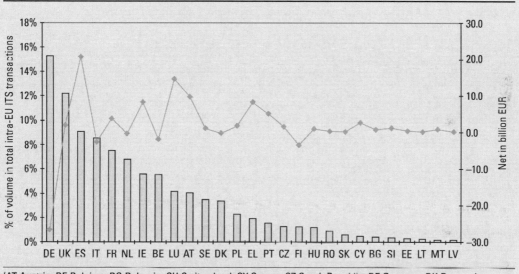

(AT Austria, BE Belgium, BG Bulgaria, CH Switzerland, CY Cyprus, CZ Czech Republic, DE Germany, DK Denmark, EE Estonia, EL Greece, ES Spain, FI Finland, FR France, HR Croatia, HU Hungary, IE Ireland, IS Iceland, IT Italy, LT Lithuania, LU Luxembourg, LV Latvia, MK Macedonia, MT Malta, NL Netherlands, NO Norway, PL Poland, PT Portugal, RO Romania, SE Sweden, SI Slovenia, SK Slovakia, TR Turkey, UK United Kingdom)

Source: Eurostat

The line represents the surplus or deficit in intra-EU trade in services per country (in €billion). Germany recorded by far the highest deficit in intra-EU trade in services (−€26.6 billion). Finland, Italy and Belgium were the other debtor countries in that year. Spain was the biggest creditor country; it registered a surplus of €20.7 billion. Luxembourg, Austria, Ireland and Greece were the other countries with significant surpluses.

Looking only at exports, the major portion of intra-EU services (53%) goes to the original six Member States (Belgium, France, Germany, Italy, Luxembourg and Netherlands) followed by the United Kingdom, Ireland and Denmark (36%).

We have looked at the importance of the different types of services and the amount of money that is involved in intra-EU trade. Table 6.4 provides information about the importance of the types of services for each EU Member State by comparing its intra-EU exports as a share of its total exports with the intra-EU share of the EU as a whole.

The index is defined as the intra-EU share of a service category in a country's total exports in that category, divided by the corresponding share of the EU total. So, if the index is greater than one, a country exports relatively more in that service category to the EU internal market than the EU as a whole; it is therefore considered to be specialized in the exporting of that service category to the EU internal market. If the index is less than one, the country's intra-EU export share is smaller than that of the EU as a whole. For instance, Belgium exports 1.9 times more services in construction than the average intra-EU export (of all Member States) in that service category. Belgium is less specialized in exporting other business services within the EU (0.8).

Table 6.4 **Intra-EU trade specialization**

	Total services	Transport	Travel	Commu-nication	Con-struction	Insurance	Financial	Computer	Royalties	Other business	Personal	Govern-ment
BE	1.1	1.3	1.2	0.9	1.9	1.6	1.3	1.4	1.8	0.8	1.6	1.7
BG	1.2	1.3	1.0	1.2	1.5	1.3	1.4	1.2	1.8	1.3	0.8	0.6
CZ	1.3	1.3	1.1	1.0	1.9	0.7	1.0	1.2	1.8	1.4	1.6	0.1
DK	0.8	0.8	1.0	1.0	0.9	0.7	1.7	1.1	1.1	1.2	1.2	0.7
DE	0.9	0.9	1.0	0.9	0.9	0.9	1.4	0.8	0.9	1.0	0.7	1.0
EE	1.2	1.3	1.0	1.2	1.9	2.0	1.0	1.3	1.0	1.2	1.3	1.2
IE	1.1	1.7	1.0	1.0	na	1.3	1.0	1.2	1.1	0.9	0.3	1.7
EL	0.9	0.6	1.1	1.2	1.3	1.4	1.3	1.2	1.7	1.5	0.9	1.1
ES	1.3	1.3	1.2	1.1	0.8	1.0	1.4	0.5	1.4	1.4	1.0	1.4
FR	0.9	0.7	1.0	0.9	0.4	1.3	0.8	0.9	0.7	0.6	1.0	1.2
IT	1.1	0.9	0.9	1.1	1.0	1.4	1.4	1.4	1.3	1.4	1.2	0.3
CY	1.3	1.3	1.1	1.1	1.7	1.3	1.5	0.6	2.1	1.2	1.1	1.8
LV	0.9	1.0	1.0	1.1	1.9	0.0	0.0	1.0	1.6	0.7	0.3	0.7
LT	1.1	1.1	0.9	1.0	1.3	2.2	1.2	1.4	0.0	1.3	1.3	1.2
LU	1.3	1.1	1.4	1.2	1.4	1.8	1.3	1.5	1.7	1.6	1.6	1.9
HU	1.2	1.5	1.0	1.2	1.6	1.7	1.2	1.3	0.6	1.3	1.0	1.1
MT	1.4	1.6	1.2	1.2	0.0	1.7	0.3	0.7	1.7	1.5	1.5	0.8
NL	1.0	1.1	1.1	0.9	1.2	1.2	1.0	1.0	1.2	1.0	1.2	0.8
AT	1.3	1.5	1.2	1.1	1.8	1.7	0.9	1.3	1.4	1.3	1.4	0.4
PL	1.3	1.4	1.1	1.2	1.7	0.6	1.5	1.3	1.4	1.5	1.4	0.3
PT	1.4	1.3	1.2	1.2	1.8	1.5	1.3	1.2	2.0	1.4	1.2	1.1
RO	1.4	1.5	1.0	1.2	1.4	1.7	1.6	1.1	1.3	1.5	1.4	1.1
SI	1.3	1.5	1.1	1.1	1.3	1.5	1.0	1.1	0.9	1.2	1.0	0.4
SK	1.4	1.2	1.3	1.3	2.0	1.7	1.7	1.3	1.6	1.7	1.4	1.0
FI	0.7	1.4	0.8	1.0	0.9	1.6	0.2	0.9	0.7	0.6	1.2	1.0
SE	0.9	1.1	0.6	1.0	0.7	0.6	1.0	0.8	1.1	1.0	1.3	0.0
UK	0.7	0.8	0.6	0.9	0.9	0.3	0.6	0.7	0.8	0.8	0.7	0.7

Source: Eurostat

A few interesting observations can be made:
- European export figures show that of all EU countries, Germany and Denmark are the biggest exporters of transportation services; however, the intra-EU share of total exports of these two countries is less than the share of the EU as a whole. Spain is the major travel destination in the EU. The proportion of receipts from travellers coming from EU countries is higher in Spain than in the EU as a whole.
- In construction services there is a much bigger variation between the countries. The intra-EU share of Slovak exports in this service category is twice as high as the share for the EU (however, Slovakia plays a minor role in this area).
- In exports of insurance services, Ireland and the UK are the major players in the EU.
- Luxembourg and the UK are by far the largest exporters of financial services.
- In computer services, Luxembourg is specialized in intra-EU exports, while in Spain the intra-EU share of exports is only half that for the EU as a whole.
- Ireland – the leading exporter of computer services – exports relatively more to the EU internal market than the other Member States.
- In the service category royalties and licence fees, the UK and the Netherlands are the major exporters. While the intra-EU share of Netherlands exports is higher than that of the EU, for the UK it is the other way round.
- The UK and Germany are the major exporters of other business services, which make up the biggest service category in terms of EU exports.
- Personal, cultural and recreational services are one of the two smallest service categories, accounting for about one per cent of total EU exports. The UK and France are the major exporters in this category.
- Government services are the other smallest category. Germany, with the same intra-EU share as the EU, is the biggest exporter.

To conclude on the subject of intra-EU trade:
The intra-EU share of trade in services is much less than that for trade in goods. This indicates that EU integration has been much stronger for trade in goods than for trade in services. In the major countries, such as the UK, Germany and France, the share of total trade in services accounted for by the EU internal market is in many categories below the EU average. In other words, in these countries a higher export share in many categories goes to non-EU member countries. Transportation, travel and other business services are the main export services within the EU. There is a pattern of specialization in intra-EU trade in services. Also, the countries that joined the EU in 2004 were able to increase their exports of services within the EU at a higher rate than their exports to non-EU countries.

Unfortunately, Member States still apply national legislation that may hinder the free movement of services within the EU. (See 6.1.2. for a more detailed discussion of this topic.)

Extra-EU trade

Since the 1990s, the volume of exports of EU goods and services has increased in a broadly similar pattern, both by about 6.5% per year on average. Consequently services maintained their share of roughly 22% of overall international trade during this period. Figure 6.5 shows that exports of services from the EU to its main partners (Extra-EU-27/EU-25, Canada, USA, Japan, Brazil, Russia, China, India and Hong Kong) in 2007 grew faster than goods exports, after lagging slightly behind in previous years. This was mainly due to the expanding international supply of many services and to the increase in transportation prices.

Figure 6.5 **EU GDP and exports of goods and services with non-EU partners, 1997–2007**
(at 2000 prices and exchange rates, annual percentage change)

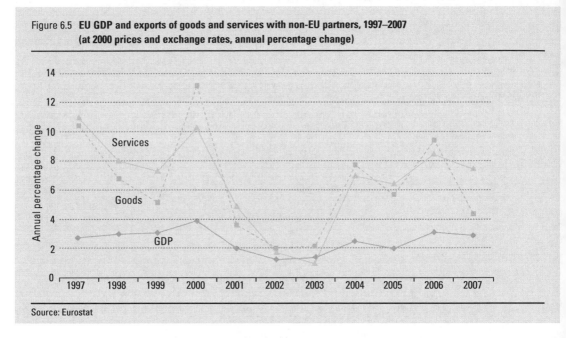

Source: Eurostat

According to figures published by the International Monetary Fund (IMF), total international trade in services (exports plus imports) in 2007 amounted to €48,18.7 billion (of which intra-EU trade accounted for €1,302.2 billion) – an increase in value of 9.5% compared with 2006.

However, the European Union continued to be the biggest global player in the international trade in services (ITS). In 2007, the EU's ITS recorded a surplus of €84.1 billion, compared to €68.5 billion in 2006 and €54.1 billion in 2005. The USA remained the EU's main trading partner. Of all the EU Member States, the UK was the biggest contributor to extra-EU transactions.

Looking at different categories of services and the trend since 2005, there is an increased surplus for financial services (to +€30.8 billion in 2007), computer and information services (to +€14.5 billion in 2007), insurance services (from a deficit to +€6.9 billion in 2007) and construction services (to +€8.1 billion in 2007). Transportation services varied between +€11.1 billion and +€15.5 billion. The significant surplus in 'other business services', which comprise merchanting and other trade-related services, operational leasing services and miscellaneous business, professional and technical services, remained stable (+€35.5 billion in 2007).

On the credit side, insurance services experienced the biggest increase in relative terms (+28.3%), followed by financial services, communication services, construction services, and computer and information services (+22.9%, +17.3%, +16.2% and +15.3% respectively). On the import side, double-digit rates of expansion were seen in financial services, other business services, royalties and licence fees and construction services.

Overall, the volume of extra-EU trade in services is about a quarter of that of trade in goods.

Figure 6.6 gives the trade in services in billions of euros with some major countries outside the EU.

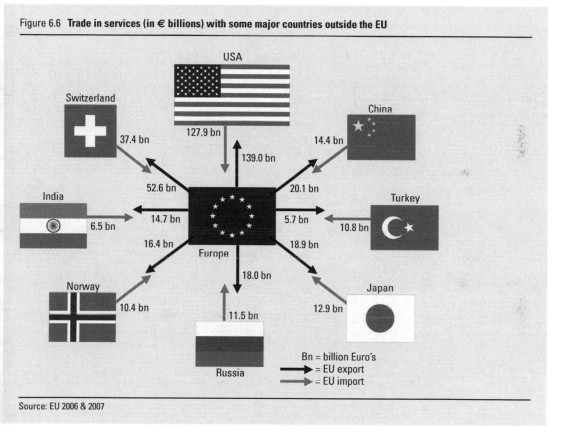

Figure 6.6 **Trade in services (in € billions) with some major countries outside the EU**

Source: EU 2006 & 2007

Within the EU-25, 53.6 million people categorized as 'Human Resources in Science and Technology' were employed in the services sector and 9.4 million in the manufacturing sector in 2004. In relative terms, Human Resources in Science and Technology employees represented 47% of total employment in services, but only 29% in the manufacturing sector.

The share of scientists and engineers among Human Resources in Science and Technology personnel varied markedly across sectors. At EU-25 level it was highest in the hi-tech 'knowledge-intensive services' sector with 35.3%, followed by the hi-tech manufacturing sector with 27.5%.

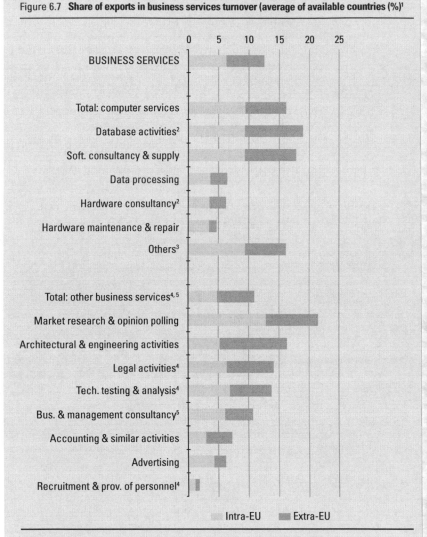

Figure 6.7 **Share of exports in business services turnover (average of available countries (%)[1]**

1 Average based on information for: Denmark, Spain, Portugal, Romania, Slovenia and Sweden (all 2005), Germany, Lithuania, Slovakia, Finland and the United Kingdom (all 2004), Estonia, Latvia and Poland (all 2003); Denmark, provisional; Poland and Sweden, including estimates.
2 Excluding Lithuania.
3 Excluding Spain.
4 Excluding Portugal.
5 Excluding Estonia.

Source: Eurostat (SBS)

The proportion of exports in relation to total turnover was highest for computer services, although the share was particularly low for computer activities related to hardware and data processing. Among other business services, market research and public opinion polling businesses had the largest non-resident market, while businesses providing recruitment and personnel services were the most concentrated on national clients. Businesses providing architectural and engineering services had the highest proportion of their exports outside the EU (see figure 6.7).

The most profitable service activities by far were renting of machinery, real estate activities, post and telecommunications, and water transport.

6.3.3 How to improve the export of services

The diversity and complexity of services preclude the formulation of a standardized and simple set of solutions to the problem of optimizing exports. However, based on 'lessons learned' and expectations of future trends, some suggestions for possible solutions can be made.

Focus on business services and the facilitation of outsourcing
Employment in EU-25 services grew by 12% overall from 2000 to 2004 compared with the non-financial business economy, which grew by 6% as a whole, and industry, which shrank by 5%. This decline in industry is also to be expected for the coming years and is explained by the automation of tasks, the relocation of industrial activities to countries with lower cost bases, and the increased use of outsourcing by businesses, which call on external service providers for non-core activities (e.g. transport, accounting and marketing services) or even for production (e.g. through temporary labour provision services).

Business services are performed in-house or outsourced, and the increase in outsourcing has led to growth in the business services sector. Service businesses include highly advanced consultancy services such as management consultancy or computer services, professional services such as engineering and legal services, marketing services such as advertising or fairs and exhibitions, labour-intensive services such as personnel services, and operational services such as cleaning and security services.

Business services are of major importance in helping the SME sector realize its potential contribution to innovation and growth. There is evidence that some of the most dynamic SMEs already make use of business services to perform the functions that cannot be undertaken in-house. The providers of business services are often small enterprises, which require the right environment to be able to flourish.

European policy on industrial competitiveness is primarily focused on manufacturing of goods. However, with the growing integration of business services into manufacturing and their importance for economic development, this policy needs to be extended and targeted on business services.

Focus on the tourism sector

According to the World Tourism Organization, Europe is the world's most important tourist destination and tourism generating region. Indeed, according to figures from the same source, more than half (54.8%) of worldwide international tourist arrivals in 2005 (estimated at 806 million) were recorded in Europe (441.5 million). Most of these were recorded within EU-27 Member States, France, Spain, Italy, the United Kingdom, Germany and Austria all figuring in the top 10 list of international tourist arrivals and together accounting for almost 30% of the worldwide total.

Simplification and harmonization of regulations

Nine per cent of European companies reported import tariffs in destination countries as a major obstacle to export (to countries within or outside the EU). Table 6.5 shows which measures were included in the Treaty of Rome (1957) to eliminate obstacles.

Table 6.5 **Specific measures in the Treaty of Rome in respect of the free movement of services**

Obstacles	Instruments
barriers to commercial, professional and artisan services	elimination of discriminating restrictions
barriers to network services	policy harmonisatie
quantitative restrictions	common transport policy
	elimination of restrictions on free delivery of services

The potential effects of the creation of an internal market allowing the free movement of services, capital and labour with respect to trade are as yet unclear, since the measures designed to ensure free movement are fairly recent. The potential effects, however, are considerable: Kox and Lejour (2006) show that intra-EU trade in services could rise by 30 to 60% and that bilateral direct investments in services could increase by 20 to 35% if regulations are harmonized. This means that GDP could increase by some 0.3 to 0.7%. The GDP effects for the Netherlands are slightly more pronounced, due to its specialization in commercial services.

6.4 The marketing of services in Europe

For a clear understanding of the complexity of the marketing of services in Europe it is necessary to understand the main features of a service. These are applicable to all types of service.

The main features of a service are intangibility (no physical elements), perishability (if the service is not used at the appropriate time it becomes obsolete), lack of ownership (a service is used, not owned, e.g. leasing, consultancy, medical treatment), heterogeneity (a service is time and place related and therefore quality is difficult to standardize) and inseparability (services may vary in completeness, but customers cannot use only part of a service, e.g. specialized and full-service advertising agencies). Therefore networking and building and maintaining a good relationship with all stakeholders is even more important for the successful marketing of services than it is for the marketing of goods.

Positioning products or services efficiently in attractive market segments in Europe is a key activity for every European marketer. Internationalization of services in the diverse and multicultural environment of Europe may give a challenging added value to a company.

A difficulty in designing an internationalization strategy for services is that often the initial success of a service is related to the features of the domestic market. Comparison of these features with those of a foreign country is therefore essential to avoid a 'country-of-origin' tendency and consequent wrong positioning of the service.

Reasons for the internationalization of services do not differ from those relating to product marketing (see section 5.6.3). However, the marketing mix for 'intangibles' offers some unique challenges (see 6.4.3).

The structure of this section is as follows:
In the first subsection (6.4.1) some features – which may be important for a commercial manager – of the European internal market are described. This is followed by some practical advice on how to conduct market research within Europe (6.4.2). 6.4.3 discusses relevant aspects for international strategies and practical considerations for introducing products and/or maintaining market share in existing markets. Finally, 6.4.4 describes the impact the internet has had and continues to have on the European services sector.

6.4.1 The EU internal marketplace

Three trends within the EU will increase the need for services and influence the type of services required:

Social change
- An increase in expenditure on leisure activities and an improved quality of life brought about by rising affluence will lead to an increase in demand for various services internationally.

Business change
- The trend towards international franchising and the creation of international standards for services such as ISO 9000
- In recent decades the services sector has grown in importance thanks to an increase in outsourcing. A growing number of businesses are outsourcing to service providers either for non-core activities (such as transport or marketing) or for part of their core activities in order to increase flexibility (for example, through the use of labour recruitment services). Another reason for the increase in outsourcing is technological development – particularly in relation to information and communication technologies (ICT), which may allow services to be delivered over considerable distances (for example, via internet sales or call centres).

Advances in technology

- Technology has cut through the constraints on the provision of services traditionally imposed by national boundaries.

Unfortunately the EU already has an efficiency disadvantage in relation to other major global markets due to the fact that it has so many different cultures and languages with relatively small domestic markets. from the relative absence of an economy of scale factor is a direct consequence of this.

The EU can generate infrastructure and regulations and harmonize the legal environment in order to stimulate companies to internationalize. This will benefit not only the internal market, but also the European (negotiating, competitive) position vis-à-vis other major economic powers like the USA, India, China and Japan.

6.4.2 Market research within Europe

Market research is employed to identify the key success factors of a service (e.g. for competitive benchmarking) by various data collection techniques such as telephone surveys, interviews, questionnaires and emails.

Conducting market research early in the development process of a service is essential for successful (new) services.

Basically the same tools are used for market research in services as in products. (See also section 5.6.2.)

However, cultural attitudes and behaviour are more critical to the successful introduction of a service than of a tangible product. In particular, services in the diverse European business-to-consumer (BtoC) markets require adaptation to each specific market.

In their research into cultural mapping, Hofstede and Trompenaars have studied and described social behaviour in many European and non-European countries and identified aspects of it that correlate to a large extent with (business) behaviour.

In any European market research where data are being collected on market features and customers' needs for the appropriate positioning of a service, these behavioural aspects must be taken into account.

There are many organizations that can carry out market research, and there are several selection criteria.

Broadly, the ideal candidate has experience and knowledge of your type of service and your cross-border target markets. Also, it should be able to use different data collection techniques.

A few major sources of information on market research organizations are briefly described below.

The ESOMAR Directory of Research Organisations (http://directory.esomar.org/) is an up-to-date, searchable resource of over 2,000 major research organizations worldwide. The Directory enables research buyers to find and select research companies, with the reassurance that all companies listed have agreed to abide by the ICC/ESOMAR International Code on Market and Social Research.
The Alliance of International Market Research Institutes (AIMRI) was founded in Bruges in 1991 and currently has nearly 100 members in 30 countries. It represents the corporate and business interests of international market research agencies. AIMRI helps members develop their businesses by connecting them with fellow professionals throughout the world. Where clients need a to carry out research in many countries, members work together to provide a global service.

All About Market Research (www.allaboutmarketresearch.com/) is a guide to the best tools, tips and services for internet market research.

Researchandmarkets, a searchable database of market research reports (www.researchandmarkets.com/info/about.asp), is a source of international market research and market data. It produces many research publications written by consultants and analysts which contain data on international and regional markets, key industries, companies, new products and the latest trends.

Global Information, Inc. (GII) offers business intelligence and market research products. It has offices in Korea, Singapore, Taiwan, Brussels, and the United States. With respect to services GII offers market research, industry forecasts and business analysis in the travel and tourism market, including hotels, accommodation, transportation, car hire, tourist attractions and tours.

Before engaging a supplier to conduct your market research, you should consider two further factors: first, since the service often involves a collaboration with the company with intensive communication, the 'chemistry' between the two organizations must be right; second, costs of market research within the EU vary markedly, and Eastern European organizations are often less expensive than their Western European counterparts.

6.4.3 European marketing strategy and operations

A European service marketing strategy must take account of the fact that access to markets varies. This applies generally to services but especially to professional services. Market access restrictions hamper not only the establishment of new domestic suppliers but also the entry of foreign suppliers. By eliminating those restrictions, including the restrictive rules for entrepreneurs' conduct, more market integration and a pan-European strategy is possible.

The structure of this section is similar to that of the equivalent section relating to goods (see 5.6.3). Like the latter, it starts by giving strategic information and ends with suggestions as to how a European marketer may put together a successful marketing mix.

First, the reasons why companies might want to internationalize are briefly discussed. Then the various ways in which a company may enter a foreign market are reviewed, including some pros and cons for each entry strategy. The next part deals with competition within Europe and how EU legislation and harmonization may help or inhibit intra-European marketing of services. Finally, operational marketing strategies in Europe are explained in terms of the marketing mix (the seven Ps for services).

Why do companies export services?
Let us first look at some data to ascertain whether the service market in Europe is a potentially profitable one.

It is a growing market: during the five-year period from 2001 to 2006, the EU-27 index of turnover increased on average by approximately 5% per annum within the non-financial services sector for which data are available. The highest rates of sales growth were reported for transport services, with average growth of 5.8% per annum for land transport and transport via pipelines, 5.6% per annum for air transport, and 5.4% per annum for water transport services. The lowest rates of turnover growth across the NACE divisions for non-financial services were registered for hotels and restaurants (3.5% per annum) and for retail trade (3.1% per annum).

The seven generic reasons for exporting are also true for exporting services. These are: opportunity development, leveraging key success factors abroad, following customers abroad, pursuing diversification, taking advantage of different growth rates of economies, exploiting product life cycle differences and internationalizing for defensive reasons (also mentioned in section 5.6.3, European marketing strategy and operations). However, extra challenges are the three Ps involving human interaction: people, processes and physical environment.

From European data collected in 2004 a clear picture emerges of the major reasons for cross-border trade. Figure 6.8 presents the five main reasons. The most common reason given by exporters for engaging in cross-border trade of services was that they had a cutting-edge or niche market product.

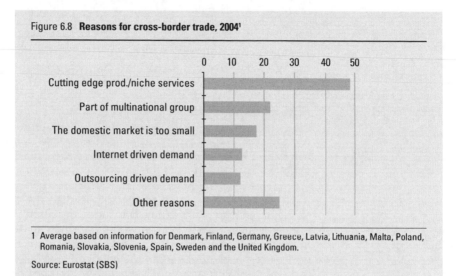

Figure 6.8 **Reasons for cross-border trade, 2004[1]**

1 Average based on information for Denmark, Finland, Germany, Greece, Latvia, Lithuania, Malta, Poland, Romania, Slovakia, Slovenia, Spain, Sweden and the United Kingdom.

Source: Eurostat (SBS)

TFS (the chapter's opening case study) had three reasons for engaging in cross-border trade: cutting-edge products, a small domestic market (Sweden) and the trend among pharmaceutical companies to increasingly outsource research & development. It improved its trading position by moving to Medicon Valley in Lund, by expanding throughout Europe (e.g. its acquisition of CDC Clinical Data Care) and by opening an office in Japan.

Competition within the EU

Market integration in the EU increases demand because businesses produce not only for the national market but also for foreign markets. In addition, competition in a larger market increases the need for businesses to innovate. Greater competition also leads to lower profits, however, as a result of which the scope for innovation diminishes.

More competition as a result of opening up markets leads to a reduction in profit margins, meaning that only the more productive businesses survive.

More trade within the EU produces more competition, which pushes prices down. This leads to higher production by a smaller number of businesses, after the least productive businesses have left the market. Average productivity per employee therefore rises if competition increases due to trade.

Financial services
Interest rates for consumers differ widely in Europe and also within the euro area. Additionally, costs for international transactions are often much higher than for domestic transactions.

The European Commission has proposed the Payment Services Directive, which will introduce uniform rules from 2012 and promote competition. This should lead to lower transaction costs. In addition there will be directives on mortgage loans and consumer credits designed to promote international competition.

Efforts to promote (European) competition in financial services can produce extensive benefits for consumers, although a possible restructuring of the financial sector and the potential elimination of bank branches can cause these benefits to be distributed unequally.

Network industries
Many markets in network sectors, such as telecommunication, electricity, gas, post and transport, have been liberalized since the 1980s. But the degree to which the Member States have liberalized their market varies widely. This impedes the European integration of network sectors.

In electricity and gas, public ownership is often the norm. The division of tasks (such as production, transport and supply) by monopolists often encounters resistance, which indicates greater trust in the government than in the operation of the market. More competition could nonetheless lead to higher productivity and lower prices. A requirement is the physical integration of the networks to transport gas and electricity. International connections are exceptions rather than the rule.

Network industries can also contribute to security of supply. The liberalization and integration of network sectors is no simple undertaking. Sound (European) supervision is necessary for security of supply in the short and long term and the protection of consumers. There needs to be a balance between mutual recognition, regulation by the host country and harmonization. Mutual recognition and harmonization can contribute to a level playing field for businesses, but harmonization in particular can lead to rigidity in regulation.

Careful regulation is essential for network industries, and further European integration in a number of these markets appears to be possible, especially if national networks are better connected with each other and the functions of the monopolists are further split up.

Old versus new Member States
The perception of how competition in an integrated EU market may stimulate the economies of the EU Member States differs between the 15 old Member States and the 12 new ones. Based on a survey carried out in 2006, 63% of all respondents stated that free competition provides the best chance of prosperity, but the 12 new members are more positive about the impact of free competition; 72% thought it provided the best chance of prosperity.

Furthermore, an internal European market that favoured competition was considered to be positive by 66%; however, 9 of the 15 old Member States had a negative opinion, compared with only two of the new Member States.

Finally, a direct consequence of strong competition is that the prices of tradable services will converge.

Single market legislation and harmonization
In order to achieve a genuine internal market for services, the European Parliament and the Council adopted in December 2006 Directive 2006/123/EC on services in the internal market – known as the Services Directive. This directive was to be transposed by the Member States by the end of 2009. The main aim of the Services Directive was to remove legal and administrative barriers to the development of service activities between Member States and to eliminate obstacles to trade in services, thus allowing the development of cross-border operations. The Directive will assure service providers of greater legal certainty in exercising two of the fundamental freedoms enshrined in the EC Treaty: freedom of establishment and freedom to provide services. This will make it easier for businesses to provide and use cross-border services in the EU.

It has been one of the most disputed pieces of EU legislation in recent years, proponents arguing that it will boost European competitiveness and critics attacking it for producing 'social dumping'. (See also 6.1.)

'Country of origin' principle versus 'Freedom to provide services'
Initially the directive stated that service providers would, temporarily, be subject to the laws of their country of origin rather than those of the country where the service is provided. They could thus test a new market without having to register with the authorities. This principle was the most controversial part of the proposal as many of Europe's older Member States worried that workers from the eastern EU countries would flock to the west, pulling down social standards.

The relevant Article was renamed 'freedom to provide services' and stipulated that Member States must 'ensure free access to and free exercise of a service activity within [their] territory' while allowing them to continue applying their own rules on conditions of employment, including those laid down by collective bargaining agreements.

Concretely, this means that service providers will not:
- need to be established in the territory in which they are seeking to operate
- need to obtain an authorization
- need to register with a professional body or association
- be banned from setting up infrastructure which they may need to supply the services in question.

Only requirements concerning public policy, public security, public health and the protection of the environment may be imposed on a service provider, so long as they are 'non-discriminatory, necessary and proportional'.

The adopted Services Directive provides that national regulation must not contain any directly discriminating provisions for service providers from other parts of the EU.

Also, there will be a single office in each country where foreign service providers can arrange compliance with local regulations. This can result in significant costs savings for businesses. The Services Directive applies to commercial services, with the exception of network services (telecommunications and energy companies), transport and financial services.

Case study 6.6 **The complexity of regulating an innovative outsourcing and IT service industry**

The 'information age' offers tremendous business opportunities. Companies delivering software and computer services support clients in a broad range of areas, in almost all economic activities. It is quite common for businesses to outsource their requirements for hardware and software to specialist providers. The trading of such services across borders has been assisted by improved telecommunications, notably growing broadband access to the internet. The world's top software and IT services businesses in 2005 are shown in Table 6.6.

Table 6.6 **The world's top software and IT services enterprise (groups), 2006[1]**

	Software and IT services revenue (€ million)	Corporate revenue (€ million)	Number of employees (units)
IBM	50 263	72 582	366 345
Microsoft	29 106	31 688	61 000
EDS	15 735	15 735	117 000
Hewlett-Packard	13 842	69 047	150 000
Accenture	13 615	13 615	123 000
Computer Sciences	11 197	11 197	79 000
Oracle	9 397	9 397	49 872
SAP	7 960	8 028	32 205
Hitachi	7 186	64 428	35 600
Capgemini[2]	7 077	7 077	59 324

1 Revenue converted at USD 1.2556 = €1.
2 Number of employees, 2005.

Source: *Software Magazine*'s Annual Software 500, King Content Co., Newton, Mass., 2006

Issues faced by this sector include the development of open-source technology, anti-trust rulings concerning the bundling of applications and operating systems, the protection of intellectual property rights and the patentability of software, and the security of software – particularly in relation to the use of the internet.

The protection of intellectual property rights is a double issue for this sector, as software suppliers must provide solutions to the management of digital rights to other content providers, as well as being concerned about protecting their own rights. One of the broader issues facing the information society is the security of communication networks and IT, and computer services have a leading role to play in this area.

In May 2006 the European Commission adopted a communication on a strategy for a secure information society – dialogue, partnership and empowerment.

Promoting cross-border transactions and stimulating competition by making national markets more accessible to foreign businesses are primary objectives of the internal market policy. For the economy as a

© Noordhoff Uitgevers bv

whole the advantages of further market integration appear to be clear, provided careful regulation is introduced.

However, differences in regulation form a significant obstacle to trade in services. The Services Directive represents a first step in this area but its economic potential is still far from realized. Given the major differences between the many service sectors, sector-specific policies are required. Accordingly, the choices made between harmonization, mutual recognition and maintaining the status quo may differ per sector.

Operational aspects of marketing

There are major differences between services. This has important implications for a company's marketing strategy. Lovelock et al. (2009) describe four broad categories of services, each of which must be marketed differently. These categories are: People processing (e.g. barbers), possession processing (e.g. refuelling your car), mental stimulus processing (e.g. education) and information processing (e.g. banking).

Service industry sectors join forces by forming associations. For TFS, this means being a member of EUCROF.

EUCROF was founded in 2005 and its aims are:
· to promote high-quality clinical research in Europe
· to form a legal entity to represent the interests of CROs in the EU, for example in transactions with regulatory bodies, the pharmaceutical/biotechnology industry and the medical research community
· to promote a close relationship and mutual understanding between the national member associations and the above-mentioned bodies.

A more global presence in the pharmaceutical (research) industry is provided by the Drug Information Association (DIA). It is a professional non-profit organization of more than 18,000 members worldwide who are involved in the discovery, development, regulation, surveillance and marketing of pharmaceuticals and related products. It has global and regional forums for the exchange of information, education and training.

For international strategy development the processing can be carried out in three ways:
· Export the service to a local service factory (e.g. study programs from universities).
· Import customers (e.g. operations in commercial clinics).
· Export information (via telecommunication) and transform it locally (e.g. international clinical trails conducted by pharmaceutical companies).

Three features of services are of primary importance for a successful marketing strategy in Europe:
· People – hence high levels of staff training in the provision of services is essential. An important challenge is achieving uniformity of the service in geographically diverse locations.
· Relationship markets – e.g. loyalty programmes linking airlines (transport services), car hire companies (transport services) and hotel chains (accommodation)
· Service delivery – which has two broad co-mponents: high-contact involvement by frontline staff, e.g. call centre operations or waiters,

and low-contact involvement by back-office staff, e.g. cleaning, laundry or general maintenance staff in a hotel.

The market for services in Europe is less integrated than the market for goods. In part this is due to the fact that certain types of service are less easily provided across long distances than goods. Many types of service, however, are increasingly suitable for cross-border trade – for reasons including improved information and communication technology and cheaper airline tickets. Examples are R&D, telemarketing and consultancy. Marketing a service in Europe includes understanding and following regulations that affect trade, including regulations targeted at foreign businesses, and studying differences in regulation between countries.

Which market entry strategies can be used?

How a service is introduced in a foreign market depends on whether it is a people, possession, mental stimulus or information processing service (see Operational aspects of marketing above).

As with cross-border marketing of goods, different avenues may be pursued: partnerships, strategic alliances, joint ventures, mergers and takeovers.

These strategies may be pursued for all activities (full service) or for some specialized activities where a minimum capacity is needed, e.g. administration, operations, marketing and sales.

Often, as a first step to a 'full' partnership, master contracts are drawn up for a limited period (1–3 years) in order to get acquainted and overcome the 'learning curve' in any collaboration. In this case, the contractor appoints the service provider as a 'preferred supplier'.

It should be noted that, in general, SMEs have a shorter life expectancy than large enterprises. In other words, it is less certain that they will still exist five to ten years from the time of an agreement. Given that complex services (e.g. R&D) can take years to provide in full, the size of the participating organizations therefore matters. The last thing a contractor wants is a supplier going bankrupt during the delivery of services. Therefore SMEs need to devise with strategies that build up trust and generate confidence in the delivery of long-term services.

TFS (the chapter's opening case study) used two market entry strategies: it opened foreign offices (in Portugal, Japan, the USA and Hungary) and took over other companies (CDC Clinical Data Care and IMRO TRAMARKO).

The marketing mix

Some practical aspects of marketing a service in Europe will now be discussed – based on the 'marketing mix', which for services is usually described by the seven Ps. Product, price, promotion and place are 'classical' but the three other Ps deserve extra attention, especially for managing the customer interface: process, people and physical environment.

Product

No matter which service you offer, your customer is paying for an expertise which is intangible and will fulfil a primary need (core product). This applies to knowledge, experience, time and transporting people or goods from A to B. Supplementary service elements are value-adding enhancements (e.g. comfort and individualized assistance).

Europe is a crowded and developed marketplace, so companies need to use branding strategies to generate loyalty and visibility. A more integrated European market will enhance EU branding which will stimulate intra-EU trade.

Continuous innovation will safeguard a company's presence in the market.

The objectives of innovation are multiple. They may include service line extensions, service or process improvements and style changes. Integration of the EU will stimulate innovation in services, causing service diversification and increased availability.

Case study 6.7 Branding and positioning of a service in Europe

With the UK recession showing no signs of easing, it might be imagined that there would be little appetite for launching a take-over of a restaurant chain. Yet in May 2009 private equity group Hutton Collins put in a bid for the Italian-style cafe and delicatessen group Carluccio's.

Founded in London in 1991 by well known Italian chef Antonio Carluccio and his wife Priscilla, Carluccio's says it aims to serve "great quality, authentic Italian food at sensible prices".
Designed in a modern canteen style, each branch includes both a restaurant – which opens all day for breakfast, lunch and dinner – and a shop selling a wide range of Italian food goods and wine.

The company proved so successful that when it was floated on the Alternative Investment Market in

2005, Antonio and his wife were able to pocket an estimated £11 million from the sale of their majority stake.

Now owned predominantly by a broad range of institutional investors, Carluccio's has a market capitalization of £56 million, and 41 outlets across the UK and Republic of Ireland.

"It is a very good brand that ticks all the boxes," says Antonio. "The interesting dynamics are that it is open all day, and has a retail space tagged onto each restaurant. In the morning it's a cafe, at lunchtime it can effectively compete with sandwich bars, and then at night it becomes a proper restaurant. This gives Carluccio's flexibility and resilience."

(By Will Smale, business reporter, BBC News, May 2009)

■ **Example 6.2 How ING finds ways to innovate**

ING is a global company offering banking, insurance and pension services to over 85 million customers in Europe, the USA and Asia. Its headquarters is located in the Netherlands. ING has 114,000 employees worldwide.

In order to facilitate innovation, ING looked at the popular gaming industry. The idea was that skills used in playing games may be relevant to the creative processes of developing new services.

By developing the X-box game for product developers, ING produced a tool to generate new insurance products.

ING developed the X-box in a joint venture with teams at the University of Amsterdam, who designed the algorithms (decision models and criteria) and at the Technical University of Delft, who developed the user interface.

Price
Irrespective of the pricing method you use (e.g. cost price plus or premium price), you must consider factors such as economic need and market attractiveness. Price setting must also take into account the investment necessary to deliver the service and the uniqueness of the service. Therefore, a price includes factors related to costs, value to the customer and competition.

It is often more difficult to trace all the costs incurred by a company providing a service than it is for a tangible product; what is the relative contribution of fixed and variable costs to the price of a service? In general, for complex services (e.g. R&D services) the activity-based costs approach is used, which means that indirect costs (overheads) are allocated to a service based on the quantities and the type of activities required to deliver the service.

Customer relationships are a main factor in price rigidity. In particular, the fear of antagonizing customers with frequent price changes seems to be the most significant cause of price inflexibility in the euro area.

For the customer the service must be worth the time and effort as well as the monetary cost.

An extra complication for cross-border price setting is that the perception by the customer of the services offered varies considerably between European markets.

Unfortunately for European consumers buying in another EU country, the differences in VAT in the EU can be substantial; in Austria, for instance, VAT on services is 20% whereas in Spain it is only 7%. Moreover, the rate of VAT may vary considerably with the type of goods or services.

The less competition there is, the more service providers can mark up prices. There is, however, considerable competition in the European market, and yet price discrimination is a common practice. This suggests that the models European companies are following is monopolistic competition, resulting in the positioning of many services with differential advantages.

In Europe, lack of cross-border trade and the as yet relatively low level of direct investment by service businesses in other EU Member States are causing unnecessarily high prices due to insufficient competition.

In most European countries the modal average number of price reviews lies in the range of one to three times per year, and in nearly all countries on which this report is based, the median average is once a year. (This is less frequent for services than for goods.)

In the business-to-business (BtoB) market, the local market tax system is a less relevant factor in accounting for price differences across countries. This factor is more important in consumer-oriented enterprises, operating in business-to-consumer (BtoC) markets, for which differences in indirect taxation are presumably more significant.

Promotion
The promotion of a service must communicate the fact that the service provider can be trusted. It is a continuous concern because public opinion can easily shift to the negative side based on only a few recent experiences.

When customers are required to participate in creating a service product (e.g. self-service restaurants and online flight tickets) – a phenomenon called co-production – much communication/promotion is educational in nature, to guide customers through a service process.

As the service is provided at a specific point of sale, the training and motivation of the international sales force are also crucial issues.

In the consumer market the cultural diversity within Europe makes it difficult to develop international promotional campaigns, though this is less of a problem in the BtoB market.

The continuous improvements in IT provide the European marketer with a dynamic and powerful new tool for promoting services.

Media service providers will benefit from modernized advertising rules, opening up attractive new avenues of finance that will ultimately stimulate the content production sector.

A challenge is to position and differentiate a service in a European market with a tremendous variety of cultures and languages and to communicate the added value of a service to a cross-border customer. For instance, what is the common denominator of advertisements for plane tickets that appeal to a large proportion of the European population?

Place (and time)
For services there are three distribution options:
· The customer goes to the service provider (e.g. hair salons).
· The service provider goes to the customer (e.g. mail delivery).
· The customer and the service provider transact remotely (e.g. telephone services).

Service distribution in Europe may take place through non-physical channels. Some service businesses are able to use electronic channels to deliver their service elements (e.g. R&D services). Distribution channels include visiting an office, using a network, and delivery by telephone and over the internet (e.g. banks).

Intermediaries may also be used. For services two intermediary structures are feasible: franchising and licensing. Each option has its pros and cons; it is beyond the scope of this book to discuss these extensively, but the trade-off factors are quality and control of the delivery of services versus costs.

Speed, and convenience of place and time are important determinants of effective service delivery; more and more services are available 24 hours a day and seven days a week.

Infrastructures that link customer relationship management (CRM) systems, mobile phones and websites to provide a great variety of services are becoming more advanced. Providing a standardized European information platform would greatly enhance intra-EU service trading (see also section 6.4.4).

Process
How a company delivers a service is at least as important as what it delivers.

Therefore it is a prerequisite for success to design and implement effective processes.

Especially in services where consumers become part of a production process that is simultaneous with consumption (people processing), the way the process is designed and implemented may vary substantially.

Furthermore, attitudes, transactional speed and quality of performance can vary widely across Europe. This makes it very difficult to control quality and ensure reliable delivery in different European countries.

Flowcharting and blueprinting are techniques for displaying and understanding the total customer service experience and how the customer is involved in the process. They show where backstage and frontstage activities interact and where things can go wrong.

Continuous training of employees, automation of tasks and adequate management of the flow of customers through service processes will improve the chance of success in European service delivery.

People
Employees are very important to a service company; they often fulfil the role of the service provider as well as the role of the seller of the service. The attitude and skills of the employees are therefore directly related to the image of the company and the quality of the service. As a consequence the service company should be focused on supporting its frontline employees.

In Europe – especially in the hotel and restaurant sectors – multi-lingual skills are always highly valued and appreciated. Additional competences include flexibility and the ability to work in a multi-cultural environment.

Therefore, selecting, training and motivating employees should be one of the core competences of service companies.

Physical environment

Tangible evidence of a company's image and service quality is provided by various dimensions of the service environment. These are buildings, landscapes, vehicles, interior furnishing, equipment, staff members' uniforms, signs and printed materials, and the use of colours, smells and sounds.

Service businesses need to manage this physical evidence carefully, because it can have a profound impact on customers' impressions. These impressions should all be favourable, e.g. clear positioning, identifiable image (brand) and quality.

This is true for a large variety of services, including shopping centres, waiting and treatment rooms in hospitals, consultancy services and interior design for restaurants and hotels.

International service companies in BtoC markets (e.g. oil companies such as Shell and BP, mobile phone service companies such as Vodafone, and hotels such as Bilderberg, Carlton and Mövenpick) need to balance brand consistency against the cultural expectations of customers in each country. Another important parameter in the equation is the cost–benefit relationship. This relationship depends on the extent of country-specific adaptation required, the market size and the expected income from each country.

Tools for determining in each European country an optimal physical environment for a service include careful observation of customers' behaviour, feedback and ideas from (local) customers and frontline staff, field experiments (measuring the effects of different kinds of music, spatial layouts, styles of furniture, etc.) and blueprinting (see also Process above).

TFS faces extra challenges in implementing a consistent and coherent service marketing mix because in its internationalization strategy it both opened offices in other countries and took over other companies in order to deliver services internationally.

In the BtoB environment TFS is operating in, international regulations and industry standards – e.g. good clinical practice and good laboratory practice – determine the basic level of its services. Beyond that, TFS needs to distinguish the company and its services from the hundreds of competitors active in this market. (See also Question 10.)

6.4.4 Electronic commerce in European marketing

As in the European market for goods (see section 5.6.4) the service marketer faces the challenge of using e-commerce most effectively. This short subsection outlines the main pointers – among them the increasing importance of the internet.

First, the provision of European marketing of services is gaining increased attention due to:
· globalization and the increased use of e-commerce in both private and business life

- a decrease in government regulations (in some countries), e.g. the deregulation of the local banking industry in many countries
- the possible avoidance of trade barriers when using the internet to solicit and deliver services
- e-commerce, which allows the international marketer to replace traditional business activity (e.g. order taking) by electronic activity (online ordering).

Second, the internet changes the dynamics of European commerce and, in particular, leads to the more rapid internationalization of small to medium-sized enterprises, including those offering services.

Third, Mobile TV is one of the new platforms for European audiovisual content. A new Audiovisual Media Services Directive will contribute to the success of Mobile TV. It will modernize the rules on television advertising and provide a coherent regulatory framework for the delivery of audiovisual media services – including on-demand services via fixed or mobile networks.

Fourth, the convergence of audiovisual media, broadband networks and electronic devices is generating new opportunities in the ICT and content sectors in Europe. It is both creating new delivery channels for traditional formats and opening the path to the development of interactive content and services.

However, piracy and the illegal sharing of movies, software and music over the internet remain burning issues. Piracy siphons off potential online revenue and deters media companies from putting content online as they fear losing control to pirates.

Finally, the service sectors that are likely to grow in the EU using e-commerce are:
- banking and finance (international money transfers, overnight money marketing, etc.)
- education (online education)
- computer software
- telecommunications
- e-commerce infrastructure (e.g. cabling and broadband communications).

■ Example 6.3 Obtaining finance via the internet

Companies can use the internet to solicit requests for finance. An international consumer may even apply for finance on the internet by completing the finance company's application form, though subsequent credit checks required by the finance supplier are likely to be done independently of the internet.

Similarly, the internet can be used for supplying insurance. International consumers wishing to be covered by a company's insurance product can complete and submit the initial application form for consideration online.

Conclusions

In sections 6.1 and 6.2 the legal basis for the free movement of services was explained. Businesses must beware of national legislation that breaches European law on the subject. There are many qualification requirements on both the provider and the service itself. Even though European legislation is actively harmonizing the requirements regarding services, businesses still need to be aware of which legislation is allowed and which legislation breaches European law.

If a Member State continues to apply national legislation that hinders the free movement of services, the companies affected should be aware that they will have to make a legal assessment of the requirements and then amass arguments sufficient to convince the national authorities in order to prevent a court case. One of the stronger arguments against national authorities is that the company will file a complaint with the Commission; this prompts the national authorities to check their legislation for compliance because they do not want to be warned by the Commission. The problem with this procedure is that it may take a long time for a final decision on the matter to be made.

The short-term solution is to continue providing the cross-border service. Companies should be aware, however, that if they take this decision they may face criminal charges or be denied the proper authorization.

The Services Directive will be of great help to businesses, not least in creating a Single Point of Contact in each Member State which will process the administrative procedures through eGoverning.

In section 6.3 the service industry and its import and export relations were discussed.

Services is an important and growing industry in Europe. Total international trade in services (exports plus imports) in 2007 amounted to €4,818.7 billion (of which intra-EU trade accounted for €1,302.2 billion) – an increase in value of 9.5% over 2006. Moreover, the European Union continues to be the biggest global player in international trade in services (ITS). In 2007, the EU's ITS recorded a surplus of €84.1 billion.

Two trends that will reinforce the growth of this industry are outsourcing and internationalization (section 6.4). Especially in the more complex service sectors such as IT and R&D, a strong expansion may be expected in the near future.

However, the diversity of cultures in Europe makes the internationalization of services challenging. The internet is a communication platform that has not only increased business in existing services, but also generated many new services.

The EU should facilitate infrastructure and generate policies that are more 'tailor made' for the service industry. The European Services Directive represents a first step in this direction but is still far from realizing the economic potential of the services sector. Given the major differences between the many service sectors, sector-specific policies are required.

Questions

Legal aspects of the free movement of services

6.1 What sort of cross-border activities might benefit from the free movement of services?

6.2 What kind of services are excluded from the free movement of services?

6.3 What exceptions to the free movement of services are allowed?

Case law

6.4 TFS would like to provide their research services to Estonia. The Hungarian subsidiary which will offer the service stumbles on several requirements under Estonian law. TFS meets all the Hungarian safety requirements and has all the necessary permits and authorizations, but for reasons of public health the Estonian legislation holds the following requirements:
1 The service provider must have a place of business in Estonia in order for the authorities to visit and check the premises for compliance with the safety rules.
2 The staff of the service provider must have had at least three years of higher education in medical research & development.
The TFS Hungary management is not sure whether they should continue making an offer to the Estonian company.

a State whether the two requirements are allowed under EU law or not. Explain your answer.

b What is your advice to the Hungarian management? In your opinion, are they allowed to make an offer?

c Explain to the Hungarian management what action the Estonian authorities can take against TFS Hungary if they are of the opinion that the company does not comply with Estonian law.

d What solutions would you propose to the TFS management for the short term and for the longer term?

Marketing

6.5 Describe three important differences between services and goods with respect to positioning strategy in Europe.

6.6 What opportunities and threats do you envisage with respect to the introduction of a transport service (e.g. taxis) in another EU country?

6.7 Looking at the 12 new EU members, identify a service that is particularly suited to these markets and give at least three arguments supporting your choice.

6.8 Prescribe briefly TFS's use of the service marketing mix.

The free movement of capital and international business strategy

7

Causes of the financial crisis and its impact on the European financial regulatory framework

In the aftermath of the 9/11 terrorist attacks, mortgage lending in the USA began to shift from low-risk or prime mortgages to high-risk or sub-prime mortgages, in which the borrower has a low credit rating, the lender does not verify the borrower's income and the amount of the mortgage exceeds 80% of the appraised value of the house. The shift was partly encouraged by sharp drops in interest rates in the USA, the euro zone and Japan.

The global financial crisis started in August 2007 as a US sub-prime mortgage crisis. Many of these sub-prime mortgages were also adjustable rate mortgages where the interest rate would periodically adjust as market rates changed. Often these adjustable mortgages had rates that were set artificially low during the first years of the mortgage but increased a lot with the increase in market rates. Many banks found that their housing assets had been overvalued. The creation of sub-prime debts with a high risk of default by the borrowers were strengthened by a large availability of liquidities in the financial markets due to larger capital inflows from Asian countries such as China, Japan and the United Arabic Emirates. US and EU banks were forced to seek better returns on their financial products (financial assets or securities).

Another cause of the global financial crisis of 2007–09 was the process of securitization in the USA and to a lesser extent in the EU. Securitization refers to the transformation of non-marketable assets into marketable instruments, whereby loans and other financial assets are pooled for sale as securities to investors who use them to finance their business activities. These so-called 'asset-backed securities' can give banks more opportunities to hedge their financial risks through transforming initially weak sub-prime loans into triple-A (AAA loans). This can give them better returns without a counter-transaction on the balance sheet.

Securitization is usually applied to illiquid assets, which are not easily sold, and it has become common in the real estate market. For example, mortgage-backed securities (MBS), whereby the underlying collateral consists of a pool of mortgages, are an off-balance-sheet activity which has gradually become a more significant part of banks' business.

Securitization has been extended to a diverse array of less well known assets, including mortgages, insurance receivables and commercial bank loans among many others. These securities are usually purchased by institutional investors, including investment banks, insurance companies and pension funds.

A critical element in any securitization is the presence of credit enhancement or liquidity support. This increases the likelihood that security holders will receive timely payment on their investments. Since investors do not originate the loan, they cannot verify the quality of the securitized loan portfolio. More or less independent credit rating agencies, such as Standard & Poor's, Moody's and FitchIBCA, assess and rate the risk and the quality of the securities. They will generally issue credit ratings and often monitor the performance of the transaction throughout its life and adjust their ratings accordingly.

In any securitization activity it is important to ensure that repayment of the securities will still be made in the event of insolvency.

It is tempting to regard the securitization process as the main cause of the financial crisis. On the one hand, securitization weakened origination standards, encouraged the extension of credit to borrowers unlikely to be able to bear the ensuing burden, and led to increased leverage on the financial system in general. It also constituted a 'moral hazard', i.e. the temptation to take more risks when you know that someone else (e.g. other banks, the central bank or government) will cover the risks if you get into difficulties.

On the other hand, securitization had many beneficial effects on the stability of the financial system. The pooling or repacking of loans facilitates investor diversification through the creation of separate tranches, each with its own risk/return ratio. Furthermore, the ability to divert credit risk away from the banking system increases financial stability and facilitates risk management by banks. Securitization also enhances the liquidity of loan portfolios and provides price signals which in turn are the basis for more prudent risk management. However, a fundamental cause of the financial crisis is the fact that the relationship between risk and return gradually became obscured.

Reconsidering a more co-ordinated and sophisticated supervision of European financial institutions

Since early 2008, not only have US banks suffered, but the US financial crisis has become a worldwide problem for all financial institutions due to the interconnectedness of the international money markets and the highly integrated and globalized capital markets. For example, in early 2008 the British institution Northern Rock was nationalized by the UK government in order to prevent its default.

One of the core competences and responsibilities of banks is to manage their financial risks in order to achieve greater coherence between risk and return on financial products. To avoid creating a moral hazard in the financial services industry, they should be in a position to assess the risks of their own investments and their products' acceptance criteria without relying on the judgement of the rating agencies, i.e. taking potential adverse market developments into consideration. Nowadays advanced liquidity and risk management plus an advanced capital requirement monitoring policy are essential if banks are to avoid bankruptcy.

On account of the capital liberalization and deregulation of the financial markets of the 1980s and the globalization and securitization trend of the 1990s, a credit crunch affects many interconnected banks in the market and will spread out like a contagion or in a domino effect within the different financial systems. On the one hand this necessitates more co-ordinated regulation and supervision on a global scale and on the other hand the re-regulation of business conduct supervision.

Due to differences in legislation between different regions (e.g. the USA and EU) and different countries this implies better co-ordinated methods of intervention and supervision by the policy makers and a reconsideration of the supervision of financial institutions on a global scale to prevent adverse spill-over effects which might endanger the stability of the overall financial system.

In order to prevent a new global financial crisis and a further economic slowdown, more emphasis will be put on strengthening prudential supervision, enhancing transparency and information disclosure, improving valuation methods and the role of rating agencies, and increasing the possibilities for risk management in times of financial crisis.

In addition, the Basel II capital adequacy ratio and its potential pro-cyclical effects need to be reconsidered . The Basel II capital adequacy ratio refers to the level of capital a bank should hold in relation to the regulatory minimum standards established under the Basel Accord (8%). The amount of capital a bank holds relates to the riskiness of its business activity. The more risky a bank's on-balance sheet assets and off-balance sheet business, the more capital it needs to hold. When default risks increase during a recession, capital requirements are likely to rise. As long as the capital requirements of a bank are connected to the extent of its risk exposure (in order to guarantee the bank's stability), the Basel II model will always be pro-cyclical and never anti-cyclical.

The big question in this period of credit and liquidity deficiencies is whether the Basel II accord, in spite of its many risk differentiation amendments, is still too pro-cyclical. A more precise fine-tuning of higher capital requirements in conjunction with the fluctuations of the business cycle might reduce this problem.

Another solution to this problem would be a less optimistic risk assessment at different stages of the business cycle by regulatory bodies and rating agencies, for instance through so-called stress tests, which are a form of testing that is used to determine the stability of a given financial system or institution beyond normal operational capacity, often to a breaking point, in order to observe the results.

Besides policy changes, the global financial crisis has led to Europe-wide discussion to strengthen the EU regulatory framework.

EU supervision is still mainly nationally oriented, since most financial institutions and markets are still national. At the same time we can see a trend towards increased consolidation and internationalization, which creates more spill-over effects and an increasing necessity for a more advanced infrastructure for EU financial supervision.

The so-called Lamfalussy procedure (or process), developed in March 2001, is considered to be the original legislation on EU financial supervision. This procedure aims to simplify and speed up the complex and lengthy EU legislative process by means of a four-level approach. It was extended to the entire EU financial sector in December 2003. According to the Lamfalussy procedure, the various EU institutions adopt a legislation framework under the auspices of the European Commission. It encourages harmonization of supervisory practices in the European market for financial services and closer co-operation with the Member States, the regulatory authorities involved and the private sector in the field of banking, securities, insurances and occupational pensions.

The framework also includes a separate European financial conglomerates committee. Financial conglomerates (sometimes called financial supermarkets) are groups of financial institutions operating in different sectors of the financial industry such as banking, insurance, securities and so on. National supervisors remain responsible for national financial institutions, while any necessary co-ordination and refinement of cross-border institutions takes place at EU level. It is highly likely that in the near future increasing steps will be taken to push forward the financial integration process, which will make an adjusted version of the European regulatory framework all the more important.

The causes of the severe financial crisis at the end of the first decade of the 21st century and its consequences for the European economies are examined in this chapter. Section 7.1 deals with the single market for capital as one of the 'four freedoms' which have fostered the change from capital restriction to free capital mobility (section 7.2) and the European integration process for financial institutions, financial markets and financial products (sections 7.3 and 7.4). The single market for capital can also be seen as a stimulus to the establishment of a single monetary policy, the creation of the European Central Bank and the launch of the euro (sections 7.5 and 7.6). Finally, the consequences for merger and acquisition activities within and between EU countries is addressed in section 7.7. Overall, the major focus of this chapter is the impact of the financial crisis on doing business in Europe.

7.1 The single market for capital

Although the European integration process started in the early 1950s with the formation of the European Coal and Steel Community, most Europeans were obliged to manage and invest their money predominantly in their home country until the 1990s.

Since the 1980s, the liberalization of capital movement and the deregulation of domestic financial sectors – which often occurred hand in hand – have improved the efficiency of the international financial markets enormously. This trend accompanied the consolidation of the single market for capital in 1992, with the result that EU citizens could conduct many operations abroad, from opening bank accounts, buying shares and bonds in non-domestic companies, and investing to purchasing real estate. For businesses in the EU, the single market principally meant being able to invest in and own other European enterprises and take an active part in their management. However, the rules concerning some of these rights remain governed by national provisions, which vary from one Member State to another.

Free movement of capital is at the heart of the single market for capital and is one of the 'four freedoms' of the single market. It enables integrated, open, competitive and efficient European financial markets and financial services. The transition from capital restriction to the free movement of capital is an essential condition for the proper functioning of the single market. It enables a better allocation of resources within the EU, facilitates cross-border trade, favours labour mobility and makes it easier for businesses to raise finance and gain access to European financial markets. The EU single market for capital can be considered as a precondition in order to establish a single market for financial services in the wholesale and retail markets.

Efforts to create a single European market for financial services has made substantial progress, but it is still far from complete. Major advances have been accomplished in particular by the implementation of various measures of the Financial Services Action Plan (FSAP) since its adoption in 1999. This has led to the emergence of more or less integrated interbank and wholesale markets, vigorously encouraged by the major corporate and investment banks.

The FSAP laid the foundations for a strong financial market in the EU and has already brought about many positive changes despite a turbulent global environment. The ultimate aim of the FSAP was to achieve full integration of the banking and capital markets by 2005. In addition, the FSAP was set up to promote a more competitive and dynamic financial services industry with more sophisticated regulation, which was expected to lead to enhanced economic growth. Consumers of financial products should obtain lower prices, and producers of such services would benefit from lower costs.

The EU's FSAP comprises measures designed to harmonize the Member States' rules on securities, banking, insurance, mortgages, pensions and all other forms of financial transaction in order to create an optimal single financial market. The success of the FSAP is considered crucial to the financial integration process.

However, the retail banking sector remains fragmented by national borders in terms of price convergence, infrastructure integration and cross-border supply of products and services. A single market for financial services requires:
· freedom of movement of capital, implying the removal of exchange controls, the ironing out of exchange rate fluctuations and the full acceptance of the right to raise capital and to invest in all EU markets
· the right of establishment by businesses in other Member States
· the right to supply cross-border services
· the acceptance of common supervisory regulations
· the harmonization of taxes in order to prevent tax arbitrage.

The first three criteria have been met, but the last two have not been fully achieved. It will be very difficult to fully meet these requirements, since the financial services industry has always been politically sensitive and highly regulated throughout Europe.

There are two important reasons for this heavy regulation. First, the risk that the failure of one bank or financial institution might endanger a country's whole financial system. During the financial crisis it became obvious that financial systemic risks had led to domino effects on various financial systems throughout the world. Since then, banks that are 'too big or too important to fail' but that cause such domino effects have been referred to as 'system banks'.

Second, there is a common assumption that purchases of financial services need a high level of consumer protection. In most countries this is supported by different types of prudential and business-conduct supervision by the monetary authorities (supervisory bodies such as the central bank and the government). The supervisory bodies are responsible for the regulation and supervision of the financial system.

With the aim of increasing financial integration, the supervision of the financial sector has followed similar trends in most European countries, namely:
- from 'sectoral' to 'functional'
- from 'off-site' to 'on-site'
- from quantitative to qualitative.

The sectoral approach of supervision is based on the possibility of separating the banking, securities, pension and insurance markets. Since the creation of financial conglomerates in the 1990s, more focus has been put on the functional type of supervision, whereby it is important to control each function within the financial services industry (liquidity, business conduct, etc.) instead of a particular branch. In addition, since the implementation of the BIS (Bank for International Settlements) directives in the domain of commercial banks, more emphasis has been put on own-risk assessments and this has changed the type of supervision from 'off-site' to 'on-site' , in other words to increased focus on qualitative rather than quantitative financial risk assessment.

Broadly speaking we can distinguish four types of supervision of the financial system in the euro zone, namely:
1 monetary supervision conducted by the European Central Bank (ECB)
2 prudential supervision conducted by the national central banks (NCBs)
3 conduct business supervision conducted by different supervisory bodies
4 system supervision conducted by NCBs.

Because financial services have such a vital role in the economy, supervisory bodies have long been reluctant to allow national markets to be dominated by foreign institutions. In general, regulation of all financial institutions operating in a country by the domestic government (host-country regulation) acted to remove many competitive advantages the foreign institutions might have had and thus tended to reinforce the general tendency towards a fragmented and inefficient financial services industry.

Before the 1980s, there had been a movement towards an integrated market in some areas of finance, such as wholesale banking, but areas such as retail banking and insurance had remained fragmented. Even for corporate business, EU national financial systems, were, by the 1980s, far from integrated, with differences remaining between them in regulation, taxation, the competitive environment and the role of the government.

The demand for a competitive and more efficient financial system across Europe led to a demand for home-country regulation (the 'single passport' principle), each bank being authorized and regulated by authorities in the country in which its head office was located. For example, the branches of a German bank in other EU countries would be supervised by the German regulatory authority and would need to comply with German laws.

The effectiveness of EU initiatives to integrate the financial services industry would be compromised if capital movements within the EU were subject to restrictions. Stimulated by the deregulation of the financial markets, the single market for capital pushed forward many reforms in the financial sector and changed the banking industry from a traditional into a modern type of business (see section 7.3).

7.2   From capital restriction to free capital mobility

The reluctance on the part of governments to relinquish control of financial institutions operating in their national markets explained the greater resistance to a single market for financial services than in other areas of production. Until the 1980s the European financial and banking sectors were mainly domestically oriented. National governments invariably acted to protect their banks from foreign influences and sometimes were themselves owners of major banks.

When the foreign exchange markets calmed down in the mid 1980s, exchange controls were eased in most Member States of the European Monetary System (EMS). Exchange controls are restrictions placed on movements of funds in a particular currency (or limitations on the convertibility of a currency) imposed by monetary authorities. These controls enabled national authorities to prevent operations by a citizen or a company in another Member State and hampered financial integration in the single market.

However, exchange controls were only one of the barriers to free capital mobility, which in turn was only one of the barriers to a single market in financial services. Despite the relative stability of exchange rates in the second half of the 1980s, significant interest rate differentials remained among Member States, and exchange rate uncertainties were to return in the 1990s. The free flow of capital was also hindered by differences in tax regimes among countries, particularly relating to the taxation of profits, and by differences among national capital markets. For example, merger and acquisition (M&A) activity by financial institutions was more difficult in Germany than in the Netherlands and the UK.

Interest rate restrictions and capital controls were common, and branch restrictions existed in some countries. For example, all countries required foreign enterprises to obtain formal authorization before they could set up branches, and Spain imposed limits on their establishment. In all countries except the UK, capital had to be provided, increasing the cost to enterprises of establishing branches abroad. Many countries retained restrictions on the acquisition by foreigners of domestic financial institutions, especially of major domestic banks, most countries requiring the declaration of anything more than minor shareholdings in banks.

The move towards harmonization of laws and restrictions among Member States reflected wider changes in the domains of economic policy, technological development, internationalization and globalization. This integration process included extensive financial liberalization and was aimed at creating a single market (a 'level playing field') for financial services.

Until the 1986 Single European Act (SEA), the EU capital markets were not well integrated. Although the free movement of capital was supported by the Treaty of Rome, the treaty provided several loopholes, which EU members eagerly exploited.

The basic problem was that, until recently, EU nations simply did not believe that unrestricted capital mobility was a good idea. For a long time, international capital flows were widely held responsible for repeated balance of payments imbalances and banking crises (see 7.2.1). Even the International Monetary Fund (IMF) was initially reluctant to promote the free movement of capital.

The Treaty of Rome imposed no formal requirements concerning capital market liberalization. The only structure was a general one against capital restrictions that inhibited the proper functioning of the common market. The EC advanced capital flow liberalization only modestly, with directives in 1960 and 1962. These included numerous opt-out and safeguard clauses, which were in fact extensively used by EU members.

The SEA of 1986 instituted the principle that all forms of capital mobility should be allowed inside the EU. The actual liberalization was implemented by a series of directives culminating in Directive 88/361/EEC), which came into effect in 1990 for most Member States, while for the rest specific transitional periods were agreed.

The free movement of capital was intended to permit movements of investments such as purchases of shares between countries. Until the drive towards EMU, the development of capital provisions had been slow. However, the Treaty of Maastricht, which came into force in November 1993, banned all national restrictions on the movement of capital. This included the prohibition of restrictions between Member States and between Member States and non-EU countries, except those required for law enforcement and national security. Since then many more countries have joined the EU. Before joining, these countries progressively removed barriers to free the movement of capital. However, transitional periods exist for certain Member States with regard to the right to purchase second homes or agricultural land.

The implementation of the SEA in 1987–90 not only removed remaining barriers but also increased harmonization, and thereby enhanced the competitiveness of European companies. As EU companies positioned themselves to take advantage of the opportunities that the SEA offered, a wave of M&As swept across the EU. Large enterprises combined their special understanding of European needs, capabilities and cultures with their advantage of economies of scale and scope (see section 7.7). Small and medium-sized enterprises (SMEs) were encouraged through EU institutions to network with one another to offset any adverse consequences of changing product standards, for example.

7.2.1 The importance of international financial movements: how a current account deficit can coincide with an appreciating exchange rate

Since the early 1970s, most of the major economies of the world have operated with 'managed floating' exchange rates. The potential these give for speculative gain led to a huge increase in short-term international financial movements. Vast amounts of money were transferred from country to country in the search for higher interest rates or a rise in the free-market exchange rate of the domestic currency with foreign currencies (appreciation).

This had a bizarre effect on exchange rates. If a country pursues an expansionary fiscal policy (e.g. an increase in government expenditure), the current account will tend to go into deficit as imports increase. The effect on exchange rates might appear obvious: the higher demand for imports creates an extra supply of domestic currency on the foreign exchange market and hence drives down the currency's value. In fact the opposite is more usually the case. The higher interest rates resulting from higher domestic demand can lead to a massive inflow of short-term finance when there are no capital restrictions. The financial account can thus move sharply into surplus. This is likely to outweigh the current account deficit and cause an appreciation of the currency.

In the context of the free movement of capital, exchange rate movements, especially in the short term, are largely brought about by changes to the financial account rather than to the current account of the balance of payment.

Equally, it is clear that monetary authorities such as the ECB will lose a monetary instrument or tool to control exchange rate fluctuations with the transition from capital restrictions to capital mobility. The main motives to restrict capital in- and outflows are to gain greater control over exchange rates and monetary policy, to protect domestic savings and key industries and to prevent tax arbitrage, i.e. trading that takes advantage of a difference in tax rates or tax systems (see table 7.1).

Table 7.1 **Motives for capital restriction**

	Short-term	Long-term
Outflow	To sustain a low interest rate; To prevent a downward pressure on the exchange rate	To protect domestic savings; To protect the domestic capital market; To prevent tax arbitrage
Inflow	To sustain domestic price stability; To prevent upward pressure on exchange rates	To maintain domestic control over key industries

7.2.2 The 'impossible trinity' principle from the ERM to EMU: a matter of give and take

The free movement of capital has advantages and disadvantages. The advantages of allowing capital to move across national boundaries are principally at the micro-economic level. They fall into two main categories, namely allocation efficiency and diversification (see Glossary for explanation). The disadvantages of international capital mobility are mainly of a macro-economic kind and can be explained by the 'impossible trinity' principle. This principle, also known as the inconsistent trinity, is the hypothesis in international economics that it is impossible to achieve all three of the following aims simultaneously (see figure 7.1):
· fixed exchange rate
· free capital movement
· independent or sovereign monetary policy.

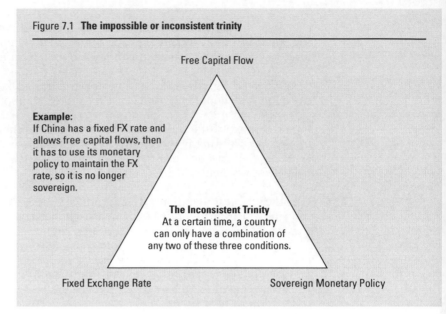

Figure 7.1 **The impossible or inconsistent trinity**

Free Capital Flow

Example:
If China has a fixed FX rate and allows free capital flows, then it has to use its monetary policy to maintain the FX rate, so it is no longer sovereign.

The Inconsistent Trinity
At a certain time, a country can only have a combination of any two of these three conditions.

Fixed Exchange Rate

Sovereign Monetary Policy

However, it is possible to achieve any two aims at any given moment. During the early EMS period, for example, many countries restricted capital movements; they could award themselves some degree of monetary independence even though they were part of the EMS. The UK dismantled its capital controls in the early 1980s and retained monetary policy independence by staying out of the Exchange Rate Mechanism (ERM), the forerunner to EMU.

The ERM, which is the EMS excluding credit facilities, consists of four elements, namely:
· a parity grid (usually set at ± 2.25%)
· mutual support, whereby members buy and sell foreign reserves
· joint management of exchange rate realignments to avoid beggar-thy-neighbour policies
· the European Currency Unit (ECU) as a symbolic official unit of account (a 'basket of currencies', weighted by the size of the member countries).

Under the ERM, each currency was given a central exchange rate with each of the other ERM currencies in the grid. However, fluctuations were allowed from the central rate within specified bands. The central rates could be adjusted from time to time by agreement, thus making the ERM an adjustable peg system, whereby exchange rates are fixed for a period of time but may be devalued (or revalued) if a deficit (or surplus) on the current account becomes substantial. All the currencies floated jointly with currencies outside the ERM. If an ERM currency approached the upper or lower limit against any other ERM currency, intervention would take place to maintain the currencies within the band. This would take the form of central banks in the ERM selling the strong currency and buying the weak one.

After the launch of the euro on 1st January 1999, the EMS-II was created as a 'waiting room' for countries of existing EU members who cannot or do not want to join the euro area. For example, Denmark and the UK have a derogation, but Denmark has adopted the new ERM-II. In the context of EU legislation, derogation implies that a Member State delays the implementation of an element of an EU regulation into their legal system over a given timescale, or that a member state has opted not to enforce a specific provision in a treaty due to internal circumstances. Sweden has no derogation but declined to adopt the ERM-II.

The new EMS-II (ERM-II plus credit facilities) differs from the EMS-I in that the euro has become a reference currency for all members and the ECB is explicitly allowed to suspend intervention. ERM membership is compulsory for all new members. They must remain in the ERM for at least two years and eliminate capital controls before joining the euro zone.

As is stressed with the example of China in figure 7.1, the impossible trinity principle holds that the price to pay for area membership is independent or sovereign monetary policy. On the road to EMU all the euro area members achieved the first two policy aims by establishing a supranational independent ECB and accepting the loss of national monetary policy with a fixed mutual euro parity rate and a single market for capital – a matter of give and take.

7.3 The European financial system and Europe's real economy

Section 7.3 describes what a financial system is and its connection with the real economy, which can be explained by monetary transmission mechanisms. The landscape of European financial institutions, regulatory measures affecting the EU financial sectors and the changing framework for the EU banking sector, thanks to a new regulatory business environment, are also discussed in this section.

7.3.1 The connection between the financial system and the real economy

The European single market for capital has been greatly affected by the current financial crisis, which provides a good opportunity to elaborate on the different components of the financial system and its relation with financial stability in Europe. The financial system comprises several distinct but closely linked components, namely:
- financial institutions (section 7.3)
- financial markets (see section 7.4)
- financial products, tools or instruments (see section 7.4)
- financial infrastructure including settlement and payment systems such as the Single European Payment Area (SEPA), which is not elaborated on in this chapter.

As both the individual components and the linkages among them constitute the financial system, the maintenance of financial stability requires their collective stability. Vulnerabilities in one component may affect the smooth functioning of others, thereby posing a threat to the smooth functioning of the financial system as a whole.

The single market for capital and the movement from capital restriction to free capital mobility in the EU have gradually made the European financial system more market driven and less bank based.

European financial institutions can be grouped into financial intermediaries and other financial institutions such as insurance companies and pension funds which directly borrow or lend money in a financial market by selling or buying securities or financial instruments (securitization). The performance of financial institutions and financial systems and its major trends is addressed in section 7.3. The most important features of the European financial markets and their instruments, including steps to be taken to encourage financial stability in the EU, are focused on in section 7.4.

Faced with a desire to lend or borrow, the end-users of most financial systems have a choice between three broad approaches, namely:
· to deal directly with each other – 'over-the-counter' trade, which is usually costly, risky and inefficient
· to use one or more of many organized financial markets (e.g. the NYSE Euronext and the Deutsche Börse, the most important European stock exchange markets)
· to deal with each other via financial intermediaries (mostly commercial banks), who also make use of financial markets (via indirect finance or trade with indirect participants, for instance through the money market or capital market, see section 7.4).

Broadly speaking, lenders like to maximize liquidity and yield (return) while borrowers like to maximize the length of the loan at the minimum cost. The aims of profitability and liquidity tend to conflict with each other. In general, the more liquid an asset, the less profitable it is, and vice versa. The major aims of a financial system are:
· to channel funds to flow from lenders to borrowers via banks
· to create liquidity and money via banks
· to provide a means of payments by financial institutions
· to provide financial services such as securities, insurances and pensions
· to provide an accumulation of a diversified portfolio of financial assets taking into account that financial institutions (banks) prefer to hold a range of assets of varying degrees of liquidity and profitability (an optimum risk-return portfolio) in order to spread their risks.

The European monetary policy strategies and the consequences for business (section 7.5), the launch of the euro and its impact on the EU business environment (section 7.6), and M&A activity in the EU (section 7.7) show the close links between the financial system and the real economy. The financial crisis has emphasized how closely the financial system is connected to the real economy.

First, in the real economy people earn and spend incomes, which generates surpluses and deficits. The financial system can reconcile those surpluses and deficits by creating for lenders and borrowers assets and liabilities which most closely match their preferences for risk and return. Second, an expanding real economy requires additional liquidity and money power, in advance of growth of output, which have the effect of raising the level of aggregate demand (AD), with an increasing effect on the price level (demand-pull inflation: inflation caused by persistent rises in AD) or the production in terms of gross domestic product (GDP). Third, in making lending and borrowing easier, a financial system must also make it cheaper, which will affect the levels of savings and investments.

From the perspective of monetary and/or fiscal policy measures to be taken by the monetary authorities, the interaction between the financial system and the real economy is often explained in terms of monetary transmission mechanisms. These mechanisms or links are causal relationships between two economic variables (e.g. the interest rate and inflation), other things being equal (*ceteris paribus*). For example, a change in the official interest rate can affect market rates, asset prices, exchange rates and market confidence, which in turn can influence inflation (see figure 7.2): the monetary transmission mechanism is basically a three-stage process.

Figure 7.2 **Monetary transmission mechanisms: the links between the interest rate and inflation**

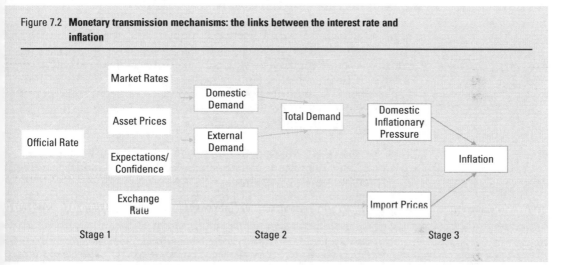

The first stage is that a change in the official interest rate set by the monetary authorities will affect market interest rates. Commercial banks and other financial institutions must react to any official rate change by changing their own savings and loan rates. The change will also affect the asset prices of shares, bonds and real estate, for instance. The exchange rate may change as demand and supply of the domestic currency adapt to the new level of interest rates. There may also be an effect on the expectations of both companies and individuals. They may become more or less confident about the future path of the real economy.

The second stage is that all these changes in markets affect the spending patterns of consumers and businesses. In other words there will be an effect on AD. Higher interest rates are likely to reduce the level of AD, as consumers are affected by the increase in rates and may look to cut their spending. There will also be international effects as the level of imports and exports changes in response to potential changes in the exchange rate.

The third stage is the impact of the AD change on GDP and inflation. This will tend to depend on the relative levels of AD and supply. If there is enough capacity in the economy, an increase in AD may not be inflationary. However, if the economy is already at full capacity, producing as much as it can, any further AD increase may be inflationary.

The strength of such transmission mechanisms varies from country to country since member countries respond differently to interest rate and exchange rate changes for several reasons. For example, countries with a high proportion of external trade (e.g. the Netherlands) tend to be more concerned about the impact of interest rate changes on the euro exchange rate with other world currencies. EU members which derive a large percentage of their GDP from trade outside the euro zone (e.g. Ireland and Belgium) will be more concerned about euro exchange rate fluctuations than members which are more focused on trade with other EU countries (e.g. Spain and Greece).

Another factor is the balance between industry and services. Germany, with a large percentage of employment in manufacturing (e.g. in the car industry), is more concerned about euro exchange rate fluctuations than Member States with higher employment in the services industry. However, southern EU countries like France, Italy, Greece, Spain and Portugal are more vulnerable to exchange rate fluctuation because of their high contribution of tourism from non-EMU countries to GDP.

There are also differences in the financial structures of EU members, which can have significant consequences for businesses trading in different Member States. For example:
- The higher the proportion of borrowing at variable interest rates, the bigger the effect on AD. For example, Austria and Italy have over 70% of borrowing on such terms, while France, Germany and the Netherlands have only around 40% (mostly long term and at fixed interest rates).
- The higher the proportion of consumer debt to GDP, the bigger will be the cost to households of servicing a rise in interest rates (and hence the bigger will be the income effect). This proportion is relatively high in the UK, Germany and Sweden and relatively low in southern European countries.
- The more rapidly banks pass on interest rate changes to their customers, the more rapid the effect on AD. In the Netherlands and Spain, ECB official interest rate changes are fully passed on into banks' short-term rates within three months, while in France and Germany the transition is much slower.
- The greater the levels of private-sector debt, the bigger will be the effect of any change in interest rates on AD. In the Netherlands the ratio of household debt to GDP is a massive 108%. In Italy, by contrast, the ratio is only 34%, so that a change in interest rates is likely to have a relatively small effect on consumer spending.

Interest rate changes, then, have different effects in different countries. For example, if we compare Germany and Ireland, the effect is likely to be less in Germany, which has lower levels of variable interest rate debt, a slower transmission of interest rate changes to banks, and a lower proportion of its trade outside the euro zone.

If the exchange rate is adjustable pegged, as in the ERM or the EMS, or is fixed (rate parity), as is the case within the euro zone, the situation will be completely different. With gradually rising costs and prices, the real exchange rate increases, and competitiveness declines with a smaller surplus or larger deficit on the current account of the balance of payments (see Glossary for fuller explanations). At the same time, lower interest rates worsen the financial account (due to less inflow of interest-bearing capital), which exacerbates the balance of payments deficit.

Committed to a fixed exchange rate, the central bank must intervene in the foreign exchange market, selling part of its foreign exchange reserves and buying back its own currency. On the one hand, this means that the central bank reabsorbs the money it has created, which increases the value of the domestic currency. On the other hand, it lowers the stock of foreign exchange reserves, which shrinks the supply of money. A country's monetary policy is less effective when exchange rates are fixed; an independent monetary policy is impossible because of the exchange rate commitment. A central bank can control either the money supply or the exchange rate but not both, as is explained by the 'impossible trinity principle' (see figure 7.1). In practice, exchange rates are rarely rigidly fixed but are usually allowed to move within bands. If the band is narrow, the room for monetary policy independence is very limited and vice versa.

7.3.2 The global credit crunch and its impact on the European financial services industry

The underlying reason for the vulnerability of the EU's financial systems is not the US sub-prime mortgage crisis. The crisis might have been contained within the financial services and housing sectors alone, but in the EU the close connection between banks and industry is deeply rooted. Unlike the USA, where the government has spent more than a century battling to break the links between government, industry and banks, this Europe has fostered collusion between banks and businesses from the very beginning of modern capitalism.

Since the 19th century, European financing and investing has been co-ordinated between banks and industry, and encouraged by the government, because industrialization was a modernizing project led by the state that did not spring up spontaneously as it did in the USA. The most famous example of this close connection between banks and private companies is the ties between Siemens AG and Deutsche Bank, a relationship which has existed for more than a hundred years. This linkage between banks and business insulates the financial system from many minor shocks, such as strikes or changes in government, but also makes it less flexible in the face of major shocks like serious recessions.

Therefore, in times of a global shortage of capital, European enterprises are left with few attractive financing alternatives.

In contrast, while banks are an important source of financing in the USA, companies there depend much more on the stock exchange market for investment. This forces American companies to compete vigorously for capital and constantly seek greater and greater efficiencies.

Apart from the effects of the US sub-prime crisis, the EU's banking system is vulnerable to three phenomena: the global credit crunch, the European sub-prime crisis and Eastern European overexposure to risk.

The global credit crunch

A credit crunch is a sudden reduction in the general availability of loans (or credit), or a sudden increase in the cost of obtaining loans from banks. Various European countries had such problems long before the US sub-prime crisis sparked the global credit crunch. Many of these were caused by the post-9/11 global credit expansion in combination with the adoption of the euro. Almost all central banks issued money into the financial system. The US Federal Reserve System (Fed) dropped interest rates to 1% and the ECB dropped them to 2%. The launch of the euro granted this low interest rate to all of the EMU countries. This easy credit environment was also spread to most of the smaller, poorer and newer EU members and caused a consumer spending boom which led to a real estate expansion or 'bubble' that, even without the sub-prime crisis and the global credit crunch, was going to burst sooner or later.

The European sub-prime crisis

The global credit crunch caused a second problem, namely the European sub-prime crisis, which is particularly acute in Spain, Ireland and non-EMU countries such as Iceland, Hungary and Ukraine that have recently experienced a lending boom stimulated by the euro's low interest rates. The adoption of the euro in Spain, Portugal, Italy and Ireland spread low interest rates normally reserved for highly developed, low-inflation economies such as that of Germany to typically credit-starved countries, granting consumers there cheap credit for the first time. The consequence was the property boom. Spain built more homes in 2006 than Germany, France and the UK combined, which led to the growth of the banking and construction industries. Banks pushed for more lending by offering liberal mortgages. In Ireland the no-down-payment 110% mortgage was a popular product, and in Spain credit checks were often waived, creating a pool of mortgages that might soon become as unstable as the US sub-prime pool. The poorer, smaller and new European countries gorged the most on this new credit, leading to the third European problem, namely Eastern European overexposure.

Eastern European overexposure

EU countries in Eastern Europe are in economic freefall as the slump deepens in the West, which is the main market for their exports. These export-led emerging markets find it more difficult to recover since world trade flows are heavily shrinking.

Unlike Asian countries, the Eastern European region has hardly any foreign exchange reserves at its disposal and also suffers from huge public debts. For instance, the Polish zloty, the Hungarian forint and the Czech koruna have recently depreciated markedly against the euro. These countries are not able to stimulate their economies by lowering interest rates or boosting public debt. Many Western European banks are severely affected by this Eastern European overexposure, since the region has grown so fast in the last couple of years. For instance, Austrian banks have lent around €278 billion to Eastern European countries (around 70% of their GNP).

As far as the Baltic countries are concerned, their growth surpassed even East Asian rates, but all on the back of borrowed money. This rapid growth caused double-digit inflation, which made it more difficult, for instance, for the Baltic states to take out loans to service their enormous trade imbalances.

The reason that growth rates were in the Balkans were low is because these countries either came late to EU membership, as with Bulgaria and Romania, or have not yet joined at all, as in the case of Croatia and Serbia, so they did not experience the full credit-expanding effect of being associated with the EU. Fuelling the surges were Italian, French, Austrian, Greek and Scandinavian banks. With their limited domestic markets, they pushed aggressively into neighbouring countries. The Scandinavian banks rushed into the Baltic countries and the Greek and Austrian banks focused on the Balkans and Hungary and the Italians and French went to Russia.

The new European states witnessed the greatest expansion in the past five years in terms of credit, by any measure, of any countries in the world with the possible exceptions of oil-booming Qatar and the United Arab Emirates. But that credit was almost entirely sourced from abroad and the easy credit environment has now collapsed, while heavy foreign ownership of even the domestic banks means that those who have the money have their core interests elsewhere.

Because Europe is very open in terms of trade, and because its financial sector is so closely integrated with the rest of the world, the region cannot avoid being significantly affected by the financial crisis. But how the crisis will play out in Europe will differ from the way it plays out in the USA because the economies are structured differently. Although the EU does not have that many complex financial products of its own and securitization is still in its infancy in many Member States, European banks owned a lot of bad US assets and were more highly leveraged than American banks.

The other difference is that automatic stabilizers are much more important in the EU than in the USA due to the size of the public sector. While this will help Europe, the unprecedented scale of this crisis will require more policy action. European leaders have adopted a co-ordinated approach to dealing with the problems in the financial system and have called for fiscal stimulus.

According to Stratford research (October 2008) into the impact of the financial crisis on Europe, government ability to address the financial crisis is weak in France, Italy, Hungary, Greece, the UK and Poland. The current financial crisis is a timely reminder to strengthen European co-operation in the area of financial stability, especially when it comes to cross-border financial institutions. There is an urgent need to deepen reforms that can tackle long-term issues such as the fiscal burden that will result from the ageing of the population and the need to improve productivity, a key goal of the Lisbon Agenda for growth and jobs.

Rescue plan to address the effects of the financial crisis
The financial crisis has led to other European monetary and fiscal policy measures as euro zone economies have propped up their banks by means of guaranteed loans, interest rate reductions, asset write-offs, nationalization of 'bad banks', interbank loan interventions and an increase in the minimum bank deposit guarantee from €20,000 to €50,000 by EU finance ministers in October 2008.

The EMU authorities, along with the British Prime Minister, Gordon Brown, met on 12th October 2008 to discuss the worldwide financial crisis. They agreed on various ways to tackle the crisis, such as guaranteeing interbank loans for up to five years and buying stakes in banks that are affected by or likely to be victims of the crisis.

However, a collective, European-wide programme was absent because the European integration process did not incorporate measures that would impinge on the financial institutions of the Member States; proposed measures were simply guidelines for Member States to follow. Nevertheless, in implementing their own, independent solutions, the main European economies quickly started putting those measures into action by infusing liquidity directly into the 'bad banks'. The comprehensive rescue plans took various forms in different countries, but all were aimed at combating the drying-up of credit and lessening the depth of the oncoming recession.

7.3.3 The landscape of EU financial institutions and financial systems

Central banks often make a distinction between deposit-taking (monetary) financial institutions (DTIs) and non-deposit-taking institutions (NDTIs). The division between DTIs and NDTIs is similar to the distinction between money-creating and non-money-creating institutions. Examples of DTIs are commercial banks and building societies, while insurance companies, pension funds, investment funds, unit trusts, leasing companies and hedge funds are examples of NDTIs (see table 7.2).

Hedge funds, which can be described as private investment funds that trade and invest in various assets such as securities, commodities, currency and derivatives on behalf of their clients, played a significant role in bringing about the financial crisis. The loss of a significant prime broker in Lehman and the counterparty implications are already being felt. As a consequence, regulatory changes, beginning with a temporary ban on short selling, can be expected in the future.

Commercial banks and building societies are considered to be financial intermediaries which, unlike brokers, act as a means of channelling funds from depositors to borrowers and create liquidity at their own account and risk. Financial intermediaries create liquidity by means of size, maturity and risk transformation through exploiting economies of scale and scope associated with their lending and borrowing activities, mismatching their assets and liabilities, diversifying their investments, pooling risks, screening and monitoring borrowers and holding capital and reserves as a buffer for unexpected losses. As a consequence there will exist more financial assets and liabilities than would be the case if the economy were to rely upon direct financing. However, mismatching can create problems in terms of liquidity risk, which is the risk of not having enough liquid funds to meet one's liabilities.

The variety of EU financial institutions can be classified in many ways, although there is inevitably some overlap in their activities – for example, DTIs versus NDTIs or a grouping according to different types of banking such as retail, wholesale, private, corporate and investment banking. During the financial crisis it has become more common to distinguish commercial banks from investment banks. Commercial banks are more involved in traditional 'on-balance sheet' activities such as booking assets and taking deposits, while investment banks focus more on 'off-balance sheet' activities, which are often fee-based, such as swaps, options and futures (see Glossary). Table 7.2 gives an overview of features of the most important European financial institutions divided into DTIs and NDTIs. It should be noted that nowadays almost all financial institutions in the EU are part of a financial conglomerate, since a wave of mergers and acquisitions has taken place since the early 1990s (see section 7.7).

The major functions of banks as DTIs are financial intermediation (interest margin business), money creation and, together with NDTIs. transmitting payments, insurances, securities and other universal banking activities (commission fee business).

From the perspective of the ECB, commercial banks are also known as deposit-taking monetary financial institutions (MFIs) and play a major role in a country's money supply and therefore a significant role in monetary transmission mechanisms (see figure 7.2). The monetary function of bank deposits is often seen as one of the main reasons why MFIs are subject to heavier regulation and supervision than their NDTI counterparts.

Figure 7.3 shows the development of the euro area MFI sector in the period 2000–2009. The most remarkable changes in this development were caused by the euro zone enlargements on 1st January 2001 (Greece), 2007 (Malta and Cyprus), 2008 (Slovenia) and 2009 (Slovakia) and the EU enlargements on 1st May 2004 and 1st January 2007 (Romania and Bulgaria). More than 80% of the euro area MFIs are credit institutions and most of the remainder are money market funds (see figure 7.4 for more information). Since 1st January 1999, the number of MFIs in the euro area has decreased by 20%, despite the euro zone enlargement as a result of Greece, Slovenia, Slovakia, Cyprus and Malta joining the euro zone. Germany and France account for 44% of all euro area MFIs (in 2008).

Table 7.2 **Some features of the most important European financial institutions divided into DTIs versus NDTIs**

European financial institution	DTI (or MFI) versus NDTI	Some features
European Central Bank	DTI	Independent supranational central bank for the euro zone countries; issues notes and coins; controls money supply; responsible for monetary supervision
European System of Central Banks (ESCB) and Eurosystem	DTI	ESCB = National Central Banks (NCBs) of all EU members Eurosystem = all NCBs of the euro zone; lender of last resort; government's banker; responsible for prudential, conduct business and system supervision
Commercial banks (wholesale and retail)	DTI	Major financial intermediary in any economy (mainly involved in 'on-balance sheet' business, but they usually offer a full range of financial services); main providers of credit to the household and corporate sector; operate in the payments mechanism (e.g. Deutsche Bank and Barclays).
Building societies (retail institutes)	DTI	Offer personal banking services; prevalent in the UK and very similar to savings and co-operative banks as they have mutual ownership and focus primarily on retail deposit taking and mortgage lending. Since 1989 most building societies have embraced demutualization, leading to a shift of assets from the mutual to the commercial banking sector.
Savings banks (retail banks)	DTI	Similar to commercial banks, the main difference being their mutual ownership. In Germany and Spain they are (quasi) public owned.
Co-operative banks (retail banks)	DTI	Similar to commercial banks; originally had mutual ownership without shareholders; typically offer retail and small business banking services.
Credit unions (retail institutes)	DTI	Mutual non-profit DTIs (especially in Ireland and, though to a lesser extent, the UK).
Investment banks or merchant banks (in the UK) (wholesale banks)	NDTI	Specialized in securities market activities with corporate customers (e.g. underwriting, mergers and acquisitions advisory activities).
Finance houses (mainly retail institutes)	NDTI	Usually subsidiaries of commercial banks and finance for the purchase of consumer durables. They raise funds by issuing commercial paper, stocks and bonds.
Private banks	NDTI	Specialist banking, investment, estate planning and tax services provided to wealthy personal customers.
Overseas banks	DTI or NDTI	Finance of international trade and capital movements and dealing in foreign exchange markets.
Insurance companies	NDTI	Protect policy holders from various adverse events.
Pension funds	NDTI	Invest contributions to pay a pension on retirement or disability.
Hedge funds	NDTI	Control billions of dollars of stocks and may borrow billions more, and thus may overwhelm intervention by central banks to support almost any currency, if the economic fundamentals are in the hedge funds' favour.

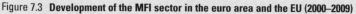

Figure 7.3 **Development of the MFI sector in the euro area and the EU (2000–2009)**

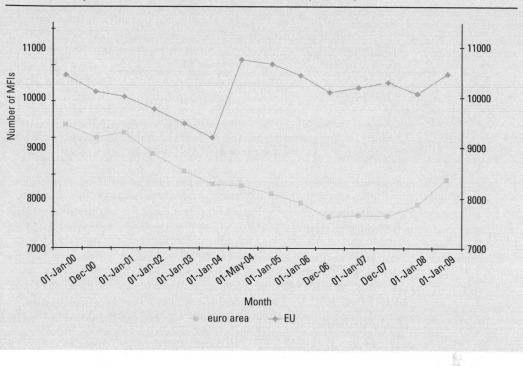

Credit squeeze hits bigger companies hardest

Contrary to expectations, large companies in the EU and USA are seeing the terms of their credit facilities tightened faster and more severely than smaller companies. Surveys by the ECB, US Fed and Germany's Ifo economics institute all show banks tightening their lending criteria the most for the largest companies. Possible reasons put forward for this shift in attitude include smaller companies enjoying a better relationship with their banks, and financial institutions shying away from making large loans and preferring to deal with local groups, rather than multinationals.

'Large companies drove the credit-fuelled expansion but, especially in November, we have seen a big reversal of that,' said Chris Williamson, chief economist of data provider Markit. André Kunkel, head of surveys at Ifo, said: 'For the last few years, big companies consistently had it easier but then, in recent months, they saw a huge worsening in credit conditions. Lending terms have dramatically tightened for big companies.'

Banks in the euro zone have tightened the credit conditions for 68% of large companies but only 56% of SMEs, according to the ECB's latest survey. Similarly, the Fed's latest lending survey shows that 95% of banks have tightened conditions for large companies whereas only 90% have done so for smaller ones. Ifo's figures for December in Germany are even more dramatic, the number of large companies reporting tightened loan terms more than doubling since August to 48%. By contrast, only 36% of mid-sized companies and 35% of small companies reported stricter terms. Some analysts suggest the difference in approach is to do with a re-evaluation of risk. 'SMEs are seen as less risky, as the risk of default for large companies is at an all-time high,' said Mr Williamson.

Philip Isherwood, European equity strategist at Dresdner Kleinwort, suggested it may be simply that banks had applied laxer conditions to larger companies previously and were 'now playing catch-up'. Large European companies are also seeing production fall faster than smaller groups, according to a survey by Markit.

7.3.4 Basel Accords and other regulatory measures affecting the EU financial sectors

The main aim of EU capital market liberalization prior to the 1980s was to facilitate real business activities. For example, national policies should not hinder an enterprise based in one Member State from setting up business in another Member State. This right of establishment covers international transfers of capital that may be necessary to set up a business.

Likewise, national policies were not supposed to hinder the repatriation of profits and wages among Member States since such obstacles act as restrictions on the free movement of goods and people.

Initiated in the 1970s by the Basel Committee on Banking Supervision, the convergence of capital adequacy requirements among the major industrialized countries that meet at the Bank for International Settlements (BIS) has become a central issue in the establishment of the 'level playing field' on which international banks need to compete. Capital adequacy is a minimum level of capital (difference between assets and liabilities) a bank should hold, as established by the Basel Accord. According to this agreement, banks must have at least 8% of their balance sheet total (or total assets) in the form of own capital. This so-called BIS-ratio (or capital or solvency ratio) varies according to the riskiness of a bank's business activity (both on and off balance sheet). The more risky the activity, the more capital a bank needs to hold.

In general, there has been a gradual shift from direct forms of control over banks' performance by national regulatory authorities (e.g. by limiting credit creation or instructing banks to prioritize lending according to the type of customer) to indirect and objective types of control (such as changing the discount rate).
The process of implementing new rules, restrictions and controls in response to market participants' efforts to circumvent existing regulations (supervisory re-regulation) has been shaped by global pressures.

The first effort to encourage convergence towards common approaches and standards at the international level started with the First Basel Capital Accord in 1988 (known as Basel I). Since then, capital adequacy standards and risk regulation have been important policy issues and fundamental components of bank's prudential re-regulation. The Basel I Accord established an international standard around a 'capital ratio' of 8% and focused on risks associated with lending (default or credit risks), thereby ignoring other types of risk.

The Basel definition of capital is made up of two elements: Tier 1 ('core capital': common stock plus disclosed reserves) and Tier 2 ('supplementary capital', e.g. undisclosed reserves, asset revaluation reserves and subordinated loans). Bank total capital is the sum of Tier 1 and 2. According to the committee, a weighted risk ratio – in which capital is related to different categories of asset and off-balance sheet exposure and weighted according to broad categories of relative riskiness – is the preferred method for assessing the capital adequacy of banks.

A major aim of EU legislation has been to reduce the barriers to cross-border trade in the banking and financial services area with the ultimate aim of creating a single market in financial services. The removal of structural obstacles has been accompanied by financial deregulation through the reduction of direct government control. At the same time it has been associated with upgrades of prudential regulation, as witnessed by the Basel II rule revision (see table 7.3).

Table 7.3 Regulatory measures that have had an impact on the European banking sector

Year	Regulation
1977	First Banking Directive: adoption of regulations, norms and procedures which removed obstacles to the provision of services across the borders of Member States and to the establishment of branches. It also harmonized the rules and conditions for issuing a licence to operate as a bank and defined authorities that supervise banks and branches of foreign banks, as well as the procedures for co-operation among these authorities.
1988	Basel Capital Adequacy Regulation (Basel I Accord)
1988	Deregulation of capital movement within the EMS: enabled the free flow of capital across EU borders.
1989	Second Banking Directive: established the rules for a single banking licence within the EU and introduced the principles of 'home-country control' (home regulators have ultimate supervisory authority for the foreign activity of their banks) and mutual recognition (EU bank regulators recognize that their rules and regulations are equivalent). The Second Banking Directive was passed in conjunction with the Own Funds and Solvency Ratio Directives, which effectively introduced capital adequacy requirements similar to those proposed by Basel into EU law.
1993	Investment Services Directive (ISD): set the legislative framework for investment firms and securities markets in the EU, providing for a single passport for investment services.
1999	Financial Services Action Plan (FSAP): aimed at developing a legislative framework for developing the single market in financial services.
2000	Directive on e-money: conceived and adopted at the height of the e-commerce boom and intended to facilitate access by non-credit institutions to the business of e-money issuance. Dealt with harmonizing rules and standards relating to such things as payments by mobile telephone and using transport cards.
2001	Directive on the Re-organization and Winding-up of Credit Institutions: created rules to ensure that reorganization measures or winding-up proceedings adopted by the home state of an EU credit institution are recognized and implemented throughout the EU.
2004	New Takeover Directive: established a common framework for cross-border takeover bids.
2006–08	Basel II: new solvency capital adequacy framework to update Basel I, which had been in effect since 1988. The new rules aimed to improve the consistency of capital regulations internationally, make regulatory capital more risk sensitive, and to promote better risk-management practices among large, internationally active banking organizations.
2007	Markets in Financial Instruments Directive (MiFID): the cornerstone of FSAP; replaced the ISD and contained measures which would change and improve the organization and functioning of investment firms, facilitate cross-border trading and thereby encourage the integration of the EU capital markets. MiFID (also called the Lamfalussy Directive) would ensure strong investor protection, with a comprehensive set of rules governing the relationship between investment firms and their clients.
2007	Payment Services Directive (PSD): provided the legal framework for the creation of an EU-wide single market for payments. At the same time the PSD provided the necessary legal platform for the Single Euro Payments Area (SEPA). From November 2009 new EU rules would allow alternative providers such as mobile phone operators to deliver payment services alongside banks and credit card companies, paving the way for a more efficient non-cash economy.
2008	Consumer Credit Directive (CCD): intended to harmonize key aspects of consumer credit legislation in Member States as part of the objective of creating a common credit market across the EU. The Directive was also intended to maintain high levels of consumer protection.

Source: ECB Eurosystem press release, Development of Euro Area Monetary Financial Institutions Sector, 8th January 2008 (adapted)

7.3.5 A changing framework for the banking sector in the EU

Since the early 1990s the regulatory environment of the European financial services industry is constantly changing, including adjustments to supervision of the financial system, government deregulation, a growing importance of financial markets outside the EU and technological changes in the form of financial innovations and automation.

In 1999 the Basel Committee on Banking Supervision launched proposals for a new capital adequacy framework (which was to become Basel II). The new accord's main aim was to introduce a more comprehensive and risk-sensitive treatment of banking activities to ensure that regulatory capital bore a closer relationship to default, market and operational risks.

In general, the performance in terms of profitability, efficiency and solvency of European banking systems has increased significantly since the creation of the single market for capital. However, there remain substantial differences in the features and performance of banks in different EU countries despite a widespread adoption of strategies aimed at boosting stock market prices and generating shareholder value for bank owners.

Table 7.3 shows that the EU is progressing with legislation aimed at removing barriers for the creation of a single European financial services marketplace as well as the implementation of the new Basel II capital adequacy rules.

In addition to the changing framework for banking in the EU, the following major trends in the European banking sector can be identified:
· consolidation or concentration of the financial services industry including M&A activity
· internationalization and globalization of financial markets
· convergence or interconnection of bank- and capital market-based financial systems
· deconstruction and specialization, with a focus on the core competences of the banking sector, low-priority activities being outsourced or offshored.

Outsourcing involves the transfer of (part of the) business activities to an external service provider, mainly because of cost advantages (e.g. call centres in India). Offshoring is an activity undertaken by institutions that are located outside the country of residence of the customer, typically in a low-tax jurisdiction (e.g. the Bahamas and Bermuda), and that provide financial and legal advantages. Offshoring is the transfer of an organizational function to another country, irrespective of whether the work is outsourced or stays within the same business. Outsourcing and offshoring are used interchangeably in public discourse despite important technical differences. Outsourcing involves contracting with a supplier, which may or may not involve some degree of offshoring.

In general, increases in competition appear to have forced a concentration of the European banking sector during the 1990s. The preference for national consolidation is that it offers opportunities for reducing costs and reduces complications in terms of handling M&A activities due to dissimilar corporate cultures. In the future, greater emphasis might be placed on cross-border M&As as domestic markets become congested and competitive regulation no longer allows mergers between major players.

Increasing improvements in ICT, the abolishment of capital controls and the deregulation of financial markets, combined with the introduction of the single market for financial services have encouraged the transition from a rather traditional into a more modern European banking system. This transformation of a relatively restricted and uncompetitive industry into a more dynamic, competitive and risk-taking business has led to the provision of more universal products and services, which in turn has accompanied a proportional increase in income from fee- and commission-based business as opposed to net-interest business. In addition, the banking sector has seen a change in strategic focus from asset size and growth objectives to return to shareholders and a move from supply-driven to demand-driven customer focus (see table 7.4).

Table 7.4 Traditional versus modern banking systems

Traditional banking system	Modern banking system
Limited number of products and services: loans and deposits ('on-balance sheet' activities)	Universal banking activities: loans, deposits, insurances, securities, pensions, etc. ('on-balance sheet' and 'off-balance sheet' activities); an increase in securitization techniques to pass on assets to other investors
'Matching' the maturity of loans and deposits (the 'golden rule' of banking)	Maturity transformation: 'mismatching' the maturity of loans and deposits
Net interest income as the main source of income; high interest margins and small transactions	Both net interest income and fee and commission income; low interest margins and large transactions; investment banks focus more on advice, market liquidity, underwriting and other fee-yielding services related to capital markets
Relatively restricted and uncompetitive environment (capital controls and regulation)	Relatively unrestricted competitive environment (capital mobility and deregulation)
Strategic focus on size (balance sheet total) and growth	Strategic focus on returns to shareholders (shareholder value approach: return on equity larger than cost of capital); greater focus on market capitalization
Relatively lax risk assessment (mainly default and liquidity risks)	Relatively comprehensive risk assessment (default, market and operational risks)
Supply-driven customer focus	Demand-driven customer focus
More market fragmentation in different regions and more segmented financial markets; a more bank-based financial system	Greater consolidation of the banking industry (higher concentration ratios) with large differences within the EU (see case study 7.1: contrast between German and British banking); financial markets are more interwoven; trend towards M&A, leading to the creation of financial conglomerates (e.g. 'bancassurance')

7.3.6 A new regulatory business environment

There is still considerable potential to reap the benefits of the increasing integration of EU banking and financial sectors. The EU is consequently pressing ahead with new legislation focusing in particular on retail market issues (even though there is more to do with respect to the structure of financial supervision in the EU, the alignment of consumer protection and contract law, and tax issues, among other things). Besides the many regulatory measures (see table 7.3), the growing importance of economies outside the EU and technological changes have had a huge impact on the European banking sector.

Regulatory measures
In the secondary markets, i.e. markets in which previously issued securities are traded, MiFID is designed to foster competition among trading venues on the basis of a level regulatory playing field and market transparency, aimed at supporting market efficiency and investor protection. The MiFID contained measures designed to change and improve the organization and functioning of investment firms, facilitate cross-border trading and thereby encourage the integration of EU capital markets (see also section 7.4). The MiFID should ensure strong investor protection, thanks to a comprehensive set of rules governing the relationship which investment firms have with their clients.

Similarly, the Consumer Credit Directive (CCD), which has been passed at EU level but has yet to be transposed into national law, aims at improving the cross-border supply of consumer loans, thereby making credit more easily available and cheaper for retail clients. The CCD was adopted by the EC in May 2008, with a deadline for completing the transposition of June 2010 for all Member States.

The Payment Services Directive (PSD) provided the legal framework for the creation of an EU-wide single market for payments. The PSD aimed at establishing a modern and comprehensive set of rules applicable to all payment services in the EU. The target was to make cross-border payments as easy, efficient and secure as national payments within a member state. The PSD also sought to improve competition by opening up payment markets to new entrants, thus fostering greater efficiency and cost-reduction for retail customers and SMEs.

Growing importance of economies outside the EU
Apart from European integration, the past decade has witnessed a remarkable shift in the global balance of power away from the industrialized countries of Europe towards emerging markets such as Brazil, Russia, India and China (BRIC). The growing importance of economies outside the EU is partly the result of a long period of transition in CEE and elsewhere from centrally planned economies to (semi-) market-oriented economies in addition to a wave of economic liberalization.

Technological change
A third key driver for changes in the European banking landscape in recent years has been technological progress, a factor whose influence can hardly be overestimated. Innovation in telecommunications and electronic data processing have considerably facilitated the flow of information between clients and banks, within financial institutions, and between them. For example, online banking activities have made gathering and exchanging information much easier for clients as well as for banks themselves.

These technological changes have not only been a precondition for the far-reaching improvements in the quality of products, in-house operations and client services, but at the same time allowed for enormous cost savings, which have benefited both banks and customers via lower prices for many standard banking services. The IT revolution, however, has not only turned upside down the way banking is conducted, but also resulted in expenditure on technology and communication becoming one of the most important cost factors for the financial services industry.

7.3.7   Major trends in the EU banking industry

Although the turmoil in the financial markets reverses a long period of improvements in profitability, solvency and efficiency and will negatively affect the earnings of European banks for a considerable time, this should not distract from the continuing development of the banking environment in Europe. The EU banking industry can identify at least four major trends, namely consolidation/concentration, internationalization/globalization, convergence of financial systems and deconstruction/specialization of financial activities. EU banking markets have become more consolidated and international banks more capital market-oriented and more specialized over the last few years.

Merger and acquisition activity and consolidation
Encouraged by the drive towards economies of scale and scope and towards diversification of income streams, the consolidation trend has led to increases in size and higher market shares. There are several reasons for consolidation, including the following:
- Consolidation leads to economies of scale and scope, particularly in cases where fixed costs are high.
- M&A among banks create more X-efficiency. Formulated by American economist Harvey Leibenstein (1922–1993), X-efficiency is an economic expression for the effectiveness with which an organization uses its given set of input to produce outputs. It describes the general efficiency of an enterprise (judged according to managerial and technological criteria) in transforming inputs at minimum cost into maximum profits. A merger between two banks can allow for the exchange of best practices and leverage of successful products, processes, and brands.
- Large banks are seen as more stable institutions. Their generally higher degree of diversification reduces their exposure to adverse movements in individual markets, which in turn strengthens ratings and lowers refinancing costs.
- Large banks can also claim that they are the only institutions able to satisfy the increasing demand for large-scale transactions that in particular require a broad capital base and sufficiently experienced personnel. As the latest boom in leveraged buy-outs and mega-M&A deals has demonstrated, volumes in the double-digit billion euro range are no longer exceptional in both syndicated loans and debt and equity underwriting.
- Finally, creating a larger bank might also be beneficial in terms of public awareness (and that of financial analysts). Wider coverage in

the media, by equity analysts, and perhaps admission to a major stock index can boost share prices as well as facilitate future business.

Internationalization
Internationalization comprises mainly three dimensions, namely that European banks increase their foreign earnings, that foreign banks enter the EU market, and that the shareholder base of banks in Europe becomes more international.

Convergence
In this context the term 'convergence' describes the tendency in recent years of capital market activities and traditional on-balance sheet banking to become ever more interwoven with each other and often complement each other. This has led to fundamental improvements in risk management and to a shift in bank activities from asset intermediation towards the provision of fee-generating capital market services.

The convergence of bank- and capital market-based financial systems suggests that the clear distinctions which have been drawn between money and capital markets for decades may no longer be valid.

Although the EU banking system is becoming more capital market-oriented, there are still huge differences among the EU countries. Historically, the more traditional German bank-based financial system contrasts highly with the more capital market-based financial system of the UK (see case study 7.1). The German financial system is characterized by greater fragmentation and focus on traditional on-balance sheet activities, while the UK banking system is more concentrated and has put more efforts into off-balance sheet activities. Although universal banking activities have now been introduced in Germany, for a long time the trend towards bancassurance was more common in Scandinavian countries, the UK and the Netherlands.

Deconstruction and specialization
A fourth major trend in European banking markets is for banks to constantly review their core businesses, identifying competitive advantages as well as relative weaknesses, in order to concentrate on their identified strengths. Similar practices are common in other industries, where business evaluate which parts of the value chain to provide for themselves and which services to procure from external sources.

Increasing complexity, the presence of economies of scale and scope, and growing international competition are increasingly forcing banks to specialize in what they really do best, diverting from areas in which they have little expertise and too small an involvement. The efficiency gains associated with a higher degree of specialization and a better division of labour have contributed to making the banking sector as a whole more effective and profitable.

The motivation behind banks' current move to scale down the scope of their activities is mainly threefold:

- First, outsourcing improves the division of labour and therefore releases efficiency gains, as banks can benefit from deeper specialist knowledge.
- Second, outsourcing reduces costs.
- Third, banks also gain from greater flexibility due to their more focused operations: they are more sensitive and pay more attention to changes in a specific market environment, to which they can then adjust more quickly.

Case study 7.1 **German banking: a contrast with British**

The German financial system was the prototype of a universal, segmented bank-based financial system with a relatively low concentration ratio. Consequently, financial flows were channelled through credit institutions rather than through markets and the system was mainly focused on on-balance sheet business activities. In the 1980s, this was considered a pillar of Germany's economic strength.

Nowadays, Germany is characterized as being overbanked and its banking system inefficient (relatively high costs), not particularly profitable and in need of radical restructuring; the need to reform the German financial system has been widely discussed. Does the British banking and financial system provide a good role model?

In any assessment of German economic development one crucial factor stands out: the role of the banks. The German banking sector was paramount in stimulating and promoting much of Germany's industrial growth, and significantly contributed to German economic success, both before and after the Second World War. Credit banks, or commercial banks, as they are more commonly known, were formed in both Germany and France in the 1850s. In both countries they had as their primary function the promotion of industrial investment. However, by 1900 the role of credit banks had been substantially widened, such that in Germany in particular they were in fierce competition with other specialized banking institutions.

Today the Deutsche Bank AG, the Dresdner Bank AG and the Commerzbank AG, the main credit banks, are the major elements in the German banking system and their influence on economic development is significant. These big commercial banks dominate the lending of funds to the giant German corporations. In fact, such lending typically exceeds the issuing of shares as a source of business finance.

In line with this position, the commercial banks have significant influence over business activity and decision making. The banks are significant shareholders in German companies, using voting rights and being represented on business supervisory boards.

A key feature of German banks is that they lend long term to the industry and are prepared to make a long-term commitment to financing investment (e.g. the close ties between Siemens AG and Deutsche Bank). From time to time they have co-operated in mounting rescue operations when businesses have fallen into financial difficulties, a situation that in Britain has been left to the government to resolve (which in practice has often meant bankruptcy). The German steel industry is a good example of such action. The 1980s recession saw the steel industry suffer heavy losses. The response was for bank lending to increase substantially.

The contrast with British banking is dramatic. British banks are not shareholders in British industry, and their lending is primarily short term. As a result, British investment has had to be financed primarily by ploughed-back profits, with new share issue as the other major source of finance.

The UK banking sector has traditionally been highly segmented, consisting of many different types of financial institution, such as building societies and merchant banks (see table 7.2). In comparison with other major European countries, the UK has a small number of banks. Since 1997, the UK financial system has become more concentrated as a result of M&A activities.

Since interest margins remained relatively high throughout the 1990s, UK banks were among the best performing European banks in terms of profitability. It is obvious that this is partly due to the fact that UK banks were more involved in risky banking activities, which eventually took them down during the financial crisis.

7.4   European financial markets and financial instruments

Financial markets deal with matching the needs and preferences of borrowers and lenders, evaluating risks and allowing for risk diversification. The financial industry has sought massive economies of scale and scope, which has affected financial institutes and markets through the emergence of financial conglomerates and large, interwoven financial markets. The deregulation of financial markets in the 1980s, the establishment of the single market for capital and the launch of the euro in 1999 have also helped to reduce barriers between financial markets and financial institutions.

These trends in the EU financial system have blurred the demarcation lines between the money and the capital markets. The money market is the market in which short-term funds are raised, invested and traded using instruments which generally have an original maturity of less than one year (sometimes two years is used as the demarcation line), while the capital market is the market for long-term funds with a residual maturity date of more than one year.

As financial innovation continues and new markets and new types of instrument are developed, the degree of interdependence between the financial markets is increasing, as has become apparent during the financial crisis. Although nowadays the European money and capital markets are more interlinked, the different markets are still distinguished from each other and have different features.

7.4.1   European money and capital markets

Financial markets can be distinguish into money and capital markets depending on the maturity of the loans they handle. The market of short-term loans is the money markets, with commercial banks and wholesale companies as the main participants. The market of long-term loans is the capital market, with institutional investors, banks and the government as the principal participants.

European money markets
There are several ways of classifying money markets. First, it is possible to make a distinction between retail and wholesale money markets. The retail money market is for SMEs, while the wholesale money market applies to large businesses. Nowadays it makes more sense to talk of retail or wholesale banking activity, rather than retail or wholesale banks, since the same banks are involved in both types of activity (and many more).

Second, there exists a money market between a central bank and commercial banks (narrow definition of money market) and an interbank money market between banks which is directly connected to the monetary policy and appeared to be indispensable during the global financial crisis.

Third, the money markets of the euro zone can be categorized as uncollateralized or collateralized (see table 7.5). An uncollateralized money market is not covered by assets that secure repayment on short-term loans and is closer to the single monetary policy. A significant exception to the generally high level of integration among euro zone money markets is the segment that deals in collateralized short-term securities (i.e. commercial paper and certificates of deposit), which has remained fragmented.

The emergence of liquidity problems in the money markets due to the global financial crisis has had an impact on the volatility of short-term money market rates. This is in particular the case with overnight rates, at which money is lent by one bank to another, to be returned the next day. Banks frequently find that they have surplus or insufficient funds at the end of the day. They settle with other banks by borrowing, and profit on any excess by lending till the next day.

European banks considered that the introduction of the euro in 1999 made it necessary to establish a new interbank reference rate within the euro zone. It was called the Euro Interbank Offered Rate (or Euribor) and is a daily reference rate based on the averaged interest rates at which banks offer to lend unsecured funds to other banks in the euro wholesale money market. It is the rate at which euro interbank term deposits are offered by one prime bank to another prime bank. Euribor is sponsored by the European Banking Federation, which represents the interests of some 5,000 European banks, and by the Financial Markets Association. It is published at 11 am. The choice of banks that may quote for Euribor is based on market criteria. They must be of first-class credit standing and are selected to ensure that the diversity of the euro money market is adequately reflected, thereby making Euribor an efficient and representative benchmark. Since its launch, Euribor has become established in the derivatives markets and is the underlying rate of many derivatives transactions, both OTC and exchange-traded. Euribor is used as a reference rate for euro-denominated Forward Rate Agreements (FRAs), short-term interest rate futures contracts and interest rate swaps. An FRA is a cash-settled forward contract on a deposit; an interest rate futures contract is an agreement to buy or sell a specific amount of a commodity or financial instrument at a particular price on a stipulated future date; and an interest rate swap is an exchange between two parties of fixed and/or variable interest rate payments. These financial products provide the basis for some of the world's most liquid and active interest rate markets.

Another widely used reference rate in the euro zone is the Euro Over-Night Index Average (EONIA), also published by the European Banking Federation, which is the daily average of overnight rates for unsecured interbank lending in the euro zone (equivalent to the federal funds rate in the USA). EONIA is calculated as a weighted average of all overnight unsecured lending transactions undertaken in the interbank market within the euro area by the contributing banks. EONIA is computed with the help of the ECB. The banks contributing to EONIA are the same as the banks quoting for Euribor. Since its launch, EONIA has been the underlying rate of numerous derivatives transactions.

The integration of the European money markets relies on the existence of a single system for refinancing the banks in the euro area or a common monetary policy. However, it also relies technically on a system of instantaneous data transfer and on the new common payment system,

TARGET, enabling real-time gross settlement. Thanks to the smooth operation of the information, communication and payment systems, a common monetary policy is realistic and the integration of the markets can take place. Such integration will, in turn, involve greater liquidity and further development of the financial markets.

A specific channel through which the monetary policy of the ECB and the TARGET system can have a direct impact on the development of the financial markets of the euro area is the requirement to have guarantees or collateral for operations with the ECB. This requirement for adequate collateral can stimulate the process of loan, especially in the case of the banking institutions of certain financial systems. The underlying assets can be used across borders, which means that a banking institution in a country belonging to the European System of Central Banks (ESCB) can receive funds from its national central bank by pledging assets located in other countries, which is also relevant from the perspective of the integration of the financial markets of the area.

European capital markets
The capital market is the market of borrowers (or savers) and lenders (or investors) of capital with a residual maturity date of more than one year. This capital market consists of an official and a private market. The official market deals in shares, bonds and mortgages, while the private market handles private loans, home mortgage loans and real estate investments.

Before the introduction of the euro, several factors acted as disincentives to cross-border financial activities, including the exchange rate risk, differences in inflation and interest rates, the substantial transaction costs of operating in different currencies, and currency restrictions on investors and banks. The adoption of the euro removed these obstacles and gave momentum to financial market integration, although to different degrees according to the market segment. Progress in financial integration has been fastest in the government bond market, where yields have converged and are increasingly driven by common factors, although local factors such as liquidity differences and the availability of developed derivatives markets tied to the various individual bond markets continue to play a role. Similarly, the advent of EMU has led to progress in the integration of the corporate bond market, as the various markets previously segmented by currency have merged into a single, diversified euro market. As a result, country-specific factors have become less important in determining corporate bond prices and spreads. The level of cross-border holdings also confirms that government and corporate bond markets are quite well integrated. For instance, cross-border holdings of long-term debt securities have significantly increased during the last ten years. Moreover, the holdings of debt securities issued by non-financial corporations have risen markedly from a very low level, suggesting that investors are increasingly diversifying their portfolios across the euro zone.

The stock exchange market (in the UK called the equity market) is where companies raise the financial resources they need for the acquisition of capital and generally develop their activities. They issue shares, which are held by individuals or by large institutional investors, such as pension funds and insurance companies.

The capital markets consist of primary markets and secondary markets. Newly formed (issued) securities are bought and sold in primary markets. One example of a transaction in the primary market is the emission of shares and bonds as examples of securities. Secondary markets allow investors to sell securities that they hold or buy existing securities. The primary markets for securities are not well known to the public because the selling of securities to initial buyers often takes place behind closed doors. An important financial institution that assists in the initial sale of securities in the primary market is the investment bank. It does this by underwriting securities: it guarantees a price for a company's securities and then sells them to the public. The secondary market plays an important role in the financial system, since it enables investors with a temporary surplus of liquid assets to buy illiquid assets (e.g. mortgages and bonds) with a long-term maturity and a high return, mainly from investment banks. In particular, during the last decade many investment banks used the secondary market to acquire more liquidity and diversify their financial risks, which partly caused the financial crisis of 2007 onwards.

Financial integration in the stock exchange markets is less advanced but shows signs of improvement. Since the early 1990s, stock market integration has proceeded more quickly in the euro zone than worldwide, although local shocks still cause considerable variance in equity returns. Since the last decade, euro zone investors more or less doubled their holdings of equity issued in other euro zone countries, whereas the share of euro zone stocks held outside the euro zone remained at a much lower level and increased only slightly. Table 7.5 gives the current state of financial integration and an overview of the main financial segments in the euro area.

Table 7.5 **State of financial integration in the euro zone: overview of the main financial segments**

Market	State of integration	Related infrastructure
Money markets:		
· Unsecured money market	· 'Near perfect'	· Fully integrated
· Collateralized money market	· Advanced	· Cash leg fully integrated; collateral leg hampered by fragmentation
Bond markets:		
· Government bond markets	· Very well advanced	· Fragmented
· Corporate bond markets	· Fair	· Fragmented
Stock or Equity market	Low	Highly fragmented
Banking markets:		
· Wholesale activities	· Well advanced	· Fully integrated
· Capital-market-related activities	· Advanced	· Fragmented
· Retail banking	· Very low	· Highly fragmented

Source: ECB Eurosystem, *Monthly Bulletin*, 10th Anniversary of the ECB: 1998–2008, p. 104 (adapted)

7.4.2 From financial integration to financial stability

The European financial landscape has changed since the introduction of the euro. The financial markets of the euro area have all benefited from financial innovation (new products, new techniques) and infrastructure development. The financial markets have also become more integrated, which enhances competition, benefits consumers, diversifies risk and therefore smoothes asymmetric shocks and ultimately fosters growth. The new phenomenon of interbank markets has transformed the financial structure of commercial bank lending, with banks in countries such as Portugal and Greece now obtaining finance from banks in other Member States rather than from non-euro zone sources. These advances in wholesale markets facilitate access to capital for financial companies and make risk sharing across the system more efficient, reducing the economic cost of financing and improving the resilience of financial institutions.

Government bond markets have also become more integrated. The spread across government bond yields has narrowed to a very low level, which may in part reflect an alignment of fundamentals, as well as the elimination of liquidity premia on debt denominated in domestic currency. Bonds issued by member countries have also been perceived as very close substitutes due to EMU.

To a lesser extent, integration has also advanced in the corporate bond and equity markets. However, the securities infrastructure, e.g. clearing and settlement systems, would need to be further improved in those segments to facilitate integration.

Historically confined to national markets, bond issuance by EU companies and banks has expanded since the creation of the euro zone. The resulting increase in competition in investment banking reduced issuance costs and provided small and high-risk issuers with better financing conditions. The elimination of currency risk has also enhanced substitutability across euro zone government and corporate bonds. However, the integration of the financial markets is still uneven.

In contrast, the retail markets suffer from a visible lack of integration. The price variations across Member States are still wide, and the volume of direct cross-border transactions remains limited. Remaining barriers such as consumer habits, culture, regulation and law markedly slow the integration of traditional retail activities.

Mortgage markets in particular are essential for financial stability because of the link between the banking sector and households' intertemporal income and wealth management. Low cross-border activity and marked price variation in the mortgage markets suggest that integration remains very limited in this segment.

7.5 European monetary policy strategies

The Maastricht Treaty specifies that the main task of the Eurosystem, referring to the ECB and the participating national central banks (NCBs), is to deliver price stability – defined as a year-on-year increase in the Harmonized Index of Consumer Prices (HICP) for the euro area below but close to 2%. Price stability is to be maintained over the medium term.

While many central banks typically announce an admissible range for inflation, the Eurosystem indicates only an imprecise target. It does not specify the meaning of the medium term, but price stability clearly has priority over objectives such as low rates of unemployment and sustainable high economic growth. Officially the highest priority of the Eurosystem is to stabilize inflation, but it might also consider secondary concerns which are indirectly connected to the final aim to stabilize the inflation rates (between 0 and 2%).

The ECB in Frankfurt

Like most other central banks, the Eurosystem uses the short-term interest rate to conduct monetary policy. The reason is that very short-term assets are close to cash. As central banks have a monopoly on the supply of cash, they can control very short-term rates. On the other hand, longer-term financial instruments such as mortgages and bonds can be supplied by both the public and the private sectors, making it nearly impossible for central banks to dominate the market and control the rate. In fact, long-term interest rates incorporate market expectations of future inflation and future policy actions. These expectations are beyond the control of the central bank, and therefore long-term interest rates cannot be steered with any degree of precision. By concentrating on short-term rates, central banks can achieve greater precision.

The problem is that central banks control short-maturity funds, whereas it is the long-term interest rate that affects the real economy because households and businesses borrow for relatively long periods, typically from 1 to 20 years. Stock prices and exchange rates (see figure 7.2), which are the other transmission variables through which monetary policy affects the real economy, also incorporate longer-term expectations, similar to those that affect long-term interest rates.

Thus central banks act indirectly on the real economy, since they affect long-term interest rates through their influence on future short-term rates and inflation. This can be explained by the so-called Fisher Effect, which describes the long-term relationship between inflation and interest rates. This relationship tells us that, all things being equal, a rise in a country's expected inflation rate will eventually cause an equal rise in the interest rate (and vice versa).

The ECB is one of the most independent central banks in the world. It has very little formal accountability to elected politicians. Although its president can be called before the European Parliament, the Parliament has virtually no power to influence the ECB's actions. There is one area, however, where the ECB's power is limited by politicians and this concerns the exchange rate of the euro. The Eurosystem is not responsible for the euro exchange rate movement, which is generally freely floating, though sometimes managed.

Under the Maastricht Treaty, EU finance ministers have responsibility for deciding on exchange rate policy (even though the ECB is charged with carrying it out). If finance ministers want to stop the value of the euro rising in order to prevent putting EU exporters at a competitive disadvantage, they will put pressure on the ECB to lower interest rates, which might run directly counter to its desire to meet inflation and money supply targets.

The monetary strategy of the Eurosystem relies on three elements, namely the definition of inflation and two 'pillars' used to identify risks to price stability. The first 'real economic pillar' consists of a broad review of the recent evolution and likely prospects of economic conditions, including growth, employment, prices, exchange rates and foreign conditions. The second, 'monetary' pillar studies the evolution of monetary aggregates and credit which, in the medium to long term, affect inflation in line with the neutrality principle (see Glossary).

The ECB uses a broad (M3) and a narrow (M1) definition of the money supply in the euro zone. The broad definition consists of cash in circulation among the public, plus overnight deposits or 'call money' (M1), deposits with agreed maturity of up to two years, deposits redeemable at up to three months' notice (M2), repos, money market funds and paper, and debt securities with residual maturity of up to two years.

Within the EU, many national central banks in countries not participating in EMU that want to maintain an independent monetary policy have adopted the so-called inflation targeting strategy as their monetary policy (including the Czech Republic, Hungary, Norway, Poland, Sweden and the UK) instead of the monetary targeting policy of the former German Bundesbank, which is closer to that of the ECB.

Inflation targeting comprises announcing a target, publishing an inflation forecast at the relevant policy horizon (usually one or two years ahead), and adjusting the interest rate according to the difference between the forecast and the target. For example, if the forecast exceeds the target, the presumption is that monetary policy is tightened, i.e. that the interest rate is raised.

The inflation targeting strategy has several advantages:
- It enables monetary policy to focus on domestic considerations, which has proved relatively easy to achieve.
- A stable relationship is not critical to its success (a stable demand for money is not a precondition).
- It is readily understood by the public and is highly transparent, since it involves the announcement of medium-term numerical targets for inflation.
- It increases the accountability of the central bank.
- It appears to ameliorate the effects of inflationary shocks.

However, it also has some disadvantages:
- Inflation is not easily controlled by the monetary authorities, so that an inflation target is unable to send immediate signals to both the public and financial markets and it might impose a rigid rule on policymakers, although this has not been the case in practice.
- If the actual inflation rate is way above the target level, the higher rates of inflation necessary to bring inflation down may cause a recession.

However, once inflation has been brought down, most countries have been relatively successful in maintaining it at the target level. This partly explains why, since the enlargement of the EU-15 to the EU-25 in 2004 and the EU-27 in 2007, many new EU Member States such as Romania and Bulgaria have implemented the inflation targeting strategy to encourage the transition to a market-oriented financial and monetary system.

Although money supply targets were adopted by many countries in the 1980s, including the UK, and proved to be very difficult to achieve, the Eurosystem wants to claim the Bundesbank heritage. To a certain extent the monetary targeting strategy of the Eurosystem is similar to inflation targeting, since there is a implicit target of 2% and an inflation forecast is published twice a year.

The main difference between the two strategies relates to the proportional relationship between money growth and inflation (which depends on the stability of the demand for money). Monetary targeting is characterized by a close relationship (thanks to a relatively stable demand for money), while inflation assumes an unstable demand for money and consequently an unreliable relationship between money supply and inflation. Monetary targeting has two main advantages: it enables a central bank to adjust its monetary policy to cope with domestic considerations, and it allows information on whether the central bank is achieving its target to be known almost immediately.

On the other hand, money supply depends on the amount of credit banks create, which is not easy for authorities to control. Monetary targeting suffers from the disadvantage that it works well only if there is a reliable relationship between the monetary aggregate and the goal variable, inflation or nominal income – a relationship that has failed to be maintained in several countries.

During the financial crisis, the ECB has played a significant role as a 'lender of last resort'. The ECB repeatedly provided large amounts of liquidity to stabilize the financial markets in the wake of crashing confidence in August 2007. The relentless turmoil in the financial markets necessitated close international co-operation and co-ordination on liquidity and monetary policy between central banks. The beginning of October 2008 saw the first internationally co-ordinated round of interest rate cuts since 11th September 2001, featuring the ECB, the BoE and the Fed as the major players.

The effectiveness of monetary policy partly depends on the magnitude and speed with which changes in interest rates affect aggregate demand and then prices. Since the outbreak of the financial crisis in Europe, the ECB has had more room for manoeuvre in cutting its official interest rate or borrowing cost for the euro zone and could add further anti-recession measures such as offering significant amounts of extra liquidity to banks for longer periods.

As the economies of the world slid into recession in 2008, central banks became more and more worried that the traditional instrument of monetary policy, namely controlling interest rates, was insufficient to ward off a slump in demand. Since October 2008, the interest rates had been cut at an unprecedented rate by the ECB (see figure 7.4) till the historical low level of 1% in May 2009, its lowest rate since the euro was launched in 1999.

The low inflation rate in the euro zone made it possible to lower the interest rate. Although the ECB was aiming to stimulate the economy of the euro zone, lower interest rates were seldom passed on to producers and consumers, since commercial banks were struggling to attract more savings. This should have increased the interest rates on savings and mortgage deposits. The problem was that there was an acute lack of willingness among banks to lend and businesses and consumers to borrow, as people saw the ongoing recession. Banks were more cautious about mortgage lending as the prices of houses fell and unemployment rose, and more cautious about lending to business as the recession deepened. Businesses did not want to invest and consumers tried to rein in debt. So the cuts in interest rates were not having enough effect on aggregate demand.

Figure 7.4 **ECB key interest rate (1999–2009)**

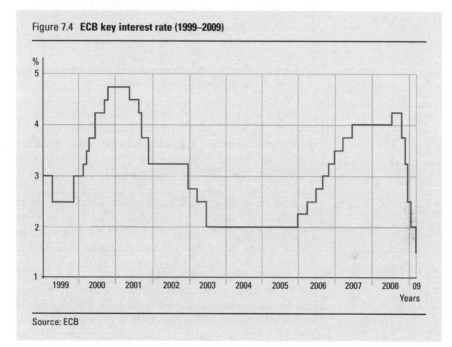

Source: ECB

Finding itself running out of monetary policy options, the ECB increased the money supply directly, in a process known as quantitative or credit easing. This involves an aggressive version of open-market operations, where the central bank buys up a range of assets, such as securitized mortgage debt and long-term government bonds. The effect is to pump large amounts of additional cash into the economy in the hope of stimulating demand and, through the process of credit creation, to boost broad money too. Under this policy, monetary authorities buy up bonds either from banks or from the commercial sector.

There are two potential benefits. The first is that the banks get cash in exchange for bonds they sell back to the authorities, and the increase in the money supply leads to an increased volume of lending. The second is that decreasing the supply of bonds pushes up their price. When bond prices go up, their yields go down, which affects long-term interest rates for overdrafts, some fixed-rate mortgage products and most business lending.

This policy was first tried in the 1930s and has been dusted off by the Fed in an attempt to get the economy moving again. It is not easy for the ECB to apply quantitative easing in the same way in 16 euro zone countries. The ECB's focus on restoring the workings of a commercial bank system reflects the latter's importance to the euro zone compared with its status in the UK and the USA, where securities markets play a large role in providing finance for mortgages as well as industry and commerce.

The dangers of the quantitative easing policy are that in the short term little credit creation may take place, since people need to have the confidence to borrow, and that if this policy is conducted for too long, the growth in the money supply may prove to be excessive, resulting in inflation rising above the target level.

7.6 The introduction of the euro and its impact on the EU business environment

Ten years after the introduction of the euro we can say that without it and the ECB the impact of the financial crisis on EMU would certainly have been far worse. The launch of the euro, Europe's answer to globalization, has eliminated exchange risks, together with the attendant economic and growth risks, within most of Europe.

Before its introduction, Europe went through several periods of economically hazardous tension in the Exchange Rate Mechanism (ERM) of the EMS, the last two, in 1992/93 and 1995, being triggered by the weakness of the dollar against the deutschmark (DM), the second most important investment and reserve currency. Since the DM not only was strong in relation to the dollar but had also appreciated sharply vis-à-vis the currencies of its main trading partners in Europe, Germany's business activity and competitiveness were at times put under severe strain. Moreover, the member countries of the ERM often had no choice but to raise their interest rates to defend their currencies' peg to the DM.

Hungary and the other new EU states unable or unwilling to join the euro zone are now experiencing the downside of standing on the sidelines. That may spur the political will there to work consistently towards joining the euro zone. In some countries the euro is increasingly being used in the corporate sector even without the prospect of euro zone accession.

Sharing a currency helps to knit the euro zone economies into a unified whole, eliminates exchange rate fluctuations, and encourages trade between euro area members. It is easier to compare the spectrum of prices, taxes and required pension contributions across national borders, and as a consequence businesses are tempted to make new investments in countries where costs are lowest and regulation is lightest. Euro zone governments are under continuous pressure in the euro zone to cut taxes, prevent excessive regulation or 'red tape' and harmonize fiscal and social policies.

Thanks to the EU Stability and Growth Pact, the EU's fiscal policy has been put into a kind of strait-jacket. The introduction of the euro provided a unique opportunity and stimulus for EMU enterprises to increase profits. For example, accounting became cheaper and easier to carry out because there was only one currency to deal with (although there was the initial cost of converting all accounting procedures to euros).

Particularly for the managers of large companies the launch of the euro was attractive because it reduced the cost of doing business in many national markets, especially by removing the effect of currency fluctuations on cross-border trade and investment.

Many companies found that they had to radically modify their pricing strategies. For instance, computer maker Dell considered various strategies and ultimately decided to be a leader in harmonizing prices across the EU. The advent of the euro made prices easier to compare, which increased competition in the EU. Companies such as Dell decided to standardize their pricing across the EU to prevent customers from shopping around the continent and making purchases in the country with the lowest price.

Case study 7.2 **The euro–dollar see-saw and its impact on business**

In the global context the euro's exchange rates, especially against the US dollar, are crucial to the price competitiveness of the EMU Member States. The euro–dollar exchange rate has undergone strong fluctuations since 1998. The euro showed a distinctly weak trend until 2002.

Why did the euro fall so much in the first two years of its existence (to US$0.83 in autumn 2000, a fall of 30% from its starting rate of US$1.1786) and increase so much in value afterwards, and how has this see-saw movement affected business?

As a new currency, the euro initially had to stand the test of international competition, while the dollar was profiting from strong US growth and attractive dollar yields. Then, amid the growing uncertainty caused by the rapidly rising US current account and budget deficits (the so-called 'twin deficits') and the Iraq conflict, foreign investors became reluctant to invest in the US economy. This meant that the euro saw a prolonged upward trend versus the dollar from 2002 onwards, resulting in a massive depreciation of the dollar and appreciation of the euro.

Over the longer term the euro has also gained ground against the yen, the Swiss franc and, since 2007, the pound sterling. The only longish break in

the euro's upward trend was after the rejection of the EU Constitution by the referendums in France and the Netherlands in June 2005 (see figure 7.5). Uncertainties over the EU's and the EMU's future politico-institutional structures weighed on the euro, which fluctuated between US$1.20 and just over US$1.30 during this phase. From summer 2007, however, the euro continued its climb amid growing signs of a weakening US economy and the subsequent financial crisis, breaching the US$1.60 mark for a while in April 2008 and again in July 2008, when the euro reached an all-time high against the dollar. This caused a huge US current account deficit in the euro zone, which has a balanced current account.

Eventually, in September 2008, with the EMU on the edge of recession and predictions that euro zone interest rates would be cut, the euro at last began to fall. It continued to do so as the ECB cut interest rates, which stood at 1% in May 2009.

What is clear from the 10 years of the euro, is that interest rate volatility and divergences in interest rates between the USA and the EMU have been a major factor in exchange rate volatility between the euro and the dollar, which is in itself a cause of uncertainty in international trade and finance.

Figure 7.5 **The euro–dollar exchange rate movement and Fed and ECB interest rate movement (1999–2009)**

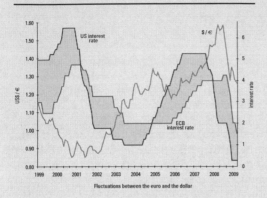

Fluctuations between the euro and the dollar

Effects of launching the euro: a double-edged sword for European business

From 2002 to 2008, the euro appreciated by a massive 82% against the dollar. If the value of the euro increases, it harms the foreign sales and profits of the EU's internationally active enterprises. A rising euro makes EU products more expensive abroad, and therefore less competitive, and yields smaller earnings to companies when they convert foreign profits to euros.

Although the introduction of the euro was intended partly to help shield the EMU from currency shocks, its greater reliance on trade means that the EU is still more sensitive to currency fluctuations than the USA. The ECB estimates that a 5% annual increase in the value of the euro can knock nearly 1% off annual GDP growth – several times the impact a similar rise in the dollar's value would have on the USA. The usual penalties of an appreciating currency, such as being priced out of export markets, hits the EU faster and harder than it does Japan or the USA.

The euro was weak in the period 1999–2001 and the ECB fought the decline by intervening in the foreign exchange market (buying euros and selling gold and foreign currencies). Since 2001, the appreciation of the euro against the dollar and the yen has resulted in falling international sales for EU companies.

To what extent is a strong euro bad for European business?

With over 22% of the EMU's GDP determined by export sales (to non-EMU countries), and a large part of those exports going to the USA, the dollar–euro exchange rate will invariably be significant. The question is how significant? The investment bank Morgan Stanley has estimated that for every 10% rise in the value of the euro against the dollar, European companies' profits fall by 3%. However, the impact of the euro's rise on EMU business was tempered by a number of factors:

- Companies are increasingly using sophisticated management and operational systems, in which value creation is spread throughout a global value chain; procurement systems are often priced in dollars.
- Companies hedge their currency risks. BMW, for example, uses forward exchange markets to agree to buy or sell currencies in the future at a price quoted today (this will cost it a premium).
- Many European companies (again, BMW is an example) have located some of their production facilities in the USA and use them to supply the US market. This helps to insulate those businesses from the effects of the rise in the value of the euro.

Nevertheless, the euro–dollar exchange rate affects enterprises within the EMU differently. Enterprises in Germany have coped relatively well with the euro's strength for some time because they have improved their global competitiveness through massive restructuring and possess a product portfolio, including capital goods, that is in global demand. On the other hand, the competitiveness of EMU members which, because of their export structure, are exposed to intense competition from the dynamic emerging economies of Asia, is under massive pressure. One example is Italy's textile industry.

The threats to Europe's economy deriving from the euro's strength are considerable given the squeeze on margins on exports to the dollar area, and a strong euro, combined with weak US growth, is likely to have an increasingly dampening effect on European exports to dollar-denominated countries.

7.6.1 EMU and the euro zone's competitiveness

The creation of the euro zone represented a unique opportunity to build a competitive advantage, since the launch of the euro involved the removal of a significant barrier between countries. As national competitive advantages diminish, companies have the opportunity to become pan-European. When companies choose the euro zone as their target area for long-term strategic investment, they must come to terms with its integrated financial markets and price transparency and the strong competition between Member States.

Since the creation of EMU in 1999, the euro zone has become even more open to the rest of the world, as measured by trade and its international investment positions. At the same time trade and capital flows among euro-area countries have risen and intra-euro trade in goods and services has increased by about 10% relative to GDP, which can be partly attributed to the creation of the euro. The single currency has also prompted an increase in the degree of intra-EMU competition and in the convergence of intra-euro zone trade prices.

As for capital flows, the euro has boosted foreign direct investment (FDI), in particular cross-border M&A activity in manufacturing, and portfolio flows across euro area countries. A number of factors associated with the euro favoured these higher capital movements among euro area countries, including the elimination of exchange rate risk, the reduction of the cost of capital, the use of common trading platforms, and the cross-border merger of stock exchanges (e.g. NYSE Euronext).

Another dimension of the euro relates to its use beyond the EMU's borders. Over the past 10 years, the euro's role in the international markets has increased somewhat, but the pace of change has been gradual and appears to have levelled off in some market segments. Moreover, the currency's international role is geographically concentrated in regions that are close to the EMU and need a closer co-ordination and co-operation between the different monetary authorities in the world.

The euro has all the qualities required of an international currency: it is the currency of the largest exporting preferential trading system of the world; it is issued by a supranational independent central bank; and it is associated with large and deep financial markets. The euro is now the invoicing currency in about 60% of EMU's exports and 50% of its imports. It has become a natural choice as the denomination of private international investments. It also has a rising share of official reserves and over 40 currencies are managed in relation to the euro.

The international role of the euro constitutes provides many benefits to members of the EMU: it allows intra-EMU trade to be carried out in a single currency; it lowers borrowing and financing costs; it constitutes a 'hard' currency and it offers business opportunities for EMU financial services providers. Perhaps surprisingly, the ECB professes a benign neglect regarding the international role of the euro (a 'leave-it-to-the-market' approach), but this can be understood as the natural behaviour of a central bank committed only to price stability.

As for the impact of the EMU on the competitiveness of euro area enterprises and their capacity to play a leading role in the world markets, recent research indicates that the euro has contributed to enhancing enterprises' competitiveness by facilitating trade by EMU countries and by contributing to the EU single market for capital. Euro zone countries are considered to be better export bases, attracting a greater number of enterprises from neighbouring countries. A larger and more integrated EMU, while allowing enterprises to benefit from economies of scale and scope, also tends to be associated with tougher competition and, therefore, richer product variety, higher productivity and lower prices. The impact of the euro on the EMU countries may vary due to differences in the quality of institutions and access to technology and research & development.

Against this background of greater competition within the EMU, the emergence of cost-competitive countries as major exporters has also increased the degree of external competition faced by the euro area countries. For example, over the last decade China has been increasing its world export market share, at an average pace of almost 13% per year – partly caused by the country's accession to the World Trade Organization (WTO). This seems to be the counterpart to the declines in export market share experienced by the EMU (1.7% yearly) and the other major trading countries over the same period (with annual declines ranging from 1.2 to 1.7%) – Germany and Ireland being exceptions.

In part, the losses in EMU export market share are due to the emergence of lower-cost competitors. However, to some extent they may also reflect the export specialization of the EMU. In particular, some EMU countries seem somewhat overweight in labour-intensive sectors, where emerging economies such as China and India have a competitive advantage.

Recently the EMU members have also gained market shares in the higher-price and higher-quality segments of mature industries and products, thereby compensating for their weaker performance in other types of export.

7.6.2 The international role of the euro

The euro's growing importance as a reserve currency is reflected in the development of the currency composition of official foreign exchange reserves held by central banks around the world. The euro share of global foreign exchange reserves rose from nearly 18% at the start of 1999 to around 25% by the end of 2003 and thus comfortably exceeded the combined share in 1998 of the legacy currencies (including the ECU) participating in the EMU (almost 17%). By contrast, the dollar share, which peaked at 71.4% in 2001, fell to 64.7% at the end of 2006. The decline in the dollar is roughly equivalent to the ground made up by the euro.

The success of the euro as a unifying force in Europe is gradually changing the international balance of power. To a certain extent, banking crises and/or reforms of the financial systems in many CEE countries, including Hungary and Bulgaria, have also enforced a process of 'euroization'. This occurs when residents of a country extensively use the euro alongside or instead of the domestic currency.

The stronger international role of the euro has made EU governments feel more empowered to challenge US policy initiatives in the world economy, while US policymakers wonder whether the euro will challenge the dollar's dominance as the world's currency of choice in international trade. In their reserves of foreign currencies, the central banks of many countries, including Canada, China and Russia, are giving more weight to the euro. The European currency's position in global foreign currency reserves is growing, eroding the power of the dollar. Many governments are increasing their euro holdings, and Asia is now significantly less dollar-centric than in the past.

The introduction of the euro in 1999 did much to promote the development of euro financial markets, and as a result the euro is eroding some of the advantages that have historically supported the pre-eminence of the US dollar as a reserve currency. Nevertheless, in terms of size, credit quality and liquidity, dollar financial markets still have an edge over euro markets.

This, coupled with the inertia typical of the launch of an international currency, suggests that the euro is not yet in a position to match the US dollar as a reserve currency. Indeed, the available data suggest that the euro's share of reserves rose during the first few years after the formation of the EMU but levelled off after 2003. In early 2006, the euro's share was still well below the US dollar's share and below even the share of euro legacy currencies in the 1980s and early 1990s. The euro comes closest to challenging the dollar in its role as a store of value. As a unit of account and medium of exchange, the dollar's role is not as secure as it once was, but the dollar is still pre-eminent.

Case study 7.3 International private and public use of the euro on the increase

Here we use the Paul Krugman matrix that differentiates between the medium of exchange, the unit of account and the store of value functions in the private and public use of money.

Private international use
Private international use of the euro comprises:
1 its role as a medium of exchange in payment and foreign exchange transactions. In terms of the volume of banknotes in circulation worldwide, the euro narrowly overtook the dollar for the first time at the end of 2006 (at around €630 billion). However, it is estimated that only 10–20% of euro notes are used extraterritorially, compared with 50–70% of dollar banknotes. By choosing not to issue €1 notes, the ECB missed

an opportunity to achieve a better international positioning of the euro against the US currency, whose $1 note is in strong demand in the international travel arena. As a transaction vehicle in the global foreign exchange markets, the EUR/USD segment was the most frequently traded currency pair in 2007, according to a BIS survey: it accounted for 27% of global foreign exchange turnover, compared with 13% for the USD/JPY and 12% for the USD/GBP.

2 its role as a unit of account in the invoicing of international trade. The data situation is, however, unsatisfactory on this count. According to earlier analyses, nearly 50% of world trade is invoiced in dollars. Oil and other commodities are billed in dollars (the exception is Iran, which invoices oil exports in euros). External trade of the euro area has in recent years been increasingly invoiced in euros (average share of around

60%). This trend also applies to EU Member States outside the EMU.

3 its store of value function, which is closely linked to the creation of dynamic euro financial markets. The financial markets for euros and dollars are now comparable in terms of liquidity and the variety of instruments. For initial offerings of international bonds in 2006, 46% were issued in euros and just 39% in dollars, whereas in the preceding years the euro had to settle for second place (with shares of between 34% and 44%) behind the dollar (39–49%). Lagging a long way behind are the pound sterling and the yen. In the circulation of international bonds the euro achieved a share of 32% in 2006 compared with some 19% in early 1999, while the dollar share fell from 50% to around 43% and that of the yen halved to 6%.

Public international use

Public international use of the euro comprises:

1 its role as an intervention currency for central banks in foreign exchange markets. Central banks have made only very limited use of euros for this purpose over the last few years. This applies to the EUR/USD market, where only in 2000 were there a few interventions to bolster the then weak euro, within the European Exchange Rate Mechanism II

(ERM II) and against the currencies of those countries whose exchange rate policy is geared towards the euro. In contrast, in the past few years, central banks in Asia have made massive interventions to support the dollar and accumulate huge foreign exchange holdings.

2 its anchor role for other currencies, the euro performing the unit of account function. According to the IMF's classification, there are some 40 countries in Europe, Africa and the Mediterranean that align their exchange rate policy with the euro, with the range of regimes extending from a currency board (e.g. Bulgaria) and the membership of ERM II to managed floating with a loose orientation to the euro (e.g. the Czech Republic). Worldwide there are some 60 countries whose exchange rate policy is geared towards the dollar. Several countries administer their exchange rate policy via a basket of currencies whose main constituents are the dollar and the euro (e.g. China, Russia). There are also countries that have unilaterally adopted the dollar as legal tender (e.g. Ecuador and Panama) and regions where the euro is legal tender (Montenegro, Kosovo).

3 its holding of foreign exchange reserves, primarily for exchange rate management via intervention.

7.6.3   The impact of the euro on financial capital flows

Financial or capital flows (i.e. international payments for financial assets or securities) have been rising faster than trade flows. This growth reflects, among other factors, the emergence of large current account surpluses in some countries and lower transaction costs of international investment afforded by technological and financial innovation.

While it is difficult to measure the specific impact of the introduction of the euro on cross-border holdings of euro-denominated assets, there are several indications of how the euro may have raised the attractiveness of assets issued in the EMU. First, for the euro to be the currency of choice for international investors, its domestic financial markets had to be liquid, deep, large, properly regulated and well serviced by ancillary financial services. The key element was not the size of the financial markets but the fact that all financial contracts issued in the euro area would be denominated in euros. This increased the substitutability and contributed to the liquidity and deepening of the EMU financial markets.

Second, the anti-inflation credentials of the ECB or euro system also play a role. In this regard, the ECB can be seen as making the same promise to international investors that it makes to EMU citizens, namely that it will aim to stabilize the inflation rate at 2%.

Third, for international investors, there are benefits of having euro-denominated equity investments as opposed to identical assets in another currency. These may seem marginal: equity investments are natural hedges against inflation and therefore less susceptible to changes in inflation, especially in diversified portfolios. However, low inflation stabilizes the real economy and in that sense a low-inflation policy conducted by the ECB will support the internal attractiveness of the EMU equity market as well. The low-inflation policy of the ECB should support the international attractiveness of the EMU's equity.

Although from a financial perspective the EMU is relatively open, especially since the introduction of the euro, the individual EMU countries are considerably more open than the EMU as a whole given the large FDI and portfolio activity that has occurred between EMU members. For example, the EMU countries, either as recipients or as sources of investment, accounted for as much as 57% of world FDI flows between 2000 and 2005. Meanwhile, EMU residents held 34% and 44% of the world's international equity and bond portfolios from 2001 to 2006. Given that EMU GDP is only about one quarter the size of world GDP, these facts suggest that the euro might have played an important role in these capital movements, particularly between the EMU countries.

The euro has boosted cross-border portfolio investment activity between EMU countries by eliminating exchange rate risk and favouring the creation of common trading platforms (e.g. the creation of Euronext through the merger of the Amsterdam, Brussels, Lisbon and Paris exchanges) and integration in post-trading market infrastructure, which have all further reduced portfolio investment trade barriers. EMU portfolio assets held in the EMU as a share of the total international asset holdings of EMU residents increased by 16% over the period 1997–2006. Moreover, all major regions of the world increased their holdings of EMU assets (as a share of their international portfolio) over this period, though by a smaller extent. This suggests that the euro might have strongly stimulated portfolio transactions between EMU countries, thereby permitting a better diversification of investment and consumption risks.

Since 1999, there has been a strong rise in FDI flows between EMU countries. FDI can provide a company with new markets and marketing channels as well as access to new technology, products and skills. For the country or foreign enterprise which receives the investment, it can provide a source of new technologies, capital, processes, products, organizational technologies and management skills, and as such can provide a strong impetus to economic development. Overall, FDI can raise efficiency in both the home and the host country. The deeper EU integration process seems to have been a magnet for FDI activity, particularly in the manufacturing sector, while an increasing share of FDI flows is taking place between euro zone countries. Since most FDI activity takes the form of M&As, EU-15 countries and the USA being the largest players, looking at cross-border M&As gives additional information on the impact of the euro on FDI activity.

7.7 Merger and acquisition activity in the EU

Since the early 1990s there has been a trend in M&A activity around the world. Figure 7.6 shows the annual evolution of worldwide total M&A deals in the period 2000 – 2006 in terms of the number and value of completed and pending deals. During the 1990s, a booming world economy went along with a last global wave of M&As, which reached its peak around 2000, and M&A activity declined with the slowing of the economy after 2000.

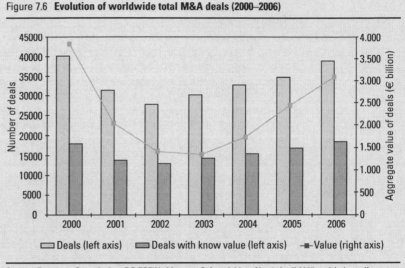

Figure 7.6 **Evolution of worldwide total M&A deals (2000–2006)**

🔲 Deals (left axis) ▨ Deals with know value (left axis) ➡ Value (right axis)

Source: European Commission, DG ECFIN, *Mergers & Acquisitions* No. 4, April 2007, p. 2 (adapted)

Since the EU enlargement in 2004, however, companies have again been showing an increasing appetite for investing in other enterprises, which is reflected in both a growing number of observed deals and higher deal values. While the majority of deals have been taking place domestically, i.e. within the same country, the average value of individual deals has been consistently higher when they were cross-border than when they were domestic. The European integration process, and the creation of the euro zone in particular, seems to have stimulated intra-EU cross-border M&A activity and to have enhanced the attractiveness of the EU's knowledge-intensive business services for non-EU enterprises.

7.7.1 Regional trends

The early 1990s saw relatively low M&A activity, as the world was in recession, but as the economy picked up, so worldwide M&A activity increased. Economic growth was particularly rapid in the USA, which became the major target for acquisitions.

There was also an acceleration in the process of globalization. With the dismantling of trade barriers around the world and increasing financial deregulation, international competition increased. Companies felt the need to become bigger in order to compete more effectively.

In Europe, M&A activity was boosted by the development of the single market, which came into being in January 1993. Companies took advantage of the abolition of trade barriers in the EU, which made it easier for them to operate on an EU-wide basis. As 1999 approached, and with it the arrival of the euro, so European merger activity reached fever pitch, stimulated also by the strong economic growth experienced throughout the EU.

By the end of the 1990s, annual worldwide M&A activity was three times its level at the beginning of the decade – and there were some very large mergers indeed. These included the €29.4 billion marriage between pharmaceutical companies Zeneca of the UK and Astra of Sweden in 1998, the €205 billion takeover of telecoms giant Mannesmann of Germany by Vodafone of the UK in 1999 and the €50.8 billion takeover of Orange of the UK by France Telecom in 2000. Other sectors in which merger activity was rife were the financial services and the privatized utilities sectors.

Currently around 80% of global M&A activity is concentrated in the EU, the USA and Asia. With the worldwide economic slowdown after 2000, there was a fall in both the number and the value of mergers throughout most of the world. What is more, the worldwide pattern of M&A activity was changing. Increasingly both European and US companies were looking to other parts of the world to expand their activities. The two major target regions were (a) the rest of Europe – especially the 10 countries joining the EU in 2004, plus Russia – and (b) Asian countries, especially India and China. These new markets have the twin attractions of rapidly growing demand and low costs, including cheap skilled labour and low tax rates.

The relatively small share of inward investment in Asia by EU companies is worrying for the EU authorities, given that China and India are the world's two fastest growing markets. Those companies which have already invested in these countries are likely to have gained a 'first-mover' advantage through establishing sources of supply and building relationships. However, in 2008, as the world economy slid into recession, so M&A activity slowed.

7.7.2   Types of M&A activity

Many M&A deals are 'hostile' or 'defensive'. In other words, the company being taken over is unwilling to agree to the deal. Such deals are often concluded after prolonged boardroom battles, with the bosses of the acquiring company seeking to build an empire and the bosses of the target company attempting all sorts of manoeuvres to avoid being taken over. This may involve them seeking deals with alternative, more 'friendly' companies. Generally companies are increasingly using the services of investment banks to help them in the process of making or warding off deals. Investment banks use their own assets to finance M&As.

Despite the growing number of horizontal mergers, whereby two enterprises in the same industry at the same stage of the production process merge (e.g. the merger in 2005 of Sony and BMG, two global recording companies), there has also been a tendency for companies to become more focused, by selling off parts of their business which are not seen as 'core activities'. For example, after Volvo unsuccessfully attempted to merge with Renault in 1993, it subsequently divested itself of several companies that it owned in a variety of industries, ranging from banking and finance to food and pharmaceuticals.

This trend of horizontal mergers has allowed companies to increase their market power in those sectors where they have expertise. Consumers may gain from lower costs, but the motives of the companies are largely to gain increased market power, something of dubious benefit to consumers.

Mergers and acquisitions are changing the structure of many industries, including banking sectors. They are not a force for change in themselves but rather a response to the forces of change and to changes in market structures. Quite often M&As change the market structure from one of monopolistic competition, with many more or less independent enterprises on the market, into an oligopoly, where a few enterprises are highly interdependent. Although the terms merger and acquisition are sometimes used interchangeably to refer to the combination of two (or more) separate companies or banks, they have slightly different connotations:
- A merger is when two, usually similarly sized, enterprises agree to go forward as a new single enterprise rather than remain separately owned and operated.
- An acquisition is when one enterprise takes over another and clearly becomes the new owner. Acquisitions are also known as takeovers and they normally occur when big institutions buy smaller ones.

Although most forms of amalgamation between two or more institutions are called mergers, in most cases they are in fact takeovers.
In order to gain a competitive advantage in a European market, the most common motives for European M&A activity are:
- growth. M&A activity provides a much quicker means to growth than internal expansion (especially in the telecommunications, media and technology sector).
- economies of scale and scope. Once a merger has taken place, the constituent parts can be reorganized through a process of 'rationalization' in order to reduce costs. For example, only one head office will now be needed. On the marketing side, two parts of the newly merged company may now share distribution and retail channels, benefiting from each other's knowledge and experience in distinct market segments or geographical locations.
- eliminating inefficiencies (e.g. X-inefficiencies by looking at the outputs that are produced with given inputs, and allocative or technical inefficiencies, by focusing on the best inputs to be using or the best outputs to be producing). Poor management may leave banks with unexploited opportunities (partly due to imperfect markets or asymmetric information) to cut costs and increase sales and earnings. Such banks are natural targets for being taken over by other institutions with more efficient management.
- reduced competition and thereby greater market power and larger profits.

- benefits to the shareholders of both companies if the merger or acquisition leads to an increase in the stock market valuation of the companies concerned.
- reduced uncertainty in the companies' market and in the economic environment generally.

Through the many cost-cutting programmes inherent in M&As, the consolidated financial institutions (sometimes called financial conglomerates or financial supermarkets) tend to become both more competitive and more efficient (e.g. downsizing, closing out-of-date plants, outsourcing, or offshoring business activities).

Technological developments, deregulation and liberalization at EU level and the launch of the euro plus the single market for financial services have played a significant role in restructuring the European financial markets. Over the last two decades, this has stimulated many M&As within the EU and has consolidated national banking markets. The reduction in the number of banks, due to the increased number of M&As, has led to an increase in the degree of concentration across European banking markets.

Although intra-EU trade has been duty free for several decades, trade among European nations is not as free as it is within any given nation. Many technical, physical and fiscal barriers make it easier for companies to sell in their local market than in other EU markets. As a result, EU enterprises can often be dominant in their home market while being marginal players in other EU markets (e.g. in the car market).

This market fragmentation reduces competition and this, in turn, raises prices and keeps too many enterprises in business. The problem is that this results in an industrial market structure characterised by too many inefficient small enterprises that can get away with charging high prices to cover the cost of their inefficiency. Due to this absence of competition, poor- and/or low-quality services and goods may accompany the high prices (e.g. the European telephone service before the liberalization of this market). M&A activity is one of the market responses.

The following trends in M&As since the early 1990s are worth stressing:
1 The distribution of M&A operations is quite varied. The big four Member States (France, Italy, Germany and the UK) have the most operations, but, with the exception of the UK, these nations' share of M&A activity is much lower than their share of the EU economy as a whole. By contrast, many of the smaller EU-15 members, such as Belgium, the Netherlands and Finland, seem to have a share of M&A activity that is higher than their share of GDP. This development shows that the EU integration process has produced the largest changes (in proportion to their economy) in the smallest members.
2 Despite many years of attempts to harmonize rules on takeovers, some members still have restrictive takeover practices that make M&As very difficult, whereas others, such as the UK, have very liberal rules. The implication of this lack of harmonization is that the restructuring effects of integration have been very different in the various Member States. The geographical focus of EU enterprises is

heterogeneous, and UK enterprises, partly due to their liberal rules, stand out for being predominantly involved in deals outside the EU.

3 Around two thirds of all intra-EU M&A activity (both domestic and cross-border) has taken place in the services sector, especially in banking (see table 7.6). However, during the early years of the single market (1986–1992), M&A activity was centred on manufacturing, with mergers often occurring in anticipation of liberalization that was scheduled. A trend since the 1990s is that in the financial services industry in particular, M&A deals predominantly occur between enterprises in the same sector. There are several explanations for the greater tendency towards national concentration ('home bias') in the banking industry than in other industries.

First, local regulations still differ. Second, cultural differences remain prevalent, and traditions in banking differ significantly from one country to another; while acquiring a foreign bank could be the easiest way of adjusting to that country's culture, problems with integrating personnel seem to deter M&As.

Table 7.6   **Decomposition of intra-EU M&A deals by sector (2006)**

Target sector:	Agriculture, Forestry and Fishing	Mining	Construction	Manufacturing	Network industries	Wholesale Trade	Retail Trade	Finance, Insurance and Real Estate	Other Services	Public Administration	Total	%
Bidder sector:												
Agriculture, Forestry and Fishing	21	0	0	10	0	6	0	14	4	0	55	0.6%
Mining	0	61	4	10	6	0	4	22	4	0	111	1,3%
Construction	0	0	127	24	7	1	4	89	28	1	281	3,2%
Manufacturing	11	10	40	1319	38	89	16	825	122	5	2475	28,6%
Network industries	0	8	31	55	567	19	8	239	67	8	1002	11,6%
Wholesale Trade	2	5	6	123	10	164	26	118	25	0	479	5,5%
Retail Trade	2	2	0	37	16	16	211	154	15	0	453	5,2%
Finance, Insurance and Real Estate	0	1	24	22	10	2	6	1272	57	5	1399	16,2%
Other Services	2	9	26	186	131	28	21	644	1319	11	2377	27,5%
Public Administration	0	0	0	1	5	0	0	6	3	1	16	0,2%
Total	*38*	*96*	*258*	*1787*	*790*	*325*	*296*	*3383*	*1644*	*31*	*8648*	100,0%
%	0,4%	1,1%	3,0%	20,7%	9,1%	3,8%	3,4%	39,1%	19,0%	0,4%	100,0%	

Source: European Commission, DG ECFIN, *Mergers & Acquisitions* No. 4, April 2007, p. 8 (adapted)

Third, the tax treatment of savings differs from country to country. Thus the choice of where to bank may be driven by tax considerations rather than by the quality of banking services. Widespread tax evasion, for example, can undermine the EU authorities' efforts to harmonize taxes. In 2005, a new agreement came into effect to combat tax evasion; all EU-based banks must now report the names of their foreign customers to their tax authorities.

Finally, the fact that M&As in the main countries are predominantly within-borders may be the result of protectionism. For instance, in 2005, the Governor of the Bank of Italy was officially warned by the EC not to interfere in attempted purchases of two large Italian banks by a Spanish and a Dutch bank; yet these attempts failed and the matter has been referred to the courts.

Since the increase in M&A activity in the mid 1990s, most banks have been consolidated at national level. Their priority seems to be to reach a size that will enable them to engage in foreign purchases. As banks merge at national level, concentration increases, which may result in less, not more, competition. This is in contrast with the effect expected from the Single European Act, which aims to generate a wave of pan-European M&As that will eventually make the single banking market a reality. While banks do not normally consolidate at pan-European level, they could still offer services across borders. This form of competition is exactly what the Second Banking Directive was meant to promote, and the elimination of exchange risk should reinforce it.

There are signs, however, that a greater emphasis may be placed on cross-border mergers in the future as domestic markets become more congested. Both the single market for capital of 1993 and the FSAP of 1999 provided a framework for an integrated market for financial services. The integration of wholesale markets, the opening of national retail markets and the harmonization of supervisory standards greatly improved conditions for cross-border provision of banking services and the emergence of pan-European banks. The financial services industry quickly responded to these opportunities in such a way that 'greenfield' investments and cross-border M&A activity in the EU gained momentum.

As market integration changes the nature of competition, it leads to two main categories of strategic reaction, which are expected to increase the number of cross-border M&As with the EU.

On the one hand, there are positive reactions, including the following:
- EU enterprises may try to become more efficient.
- They may enter new markets through M&A in order to increase their sales, thereby reducing their average costs. This may be possible due to the acquisition of an international distribution network or a well known brand name, for example.
- EU enterprises may also acquire other enterprises with the aim of reconstruction as they try to exploit economies of scale and scope and divest themselves of production processes for which they now have suppliers offering better terms. These divested businesses offer new opportunities for acquisitions.

On the other hand, increased competitive pressures may lead to defensive M&As as enterprises are motivated by strategic concerns or actual competitors in order to restore market power that has been weakened by economic openness.

Besides the fact that EU integration should boost intra-EU M&A activity, it should also increase the attractiveness of EU enterprises as targets for non-EU companies and reinforce their position as acquirers outside the EU. Figure 7.7 shows that there was an upward trend in intra-EU cross-border M&As, in both value and number, from the beginning of the 1990s until 2000. During this period, the proportion of intra-EU cross-border M&As in the total number of acquisitions in the EU also increased, suggesting that M&As were increasingly used as a channel for cross-border market access within the EU.

However, this trend should not only be interpreted as reflecting a deeper European integration process. First, M&A activity in the EU followed a global wave of M&As caused by fluctuations in the business cycle and the stock exchange markets. Second, it is difficult to distinguish the impact of EU (as distinct from world) market integration on M&A activities.

Figure 7.7 **Intra-EU cross-border deals (1992–2005)**

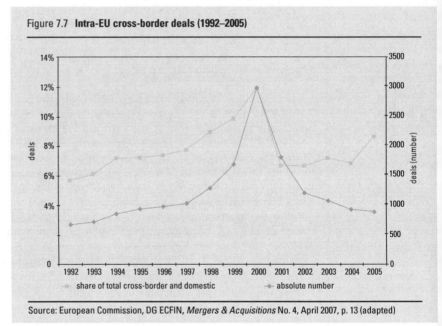

Source: European Commission, DG ECFIN, *Mergers & Acquisitions* No. 4, April 2007, p. 13 (adapted)

Conclusions

Although there are plenty of reasons for the financial crisis which started as a US sub-prime mortgages crisis in August 2007, some major underlying determinants were already established in the 1980s through deregulation of the financial markets and liberalization of capital movement.

Within the EU the establishment of the single market for capital in 1992 encouraged a single monetary policy, the launch of the euro, cross-border financial activities, and a closer inter-connection between inter-bank transactions. Besides the globalization of financial services activities in this decade, the expansionary monetary policies introduced just after the 11th September 2001 terrorist attacks on the USA, securitization activities and moral hazard problems have contributed significantly to the financial crisis.

As a result a more co-ordinated supervision and re-regulation of European financial institutions, financial markets and financial products should be considered in the near future. Current EU supervision is still mainly nationally oriented, since most financial institutions and markets are still nationally oriented.

The EU banking industry can identify four major trends in EU banking, namely consolidation/concentration of the industry, internationalization/globalization, convergence of financial systems and deconstruction/specialization of financial activities. EU banking markets have become more consolidated and internationalized and banks more capital market-oriented and specialized over the last few years. The trend towards consolidation, through M&A activities and conglomeration, can be interpreted as a response to increased pressure to realize potential economies of scale and scope.

Internationalization and globalization are expected to increase competition in most areas of financial services and will lead to an increasing necessity for a more advanced infrastructure of EU financial supervision. The so-called Lamfalussy procedure is considered to be the original legislation on EU financial supervision. It encourages harmonization of supervisory practices in the European market for financial services and closer co-operation between Member States, the regulatory authorities involved and the private sector in the field of banking, securities, insurances and occupational pensions. It is very likely that in the near future increasing steps will be taken to push forward the financial integration process, which will in turn necessitate changes to the European regulatory framework.

There are still many differences in financial structure among EU members, which might have huge consequences for doing business in the different Member States. For example, the proportion of borrowing at variable interest rates, the ratio of consumer debt to GDP and the degree to which banks pass on interest rate changes to their customers differs between states.

There is still considerable potential to reap the benefits of deeper market integration in the EU financial sectors. The EU is consequently pressing ahead with new legislation focusing in particular on retail market issues. Besides many regulatory measures, the growing importance of economies outside the EU and technological changes have had a huge impact on the European banking sector.

The European financial landscape has changed drastically since the introduction of the euro. Changes in the international regulatory environment are also having a growing influence on European banks. However, the integration of financial markets is still uneven. In contrast, retail markets suffer from a visible lack of integration. Price variation across Member States is still wide, and the volume of direct cross-border M&A activities remains low. Remaining barriers such as consumer habits, culture, regulation and law certainly slow the integration of traditional retail activities.

Questions

7.1 a What does a single European market for capital mean and how might it affect European business?
b Why is the wholesale banking market more affected by the single market for capital than the retail banking segment?

7.2 a Explain the conflict between a low, stable ECB inflation policy (between 0 and 2%) and a weak euro exchange rate.
b What is the primary objective of the ECB?
c Which kind of monetary policy – expansionary or contractionary – is the ECB forced to implement during the current financial crisis in order to reach its primary objective? Explain.

7.3 a To what extent is the ECB an independent central bank and how might this affect doing business in Europe?
b Give some arguments in favour of an independent central bank and some counter-arguments.

7.4 Outline some important trends in the EU banking industry since the early 1990s.

7.5 What were the most important financial risks addressed by the Basel II Capital Accord?

7.6 Describe two important features of the 1989 EU Second Banking Co-ordination Directive on EU banking?

7.7 a Has a single market in financial services yet been achieved in the EU? Mention two policy-induced obstacles.
b Why is integration in the retail financial services sector still quite limited? Give two reasons.

7.8 The money market of the euro zone can be divided into collateralized and uncollateralized segments.
a What is meant by financial collateral?
b Give an example of the collateralized and the uncollateralized segments of the money market.
c Which segment is more fragmented? Explain.

7.9 The conflict between profitability and liquidity may have sown the seeds for the financial crisis or2007–09.

   a Why do banks hold a range of assets of varying degrees of liquidity and profitability?

   b Does securitization necessarily involve a moral hazard problem? (See glossary for explanation of terms.)

7.10 Why will European trade with the USA be more affected by euro–dollar fluctuations than the other way round?

7.11 A key feature of European banking systems in recent years has been the consolidation trend, which has led to a small number of banks having dominant positions in various banking systems.
Explain why there has been a preference for national consolidation and why a greater emphasis will be placed on cross-border mergers in the future.

7.12 Germany and the United Kingdom are two of the most important economies within the European Union.
Describe two important differences between the banking systems of Germany and the United Kingdom.

7.13 Assuming that interest rates and exchange rates are determined only by the market and there are no capital restrictions, what determines the amount by which real output falls (with a lower GDP and lower price levels) as a result of a tight monetary policy (*ceteris paribus*)?

   a Explain how a drop in the official interest rate affects the inflation rate in at least three steps or stages (see figure 7.2).

   b Mention two factors that determine the impact of transmission mechanisms on GDP and inflation rates.

7.14 Why might the relationship between the demand for money and the rate of interest be a less stable and less predictable one for all EMU-15 members than for Germany?
What are the consequences for the effectiveness of monetary policy?

7.15 Explain the essential difference between monetary targeting (conducted by the ECB) and inflation targeting (conducted by the Bank of England).

The free movement of people and international business strategy

8

Florijn

After the EU enlargement of 2004, Berry Florijn, a Dutch entrepreneur, established a company in Bogatynia, Poland. The main reason for setting up in Poland was the size of the workforce. A secondary reason was that Florijn could benefit from local tax rules.

Setting up the company was not easy, since the same Polish rules applied to the Dutch businessman as to Polish entrepreneurs. It was to be a limited liability company (Spółka z ograniczon odpowiedzialno ci). A company charter had to be drawn up and notarized, and registration was necessary with several institutions, including the court, the tax authorities, the social insurance institution, the national labour inspectorate and the chief sanitary inspectorate.

After establishing the company, Florijn rented an office building in Maastricht, Netherlands. From this centrally located office in Europe, Florijn contacted his network in the agricultural industry in the Netherlands. He found out in which areas there was a demand for workers and discovered that the greenhouse business was short of people who were willing to handpick vegetables. He then contacted the larger greenhouse companies to arrange with them to contract temporary workers.

The Florijn Company acts as an intermediary. It ascertains the demand for workers in, say, the greenhouse business on the one hand, and on the other hand it informs the workforce in, for instance, Poland about the job opportunities in the Netherlands. The new company in Poland promoted the fact that in the Netherlands there were opportunities for relatively highly paid unskilled jobs to be had. Between 2004 and 2006 it was necessary to arrange work permits for Polish workers, but after 1st January 2007 there was no longer such a restriction. Florijn also arranged the travel and accommodation in the country of employment. For bringing employees and employers together Florijn receives a fee, which the Dutch growers were happy to pay.

The advantage for Polish workers was that they could earn substantially higher wages than in Poland, even if they were working for Dutch minimum wages. The workers were legally in the Netherlands and had the right to return to their country at any moment. The advantages for Dutch employers in the horticultural industry were that they could fill a large number of vacancies and they faced less risk than by employing workers with fixed contracts. Instead, they temporarily employed workers on the minimum wage, whereas local employees would have cost more. The main advantage for Florijn was that the company could send Polish workers to any country in the EU (except Romania and Bulgaria). Another advantage was that Florijn would pay corporate tax in Poland. The corporate income tax rate in Poland was (and still is) 19%. In the Netherlands it was 34.5% in 2004 (Dutch corporate tax is currently 25.5%, which still makes the Polish tax rate 6.5% lower).

At the moment, Florijn is focused on the Dutch and Polish market, but it is considering expanding its business throughout Europe. Florijn is also considering moving its registered seat to Cyprus, where the corporate tax rate is 10%.

Since the first steps in 1950 by Robert Schuman to develop a united Europe, free movement has matured into a fundamental right of every EU citizen. The founding treaties were not so much focused on people in general but were primarily targeted at the working population. The Schengen agreement, however, made free movement available to every individual living in the Member States that co-operated in this agreement.

Today EU citizens and their families, workers and companies all enjoy this basic right to free movement. For companies and self-employed people, this right also includes the freedom to establish a company anywhere within the EU. In order for this right to be effective, it was necessary to lift limitations to workforce mobility. The development of the Treaties and the introduction of legislation to enable people to enjoy the right to free movement has had a significant impact on the business environment. Since it has become easier to work across borders within Europe, large numbers of workers have chosen to be employed outside their home state. But it is not only workers who have shown cross-border mobility; companies have also become quite mobile within Europe. As a result of decisions by the European Court of Justice (ECJ), companies can freely establish themselves throughout Europe or open up branches or subsidiaries more easily to operate across national borders within the European Union.

8.1 The influence of the free movement of people on European business

This section describes how the introduction of free movement of people changed the European business climate. After the success of legislation to permit the free movement of goods, the European Community countries decided that other production elements should also be able to cross borders without obstacles – i.e. people, capital and services. The free movement of people was introduced in various steps. These steps were anchored in international agreements or treaties. This section outlines the obstacles that existed, and in some cases still exist, regarding the cross-border movement of people in Europe. The section ends with examples of how both employers and employees have benefited from the free movement of people.

8.1.1 Union citizenship

The Treaty on European Union (TEU), signed in Maastricht on 7th February 1992 and therefore known as the Maastricht Treaty, expanded the rights of EU nationals to move around the community. Before then, the ability to reside outside one's home state depended foremost on economic status. Before the Maastricht Treaty, only the free movement of workers, the right of business establishment and the freedom to provide services were recognized.

The TEU introduced the concept of Union citizenship (Articles 17–22). Article 17 states that every person holding the nationality of a Member State shall be a citizen of the Union. The result is that a 'Union citizen' is determined by national law and not by European law. Being a Union citizen means that you can exercise rights of movement and residence and political rights, as well as the rights connected to national citizenship.

Several court cases have strengthened the notion of Union citizenship. In the Grzcelczyk case (Case 184/99) the ECJ ruled that: 'Union citizenship is destined to be *a fundamental status* of nationals of the Member States, enabling those who find themselves in the same situation to enjoy the same treatment, irrespective of nationality, subject to such exceptions as are provided for.' And in the Baumbast case (Case 413/99) it was established that Article 18 of the TEU is directly effective, which means that every citizen has the right of entry and residence and that, if necessary, this right will be upheld by the national court.

8.1.2 Directive 2004/38

This directive came into force in 2006, providing citizens and their families with details of their rights concerning entry and residence. It is in fact a detailed implementation of Article 18 of the EC Treaty. (The EC Treaty has been supplemented in this respect by several directives, of which Directive 2004/38 is the most important.) According to Article 18, every citizen of the Union shall have the right to move and reside freely within the territory of the Member States, subject however, to several limitations and conditions.

Free movement rights can be divided into a right of travel and a right of residence. Regarding the right to residence, a distinction can be made between economically active 'natural persons' or 'legal persons' (employees, the self-employed and companies) and persons who are not economically active. According to Directive 2004/38, the family of EU citizens also enjoy the right of entry and residence.

Travel rights include the right to enter or to exit a Member State under the condition of carrying a valid passport or identity card.

Under the Directive there are three categories of citizens' residence rights:
1 for a maximum of three months (short-term stay)
2 for a temporary period more than three months (long-term stay)
3 on a permanent basis (permanent stay).

Category 1: Citizens can freely travel throughout Europe and stay anywhere for up to three months on production of a valid identity card or passport.

Category 2: Citizens and their families can reside for a period longer than three months if they meet at least one of the following conditions:
- They are engaged in economic activity (employed or self-employed) in the host Member State.
- They have comprehensive sickness insurance and sufficient resources for themselves and their family in order not to be a burden on the social security system of the host Member State.
- They are studying or following a course, at a public or private institution, which is accredited by the host Member State. Students must have comprehensive sickness insurance and sufficient resources for themselves and their families.

Category 3: Citizens who have legally lived in an EU country for five years or more are granted permanent residence rights. Members of the family of the Union citizen can also benefit from this rule (Article 16 of Directive 2004/38).

There is no need for an EU citizen to have a residence permit. Member States have the authority to require registration with the competent authorities within three months of the date of arrival. For this, Member States can require citizens to show a valid identity card or passport, confirmation of engagement by an employer, proof of comprehensive sickness insurance and/or proof of sufficient resources. EU citizens or their families can be denied access to a Member State or can be expelled on the grounds of public policy or public security. This is the case if their behaviour represents 'a genuine, present and sufficiently serious threat' to one of the fundamental interests of society.

8.1.3   Schengen

In 1985, Germany, France, the Netherlands, Belgium and Luxembourg decided to create a territory without internal borders for people. The Schengen area brought a halt to border checks between these countries. By 1997 the territory had expanded to 13 Member States. With the Treaty of Amsterdam in 1999, the Schengen agreement was incorporated into EU law.

To combat potential problems such as terrorism and organized crime, the Schengen Information System was set up. This is an information system that allows the police, customs and judiciary to work together in a more organized way. Via the system it is possible to obtain cross-border information about the identity of people and objects. There are currently 25 Schengen countries. Though not a member of the EU, Switzerland joined in December 2008 and became fully integrated in March 2009. Liechtenstein will join by November 2009 and Bulgaria and Romania are scheduled to enter in 2011. Cyprus has signed but there is no date set as to when the agreement will come into force.

8.1.4 Lisbon

According to the EC Treaty, Member States were required to create an area of freedom, security and justice in which the free movement of people would be secured within five years. The Treaty of Lisbon (ToL), signed on 13th December 2007, was more specific and far reaching than the EC Treaty. Key changes regarding the free movement of people were:

- that the Union is required to develop a special relationship with neighbouring countries, with a focus on close and peaceful relations based on co-operation. There are likely to be special arrangements for citizens from neighbouring countries regarding entry.
- a new article, Article 61, to the EC Treaty: 'The Union shall constitute an area of freedom, security and justice with respect for fundamental rights and the different legal systems and traditions of the Member States.'
- that the Union will further undertake a wide range of measures, from a common policy on asylum, immigration and border control, to combating crime, racism and xenophobia.

8.1.5 Free movement of workers

The EC Treaty enshrined specific rights for the free movement of workers. In particular, the right in Article 39 EC concerning the free movement of workers proved to be of great social and economical value to the community. However, the rights of free movement specified in the treaty and secondary legislation applied only to EU workers. A core component of Article 39 EC was the fact that any form of discrimination based on nationality in relation to employment was forbidden.

The main rights under Article 39 EC (subjected to limitations) are:
- the right to accept actual job offers
- the right to move freely within the EU finding search of a job
- the right to stay and work in a Member State under the same conditions as the other workers
- the right to stay in the Member State of employment after termination of the employment.

These rights are subject to detailed conditions, which can be found in Directive 2004/38. Since this directive, there has been a lot of worker movement throughout the EU – primarily from economically weaker areas to more prosperous areas. A 2006 report by the European Commission (Report on the Functioning of the Transitional Arrangements set out in the 2003 Accession Treaty, 30th April 2006) concludes that the free movement of workers was a positive measure. Workers' mobility from new EU Member States in Central and Eastern Europe to old Member States had had positive effects. These workers had helped to relieve labour market shortages and contributed to better economic performance in Europe. Countries that had not applied restrictions (on the basis of public policy, security or health – see below) after May 2004 (principally the UK, Ireland and Sweden) had experienced high economic growth, a drop in unemployment and a rise in employment.

8.1.6 Workers, jobseekers and the unemployed

Since the EC Treaty does not define the term *worker*, a definition was developed through ECJ judgments. Workers are considered to include:
- people who have lost their job but are capable of finding another
- part-time workers, if the work is 'real' work of an economic nature and not nominal or minimal
- part-time workers with extra government benefits
- people who, as members of a (religious) association, are paid pocket money but no wages and are commercially active, this activity forming a genuine and inherent part of their membership.

The key qualifying criterion is that a worker must perform a real and genuine activity that serves some economic purpose.

Directive 2004/38 had a major impact on unemployed people, who retained the status of workers:
- if the unemployment was caused by illness or accident
- if the unemployment was involuntary and lasted for more than one year on the condition of the citizen being registered as a jobseeker (if the unemployment was involuntary and lasted for less than one year, the citizen retains the status of worker for six months only)

If the unemployment was voluntary, citizens are entitled to stay in the host state for a 'reasonable' period (determined by the ECJ to be six months) to look for a job.

8.1.7 Limitations on free movement

The limitations on free movement can be found in Directive 2004/38 and apply irrespective of the category in which a citizen enjoys free movement rights. The limitations apply both to free movement under Union citizenship and to free movement as a worker.

First, Union citizens can be denied entry and residence on grounds of public policy, public security or public health. Such measures may vary from state to state but must comply with the principle of proportionality and be based exclusively on the conduct of the individual concerned. Proportionality means that the reason for disallowing entry or residence should be in proportion to the justification. Failure to renew a passport or ID card, for instance, is not a 'proportional' justification for deportation. Conduct must represent, according to Article 27 of the Directive, 'a genuine, present and sufficiently serious threat' to one of the fundamental interests of society. In other words, a citizen can be denied entry and residence if they pose a serious threat to society. A conviction for theft, for example, is not such a threat.

Second, workers from the Accession States have been, and still are, subjected to limitations in respect of the labour market of the old Member States. Transitional measures restrict their access to the labour market in three phases:

Phase 1 (from 1st May 2004 to 1st May 2006): Work permits were required in some Member States for some Union citizens.

Phase 2 (1st May 2006 to 1st May 2009): Measures depended on the Member State.

Phase 3 (1st May 2009 to 1st May 2011): only with Commission permission in case of serious disruptions of the labour market.

Transitional measures must come to an end by April 2011, except in Romania and Bulgaria – where there are still a lot of transitional restrictions, such as the requirement for a work permit. The cut-off date for these measures in these two countries is 2014.

Finally, there are limitations on the free movement of workers employed in the public service. According to article 39 of the EC Treaty and case law of the ECJ, not all employment in the public service is limited: only employment in which activities are connected with the exercise of official authority. Employment in the police, the judiciary, the military and other public fields is not subject to free movement rights.

8.1.8   Influence on business

For entrepreneurs in the 15 old Member States, free movement brings many advantages, since they have access to a workforce which is eager to work and is used to earning much lower wages. Therefore, by hiring workers from Eastern and Central Europe, employers can reduce their personnel costs considerably.

The other positive effect for entrepreneurs is that migrant workers help to relieve specific shortages in the labour market, as was the case with Cleanair (see chapter 3), which hired Polish workers to work for its Dutch subsidiary.

Another interesting aspect of the legislation is that jobseekers are protected by article 39 of EC Treaty. This states that unemployed people (even those with a right to unemployment benefit in their home country) can look for a job in any other Member State of the European Union. The ECJ has determined that a jobseeker can look for work in another country for a 'reasonable time'. 'Reasonable' is considered to be six months. The EU national cannot be deported even after six months if he can prove he is still looking for work and has a good chance of finding it. This creates extra flexibility for both workers and employers.

8.1.9   Business examples

Case study 8.1 **The Bosman case**

Jean-Marc Bosman is a professional football player from Belgium. He plays for the Belgian club RC Liège. When his contract ended, in the summer of 1990, Bosman wanted to transfer to the French club US Dunkerque. Liège quoted a transfer fee to Dunkerque, which declined to pay it. Bosman claimed that the rules of the Belgian football association, which stated that a club was entitled to charge a transfer fee even when a player's contract had ended, violated Article 39 (and Article 81) of the EC Treaty.

Bosman sued RC Liège, the Belgian football association and finally the European football union (UEFA) before the Belgian court. The case was referred to the ECJ in Luxembourg and in 1995 it passed a judgment in favour of Bosman. The transfer rules were incompatible with European law because they restricted access by players to the labour market of other Member States, thus hindering the free movement of workers.

When a professional footballer's contract expires, if the player is a citizen of the Union, the club previously employing him cannot prevent him from signing a new contract with another club in another Member State. It is also prohibited for the old club to make the transfer more difficult by asking the new club for a transfer fee. Limitations regarding the nationality of the player are also prohibited.

After this judgment, all professional athletes were transfer-free after the expiration of their contracts. Moreover, limitations on the number of foreign players who could play for a team were lifted. As a result, football players (and other professional athletes) began to change clubs far more often, and their salaries increased dramatically. Another result was that the international football federation (FIFA) started negotiations with the European Union in order to develop an agreement that would be acceptable to both players and clubs. Since the Bosman case, all national transfer rules have either disappeared or been extensively altered. (URBSFA v. Bosman, Case 145/93, 1995)

Case study 8.2 The Baumbast case

The Baumbast case concerns a German–Colombian family which moved to the United Kingdom, the father, a Union citizen, having found a job there. Then the parents' marriage failed and they decided to divorce; the father also lost his job. Two important questions arose:
1 Did the father still have the right of residence in the UK?
2 What rights did the mother and the children have once the father was no longer economically active?

The ECJ ruled that children have residence rights for the duration of their education. Mothers have residence rights because they are the principal caretakers of the children. It makes no difference to moth

ers and children whether the fathers are employed after a divorce or not.

Once his right of residence on the grounds of free movement had disappeared after he lost his job, Baumbast was allowed to stay in the UK under Article 18 of the EC Treaty. The conditions under Article 18 were having sufficient means of support and having health insurance. The ECJ ruled that these conditions had to be applied under the proportionality principle, which applies to all Union citizens. A relatively small shortcoming in the coverage of the insurance should not work against the long-term stay of Mr Baumbast. On the basis of Union citizenship and the proportionality principle, Baumbast had the right of residence in the UK. (Baumbast, Case 413–99)

8.2 The influence of the right of establishment on European business

The right or freedom of establishment is an extension of the right of the free movement of workers. The term establishment is not defined in the EC Treaty or in secondary legislation. According to Article 43 of the EC Treaty, however, individuals and companies may establish a company in another Member State without obstruction. Establishment includes the right to take up and pursue activities as a self-employed person as well as setting up a company. In Article 48, on establishment, a distinction is made between natural and legal persons (individuals and companies).

8.2.1 Right of establishment

According to Article 48, companies as well as individuals enjoy the right of establishment if they are established under the law of a Member State and have their real seat in a Member State. In a series of recent decisions the ECJ has clarified the freedom of establishment, allowing companies to locate their seat in one Member State and their activities in another (e.g. Centros, Überseering and Inspire Arte). This freedom allows enterprises to migrate from one Member State to another in order to benefit from corporate, tax and securities laws.

There is some concern among Member States, however, over the so-called Delaware effect. The state of Delaware in the United States has a very favourable tax regime for companies. Companies therefore establish and register themselves in the state of Delaware but carry out their activities elsewhere in the USA. Thus a cluster of tax-avoiding companies is created in one location. The result is that other states receive less tax income. With the new system in Europe, the same situation might occur. In fact, many companies are shifting their headquarters to countries with low corporate taxation.

8.2.2 Limitations on establishment

Articles 45 and 46 of the EC Treaty make an exception to the freedom of establishment. First, Member States can restrict the establishment of companies by foreign nationals on grounds of public policy, public security or public health. A Member State can also restrict activities which are connected with the exercise of official authority, i.e. authority granted by the government, which applies to certain professions. For instance, a bailiff or repossessor has official authority to seize assets, and a police officer has the authority to arrest criminals. Some self-employed people also have a form of official authority, which makes the profession vulnerable to government restrictions.

The report on the case Commission v. Germany (Case 54/08) explains how official authority and establishment should be interpreted. The Commission reprimanded Germany for appointing only German nationals as notaries. The relevant provision published by the Bundesnotarordnung discriminates on the basis of nationality and infringes on the freedom of establishment of nationals of other Member States by preventing them from exercising the profession of notary in Germany. The Commission took the view that the activities of notaries do not fall within the exception relating to the exercise of official authority so that freedom of establishment is applicable to that profession.

In the Gebhard case, the Commission specified the extent to which Member States may restrict the freedom of establishment: '... certain self-employed activities may be conditional on complying with certain provisions laid down by law, regulation or administrative action, such as rules relating to organization, qualifications, professional ethics, supervision and liability. A particular activity can be restricted to holders of a diploma, certificate or other evidence of formal qualifications, to persons belonging to a professional body or to persons subject to particular rules or supervision, as the case may be. They may also lay down the conditions for the use of professional titles, such as avvocato. Where the taking-up or pursuit of a specific activity is subject to such conditions in the host Member State, a national of another Member State intending to pursue that activity must in principle comply with them. National measures liable to hinder or make less attractive the exercise of fundamental freedoms guaranteed by the Treaty must fulfill four conditions:

1 they must be applied in a non-discriminatory manner;
2 they must be justified by imperative requirements in the general interest;
3 they must be suitable for securing the attainment of the objective which they pursue;
4 and they must not go beyond what is necessary in order to attain it.'

8.2.3   Establishment and Directive 2004/38

Directive 2004/38 applies to the free movement of people (as discussed in 8.1.2), as well as to the freedom of establishment (Article 43 EC). Article 43 applies to self-employed people and to companies. EU citizens can start up a business in any Member State and enjoy the right of residence as long as they do not become an unreasonable burden on the social security system of the host Member State. Even if they have recourse to this social security system, this is never a reason for expulsion. Article 7 of Directive 2004/38 provides a right of extended residence (more than three months) for citizens of the Union and their families. One of the requirements for the extended stay is that these citizens must be economically self-sufficient.

The extended right of Article 7 is focused more on the right of establishment. The general right of residence in Article 6 is of greater relevance to citizens exercising the right to receive and provide services. The extended right of residence is subjected to certain conditions. To be entitled to the right of extended stay, EU citizens must:

a be engaged in an economic activity in the host Member State on an employed or self-employed basis
   or
b have adequate health insurance and have sufficient resources for themselves and their families, in order not to become a burden on the social assistance of the host Member State.

Non-EU family members also enjoy the right to extended stay, provided the EU citizen they accompany satisfies the conditions for the extended stay according to Article 7.

In the event that an EU citizen tries to set up a business in another Member State but after some time the business fails, or that an EU citizen finds a job in another Member State but after a while the job is discontinued, the question is whether they should retain their status of self-employed person or employee and whether they may still exercise their rights regarding extended stay in the host Member State. Directive 2004/38 provides – in Article 7(3) – that they shall retain their status as worker or self-employed person:

- if they are unable to work due to an illness or accident
- if they are in duly recorded involuntary unemployment after working for more than one year, and if registered as a jobseeker
- if they are in duly recorded involuntary unemployment after working on a fixed-term contract for less than one year or having become unemployed during the first 12 months, and if registered as a jobseeker
- if they embark on vocational training related to the previous job, unless they are involuntarily unemployed.

EU citizens who establish a business in another Member State do not have the same rights as cross-border employees regarding social welfare. An employee is entitled (on the basis of Article 7 of Regulation 1612/68) to receive social assistance after a period of unemployment, in the same way as nationals. Several court cases and the application of the general anti-discrimination Article 12 of the EC Treaty have eliminated this difference between employees and the self-employed.

8.2.4 Business example

Most cases brought before the ECJ in connection with Article 43 of the EC Treaty have to do with the free professions. These include the legal and medical professions, architects and veterinarians. An example of a Dutch national wanting to enter the Belgian bar as a barrister can be found in chapter 2 (Reyners v. Belgian State, Case 2/74).

■ Example 8.1 Lawyer

Thieffry is a Belgian national with a Belgian law degree who wanted to start practical training for the French bar. The French Bar Council refused to allow the training. The University of Paris had recognized Thieffry's law degree and he also held a certificate that he had practised in France as a lawyer. The court ruled: 'When a national of one Member State wishes to practise a profession such as advocate in another Member State, having obtained a qualification in his own country recognized as equivalent by the other Member State, it contravenes Article 43 EC to demand the national diploma as a further prerequisite to the special qualifying examination.' (Thieffry v. Conseil de l'Ordre des Avocats à la Cour de Paris)

8.2.5 The influence of the freedom of establishment on European company law

According to Article 43 of the EC Treaty, 'natural persons' (individuals) and 'legal persons' (companies with 'legal personality') may establish businesses anywhere in the EU without restriction. Since the creation of the single market and the removal of restrictions there has been considerable company movement.

As explained in 8.2.2, Member States may impose restrictions regarding the establishment of companies by foreign nationals. When companies establish themselves in other Member States, or move their administration to another Member State, they can therefore face conflicts of laws. In this respect there are two main theories: the real seat theory and the incorporation theory. They deal with the question which law applies to the newly established company: does the law of the country where their business activities take place apply, or the law of the country where the company is officially registered? The implementation of the two theories has completely different results. Following a series of ECJ cases, the real seat theory has become obsolete.

Real seat theory

According to this theory, a company is governed by the law of the place where it has its centre of administration. In other words, the law of the state where a company was founded does not apply, but rather the law of the state where the company has its head office. The head office or 'real seat' can be characterized as the place of central control where the main company decisions are made and management tasks allocated. A company may have only one real seat.

If a company moves its seat to another country, this leads to the application of the law of the state the company moves to. The company must comply with all local rules and regulations applicable to comparable types of company. If, for instance, a limited liability company relocates its seat but does not obey the national rules, it will not be recognized as a legal body. This means it has no limited liability and no legal capacity. Therefore, it needs to reincorporate the company in the new country. Reincorporation in the country of the new seat is expensive for the entrepreneur because of administration costs and taxation.

Companies can be set up under the real seat theory in two ways. The first possibility is to set up a 'new' company in the other country, which acquires all the shares of the 'old' company. The other way is to transfer all assets and liabilities from the old to the new company. The shareholders or the company are usually taxed on any profits from the share transfer.

Real-seat-theory advocates claim that the incorporation theory facilitates the establishment of 'letterbox' companies, which government authorities may not be able to control effectively.

Incorporation theory

According to the incorporation theory, a company is governed by the law of the country of incorporation. Companies can therefore be established in the country with the most favourable law. The company will have legal personality and legal capacity in other states. The central advantage of this theory is legal certainty, because the statute seat of a company can easily be identified. Second, cross-border mobility is greatly encouraged. Third, companies can benefit from less restrictive legislation on, for instance, capital requirements, directors' liability, taxation and employee participation.

In short, the incorporation theory makes it possible to choose the most suitable legal system and develop activities in other states without losing the original status of the company. The company is recognized in other countries by the applicable legislation in the country of establishment. The real seat theory, however, allows countries to shield their markets from pseudo-foreign companies by denying them legal status.

8.2.6 Case studies

© Noordhoff Uitgevers bv

The ECJ's case history does not provide a definitive preference for either the real seat theory or the incorporation theory, though it has certainly inclined towards the latter. The reason for this is that the freedom of establishment is a necessary principle, as it is the sole way to an effective single market. The positive aspect for entrepreneurs is the fact that this principle cannot be compromised, even when the primary intention of movement is circumvention of the law.

8.2.7   Effect of the changes on European business

The freedom of establishment, instituted in legislation and elaborated in recent court cases, has resulted in two tendencies. The first tendency is for entrepreneurs to incorporate their business in a jurisdiction that offers them a better deal than the country they intend to do business in. The second tendency is for Member States to change their standards by legislation in order to make their jurisdiction more attractive to foreign companies.

Evidence of these tendencies be seen in the above-mentioned court cases, such as Centros, the Daily Mail and Überseering. Moreover, statistical data from Eurostat, the European Restructuring Monitor, and a Dutch survey by Drury support the idea that the freedom of establishment has had a tremendous impact on European business.

Several French studies show that, of all recorded investment operations, about 10% could be classified as company relocation. Most relocations are by manufacturing companies to Eastern Europe. Companies have also set up so-called offshore companies in Cyprus, Malta, Liechtenstein, Monaco and other 'tax havens'. An offshore company or non-resident company is a company that is incorporated in a foreign territory. Typically, an offshore company does not conduct most of its business in the country where it is officially based. The main reason is beneficial government regulation and lower taxation.

8.2.8   Business examples

■ **Example 8.2 Schindler – departure from Austria**
Schindler is a company manufacturing lifts, escalators and moving walkways. The production line was relocated from its Austrian subsidiary to Slovenia in order to bring together various activities in a relatively low-wage area. The scale of the job losses in Austria was not large, but it involved the dismissal of many skilled as well as unskilled manual workers, as has been the case in many manufacturing sectors in the EU in recent years.

The relocation plans were announced in January 2006. All activities relating to the manufacture of components for lifts and moving walkways were then relocated from Vienna to Slovakia. Hans-Peter Schwarz, CEO of the company, reasoned that increasing cost pressures would require a relocation of the core activities related to lifts to the 'low-wage country' Slovakia. Since an assembling plant had already been set up in Slovakia, there were synergy benefits to be expected.

■ Example 8.3 Schneider Electric – departure from Ireland

Schneider Electric Ireland manufactures electrical components used in industry. The company decided in 2004 to relocate its manufacturing part for electronic components from Ireland to the Czech Republic. This relocation gave an early warning that manufacturing, in international companies, was vulnerable to competition from the new Member States. The relocation from Ireland was announced in September 2003 and concluded in April 2004. The reasons for relocation to the Czech Republic were lower operating costs and the fact that the plant was going to be closer to the company's fastest-growing markets. The company's senior vice-president in Europe also said that rising labour costs in Ireland had contributed to the decision to move.

As a result, several organizations called for national policy to address the strategic needs of the manufacturing sector and, in particular, to examine aspects such as tax reforms. The possible effect is that Ireland has at the moment one of the lowest corporate tax rates (12.5%) in the European Union.

■ Example 8.4 Thomson Technicolor – departure from Luxembourg

The Thomson group specializes in digital video technologies. The Foetz plant in Luxembourg, which was part of the Thomson Technicolor Entertainment Service (THES), was one of the company's three plants. The other two are in Wales and Poland. THES produces DVDs and CDs, it copies cinema films onto DVD and produces music CDs and computer programs.

The relocation of the Luxembourg activities to Poland was announced in January 2007 and the plant was transferred to Poland in June 2007. As far as the management of Technicolor was concerned, it was a commercial and strategic decision. A comparison of production costs had showed that it was more profitable to concentrate activities in one location than to have them spread across the three sites in Luxembourg, Poland and the UK. The relocation took place in one go and the plant was entirely closed.

■ Example 8.5 Texas Instruments – departure from the Netherlands

Texas Instruments had a plant in Almelo, Netherlands. It produced electronic parts for the dashboards of motor vehicles. The Dutch plant employed 315 people. After the relocation to Hungary (and Mexico) in 2006, only 200 workers remained at the Dutch plant. The main reasons for relocating activities from the Netherlands were cost saving and a more favourable tax climate. It can be assumed that, because of the very tight labour market in the Netherlands, the majority of workers affected have been able to find other comparable jobs. The plant was eventually sold to the American investment group Bain Capital during the relocation process in April 2006. It continues under the name of Sensata Technologies.

8.3   Cross-border labour and social security issues

On a social level, the internal EU market is characterized by differences in social rules and circumstances between the Member States. Because of these, workers have been attracted to Member States with more attractive social circumstances. According to statistical data from Eurostat, the number of EU-27 citizens migrating to other Member States has increased by 10% per year since 2004. On the other hand, the absence or low level of social security laws in some Member States has been a magnet to companies. This potentially unbalanced situation needed to be resolved by the harmonization of certain social rules across the Member States.

On the basis of the EC Treaty, numerous directives have been made in order to decrease the social differences between Member States. More about these directives can be found in section 8.3.1, on social policy in the European Union.

8.3.1 Social policy

The EU's social policy can roughly be divided into two categories:
1 social policy in general
2 social policy for migrating workers.

In the EC Treaty there are several rules and requirements for a general social policy. These are set out in Articles 136–145. Their provisions have been the basis for a range of directives on social policy. The directives cover amongst other things:
- working time
- safety and the protection of the health of young workers
- maternity leave
- labour circumstances of young people
- equal treatment for men and women
- dismissal protection.

If workers decide to work elsewhere in the EU, their social rights can be at stake. These might be the right to an old age pension or to unemployment benefit. However, Article 42 of the EC Treaty protects the social security rights of migrating workers.

This rule is necessary to ensure that:
a by leaving their country of birth or residence, workers do not lose their social security rights and
b that workers can enjoy the same social security rights in the country of arrival as national workers.

8.3.2 Social security rights

Every Member State of the European Union has some form of contributory social security system. Such systems are constructed in order to provide people with an income at times when they are unable to provide for themselves. Situations in which people need income through social security include old age, disability and invalidity, unemployment, sickness, widowhood, pregnancy and parenthood. In general, people contribute to the system either mandatorily or voluntarily by paying part of their income to an insurance scheme. In the event of need, the contributor receives benefits from the social security organization.

The problems with social security in cross-border labour situations are that workers can lose out on the contributions they have made in the home state, and they might also not be entitled to benefits in the host state, because they have not contributed sufficiently or for long enough.

Article 42 EC and Regulations 1408/71 (amended by Regulation 2001/83) and 574/72 (amended by Regulation 1247/92) facilitate the protection of social security rights in cross-border labour situations. Article 42 EC entitles migrant workers to take their accumulated rights with them. Contributions made in the home state are taken into account in the host Member State, and contributions in the host Member State are calculated when workers return to their home state.

Article 42 EC is not intended to equalize social security benefits throughout the EU. It is rather aimed at making sure migrant workers obtain equal treatment within all local social security schemes. This is, however, a rather complex issue, since there are enormous differences in national social security schemes throughout the Union.

The beneficiaries of regulations 1408/71 and 574/72 are EU citizens who are employed or self-employed, and who are, or who have been, subject to social security legislation in more than one Member State. The principal beneficiaries' family and survivors are also covered.

Whether a person is entitled to social security benefits depends solely on the amount of contributions they have made to the national social security scheme. It is therefore not necessary for the person to be classified as a 'worker'.

A crucial aspect of Regulation 1408/71 is the fact that beneficiaries are subject to the same obligations and entitled to the same benefits under the legislation of a Member State as the nationals of that state. The main purpose of this is to prevent any form of discrimination.

The Palermo case shows that the ECJ follows this rule very strictly. French women are granted an allowance under the French Social Security Code if they meet the following criteria: at least 65 years old, married, without sufficient means and having brought up at least five children of French nationality for at least nine years before the children's 16th birthday. An Italian woman was denied the allowance by the French government because five of her seven children were Italian and not French. The ECJ ruled that payment of a benefit could not be made conditional on the nationality of the claimant or her children if they were EU citizens.

The same regulation also applies to the situation in which a worker has contributed all his working life to a national insurance scheme in one Member State and wants to retire in another Member State. In such a situation the person is entitled to full payment in the Member State of his choice. This rule is called the portability principle. This principle applies only to benefits which are exportable such as unemployment benefit (up to three months), invalidity and old age pensions, and pensions for accidents at work. It is a citizen's right to receive a benefit from the state of origin, and this is attached to the person as they travel around the EU.

The portability principle does not, however, apply to benefits classified as social assistance. Only social security benefits mentioned in Article 4(1), Regulation 1408/71, are exportable. Social assistance is available only in the host Member State and only to those who have the status of worker and to members of a worker's family.

8.3.3 Equal treatment policy

The equal treatment policy is primarily applicable to foreign workers in the country where they are working or will be working. The equal treatment policy is a non-discrimination rule, defined by Article 39(2) EC. Rights as to equality of treatment, which can be found in Articles 39(2) and 39(3a and b) are implemented by Regulation 1612/68 EC. These rights can be divided into two categories:
- eligibility for employment
- equality in employment.

Eligibility

Jobseekers are entitled under Regulation 1612/68 of the EC Treaty to take up and pursue employment in another Member State under the same conditions as the nationals of that country. Non-nationals may not be hindered in any way and may not be discriminated against when they look for a job in another EU country. Member States can discriminate by setting a quota for applications, advertising or job offers for non-nationals. States can also discriminate by setting out special recruitment procedures for non-nationals or specifying the percentage of non-nationals to be employed in a certain business or in any particular activity. Non-nationals do have the same right to assistance in job seeking as nationals. Member States are, however, allowed to stipulate conditions for non-nationals concerning linguistic knowledge required by the nature of the job, or to ask explicitly for vocational tests when making a job offer to a non-national.

Equality

Workers are also protected by Regulation 1612/68 EC in relation to conditions of employment, remuneration, dismissal and reinstatement or re-employment. Foreign (EU) workers are even entitled to the same social and tax advantages as national workers.

8.3.4 Business examples

The following two examples specifically relate to labour law (rules concerning working people and their organizations) and the next two to social security law (rules concerning the protection of the public against socially recognized conditions, including poverty, old age, disability and unemployment).

■ **Example 8.6 Labour law (1): unemployment benefit for cross-border job seekers**
The host country is not allowed to require a work permit, though it may choose to provide the cross-border worker with a residence permit. This permit is valid for five years and will automatically be renewed. Belgium and Italy operate this system. If a worker has worked and resided for three years in a

particular Member State and subsequently become a cross-border worker, they are entitled to live in the first Member State. It is, however, necessary in principle that people employed in the territory of another Member State return at least once a week to the territory of residence.

Unemployed people are allowed to look for a job in another Member State for a maximum of three months while receiving unemployment benefit. In the Netherlands, unemployed people who wanted to exercise this right used to be obliged to register with the foreign police. After a question from a member of the European Parliament, the Commission ruled that this requirement violated Community law. The right to look for work elsewhere in the European Union could not be connected to registration or the granting of a permit. (Written question E2207/94, Official Journal no. C055, 06/03/95 p.0043).

■ **Example 8.7 Labour law (2): cross-border university professor**
After working for at least 15 years, professors at the University of Innsbruck, Austria, are entitled to a length-of-service increment. Professor Köbler had 15 years' experience, if his working time for other European universities was included. However, the national law of Austria did not allow the periods he worked at a university in another Member State to be taken into account. The ECJ held that this was incompatible with Article 39 of the EC Treaty and Regulation 1612/68. The court found that there could be a pressing public interest reason which was capable of justifying the obstacle to free movement, but in this case the court held that the obstacle which this would create for the right to free movement could not be justified.

■ **Example 8.8 Social security (1): frontier worker**
Mr Hosse is a German frontier worker. He works as a teacher in Salzburg, Austria. He had paid taxes and social security in Austria and was entitled to sickness insurance in Austria. But he lives in Germany, near the Austrian frontier, with his daughter Silvia Hosse, who is severely disabled. Mr Hosse made an application for a care allowance for his daughter under a law of the Province of Salzburg. The application was rejected for the reason that the person dependent on care must live in the Province of Salzburg in order to qualify for the allowance.

The ECJ held that the care allowance should not be conditional on the residence of the members of the worker's family in the country of employment and that it was contrary to Regulation 1408/71 to deprive the daughter of a worker of a benefit she would be entitled to if she were resident in that Member State. According to the court, Silvia Hosse could claim the care allowance provided she meets the other requirements for the allowance and is not entitled to similar benefit under the legislation of the State in whose territory she resides.

■ **Example 8.9 Social security (2): fare reduction card**
An Italian worker had been living and working in France for a considerable number of years. He claimed a public transport fare reduction card issued to the parents of large families. When he died, his wife claimed the reduction card. The French government rejected the claim. The ECJ held that Article 7(2) of Regulation 1612/68 applies to all social and tax advantages, whether or not deriving from contracts of employment, and since the family had the right to remain in France under Regulation 1215/70 they were entitled to equal social advantage (Fiorini v. SNCF, Case 32/75). This was a rather liberal

interpretation by the ECJ of the phrase 'the same social and tax advantages as national workers'.

Conclusions

The core of the European Union is its internal market. The internal market mainly consists of the four freedoms. The free movement of people is indispensable for the effective working of the internal market. Free movement of people is regulated for EU citizens in general according to Article 18 of the EC Treaty. Union citizenship includes the right to move freely and reside outside the home state, independent of economic status.

The free movement of a specific group of people, workers, depends on economic status. The free movement of workers is regulated by Article 39 of the EC Treaty and in Directive 2004/38. According to these regulations, EU citizens have travel rights and residence rights. Residence rights can be divided into short term, long term and permanent rights. If a person wants to reside for longer than three months in another EU country, they must meet certain requirements. A long-term stay is possible if a citizen is employed or self-employed, has enough means to support themselves or is following a study course.

The family of a citizen who meets one of these requirements are eligible for a long-term stay. The Schengen Agreement is responsible for a European Union without internal borders for people. The Lisbon Treaty went further, increasing free movement rights for citizens. Member States may limit the right of free movement only on grounds of public policy, public security or public health. And workers from the Accession States can be denied access to a Member State in accordance with transitional measures. These measures should cease to exist completely for all Member States by 2014.

Companies also enjoy 'travel and residence' rights. A company can, for instance, sell its goods or services throughout the Union from its home state. This falls within the scope either of free movement of goods or of free movement of services. Companies can also establish themselves anywhere in the Union.. Even the seat of a company can be transferred from one country to another. The European Court of Justice has confirmed this in a series of cases questioning the freedom of establishment. This creates opportunities for companies to benefit from another legal or tax regime. Many companies, for example, have transferred their bases to Eastern European countries, where wages and labour and social security laws are more favourable.

When workers choose to work 'cross-border' they can face a few obstacles. One such is a difference in labour laws. Specifically, there can be dissimilarities in working time, working hours, safety measures and so on. Workers must also consider that cross-border labour can result in the loss of social security rights in the home state and that they may not have built up enough rights in the host state to enjoy social security rights. Migrant workers are protected by the EC Treaty and several specific directives, although case law seldom relates to cross-border protection, which must therefore often be fought for in court. Hopefully, new legislation will extend workers' rights in the future.

Questions

8.1 Explain the difference between the right to free movement of people and the right to free movement of workers.

8.2 Explain the purpose of the Schengen Agreement.

8.3 Give an overview of the pros and cons of the Schengen Agreement.

8.4 Under what conditions can Member States restrict the free movement of people or workers within the European Union?

8.5 What has been the influence of the Bosman case on professional athletes in Europe?

8.6 Under what conditions can Member States restrict the freedom of establishment in the European Union?

8.7 Explain which theory is more advantageous for entrepreneurs, the incorporation theory or the real seat theory.

8.8 Give one exception to the rule that Member States may not hinder cross-border labour.

8.9 Explain under what conditions jobseekers and the economically inactive are entitled to benefits.

8.10 Is a Dutch national who is fired from his job in Germany entitled to German or to Dutch social security benefits?

EU integration and challenges for business

Invest Bulgaria Agency

Most countries have a government agency whose function is to convince foreign enterprises to invest in its country. These agencies also provide all kinds of support to companies in terms of information, administrative services, identifying suitable locations, finding local business partners, etc. In the UK, the agency is called UK Trade & Investment; in Germany, Germany Trade and Invest; in the Netherlands, Netherlands Foreign Investment Agency. In Bulgaria, it is named Invest Bulgaria Agency.

Most agencies promote their country by listing the advantages of investing and doing business there on their websites. On its website (in September 2009), under the heading 'Why Bulgaria', the Bulgarian agency mentions the following advantages of the country:
- Highly-skilled, multilingual workforce at Europe's most competitive wages
- Stable and predictable business and political environment
- EU membership
- Free trade with the EU preferential trade partners, including EFTA, Turkey, Mediterranean countries, Western Balkan countries, South Africa, Mexico, Chile, etc.
- 10% corporate income tax rate
- 10% personal income tax
- VAT exemption on equipment imports for investment projects over €5 million
- Annual depreciation rate of 30% for machinery and equipment, 50% for new equipment used in new investments and 50% for software and hardware
- Treaties for avoidance of double taxation with 61 countries
- Agreements on mutual protection and promotion of foreign investment with 60 countries
- Acquisition of land and property through a Bulgarian registered company with up to 100% foreign ownership
- Fast administrative services through Invest Bulgaria Agency
- Natural and cultural landmarks, tasty food and hospitality.

The website also features a number of success stories, grouped by industry sector. For the food industry the story of Nestlé S.A. is presented:

'The world's largest food company, Nestlé S.A., established itself as one of the leading investors in Eastern Europe and by the end of the 1990s the firm possessed 23 factories in the region. Despite the heavy cost of investment, this was a step in the right direction for the Swiss food producer and the increase in sales proved it.

In 2000 alone, Nestlé S.A. achieved sales growth of 18% in Eastern Europe, outperforming Western Europe tenfold and by far exceeding the corporate global average sales growth of 4.4%.

Nestlé's strategy to become the dominant food company in Eastern Europe has been carried out through acquiring major local producers, modernizing them and bringing them in line with the corporate standards. As a result of its strategy, Nestlé took by storm the position of market leader in confectionery throughout Eastern Europe.

Nestlé S.A. entered the Bulgarian market in 1994 after the purchase of the largest confectionery plant in the country, located in the outskirts of the capital Sofia.

In June 1994 Nestlé Sofia AD was established. The company produces chocolate bars, boxed chocolates, wafers and biscuits. Its brands Nestlé Classic, Mura, Adventure, LZ, Taralejki and Jiten Dar are well known in the Bulgarian market and all products are appreciated by Bulgarian consumers. For the last seven years Nestlé has invested in Bulgaria more than USD30 million (excluding acquisition), renovating its manufacturing process, innovating its products, elaborating efficient marketing, distribution and control systems, and developing effective experts and managers. Special attention has been paid to the research & development process, as well as to quality, environmental protection and safety issues.

Utilizing local experience, since the year 2000 Nestlé Sofia has expanded its activities into the commercialization of imported international Nestlé products: Nescafé, Nesquik, Maggi, Breakfast Cereals, Infant Nutrition, etc.

Operating in the changing business environment in Bulgaria, the company has lived with all the difficulties of the transition period. Last year it already experienced dramatic business growth and foresees this trend to be profitable and sustainable.'

Other success stories include the Bulgarian activities of (originally) French company Solvay (chemicals), Swiss/Swedish Asea Brown Boveri (ABB; electrical engineering), German SAP (ICT) and British Lifton (mechanical engineering).

In this chapter, the challenges for companies in relation to EU integration are discussed. In section 9.1 some macroeconomic data and the tax rates of selected EU Member States are presented. The European business environment is highly diverse and there are significant disparities between the various Member States and regions in terms of macroeconomic factors, taxes and technological and scientific know-how. This results in many business opportunities for exports, imports, outsourcing and investment.

In section 9.2 the methodology for selecting a country or region for international operations within the EU is reviewed. The selection of a country depends not only on the country's characteristics but also on the company's strategic aims. In principle, every Member State has advantages, ranging from low production costs to strategic location and more advanced factors, such as abundant research facilities and technological know-how. The selection should be based on a good match between the company's objectives and the country's characteristics.

9.1 European integration and new business opportunities

European integration has resulted in numerous opportunities for enterprises in international trade and investment. First, although many barriers remain, the deepening of European integration has made it much easier for enterprises to export, to establish branches or subsidiaries, to import, and to outsource or hire staff in other European countries. Second, the recent EU enlargements have given companies in Europe easy access to rapidly emerging markets and a vast supply of cheap resources. There are large disparities in European Member States in terms of income levels, growth rates, productivity, labour costs, inflation, tax rates, etc. From a company point of view, these differences can offer interesting business opportunities for international expansion, including new markets and cheaper production locations. They are also a threat to a company, as competitors can seize opportunities.

Key economic indicators

In table 9.1 some key economic indicators for selected countries are presented. There are, for instance, striking differences in terms of labour costs between the various countries. Sweden (after tiny Luxembourg the most expensive country in terms of labour costs) is almost 17 times as expensive as Bulgaria, (by far) the cheapest country in the EU. Also in terms of corporate income tax, there are substantial differences – from the top rate of 34.4% in France to the lowest of 10% in Bulgaria.

These remarkable figures for Bulgaria are, of course, used by the Invest Bulgaria Agency to promote its country as a very attractive investment opportunity, in particular for setting up production facilities. Other former socialist countries in Central and Eastern Europe (CEE), such as Poland, the Czech Republic, Hungary, Slovakia and the Baltic States, are doing the same. A further advantage is that enterprises setting up operations in these countries might qualify for support from the EU structural funds, which are aimed at supporting regions and countries that are lagging behind in economic development.

Does this mean that these countries are the only – or at least the most interesting – countries for business development? Not necessarily, as we will see: these countries have drawbacks as well. First, low labour costs are in part offset by lower labour productivity, which is about three times higher in developed countries, such as France, Germany, the Netherlands and Sweden, than in Bulgaria and about twice as high as in Poland. The latter countries might also lack specific expertise in certain fields, which might be more widely available in western (and northern) parts of Europe.

Second, purchasing power in the emerging countries of CEE is still relatively low, although it is rapidly catching up. The growth of GDP is very important in this context; growth rates in most of Eastern Europe exceed the rates in the more mature economies by far.

Third, inflation in the new Member States in the east of the EU is far higher than in Western European countries: from 2000 to 2008 they ranged from less than 2% in Germany and France to 3.5% in Poland

and 6.6% in Bulgaria. Price levels in Eastern Europe seem to be converging with Western European levels.

Fourth, the political and economic stability of the former Eastern bloc countries is significantly weaker than in the richer part of the EU. Corruption and organized crime is very high in, for instance, Bulgaria and Romania.

Table 9.1 **Key economic indicators for selected countries**

Macroeconomic data	Germany	France	Netherlands	Spain	Sweden	UK	Bulgaria	Czech Rep.	Poland	Romania
Population (2009; million)	82.0	64.4	16.5	45.8	9.3	61.6	7.6	10.4	38.1	21.4
GDP (2008; € billion)	2,491	1,950	595	1,905	328	1,812	34	149	362	137
GPD/capita (2008; EU-27 index = 100	116	107	135	104	121	117	40	80	57	46
Real GPD growth rates • (2009, forecast; %) • (2000-2008; %)	−5.4 1.4	−3.0 1.9	−3.5 2.2	−3.2 3.3	−4.0 2.6	−3.8 2.5	−1.6 5.6	−2.7 4.3	−1.4 4.2	−4.0 5.8
Inflation • (2008; %) • (2000–2007; %)	2.8 1.7	3.2 1.9	2.2 2.5	4.1 3.2	3.3 1.6	3.6 1.6	12.0 6.6	6.3 2.4	4.2 3.5	7.9 18.8
Prices (2006; EU-27 index = 100)	103	107	104	93	118	110	44	60	63	58
Monthly labour costs (2007; average gross full-time)	3,930	3,220	4,020	2,280	4,677	4,512	280	1,201	997	527
Labour productivity per full-time person employed (2008; EU-27 index = 100)	108	121	115	105	111	110	36	72	63	48
Imports of goods & services (2006; % of GDP)	39	28	63	32	43	32	88	72	42	45
Exports of goods & services (2006; % of GDP)	45	27	70	26	52	28	64	76	40	33
Taxes										
Top corporate income tax rate (2009; %)	29.8	34.4	25.5	30.0	26.3	28.0	10.0	20.0	19.0	16.0
Top personal income tax rate (2008; %)	47.5	45.8	52.0	43.0	56.4	40.0	10.0	15.0	40.0	16.0
Social security paid by employer (2007; % of total labour costs)	22.9	28.5	21.0(e)	25.0	30.6	18.0	19.8	26.9	16.6	25.0
VAT (2009; standard rates)	19	19.6	19	16	25	15	20	19	22	19

Source: Eurostat, June 2009

Most of the new Member States have not yet adopted the euro, making them more vulnerable to external shocks like the 2008 – 2009 financial crisis. Hungary and Latvia, for instance, were (in 2009) on the brink of bankruptcy. When dealing with these countries, entrepreneurs are still highly exposed to currency risks. The Hungarian forint is wildly fluctuating: between June 2008 and March 2009 it lost almost 30% of its value vis-à-vis the euro, before it started to recover. The Polish zloty also decreased by around 30% between July 2009 and June 2008.

Nevertheless, the new Member States in CEE have offered tremendous business opportunities since they joined the EU, even if the disadvantages and risks are taken into account. These opportunities, of course, have presented themselves not only to enterprises from the old Member States, but also to companies from the new Member States. The latter will have relatively easy access to markets in Western Europe and can be successful if they capitalize on their competitive advantage by exploiting low labour costs in particular.

For non-European enterprises, European integration can have advantages as well: they can set up production facilities in places with specific advantages (so-called location-specific advantages – see below) within the EU and serve the EU market from there. This might be a good strategic option if these companies are faced with high external EU trade barriers or high transport costs or if they want to have production facilities close to their markets in Europe. The last two reasons can be a good rationale for European companies as well.

Nestlé S.A. in Bulgaria (see opening case study) offers an example of this: the company established production facilities in many Central European countries, mainly to serve local markets. Another example is car manufacturers, which also set up many plants in central Europe (see case study 9.1).

Germany is still by far the leading car producer in Europe, but in terms of share of turnover, value added and employment (as a percentage of the total per country) Slovakia, the Czech Republic and Hungary are at about the same level. German car makers in particular relocated part of their production to neighbouring regions in Central Europe. Car manufacturing investment in this region was done for a different reason than the Nestlé investment, however. It was not only meant to serve local markets but also to export to other – and in particular more prosperous – countries in Europe. Both cases, Nestlé and the car industry, are clear examples of a manufacturing-based entry strategy (see chapter 5, section 5.6.3).

Usually, international trade (export and import) and foreign direct investment (FDI – direct investment in business operations in a foreign country) are interrelated. Export, for instance, can be done without any investment in a country, if the exporter sells directly to customers abroad or via agents, international trading companies or (independent) distributors (importers). But in many cases the exporting company will invest in a sales organization, co-operate with local partners or even establish its own plant in the target country. For imports, similar observations can be made. The car industry is a typical example of this kind of complex business operation: it is simultaneously involved in export, import and investment activities.

Case study 9.1 Carmaking in central Europe: no Skoda jokes, please

Cars have been built in the Czech Republic for more than 100 years, ever since Vaclav Laurin and Vaclav Klement switched from making bicycles to producing four-wheeled vehicles. Laurin & Klement is now better known as Skoda, but the duo's manufacturing base remains in Mlada Boleslav, at the heart of a region that is fast becoming a new carmaking powerhouse. Total production last year in the Czech Republic, Slovakia, Slovenia, Poland, Hungary and Romania was 2.4m vehicles – more than Britain (1.6m) and just behind Spain (2.8m).

The dominant producer in the region is the Czech Republic, where production has increased from 450,000 in 2004 to 850,000 in 2006, overtaking Poland. But it may in turn be overhauled by Slovakia, which produced 295,000 cars in 2006, and whose fortunes have been boosted by the arrival of Kia, a South Korean carmaker, joining PSA Peugeot Citroën and Volkswagen. Indeed, it is thought that Slovakia, with a population of 5.4m, could become the world's leading carmaking country measured in output per capita. Kia's greenfield factory in Zilina, which started operating at the end of

2006, has the capacity to produce 300,000 cars a year. Peugeot's factory has a similar capacity. And Volkswagen, which builds SUVs in Slovakia for export, produced 238,000 cars last year.

All this has attracted a new wave of international suppliers. Many South Korean firms have followed Kia to Slovakia and will soon start to supply its parent company, Hyundai, which has just started building a €1 billion new factory over the border in the Czech Republic, due to open in October 2008. (Hyundai and Kia have some something similar in America, positioning their supplier base between two manufacturing sites.) The Czech government, which has provided around €200m in incentives, hopes this will create a total of 12,000 new jobs in a region with high unemployment. A joint venture between Toyota and Peugeot, which got going in the country two years ago, created 2,000 jobs and now makes 300,000 cars for export.

Central Europe is an attractive place to build cars for many reasons. Labour costs are lower than elsewhere in Europe, many countries now have established car-parts industries, and Japanese and South Korean firms value the proximity to western European customers. "If we try and do everything from South Korea, we cannot know exactly what European customers want," says Bae In Kyu, the boss of Kia's Slovakian plant. Making cars in Slovakia also cuts delivery times and sidesteps important taxes.

But is not all good news, warns Marcel Brouiller of Renault. Recruiting staff is getting harder, and infrastructure in the regions is under strain. Most of the roads that serve Renault's plant in Novo Mesto, 40 miles east of Ljubljana, are only single carriageways. Even so, Laurin and Klement would surely be delighted that their legacy lives on.

Source: *The Economist* print edition, 21st June 2007

9.2 The selection of destinations for international trade and investment within the EU

In this section, the methodology for selecting a foreign country for cross-border trade and foreign direct investment is analysed.

Obviously, there are attractive countries and regions in the EU for trade and investment other than Central Europe – at least according to the relevant national investment agencies. Low labour costs and taxes are definitely not the only reason to invest in a country. The UK Trade & Investment agency gives 20 reasons to do business in the UK on its website, including the following:

- the easiest place to set up and run a business in Europe
- an internationally competitive tax environment
- one of the most flexible labour markets in Europe
- the least number of barriers to entrepreneurship in the world
- a world leader in innovation
- uses the international language of business
- top education: the top six universities in Europe; many Nobel prizes won
- a springboard to Europe
- the number one location for European headquarters (for overseas companies)
- productivity rapidly increasing.

The Netherlands Foreign Investment Agency gives the following reasons to invest in the Netherlands:
- strategic location in Europe
- international business environment
- superior logistics and technology infrastructure
- highly educated, multilingual and flexible workforce
- high quality of life
- favourable fiscal climate.

The attractiveness of a country for a company seeking business opportunities abroad does not only depend on the country itself but also on the company and its strategic aims. For example, it is important to know whether the company's priority is to export, to import or to invest – keeping in mind that investment and import/export could be interrelated. The following aims could be linked to the reasons for companies to internationalize, as identified in section 5.6.3:

1 opportunity development
2 leveraging key success factors abroad
3 following customers abroad
4 pursuing diversification
5 taking advantage of different growth rates of economies
6 exploiting product life cycle differences
7 internationalizing for defensive reasons.

1   **Opportunity development**
This could involve, for example, finding new markets for export. Countries with high or fast-growing GDPs would normally be top of the list. However, if the relevant market in the high-GDP countries is mature, then the emerging markets might be more attractive. A typical example is Nestlé (see opening case study): in 2000, the company realized an 18% sales growth in Eastern Europe, against a mere 4.4% corporate global growth in that year. For advanced, new or expensive products, such as iPhones, Blue Ray recorders or new medicines, more developed markets are probably more attractive.

Opportunity development can also include opportunities for decreasing the costs of production by means of importing cheap components or materials or relocating plants. In this case, the countries in the east of the EU offer good opportunities, as can be seen in case study 9.1. In general, enterprises might look for places with location-specific advantages. These are the advantages that arise from the availability of resources or assets in a particular foreign location. These resources are not necessarily cheap (e.g. labour): they might be specific (e.g. knowledge or skills) or strategic (e.g. location).

Research & development (R&D) centres are mostly in advanced countries. For instance, fashion and design businesses are concentrated in the north of Italy because of the special expertise, experience and tradition that are found there. That is why the UK Trade & Investment website proclaims that the UK is 'a world leader in innovation' and also the home of the top six universities in Europe, suggesting that the UK is *the* place to be for R&D.

Case study 9.2 provides a typical example of this. In 2009, the Japanese drug company Eisai established a European Knowledge Centre (EKC) in Hatfield, UK. It includes – in addition to a factory and offices – a large research laboratory. The EKC is also meant to be the European headquarters of Eisai, indicating that Eisai believes that the UK could indeed be a 'springboard to Europe', as advertised on the UK Trade & Investment website. Another major advantage of the UK is probably the language.

Germany is well known for its know-how in the field of engineering: car makers might relocate parts of their production facilities to the eastern Member States of the EU, but the major R&D centres remain in Germany.

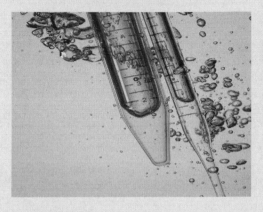
2   Leveraging key success factors abroad

Many SMEs have become successful with a particular product, which they sell in their home markets. The product might be the result of some specialist knowledge or unique competence. But if the company is successful in the home market, its products might sell abroad as well. There might even be a need to export, because the home market is simply too small. In many cases, such companies start to export to neighbouring EU countries (see interview in chapter 1 opening case study with Mr Alting of the North Netherlands Chamber of Commerce). If this turns out to be successful, they might start to export to more distant countries as well, even outside the EU. For companies in Western Europe, the initial target countries will probably be the more developed economies, particularly if they operate in the more advanced sectors such as biochemistry, medical devices, life sciences, ICT, nana-technology or sensor technology. Companies active in consumer markets might opt for countries with high purchasing power.

3   Following customers abroad

If a company has close links with its major clients, it can be a wise move to follow these clients if they set up operations abroad. This situation might occur in the context of joint development or quality control, just-in-time deliveries, flexible and tailor-made production runs, etc. The car industry is a typical example: many subcontractors followed the big car companies, Volkswagen, Peugeot Citroën, Renault, Kia, Hyundai and others, to CEE (see case study 9.1). The decision to invest in a specific country depends on the customer in this case.

4 Pursuing diversification

Diversification can occur if companies want to spread their risk: different markets can develop differently. Diversification into a foreign market can be driven by a desire to take advantage of differences in purchasing power. For example, Renault took over the Romanian carmaker Dacia in 2004 and started producing the Logan. Costing less than €5,000, the new model was initially destined for the CEE markets. More expensive versions later became available in Western European markets. The more sophisticated Renault models are primarily intended for markets in Western Europe, however.

5 Taking advantage of different growth rates of economies

Countries experience different GDP growth rates. These growth rates might not be stable; economic performance can vary from year to year. A fast-growing economy in one year can be surpassed by others or even have a severe economic dip in the next year. Therefore it is not wise for a company to put all its eggs in one basket. Companies selling to several countries lower their risk, particularly if they can switch their sales efforts quickly from one country to another.

This driver for internationalization might also apply to companies selling their products in saturated or mature (home) markets. The confectionary industry in the opening case study (Nestlé) and the car makers in case study 9.1 are typical examples. In contrast to the mature markets in Western Europe, the emerging markets in CEE offer possibilities for growth.

6 Exploiting product life cycle differences

The product life cycle (PLC) theory analyses the relationship between the life cycle of products and their production location. It is assumed that many products have such a life cycle, consisting of four stages: introduction, growth, maturity and decline.

The *introductory* stage requires research & development, leading to innovation. Mostly this is done in advanced countries, because these countries have the necessary knowledge and resources. Initially, the new product is expensive and only sold in the country where the product was introduced.

During the *growth* stage the product is marketed and produced in other industrial countries as well. The number of competitors increases, production becomes more standardized and prices fall.

At the *maturity* stage, the markets in industrialized countries are more or less saturated, but demand in developing countries is rising fast. Production is highly standardized and production facilities are (partly) relocated to developing countries. Competition is increasing and prices are falling even further. At the maturity stage, both demand and production are declining, while both have largely shifted to developing countries.

In the *decline* stage, all production has been shifted to developing countries and is exported from there to declining markets in developed countries.

It is easy to recognize these stages in the life cycle of products such as TV sets, video recorders, photocopiers, cars and medicines (if we consider a new generation of such products as 'new'). All these products were invented and initially produced and sold in advanced countries as the United States, the UK or Germany. Later on, they became more or less standardized mass-market products sold and produced in other countries as well.

Coming back to the EU, it can be noticed that a number of products are at a kind of maturity stage in the more developed countries: cars, food products, consumer electronics. Growth can be achieved only by (a) market development in the emerging markets in CEE or (b) product development in the west. The more standardized and labour-intensive parts of production (such as assembly for cars) are carried out in new Member States, while the knowledge-based parts, such as research & development, management and marketing, remain in the advanced countries.

7 Internationalizing for defensive reasons

This driver can have different backgrounds:

- If foreign competitors come to your market, one of the logical responses is to export to other countries, in order to maintain sales levels.
- Domestic competitors may find cheaper sources of components, materials or labour or relocate (part) of their production to countries with low production costs or other location-specific advantages. In order to survive, your company must follow suit.
- The competition is penetrating new markets. If successful, it might lead to a wider cost base (economies of scale and scope). If you do not follow them, they might take over the whole market and block entry for newcomers at a later stage.

To summarize: there are many reasons for companies to go abroad and get involved in international business relations. The choice of target countries depends on the companies' strategic aims on the one hand, and the attractiveness of countries' specific economic and business characteristics on the other.

Conclusions

This chapter reviewed the challenges for business in the enlarged European Union. The business environment in the EU differs strongly from country to country and is characterized by huge disparities in terms of income growth and income levels, inflation and tax rates, labour costs and productivity levels, and technological and scientific know-how.

This highly diversified environment offers many opportunities for companies to increase sales, find cheaper resources, decrease costs and become more competitive in world markets.

A necessary condition for realizing this potential is that the single market functions effectively. Barriers to international trade and services, investment and the free movement of people will prevent companies and individuals from reaping the full benefits of the single market. As we have seen in chapters 5–8, the single market is still not completed and may never be. For instance, integration of the EU retail banking markets is still in its infancy. And apart from the legal and administrative hurdles, there are still many cultural, social and language barriers. But the single market project has lowered the obstacles for international business within the EU considerably.

From a business point of view, each country has advantages (and disadvantages); the selection of a specific country or region to do business in depends on a company's strategic aims and objectives. Low-cost production locations and a fast-growing market are found in the new Member States in CEE, while opportunities for research & development, product innovation and the introduction of new or expensive products are found in the more advanced economies in the western and northern parts of the EU. Of course, this situation might change, as the emerging economies in the east converge towards average EU levels.

For an increasing number of EU companies, internationalization is a *must*. Triggered by the ongoing expansion and integration of the EU, competition in many markets is intensifying. Internationally operating competitors have access to cheaper resources and more knowledge and are thus better equipped to realize product innovation. This may result in lower prices, better products, shorter product life cycles, etc.

Although their number is growing, only a minority of EU companies is involved in international business operations. Less than 30% of large companies in the EU reported export sales (in 2007); for SMEs the percentage in that year was less than 10%. There are still plenty of opportunities (and challenges) for businesses in the new Europe.

Questions

9.1 Analyse the impact of the accession of new Member States in Central and Eastern Europe on:
- the profitability of Dutch road transport companies
- the competitiveness of German car makers on the world market.

9.2 What could be the reason(s) that the involvement of SMEs in international business is lower than the involvement of large companies?

9.3 TFS Trial Form Support International AB (opening case study of chapter 6) established new regional headquarters in 2008 in Budapest, Hungary. What could have be the reasons for TFS to expand its activities to this part of Europe?

9.4 Assume that a Dutch company specializing in water purification wants to expand its market in the EU.
- What country or countries would you recommend and why?
- Which of the seven drivers for internationalization, mentioned in section 9.2, could have played a role in the company's decision to expand internationally?

List of abbreviations

AAA	Triple A loans
ACP	African, Caribbean and Pacific group of states
AD	anti-dumping duty
AG	Aktiengesellschaft (German) = incorporated stock company (Inc.)
AIDA	Attention, Interest, Desire, Action
APEC	Asia-Pacific Economic Co-operation forum
ASEAN	Association of South-East Asian Nations
B2B	business to business
B2C	business to consumer
Benelux	Belgium, the Netherlands and Luxembourg
BIC	Bank Identifier Code
BIS	Bank for International Settlements
B/L	bill of lading
bn	billion
BoE	Bank of England
BRIC	Brazil, Russia, India and China
Brussels I	Regulation 44/2001 on Jurisdiction and the Recognition and Enforcement of Judgments in Civil and Commercial Matters
CAP	Common Agricultural Policy
CARICOM	Caribbean Community
CCD	Consumer Credit Directive
CE	Conformité Européenne (CE marking)
CEE	Central and Eastern Europe
CEN	European Committee for Standardization
CER	Australia and New Zealand Closer Economic Relations
CET	common external tariff
CFR	Cost and Freight (Incoterm 2000)
CIF	Cost Insurance and Freight (Incoterm 2000)
CIP	Carriage and Insurance Paid to (Incoterm 2000)
CISG	United Nations Convention on Contracts for the International Sale of Goods
CM	common market
COE	country-of-origin effect
CPI	Consumer Price Index
CPT	Carriage Paid To (Incoterm 2000)
CRO	Contract Research Organisation
CU	customs union
CVD	countervailing duty
DAF	Delivered At Frontier (Incoterms 2000)
DDP	Delivered Duty Paid (Incoterms 2000)
DDU	Delivered Duty Unpaid (Incoterms 2000)
DEQ	Delivered Ex Quay (Incoterms 2000)
DES	Delivered Ex Ship (Incoterms 2000)
DESTEP	demographic, economic, social, technological, ecological and political analysis
DG	Directorate General
DM	Deutsche Mark
DTC	data transmission centre

DTI	deposit-taking institution
EASA	European Advertising Standards Alliance
EC	European Community/Communities
ECA	European Community for Atomic Energy
ECB	European Central Bank
ECOWAS	Economic Community of West African States
ECR	European Court Reports
ECSC	European Coal and Steel Community
ECSR	European Committee of Social Rights
EcU	economic union
ECU	European Currency Unit
EEA	European Economic Area
EEC	European Economic Community
ECJ	Court of Justice of the European Communities (European Court of Justice)
EFTA	European Free Trade Association
EMS	European Monetary System
EMU	Economic and Monetary Union
EN	European Standard
EONIA	European OverNight Index Average
ERM	(European) Exchange Rate Mechanism
ErP	energy-related product
ESCB	European System of Central Banks
EU	European Union
EU-15	the European Union before 1st May 2004
EU-25	the European Union between 1st May 2004 and 1st January 2007
EU-27	the European Union since the accession of Bulgaria and Romania on 1st January 2007
EuP	energy-using product
Euratom	European Atomic Energy Community
Euribor	Euro Interbank Offered Rate
Euromed	Euro-Mediterranean Partnership
EVD	Dutch Agency for International Business and Co-operation
EXW	Ex Works (Incoterms 2000)
FAS	Free Alongside Ship (Incoterms 2000)
FCA	Free Carrier (Incoterms 2000)
FDI	foreign direct investment
Fed	US Federal Reserve System
FOB	Free on Board (Incoterms 2000)
FRA	Forward Rate Agreement
FSAP	Financial Services Action Plan
FX	foreign exchange
FTA	free trade agreement/area/association
GATT	General Agreement on Tariffs and Trade
GCC	Gulf Co-operation Council
GDP	gross domestic product (= GNP minus net income from abroad)
GmbH	Gesellschaft mit beschränkter Haftung (company with limited liability)
GM	genetically modified
GMM	genetically modified micro-organism
GNP	gross national product
GPA	Government Procurement Agreement
GSP	Generalized System of Preferences
HICP	Harmonized Index of Consumer Prices
IBAN	International Bank Account Number

ICC	International Chamber of Commerce
ICES	International Council for the Exploration of the Sea
IC(T)	Information and Communication (Technology)
ISD	Investment Services Directive
Incoterms 2000	International Commercial Terms published by the ICC in 2000
IMF	International Monetary Fund
JPY	Japanese yen
LAIA	Latin American Integration Association
L/C	Letter of Credit
LIBOR	London Interbank Offered Rate
LSE	large-scale enterprise (employing at least 250 workers)
MBS	mortgage-backed securities
M&A	merger and acquisition
MEQR	measure having an equivalent effect to quantitative restrictions
Mercosur	Mercado Común del Sur (Argentina, Brazil, Paraguay, Uruguay and Venezuela)
MFI	monetary financial institution
MiFID	Markets in Financial Instruments Directive
MNE	multinational enterprise
NACE	Nomenclature générale des Activités économiques dans les Communautés européennes (industrial classification used by Eurostat)
NAFTA	North American Free Trade Agreement
NATO	North Atlantic Treaty Organization
NCB	national central bank
NDTI	non-deposit-taking institution
NTB	non-tariff barrier
NYSE	New York Stock Exchange
OCA	optimum currency area
OECD	Organisation for Economic Co-operation and Development
OEEC	Organisation for European Economic Co-operation
OTC	over the counter
(4)Ps	Product, Price, Place and Promotion
(7)Ps	Product, Price, Place, Promotion, Process, People and Physical environment
PECL	Principles of European Contract Law
PJCC	police and judicial co-operation in criminal matters
PPP	purchasing power parity
PSD	Payment Services Directive
PTA	preferential trade/trading arrangement/area
R&D	research & development
REACH	Registration, Evaluation, Authorization and restriction of Chemical substances
Rome I	European Community Convention on the Law applicable to Contractual Obligations
RoO	rules of origin
SEA	Single European Act
SEM	Single European Market
SEPA	Single Euro Payments Area
SGP	Stability and Growth Pact
SME	small & medium-sized enterprise (employing fewer than 250 workers)
SRO	self-regulating organization
TARGET	Trans-European Automated Real-time Gross Settlement Express Transfer System

TB	tariff barrier (customs duty)
TEcU	total economic union
TEN	Trans-European Network
TEU	Treaty on European Union
TFU	Treaty on the Functioning of the Union
ToL	Treaty of Lisbon
ToN	Treaty of Nice
UK	United Kingdom
USD	United States dollar
VAT	Value Added Tax
WTO	World Trade Organization

Adjustable peg system (or adjustable par value system): an exchange rate system whereby exchange rates are fixed for a period of time, but may be devalued (or revalued) if a deficit (or surplus) becomes substantial (e.g. ERM and EMS).

Allocation (or technical) efficiency: focused on using the best inputs or the best outputs.

Anti-cyclical effects: effects of economic measures which decrease the fluctuations of the business cycle (e.g. by reducing the capital requirements on banks).

Appreciation: a rise in the free-market exchange rate of the domestic currency vis-à-vis foreign currencies.

Arbitrage: buying a real or financial asset in a market where it has a lower price and selling it again in another market where it has a higher price, thereby making a profit.

Asset-backed securities: collateralized securities backed by real or financial assets (e.g. real estate).

Attribution principle: European institutions are allowed to act only according to the articles of the EC Treaty. They do not have unlimited authority.

Automatic fiscal stabilizers: tax revenues that rise and government expenditure that falls as national income rises. The more they change with income, the bigger the stabilizing effect on national income.

Bailout: an injection of liquidity given to a bankrupt or nearly bankrupt entity, such as a corporation or a bank, in order for it to meet its short-term obligations. Often bailouts are by governments, or by consortia of investors who demand control over the entity as the price for injecting funds.

Balance of payments (BOP): a measure of the payments that flow between any individual country and all other countries. It is used to summarize all international economic transactions for that country during a specific period, usually a year. The BOP is determined by the country's exports and imports of goods, services and financial capital, as well as financial transfers.

Bank-based financial system: a financial system in which banks are businesses' key source of financing. In others, firms look mainly to financial markets to meet their financial needs (examples are Germany, China and Japan).

Basel II: the second of the Basel Accords conducted by the Bank for International Settlements (BIS), which are recommendations (directives) on banking law and regulations issued by the Basel Committee on Banking Supervision.

Beggar-my/thy-neighbour policies: strategic policies that increase the welfare of a country or a group of countries (e.g. the EU) at the expense of other countries (e.g. the USA).

Bilateral convention:	an agreement between two countries, especially one dealing with a specific matter.
Bologna Treaty (1999):	an agreement which aimed to make it easier for students and researchers to understand and access European education systems. The two main guidelines of this treaty were the standardization of a learning achievement evaluation system to facilitate student mobility (European Credit Transfer and Accumulation System, ECTS) and the promotion of European co-operation on establishing criteria and methods of evaluation. Now signed by 45 countries and reinforced by the Lisbon Treaty on research, this treaty reaches beyond European boundaries.
Budget deficit (surplus):	an excess of central government spending over tax receipts.
Capital adequacy:	the level of capital (difference between assets and liabilities) a bank should, established by the Basel Accord. The so-called BIS ratio (capital or solvency ratio) varies according to the riskiness of a bank's business activity (both on-balance and off-balance sheet). The more risky the activity, the more capital a bank needs to hold.
Capital market:	long-term financial market where capital funds (debt and equity) are issued and traded. This includes private placement sources of debt and equity as well as organized markets (e.g. futures market) and exchanges.
CE marking:	proof of European conformity. Allows manufacturers and exporters to circulate products freely within the EU. It indicates that the manufacturer has satisfied all assessment procedures specified by law for its product.
Certificate of deposit:	a negotiable certificate issued by a bank as evidence of an interest-bearing wholesale time deposit.
Collateral:	an asset that secures repayment on a loan (e.g. real estate).
Collateralized money market:	market with short-term financial products covered by assets that secure repayment on a loan (e.g. commercial paper).
Commercial paper:	short-term unsecured instrument that promises to repay a fixed amount representing the cost of borrowed funds plus interest, on a certain future date at a specific time.
Common market:	also known as a single or internal market, establishes free mobility of factors of production within the designated group of member countries as well as a common trade policy with non-members. The Single European Market established the 'four freedoms': free movement of goods, services, capital and labour.
Common policy:	policy developed by the EU Member States whereby only European law applies to certain activities, such as customs and fisheries.
Competitive devaluations:	manipulation of exchange rates by governments and central banks (or monetary authorities) in order to remain competitive.

Cost-push inflation: continuing rises in costs of production (independently of demand).

Cohesion fund: a means of providing economic development aid to countries whose per capita GDP is less than 90% of the EU average.

Credit crunch: sudden reduction in the general availability of loans (or credit), or a sudden increase in the cost of obtaining loans from banks.

Credit rating agencies: businesses that assign credit ratings to issuers of certain types of debt obligation as well as to debt instruments themselves. They will generally monitor the performance of a transaction throughout its life and adjust their ratings accordingly.

Current account of the balance of payments: balance of trade plus net incomes and current transfers from abroad.

Customs union: the establishment of tariff-free circulation of goods and services within the collective borders of the EU Member States and a unified set of trade tariff and non-tariff barriers with respect to imports originating from non-member countries.

Default risk: the risk of being unable to fulfil a contractual obligation when it falls due or the likelihood that a borrower will be unable to repay the principal or interest on a loan (credit risk).

Deflection of trade: imports from outside a free-trade area being routed via the country with the lowest external tariff.

Demand-pull inflation: inflation caused by persistent rises in aggregate demand.

Deposit-taking financial institution: a financial institution that obtains its funds mainly from accepting savings and/or demand deposits from the general public and provides regular banking services (e.g. commercial and savings banks).

Depreciation (of currencies): a fall in the free-market exchange rate of the domestic currency vis-à-vis foreign currencies.

Deregulation of the financial markets: the process of removing or reducing the rules and regulations that apply to the financial industry with the objective of improving economic efficiency, competition and innovation.

Derivatives: contracts involving rights or obligations relating to purchases or sales of underlying real or financial assets, or relating to payments to be made in respect of movements in indices.

Derogation: in the context of EU legislation, a delay by a Member State in the implementation (transposition) of an element of an EU regulation into its legal system over a given timescale, or the decision not to enforce a specific provision in a treaty due to internal circumstances.

Direct financing: the raising of funds without using an intermediary.

Diseconomies of scale: where costs per unit of output increase as the scale of production increases.

Disintermediation: the diversion of business away from financial institutions which are subject to controls.

Diversification: where an enterprise expands into new types of business. Benefits are presumed to arise from totally different products. In financial terms it refers to the holding of many assets (a collection or 'portfolio') rather than a few assets in order to avoid the danger of 'putting all one's eggs in one basket'.

Dynamic efficiency: arises when regional economic integration induces changes in the quantity and quality of factors of production, technological progress and changes to the competitive environment.

Dynamic effects of economic integration: the overall growth in a market and its impact on an enterprise due to expanding production and the enterprise's ability to achieve greater economies of scale and scope.

Economic integration: the elimination of economic frontiers between two or more economies.

Economies of scale: when increasing the scale of production leads to a lower cost per unit of output.

Economies of scope: when increasing the range of products produced by an enterprise reduces the cost of each one (i.e. making use of complementarities in an efficient way).

Euro system: all national central banks (NCBs) of the euro area.

Exchange controls: restrictions placed on movements of funds in a particular currency (or limitations to the convertibility of a currency) imposed by monetary authorities.

External (dis) economies of scale: where an enterprise's costs per unit of output decrease(/increase) as the size of the industry as a whole grows.

Extra-area trade: trade with countries outside the EU, known as 'third-party countries'.

Factor mobility: free movement of factors of production (labour, capital and land).

Federalism (supranationalism): a system in which the power to govern is shared between national and state governments, creating what is often called a federation.

Financial account of the balance of payments: record of the flows of money into and out of a country for the purposes of investment or as deposits in banks and other financial institutions (e.g. portfolio and foreign direct investments).

Financial conglomerates (sometimes called financial supermarkets): groups of financial institutions operating in different sectors of the financial industry such as banking, insurance and securities.

Financial intermediaries:	agents who channel funds from depositors to borrowers and create liquidity at their own account and risk (indirect financing).
Financial liberalization:	process of opening up a financial market and the relaxation of restrictive practices (e.g. capital controls). The liberalization of capital movements can be considered as an example of financial liberalization. Deregulation is required for financial liberalization to take place.
Fiscal policy:	policy designed to affect aggregate demand by altering the balance between government expenditure and taxation (this policy can be either expansionary or contractionary).
Fisher Effect:	the long-term relationship between inflation and interest rates. This relationship tells us that, all things being equal, a rise in a country's expected inflation rate will eventually cause an equal rise in the interest rate (and vice versa).
Forward (contract):	an agreement between two parties to exchange over the counter (OTC) a real or financial asset on a prearranged date in the future for a specified price.
Forward rate agreement (FRA):	a common type of forward contract that gives the agent involved the opportunity to hedge against interest rate risk, thereby 'locking in' the future price of assets.
Four freedoms:	free movement of goods, services, capital and persons.
Four (founding) treaties:	refers to the European Coal and Steel Community (ECSC) Treaty, the European Economic Community (EEC) Treaty, the Euratom (European Atom Energy Community) Treaty and the Treaty on European Union (Treaty of Maastricht).
Free trade agreement:	an intergovernmental arrangement whereby all tariff barriers and quotas (i.e. quantitative restrictions) impeding trade between the participating Member States are removed, creating a free trade area.
Globalization:	worldwide integration of national economic systems.
Government debt (also known as public debt or national debt):	money (or credit) owed by any level of government, whether central, federal, municipal or local.
GDP:	gross domestic product, which is the market value of all final goods and services made within the borders of a nation in a year.
Harmonization:	the establishment of common rules and consistent policies which foster uniformity.
Hedge fund:	a private investment fund that trades and invests in various assets, such as securities, commodities, currency and derivatives, on behalf of its clients.

Home-country regulation (principle):	principle that an enterprise is authorized and regulated by authorities in the country in which its head office is located (the single passport principle).
Host-country regulation (principle):	principle that an enterprise is authorized and regulated by the domestic authorities of the country in which it is doing business.
Inflationary targeting:	a monetary policy whereby a central bank posits an inflation rate and then tries to achieve it by altering the interest rate, etc.
Incoterms 2000:	the International Commercial Terms published by the International Chamber of Commerce, based in Paris, France.
Inflation:	a rise in the general level of prices of goods and services in an economy over a period of time.
Infringements:	• financial: decisions by national authorities to levy taxes or apply other financial burdens on cross-border trade between businesses in the EU. • physical: disruption by national authorities of the free movement of goods in a non-financial manner.
Infringement procedure:	the procedure (outlined in Article 226 of the EC Treaty) by which the Commission starts investigations and sends warnings and reasoned opinions to a Member State which breaches EU law before it can take the Member State before the European Court of Justice.
Institutional investors:	investment banks, insurance companies and pension funds.
Intergovernmental co-operation:	co-operation between countries where the countries remain in control of the matters that are agreed on. They have a right of veto enabling them to retain control of all political and legislative matters.
Inter-governmentalism:	an approach to integration that treats states, and national governments in particular, as the primary actors in the integration process.
Internal market:	see Common market.
Internationalization:	a process by which an enterprise enters a foreign market.
Key Success Factors (KSFs):	the resources, skills and capability of an enterprise that are essential to deliver success in the market.
Lamfalussy Procedure:	established in February 2001 by a committee chaired by Alexander Lamfalussy to improve the effectiveness of the EU's securities market regulatory process.
Lender of last resort:	the central bank, which will always lend money to banks experiencing a crisis if they cannot obtain finance from market sources.
Level playing field:	an environment in which all businesses in a given market must follow the same rules (infrastructure) and are able to compete on equal terms (an optimum currency area can be considered as an example).

Leverage:	generally refers to using borrowing funds or debt in an attempt to increase returns to equity. De-leveraging is the action of reducing borrowing.
Liquidity:	the ability of an institution to pay its debts when they fall due.
Location-specific advantages:	advantages that arise from the availability of resources or assets in a particular location.
Qualified Majority Voting:	system used in situations requiring more than a simple majority (50% + 1) of the votes to ratify a decision whereby each Member State is awarded a particular number of votes in accordance with its size, etc.
Managed floating:	intervention by the monetary authorities in a system of flexible exchange rates to prevent excessive fluctuations (The euro–dollar, euro–yen or euro–sterling exchange rates are determined by this managed floating exchange rate system).
Market-based financial system:	system whereby firms look mainly to financial markets instead of banks to meet their financial needs (examples UK and USA).
Marketing mix:	a set of marketing tools (consisting of seven Ps: product, price, place, promotion, people, process and physical environment) used by organizations to realize their marketing goals.
Monetary aggregates:	the broad definition of the supply of money (M3) in the euro area, consisting of cash in circulation with the public, plus overnight deposits or 'call money' (M1), deposits with agreed maturity up to two years, deposits redeemable at up to three months' notice (M2), repos, money market funds and paper, and debt securities with residual maturity up to two years.
Monetary policy:	policy of the monetary authorities (central bank and/or government) to affect aggregate demand by altering the supply or cost of money (rate of interest). Monetary policy can be either expansionary (increase in the supply of money or decrease in the interest rate) or contractionary/tight (decrease in the supply of money or increase in the interest rate).
Monetary targeting:	a strategy which involves the use of monetary aggregates as an intermediate target with an ultimate goal such as price stability.
Money market:	short-term financial market usually involving large value (wholesale) assets with less than one year to maturity.
Moral hazard problem:	phenomenon which arises when a contract or financial arrangement creates incentives for the parties involved to behave against the interest of others. In the banking and finance literature this phenomenon is often used when a commercial bank deliberately takes too many financial risks, knowing that it will ultimately be supported by the central bank and/or government as 'lenders of last resort'.
Mortgage-backed securities:	securities traded mainly in the USA which pay interest on a semi-annual basis and repay principal either periodically or at maturity, and where the underlying collateral is a pool of mortgages.

Multilateral convention:	an international agreement between more than two countries.
Mutual recognition:	EU principle that one country's rules and regulations must apply throughout the EU. If they conflict with those of another country, individuals and businesses should be able to choose which to obey. If goods are lawfully sold in one Member State of the EU, they are presumed to be safe for sale in all EU Member States.
Non-tariff barriers:	all trade barriers except tariff barriers, e.g. quotas, subsidies, dumping and standardization of products.
Negative integration:	deregulated or market-oriented type of integration whereby the range of national policy choices is reduced (e.g. integration through a common market with free flow of goods, services, capital and persons).
Neutrality of money (neutrality principle):	theory stating that the rate of inflation is driven by the rate of growth of money, at least in the long run (proportional relationship between money growth and inflation given a stable demand for money).
Nominal exchange rate:	money value of a currency in relation to other currencies, i.e. without adjustment for inflation.
Off-balance sheet activities:	banks' business, often fee-based, other than booking assets and taking deposits. Examples are guarantees, commitments, securities underwriting, derivatives trading in swaps, options and futures.
Offshoring:	activity undertaken by institutions that are located outside the country of residence of the customer, typically in a low-tax jurisdiction (e.g. Bahamas and Bermuda) and that provide financial and legal advantages.
Off-site financial supervision:	assesses quantitative risks (e.g. liquidity, solvency and profitability risks) with the use of financial ratios. This is meant to ensure the safety and soundness of insured financial institutions and takes the form of continuous evaluation of the financial conditions and performance of insured banks and monitoring compliance with prescribed prudential guidelines.
Oligopolistic collusion (or collusive oligopoly):	when oligopolists agree (formally or informally) to limit competition between themselves.
On-site financial supervision:	supervision of the way banks manage and assess financial risks which cannot be quantified through a calculation of the liquidity ratio, for example.
Open-market policy:	the sale (or purchase) by the monetary authorities of government securities on the open market in order to reduce (or increase) the money supply or influence the interest rate and therefore the amount of money in the economy.
Option:	a contractual right, but not the obligation, to buy or sell a specific amount of a given financial instrument at a previously fixed price or at a price fixed at a designated future date.

Outsourcing: the transfer of part of a business's activities to an external service provider mainly because of cost advantages (e.g. call centres in India).

Ploughed-back profits: an important source of internal or self financing by an enterprise. It refers to the process of retaining a part of the enterprise's net profits for the purpose of reinvesting in the business. This reduces its dependence on funds from external sources in order to finance regular business needs.

Positive integration: the standardizing and harmonizing of certain national policies among the Member States, as well as the establishment of supranational institutions (e.g. the European Central Bank).

Preliminary ruling: ruling by which the European Court of Justice explains European law to a national court in accordance with Article 234 of the EC Treaty. Legal proceedings in the Member State are suspended until the explanation is given.

Primary European Law: the law laid down in the EC Treaty and its amendments.

Primary (security) market: market in which securities are traded between issuers and investors, thereby raising funds for the issuing company.

Private equity firm: firms which purchase businesses privately, without the use of shares traded publicly on the stock market. Private equity firms have lots of cash and access to vast amounts of cheap debt. Their capital costs are lower than those of publicly owned companies, which means they can pay higher prices and win more deals than other sorts of buyer.

Private law: the law relating to contracts, tort and property law.

Pro-cyclical effects: effects of economic measures which increase the fluctuations of the business cycle (e.g. increasing the capital requirements on banks.

Procurement policy: government procurement policies can function as indirect form of non-tariff barrier, especially in countries with a relatively large public sector. A common procurement policy ensures the absence of special treatment by member governments of their own domestic industries.

Product life cycle theory: theory analysing the relationship between the life cycle of products and their production location.

Public law: the part of the law that grants government authorities authority that ordinary citizens do not have.

Quantitative easing: an extreme monetary policy used to stimulate an economy where interest rates are either at or close to zero. The central bank increases the monetary base by a calculated amount through the open-market purchase of government bonds or other securities from banks.

Real exchange rate: a country's exchange rate adjusted for changes in the domestic currency prices of its exports relative to the foreign currency prices of its imports. If a country's prices rise or fall relative of those of its trading partners, the real exchange rate will rise or fall relative to the nominal exchange rate.

Recession:	a reduction in economic output during at least two consecutive quarters of a year.
Re-regulation:	the process of implementing new rules, restrictions and controls in response to market participants' efforts to circumvent existing regulations.
Rules of origin:	rules that detail the conditions under which a good is classified as deriving from a Member State or not.
Schengen Agreement:	an agreement that created a territory without border checks on people. Incorporated in EU law since 1999, it now covers 22 EU Member States plus Iceland, Norway and Switzerland.
Secondary European law	the European law embodied in legal decisions and in legislative measures such as directives and regulations.
Secondary market:	market in which previously issued securities are traded.
Securitization:	the process by which traditional bank assets (mainly loans and mortgages) are converted into negotiable or marketable securities, which are usually purchased by institutional investors. Securitization often leads to disintermediation of the banking system, as investors and borrowers bypass banks and transact business directly.
Service Directive:	Directive 2006/123/EC of 12th December 2006 aiming to remove the last barriers to the free movement of services.
Short selling (or shorting):	selling financial securities that the seller does not own at the time of the sale. Short selling is done with the intention of later purchasing the financial security at a lower price.
Single market:	see Common market.
Solvency:	the ability of an institution to repay debts ultimately.
Sovereignty:	the exclusive right to control a government or a country, a people or oneself.
Speculation:	buying or selling decisions based on anticipations of future prices. Speculation can be either stabilizing (based on probable predictions about the future) or destabilizing (based on uncertain predictions).
Static (or allocative) efficiency:	optimal allocation of scarce resources to obtain the best possible combination of outputs (in terms of income, value added or employment) from the existing inputs or factors of production (in terms of labour force, capital and raw materials).
Static effects of economic integration:	the shifting of resources from inefficient to efficient businesses as trade barriers fall.

Sub-prime debt: debt where there is a high risk of default by the borrower (e.g. mortgage holders on low incomes facing rising interest rates and falling house prices).

Sub-prime lending: a loan to market participants who have poor, non-existent or insufficient creditworthiness.

Subsidiarity principle: within the context of the EU integration process, the principle that decisions should be made as close to the people as possible, and that the EU should not take action unless it is more effective than action taken at national, regional or local level.

Supranationalism: the granting to a supranational organization of powers that were formerly traditionally exercised exclusively by national authorities.

Swap: financial transaction in which two parties agree to exchange either interest or currency streams of payment over time according to a predetermined rule.

System banks: banks which are 'too big' or 'too important' to fail.

Systemic risk: the risk that problems in one bank will spread throughout the entire sector, via contagion.

Tariff barriers (or import levies): taxes on imported products, i.e. customs duties.

Tax arbitrage: trading that takes advantage of a difference in tax rates or tax systems.

Trade creation: a situation where, upon joining a regional trade bloc, trade in a given country shifts from a higher-cost domestic producer to a lower-cost producer in another country within the trading bloc (e.g. EU).

Trade cycle: periodical fluctuations in national production (GDP) or income.

Trade diversion: occurs when, subsequent to the establishment of a trading bloc, an importing country decides to acquire products from a higher-cost partner producer instead of the low-cost producer outside the trading bloc from which it has been importing.

Transposition (of a directive): the implementation of the required result of a directive into national legislation in accordance with Article 249 of the EC Treaty.

Trias politica: the division of governmental power between separate branches (legislative, executive and judicial) to prevent abuse of power.

Twin deficit: budget deficit plus trade deficit (usually referring the US situation during the Bush administration).

Universal banking: business which covers all aspects of financial service activity, including securities operations, insurance, pensions and leasing.

Viner's Ambiguity: an analysis, first introduced in 1950 by Jacob Viner, of the ambiguity of the short-term effects of regional integration, which can be either welfare-enhancing (trade creation) or welfare-reducing (trade diversion).

X-efficiency: the general efficiency of an enterprise (judged on managerial and technological criteria) in transforming minimum-cost inputs cost into maximum profits.

1   European Union websites

European Union Web portal
www.europa.eu/
Official EU-website for the European Union in 23 different official languages. Nearly everything to do with the European Union can be found here, including all the treaties and other legal documents.

Eurostat
http://epp.eurostat.ec.europa.eu/
Official EU website with statistical information about the European Union, the European Community and the Member States.

European Commission
http://ec.europa.eu/
Official EU website for the European Commission, the executive institution of the European Community. Comprehensive information about Commission matters in 23 different languages.

European Commission trade website
http://ec.europa.eu/trade/

European Commission internal market website
http://ec.europa.eu/internal_market/ext-dimension/enlargement/index_en.htm

European Union glossary
http://europa.eu/scadplus/glossary/index_en.htm

2   Bank websites

European Central Bank
www.ecb.int/

Bank of England
www.bankofengland.co.uk/

Deutsche Bank
www.dbresearch.com/

World Bank
www.worldbank.org/
The World Bank is a source of financial and technical assistance to developing countries around the world:

Bank for International Settlements
www.bis.org/

International Monetary Fund
www.imf.org/

Federal Reserve Bank
www.federalreserve.gov/

3   Other (international) organizations

World Trade Organization
www.wto.org/

Centre for European Policy Studies
www.ceps.be/

College of Europe
www.coleurop.be/eco/publications.htm
A university institute of European studies.

4   Business magazines

EU Observer
www.euobserver.com/
Dedicated news website with all the latest news, opinions and blogs about
EU and European issues.

EU Business
www.eubusiness.com/
Dedicated news website which focuses on the business aspects of EU and
European news events.

The Economist
www.economist.com/

Financial Times
www.ft.com/

5   Country and marketing information websites

EU country information
http://geography.about.com/od/lists/a/eumembers.htm

UK Trade & Investment
www.ukinvest.gov.uk/

Germany Trade & Invest
www.gtai.com/web_en/homepage/

Czech Invest
www.czechinvest.org/en/

Bulgarian Investment Agency
www.investbg.government.bg/

Netherlands Foreign Investment Agency
www.nfia.nl/

EVD market comparisons
www.evd.nl/marktvergelijkingen/

Market research in the EU
www.eubusiness.com/market-research/

Internet World Stats
www.internetworldstats.com/
Up-to-date world internet usage, population statistics and internet market research data for over 233 countries and world regions.

Europages
www.europages.com/
A comprehensive search engine for BtoB companies.

Market research firms in Europe
www.business.com/directory/advertising_and_marketing/market_research/consultants/europe/

Market Research Organizations and Associations
www.allaboutmarketresearch.com/associations.htm#european/

Index